EDITORIAL COORDINATORS
Natasha de Caiado Castro, Daniela De Luca, Luciana Palmeira Langer, Melissa Magnus, Vanessa Martin, Roberta Suplicy and Maria Paula.

Cover art: Nathalie Cartolano

Copy Editor: Ana Silvani

2ª Edition / February 2024

International Cataloging in Publication Data (CIP)

Rise and Raise Others. — 2. ed. — WeBook Publishing, 2024.

      Various authors.
      Various coordinators.
      Bibliography.

      ISBN 979-8-9886684-1-1

      1. Activism 2. Personal growth 3. Professional development 4. Empowerment Feminism 6. Women - Social aspects 7. Women - Life stories 8. Protagonism.

Indexes for systematic catalog:

Women: History: Sociology 305.42

Library of Congress Control Number (LCCN): 2023918749

#riseandraiseothers
#umasobeepuxaaoutra

2nd edition

RISE
AND RAISE
OTHERS

Real life stories from inspiring women.

Prologue by Fernanda Montenegro
Preface by Lee Cockerell, Cover by Hugh Forrest and Edu Lyra
Cover art by Nathalie Cartolano

SUMÁRIO

PROLOGUE BY FERNANDA MONTENEGRO

Fernanda Montenegro
Brazilian actress, Oscar nominee and Member of the Brazilian Academy of Letters.

FREEDOM BEHIND CONVENT DOOR

A journalist once visited a Carmelite Convent where he conducted an interview with a nun who remained concealed behind a closed door. They were unable to see each other, yet the conversation revolved around the concept of **freedom**. The journalist, intrigued by this paradox, inquired, "Ma'am, it seems paradoxical to discuss freedom from behind a closed door, where you lack the permission to even see me. Could you elaborate on this?" In response, the nun said, **"For me, freedom is when a person can be wherever their heart truly longs to be."**

PREFACE BY LEE COCKERELL

Executive Vice President (retired and inspired) Walt Disney World® Resort and author of Creating Magic...Ten Common Sense Leadership Strategies From a Life at Disney.
Website: www.leecockerell.com / www.cockerellacademy.com

RISE AND RAISE OTHERS

I wholeheartedly recommend "Rise and Raise Others" to anyone seeking a profound exploration of empowerment, inclusion, diversity, leadership, and management. Written with passion and expertise, this book provides invaluable insights into the experiences, challenges, and triumphs of women across various walks of life. I believe women are superlative leaders because they lead with empathy and discipline. They manage with fairness and firmness. They use both heart and brain to solve complex problems, which is, as we all well remember, how we learned from our mothers.

From my 8 years at Hilton Hotels, 17 years at Marriott International and 16 years at the Disney Company, I have worked with many amazing women. They were committed to excellence and were some of my best leaders.

As an executive at these organizations, I mentored and promoted women to the highest levels of leadership, and I was never disappointed. We all need to set aside what gender or age a person is and focus on their performance. In my experience women perform just as well as men, if not better. Women executives consistently demonstrate courage, and they possess an amazing capacity for attention to detail.

One of the book's greatest strengths lies in its exploration of empowerment. It highlights the transformative journey that women undertake to discover their inner strength, recognize their worth, and embrace their potential. Through inspiring narratives, practical advice, and thought-provoking anecdotes, "Rise and Raise Others" encourages readers to harness their personal power, overcome societal barriers, and create meaningful change.

Important to note, the book places a strong emphasis on inclusion and diversity. It delves into the importance of fostering an inclusive society that values and respects the contributions of women from different backgrounds, cultures, and perspectives. By showcasing diverse stories and perspectives, the book encourages readers to challenge biases, foster empathy, and embrace the power of diversity as a catalyst for growth and innovation.

Another aspect that makes "Rise and Raise Others" a standout is its comprehensive exploration of leadership and management. It sheds light on the unique leadership qualities that women possess and how they can leverage these strengths to make a positive impact in their personal and professional lives. The book also provides practical strategies, tools, and frameworks for women to enhance their leadership skills, navigate obstacles, and thrive in positions of influence.

The authors' meticulous research, combined with compelling storytelling, creates a captivating reading experience. Each chapter is filled with real-life examples, relatable anecdotes, and expert analysis, making the content accessible and engaging. Moreover, the book strikes a perfect balance between theory and practice, ensuring that readers gain both theoretical insights and actionable takeaways. "Rise and Raise Others" is more than just another book for your shelf; it is a call to action. It urges individuals, organizations, and society as a whole to actively support gender equality, break down barriers, and create a more inclusive and equitable world. It serves as an indispensable guide for women seeking empowerment, as well as for men who wish to be allies in the journey towards gender parity.

"Rise and Raise Others" is an outstanding book that encompasses the essential themes of empowerment, inclusion, diversity, leadership, and management. Its compelling narratives, insightful perspectives, and practical guidance make it a must-read for anyone interested in championing gender equality and harnessing the full potential of women. I highly recommend this book to individuals, organizations, and institutions committed to fostering positive change and creating a more inclusive society for all.

Introduction

NATASHA DE CAIADO CASTRO

CEO - Wish International Events Management
Founder - Rise and Raise Others
University Professor | International Press | Board @ United Nations | Speaker @ SXSW
Website: www.wish.international
E-mail: natashafromwish@gmail.com
LinkedIn: www.linkedin.com/in/natashadecaiadocastro
Instagram: @natashacastro1

It was June 2022, in Cannes, South of France during the Advertising Festival. The first event post-pandemic was where our creative people would gather. FOMO (fear of missing out) took over and we wanted to be "everywhere-all-the-time". Resting was not an option.

I arrived earlier in the month to produce my client's marketing endeavors... booth, events, exhibitions and during my free time I started to post on this "by invitation women Whatsapp groups", all fun stuff that was buzzing in France. The behind-the-Scenes Cannes Festival.

Everyone was eager for information, so the group boomed.

By logging we'd know where to be when and meeting who. Fun times ...

The Festival was about to end and Malala, the Nobel Prize Laureate and female education activist was giving a talk and mentioned that "for all global movements, someone has to start, and others would follow".

I had the "Rise and Raise Others" t-shirt on.

Listening to her statement, I urged to take a picture with Malala, wearing my "superpower" t-shirt, and invited Elisangela Peres, sitting by my side, to come to the green-room on backstage. Her answer was "That is an impossible task, my friend".

It took me less than 5 minutes to find my way and have the picture taken, but one week to have it released by Malala's crew. An entire chapter could be written about this.

Finally, I could post the picture and change the name of our group from "Elle" (her in French) to "Rise and Raise Others" or "Uma sobe e Puxa a outra" in Portuguese.

I remember the exact moment when the Festival was over, and we decided to extend the "expiration date" of the group. I Invited 5 of the members to compose our board (Dani De Luca, Eli Cassandre, Helô Santana, Fabiola Kassin, Glaucimar Peticov), suggested some pillars that we could cover and who should manage each (they immediately accepted), and started to invite the women we most admired, to join.

Party time!!

The timing was perfect.

Cabin Fever was being replaced by meeting the very interesting new person we could, from all over the globe. Most of our engagements were virtual and amusing.

I was living in Paris at Ille de Saint Louis at the time. Most of the members were in Brazil but some were in California, China, and Indonesia. Different time zones would keep a 24/7 active feed of sharp, smart, interesting talk.

When we started to introduce ourselves, the surprise choked us. Those super-powerful leaders were taken by underdog syndrome. Their introductory pitch started chronologically, almost trying to justify why they have reached their professional C-suite positions. We had several CMOs of global companies, Unicorn leaders, global entrepreneurs, Deans ... women easily "Googleable" starting the pitch with family information instead of a real professional introduction.

Not knowing the reason for it we chose 4 pillars to talk about, invited the main specialists, and started virtual talks. The lecturers were given by top experts on the subjects. And the experts were members of the group. If there were any information gaps, we'd invite new members to cover and after one month of very intensive classes, we had Rebooted everyone, giving them new tools on personal, professional, social, and intellectual levels. By that, we also boosted their self-confidence.

And the spirit of collectiveness had been spread.

The only non-member invited to lecture was Lee Cockerell, former Executive Vice-President at Walt Disney World, and my former boss. He gave us the honor of Prefacing this book.

By that time one of the members asked to help her with votes. Carolina Videira had just lost her child and needed to raise her voice to talk about inclusion. João was a special child and his story is in this book as well.

I asked her to contextualize her request and her post to our group and she did it and her story got everyone's sympathy and tears.

We engaged, as a group, in making it viral, asking for votes.

Made some math, got our strategists on board, and ended up with 380 thousand votes from all over the globe, 38 thousand in the last 24 hours, and gave her not only the prize but the voice she needed and deserved.

She is now changing thousands of lives with her Turma do Jilo Institute.

During the same time, some of the women full of great content and known in several innovation festivals globally were eager to step on SXSW stages, the far most interesting creative festival we have today, headed by Hugh Forrest. One of the top most admirable people on my list.

The "why not" mindset took over and I e-mailed him asking for some tips on how to participate in the Panel Picker, their voting system for electing talks. He most generously agreed to talk to us, resulting on 17 different panels registered, 7 from which were chosen to be on 2023's stages.

Another impressively fun moment. We always joke about how we stalked Hugh on social media. Can you imagine 250 women, leaders poking someone at the same time? He can!!

The genius behind the magic at SXSW is also here in our book. He has just received the award for Diversity and Inclusion in Texas, where he is originally from.

Another fun story is the United Nations Award.

I am a Board Member for UM Women USA as I spend part of my time in between my Silicon Valley and Florida offices.

I suggested embedding a Rise and Raise Others Award in our Chapter and it was accepted with our commitment that the operation would be outsourced as the UN had no arms at the time.

Our members were able to put together a Global Award rendered in the most important Stage for Women Empowerment in the USA and given to 32 amazing women from all over the Globe, from Bali to India, Poland to California, including 4 Brazilians voted by 10 thousand specialized jurors. Regina Markus a neuroscientist, Carola Videira and Carmela Borst Social Entrepreneurs and Marienne Coutinho an Executive.

The award raised the voices of leaders talking about human traffic, education, inclusion, and science. The scope was modeled on the UN sustainable development goals and has already changed the status quo of several scenarios worldwide. We are very proud of it.

The very idea of the book came from several sources in the group. It turned into one of our main communication Boulevards. Our courageous "Titans" had one week to write their chapters and each of the 2 volumes was launched in one month. Both were ranked top sellers on the launching day and they carry 113 stories of resilient women that question everything that is not right. They push the boundaries with their resilience, curiosity, sense of justice, and sisterhood. In every book signing moment, we had during our book tour, a funny event occurred. From stopping the country's Senate session for 30 minutes as the politicians wanted to talk about the book. Or cause a major traffic jam in the most important city in Brazil on a Wednesday afternoon. We are troublemakers, on the good end of it.

By the time this book is released, we will be celebrating one year of existence. It feels like a lifetime as we have touched so many lives and made a positive impact on so many ideals.

Our structure has been solidly built on ethics, generosity, gratitude, and respect.

We see no colors or shapes or sizes or time frames. We value ideas and try to find ways to make them happen using all resources we have from our personal and corporate environments. Including our amazing network that combined, can reach the impossible.

By the way, leading those Titans became the best part of life as they are the real AAA people.

Sometimes it can get scary to manage so much intense personalities combined. But during the rest of the time ... it is such a fun way of investing time.

Can you imagine a world where you wake up thinking "Who are we going to make happy today?"

And by the end of the day, you, do it?

I can!!!

Does that make me the luckiest person on Earth?

Cheers to the destiny that provided me with all the necessary dots and the time to magically connect them so we can now Rise and Raise Others!!!

Introduction

GLAUCIMAR PETICOV

C-Level, Human Resources, Sustainability, Corporate Education, Women's Leadership. Ambassador of the mentorship program for women "Nós por Elas" ('Us for Them') from the Vasselo Goldoni Institute (IVG)
Instagram: @glaupeticov
LinkedIn: www.linkedin.com/in/glaucimarpeticov

Through ups and downs, successes, and numerous initiatives, I believe there are few who do not share the perception that women have made progress in just over a century. Advances driven by connection, which brought similar realities together, amplified voices and causes have provided understanding and disseminated rights. The awakening of female power has never been a coincidence, but rather the result of a great deal of struggle; but there have also been many exchanges, where those who refuse to recognize the woman's role as a protagonist live in an anachronism.

Without exaggeration, it is possible to say that rapid evolutionary change is underway, and the numbers prove it. There have been significant advances on all fronts, but certainly not to the extent we desire. Any analysis, no matter how simple, confirms that relationships between people have been renewed and that leadership, once determined mostly by the power of position, is now perceived by companies that are connected to the world, being effective through example and inspiration. It is fortunate that we are witnessing the abandonment of a command-and-control mentality. This evolution, it is worth noting, has been accompanied by a very positive movement to make companies much more receptive to innovation and everything special that comes with it: diversity, equity, inclusion, and plurality.

Narratives help, and among many factors, the presence of a keen perception reveals that over the years, women have fought hard to acquire their rights and the recognition of their voice in society. We have lived through periods, in their broadest composition, when we were presented as fragments and appendages of history. Therefore, we have a world where women were neglected, and their voices were silenced. On the other hand, it is incredible to see the important roles that women currently occupy, although often underestimated and excluded from positions of power.

However, over time, as a result of our struggles, we have gained more space and rights, making our presence felt in different areas.

Currently, we perceive that changes are everywhere; women have realized the need to demand representation. In fact, the lack of representation was perpetuating stereotypes and limiting our talent and potential as human beings. Thus, little by little, women have historically positioned themselves to their advantage by portraying their experiences, perspectives, and thoughts in a positive light. In this way, we have been able to identify with and feel the fulfillment of being represented.

With pain and trauma, we are at the forefront of changes for our lives and society because we know that our voice brings visibility and recognition to the issues and struggles faced by women in real life. We encourage empathy and solidarity, contributing to the construction of a more equal and just world.

For example, the American activist Susan B. Anthony fought for women's suffrage rights in the late 19th century, while the Brazilian writer Carolina Maria de Jesus brought to light issues of poverty and racism in her work "Child of the Dark."

In science, female participation has also become increasingly significant. One of the most notable examples is the Polish scientist Marie Curie, who discovered radioactive elements and won the Nobel Prize in two different categories. Today, there are many women working in various fields, making significant contributions to the advancement of humanity.

Our increasingly growing participation allows us to have positive role models and references that inspire us to pursue our goals, which strengthens us with each victory.

We are far beyond simply the recognition of trends; we are talking about justice and equality, contributing, and representation in various realms. Our experiences, perspectives, ideas, and ways of thinking enrich the world and contribute to the larger realm of valuing diversity.

For centuries, women have been proving that they possess talent and competence to contribute to the development of humanity, despite the barriers and obstacles encountered.

In the corporate world, we still face challenges regarding wage equality and representation in leadership positions. However, over the past few decades, more women have entered the workforce and shown their competence in all areas, achieving significant leadership positions in companies and organizations.

The "care economy" is another issue that directly impacts the careers of millions of women. Historically, the responsibility for caring for others from infancy forward has always fallen on women. Engaged for many hours with household chores, childcare, or caring for elderly or sick family members, these women are distanced from financial autonomy. This is unpaid and often invisible work, which not only causes overload and exhaustion but also exacerbates income inequality.

And while there is still much to be achieved in terms of gender equality, the fight for a fairer and more balanced world continues, with more and more women claiming their rightful place in history.

Regardless of barriers and inequalities, our determination and preparedness are growing, and the effects are becoming increasingly visible. Therefore, we must continue to support and inspire each other to move forward, because together we can make a real and lasting difference in the world.

We are many, actually the majority of the Brazilian population, and let's not forget that the other half are our offspring. Just imagine the strength that arises when this legion comes together. It is collective action that truly drives change. We are capable, as history shows, but we must recognize the power of our authenticity, understanding that each of us has something unique to offer.

Being aware of the greatness of women allows us to break free from cycles that have imprisoned women for years, where our talents were confined within labels and stigmas that never belonged to us. But here we are, visible, making ourselves seen and noticed, in continuous and constant motion, rowing together against the tide and conquering new and old territories. After all, we exercise the motto, "One rises and pulls the other up" at every moment.

Much of this movement that encourages female talent stems from sorority, the empathy that generates unity and female empowerment. It is a lens that allows us to see that which is invisible to the naked eye. This lens is known as empathy. Empathy is not about feeling someone else's pain; it is about being able to connect with others. This ability helps us better understand and interpret the needs, vulnerabilities, and pain of others. Not all of us are born empathetic, but we can all practice it; empathy is also a skill that can be developed.

The further we advance, the greater our responsibility to fight for the growth of more women. Sharing privilege is sowing the seed for more equitable and inclusive environments. It is moving the pieces on the gameboard, using our privileged position for good. Each of us has a capacity to create change and transform the world around us.

A question that can assist in this process is: "What do I bring new to the table?" or "What contributions have I been making?" Immersing oneself in one's purpose, in one's dedication, can reveal valuable treasures for life and career. Understanding one's own vastness is an ongoing quest. The writer Rubem Alves once said in one of his chronicles that, in order to recognize the enchantments around us, we must first see the beauty within ourselves. I would add that admiring the surroundings, the small details of everyday life, the stories of other women, and nature can help us return our gaze with more delicacy and kindness towards ourselves.

We need to learn to believe in ourselves and our potential. The more we put our potential into action, the more confidence we gain, creating a virtuous circle. All of us, regardless of our position or level of knowledge, go through phases where our confidence falters, but when we learn to keep moving forward together , the obstacles become smaller and smaller.

Acquiring knowledge and skills, honing our authenticity with dedication and commitment, are resources that will always keep us in motion. In this constantly changing world, we must not fear change but remain in motion to achieve results, with the courage to confront inequality, prejudice, and stereotypes without giving up, standing firm.

It is common for us to waste more time and energy than men by striving to please or secure the acceptance of others. Excessive self-demand, which is so common among us, inhibits talented professionals who end up not being proactive, hiding behind a false layer of self-protection. However, by becoming aware of these facts, we gain the freedom to redefine these patterns, and one of the most effective ways to overcome these feelings is by connecting with others and sharing our experiences.

Tamara Klink, the youngest Brazilian to cross the Atlantic, shared n her book that the drive to face this challenge was not courage. She said that courage would have been staying in the same place and thus giving up on the small possibility of her dream. And every day, making the same decision to postpone her self-discovery. Dreaming is wonderful but achieving is fantastic.

I believe in the power of self-discovery because, after all, we all share the search, the desire to learn, to improve, and those who choose the search cannot refuse the journey.

In these incredible testimonies, we clearly see the representation of the exercise of being human and, at the same time, refining and expanding the level of our perception because growing means becoming bigger, evolving means becoming better, and that's it, as simple as that.

That is why this collection of journeys is an invitation to one of the wonders we have in life: inspiration. Opening up space for admiration is like activating a powerful GPS that guides us through the paths of possibilities, which, as beautiful and complex as they may be, become the breath of magic when we discover the countless times that we can reinvent ourselves and go further.

By writing their stories, these women generously allow us to access the backstage of their careers and lives, their first steps, challenges, and obstacles before becoming role models. They prove that there are no ready-made answers or a single path that leads to the finish line; however, upon reaching it, it is possible to expand the space with courage to include and move others.

The great writer Clarice Lispector said, "The grandeur of life is to launch oneself," and for me, launching oneself is related to taking positive steps towards others; it is simultaneously moving in our favor, collectively, as a group.

Undoubtedly, "Rise and Raise Others" presents us with a mirror in which recognition occurs at different moments, making us see what is close but not always visible. And it is in this face-to-face encounter with reality and the obstacles faced by each individual that we are transported to our own unique universes, pointing out new paths.

With each new paragraph, with each new life we encounter within these pages, we grow a little stronger. We embrace the insights, the discomfort, the impulse, and the encouragement, and become protagonists. To build a new tomorrow, we must first dream and ensure that our stories continue to be told. It is in this way that our girls and all women will continue to nurture dreams that become realities.

Congratulations to all the participants in this work, who showcase the strength of those who drive transformation, the power of present action, and the importance of walking through the open doors that have been opened by other women, opening new doors, and holding doors for women who are walking alongside us, inspiring each other so that every day, enchantment is not just about shining but about illuminating paths.

Wishing you an excellent journey!

Introduction

MANZAR FERES

General Manager, Advertising at Globo, board member, investor
LinkedIn: www.linkedin.com/in/manzarferes
Instagram: @manzarferes

This book tells stories of women. In general, very different stories. But, in all of them, you will notice something in common: these women don't shy away from the fight.

The authors are part of a group called Rise and Raise Others. It was founded in 2022 and has since been bringing together women who have the purpose of forming a large support and inspiration network so that others don't give up on their dreams. Does it sound simple in your view? If yes, then this book is for you.

Every day is a struggle to ensure that all women and girls have open and safe spaces in society and companies. But I like International Women's Day and its significance. It is mobilizing. It's a day when the whole world talks about this subject -- so, long live Women's Day!

I am a white, cisgender woman, and I have had a life with certain privileges. I could study whatever I wished, in any institution I chose. Languages, classical music, and ballet were part of my childhood and adolescence. I started working early in my family's business, importing and exporting food products. For those who don't know me, I have this unusual name because it was my paternal grandmother's name, born in Lebanon, just like my grandfather, who was also Lebanese. I studied Electrical Engineering and pursued a specialization in Systems and Computing. Passionate about technology since I was very young, I switched from the wholesale business of my family to the world of systems engineering. Sometime later, I transitioned to a consulting career at PwCC and later at IBM, where I worked for 12 years in 3 completely different jobs. During my last 4 years at IBM, I held a global role that brought me opportunities to work with countries and cultures that were very different from each other. I had teams, clients, and peers in China, Russia, Belgium, the USA, Mexico, Argentina, and Brazil. I learned a lot about respecting difference by understanding that different is neither better nor worse, it's just different.

After the "IBM school," I worked at Experian Brazil. They wanted to transform the business and the company's positioning in the local market. Still a Credit Bureau, but with a much larger and more diversified portfolio. A technology and data company, lots of data. I spent 4 years "living" that project, which I am very proud of.

Then came Globo in 2019. A major career change that, I confess, I had to dive into using a bit of intuition to decide that it would be a good move and would make me happy. And it did. I took over the commercial area of Globo at the end of 2019 with the challenge of designing and implementing a new market approach for the company to accelerate the digital transformation of its acvertising business, aligned with the operational model defined by the "Uma Só Globo" (One Globo) project. The change would take place beginning in January 2020, when its broadcast TV, pay-TV channels, websites, and streaming service (Globoplay), which were previously separate entities, would be consolidated into a single company. Everything was set. We flipped the switch, the model was implemented, a new organization, mixed teams, a robust change management process to be executed. And then the pandemic came, everyone at home, challenges that were not mapped out. And what did we do? We learned and moved forward. It was tough, but there were many rewards.

In 2021, I took on the General Management of the Globo Advertising Business Unit. And by the way, I was the first woman in that position ever. When I took over, I was also the only woman in the executive leadership of that unit. All the directors reporting directly to me were men. With great pride, one year later, we achieved a 50/50 gender balance.

Imagine, a woman, a Middle Eastern family background, an engineer, and the majority of my professional life in technology companies. I began my fight (structured, with goals and all) for gender equality in 2008, still at IBM, which was a pioneering company in Brazil to implement a program focused on women's careers. Many stories are told, and many lessons were learned during this time. We already have better numbers than our peer companies for women in the corporate world in Brazil, but we still have a great struggle ahead in order to continue this trajcectory. I fight for my two daughters, for my two sisters, for my nieces, but also for all women and girls who deserve, at the very least, a safe and prejudice-free place in the job market and in society.

A few years ago, I was confronted with the issue of women suffering domestic violence. I took a position on the board of Instituto Bem Querer Mulher (Wellbeing Women Institute), an NGO aiming to provide legal, psychological, and social support to battered women. In Brazil in 2022, every 4 hours, a woman suffers some form of violence. Every 6 hours, a woman is killed just for being a woman. So let's fight!

There is still so much to do. May Women's Day be dedicated to black women, trans women, women with disabilities, and all those who face greater social and economic challenges than many of us.

Enjoy reading, and I hope you finish this book with more inspiration, reflections, and a strong desire to join our fight!IntroductionIntroduction

Introduction

EDU LYRA

Founder and CEO of Gerando Falcões
Instagram: @edulyrag.f
LinkedIn: www.linkedin.com/in/edu-lyra/

I want to start by saying that nothing would be possible without the support of my wife, Mayara, or my daughters, Lara and Luíza. However, the phrase that has always been the greatest reference in my life is "it doesn't matter where you come from, but where you're going," by Mrs. Maria Gorete de Brito Lyra. Interestingly, the tone of optimism that has always guided me came from a woman who didn't have many opportunities in life. My "preta," as I often call her, always worked hard and stood firm during my father's absence - he was imprisoned when I was still a child. My mother's story is not so different from the accounts of millions of Brazilian women. There are still many Maria Goretes suffering from the lack of opportunities stemming from a historical machismo that still afflicts our country. More than speaking, I prefer to show. In Gerando Falcões, the NGO I lead, 70% of the total leadership is female, and we have 63% of women in senior leadership positions. In total, 39% of all employees are black women. This is a daily goal and a constant evolution so that women feel represented, welcomed, and respected. They are the ones playing in attack and turning the poverty of the favela into a museum piece. It is inspiring to see that 44 women of such relevance are empowering others with messages of support, transformation, and female emancipation. You are not only pulling each other up; you are pulling all of us, showing the importance of diversity and inclusion. I am very proud and grateful for the invitation to write about this because this book cannot be just a work; it needs to be a manual. A manual that will teach us and show us that we have a new path to follow, one that is much fairer and more egalitarian

Introduction

MARIA FERNANDA DELMAS

Journalist
LinkedIn: www.linkedin.com/in/maria-fernanda-delmas-2436a2b0/

There was a time when we used to wear a pantsuit - gray, black, or pastel - to be taken seriously in a meeting. A time when colored hair, flat shoes, and large accessories were seen with strangeness at work. Today, we show ourselves more the way that makes us feel good - including in a pantsuit.

It's a simple example to say that, yes, we have progressed. But we're still far away. The most recent edition of a study by the World Economic Forum on gender inequality shows alarming data. If the current pace of progress is maintained, the world will need 132 years for total equality in economic opportunity, level of education, health and survival, and political empowerment.

Life is still tough for women. There are even more obstacles for black women, the poor, LGBTQIA+ individuals, and those with disabilities. But every story of success and generosity moves us, like the ones you will find in this book.

However, may books like this become library relics, studied as a past where success stories were more the exception than the rule.

May in much less than a hundred and a few years we can say: "There was a time when one would rise and pull another up, now it's just a matter of looking to the side and finding a bunch of companions to hold hands with.

ADRIANA ALCÂNTARA

Audible Country Manager – Brazil
Instagram: @alcantaraadri
LinkedIn: www.linkedin.com/in/adrianaalcantara/

REPERTOIRE AND CONNECTIONS

We are all unique, and our experiences and references build each of us as individuals, with a repertoire of potential to create endless connections.

I graduated in Performinç Arts from The Lee Strasberg Theatre & Film Institute and Advertising and Marketing from FAAP, and earned a Master's degree in Social Arts and Business at New York University. Over the past 25 years, I have held executive positions in companies such as Apple, NBC, Globosat, Nickelodeon, Disney, Food Network, Oi TV, and Warner Media. For 14 years, I was a professor at FAAP. I also lead the Brazilian branch of the NGO Protect Us Kids. It may sound like a path I accomplished alone, but I was raised up by others so many times that I can't even count.

My father was an only child and my mother has one sibling, but instead of keeping the family small, they changed the formula. There are two brothers from my father's side with my mother, Fernando and Renato, then a half-sister from my mother's second marriage, Elôra, and another half-sister from my father's second marriage, Duda, and then my stepmother's daughter, Priscila. Priscila, in turn, gained another sister from her father's second marriage, Giorgia, so now we siblings are five women and two men. I'm the oldest, and for four years, I was an only child. I think it all started during that period when my desire for companionship was so strong that I learned to connect with anyone. My father always tells the story of when I was little, and we would go to hotels for the weekend- I would always make friends. Once, there was only an older gentleman in the pool, and that day, my father thought I would be alone. But when he returned, I was racing the elderly man in the water! Even standing in a line to get coffee creates an opportunity to make a connection, have a chat, and create something interesting. I also have countless contacts that I met on airplanes. Once, I met an executive who sold energy-saving devices for hotels. I was living in New York and finishing my master's degree. After ten minutes of conversation, I became his company's translator, as they were expanding into Brazil. Another person I met on a plane, from the oil and energy sector, became a work contact for my husband Renato Tocantins. In the elevator of the building where I lived in New York, I met a woman who would always go downstairs to walk her dog. After bumping into her twice, I noticed she was wearing an NBC cap. Months later, I was working at MSNBC, obtained my work visa and enjoyed several wonderful professional years. It's like those connect-the-dots books that were so prevalent during my technology-free childhood. I loved them because until the dots were connected, we had no idea what the picture would turn out to be. see life a bit like that—never knowing where the best project, idea, or friend will come from. That's what makes life a wonderful box of surprises. Not all surprises are immediately good, but I believe I've learned to always take away something positive that can lead me to a special place.

That's how it was when, in 1987, in the midst of my adolescence, my stepfather and mother decided to move to Baghdad with the whole family at the invitation of the construction company Mendes Junior. Iraq had been at war with Iran for several years. My mother always had the courage to take on new experiences, which inspired me and gave me different perspectives on seeing opportunities everywhere. She faced head on the challenges of Iraq with four children, being one (me) a teenager. I left behind my father, to whom I am very attached. I tried to focus on the advantages, like attending an international school and becoming fluent in English. The Baghdad International School, was operated by the United Nations and, consequently, "safe" for the local standards. We had weekly drills to train us how to react in case of a bombing. Once, I was in the bathroom, and the alarm went off. I didn't hear it. In a panic, the principal came in to get me. I remember feeling so embarrassed walking out with him while the whole school was looking at me. Living in Baghdad gave me an incredible sense of adaptability and resourcefulness. I became fearless, with strength and the willingness to face any situation. When the Gulf War began, I was still a teenager and a fan of *Capricho* Magazine. I sent them an article about my time in Iraq that they published, which I consider my first professional publication! There is always a lesson to be learned, a bright side, and a way to maximize results. Today, when I mention to someone that I lived in Baghdad, I enjoy seeing their reactions.

My father always believed in me, even though he disagreed with my career choice. When I decided to study Communications, he would say that I already communicated too well; now, he says it's tough to argue with me! I am aware that my level of privilege is extraordinary, and I am committed to helping others.

I was strongly encouraged by my mother and stepfather (who is actually the author of several law books published in multiple languages) to appreciate the arts. Every weekend, they would take us to the children's theater. I've done ballet and various types of dance throughout my life. This passion for the arts became closely intertwined with my professional choices. I engaged opportunities on every possible front, danced hundreds of choreographies, participated in two professional theater plays. I acted in a miniseries on Globo, a soap opera on SBT, and another one on Record. I hosted a TV show called "Walking Show" for two years. This artistic side, that seemed to be a distraction from my choice to pursue an executive career in the audiovisual field, actually gave me an advantage. I must say, however, that it was not a calculated strategy but rather my heart following my passions while, at the same time, keeping my feet on the ground and striving for a career that would provide financial stability. In practice, the actress (me!) became a children's director, who almost overnight turned into a TV program host. My eye became trained to spot potential in a way that has always helped me, even during interviews in which I now recruit executives for my team. My experience in theater gave me agility in executive presentations, interviews with media outlets, and an immense energy when I have an audience in front of me. Any opportunity to communicate ignites a fire within me. I get excited and show my best self. Considering this, I accepted the invitation to teach at FAAP, the college where I studied. At the age of 28, I faced my first class. When I arrived, nobody entered the room because they thought I was a student. After the initial embarrassment, I loved and continued teaching for 14 years. In addition to my connections, my learning grew exponentially! Each class had about thirty people to meet and share. Today, I still continue to cross paths professionally with many who were once my students. A subset of them have been part of my teams. Through all these collaborations, I built many friendships that continued on a parallel journey, exchanging, learning, giving, and receiving.

One of the most challenging phases of my professional life was my departure from the Cartoon Network after a restructuring process. It was this professional challenge that I consider to be the pinnacle of my career. Not so much because of the challenge itself, but because it was when all the skills I had developed, and the maturity I had acquired, were put to the test, generating great results. During a period of over three years, every day was a new opportunity to excel through out-of-the-box ideas, with a team that empowered me. As a team, we experienced no sense of limits. Until the day of the restructuring, when I was laid off, all our projects exceeded expectations. Truly, we never know what tomorrow holds. At the age of 48, fearful that I wouldn't be able to find a new position. A few weeks later, Christmas came, and under the tree, a huge green box. Inside, there were letters from all the team members with photos, memories, and a message saying "thank you". We can't control everything in life, but the more references and connections we have, the easier it is to rise when we fall. That team and those letters prevented my self-esteem from being shaken. These friends continued to support me in my job search, cheering me on in every interview I had, until I landed my current position. Today, two years later, I face a different challenge, with even more responsibilities. An ex-Cartoon Network colleague, Renata Gasperoni is in my current team, and another, Vivi Arias, works as a freelancer. I still exchange tips about projects with this former team regularly. I think we are closer now than we were when I was there.

Cartoon Network was not my only setbacks. Before that, after my maternity leave, I left Oi TV in Rio de Janeiro for Apple in São Paulo. I moved, bringing my husband, Renato Tocantins, and our daughter, Maria Victoria, from Rio to São Paulo. My challenge was to launch iTunes in Latin America as the Head of Movies for Latin America and Iberia. It seemed incredible, but it turned into a nightmare. The challenge was to launch local iTunes stores, grow the user base, and negotiate contracts with local independent distributors for a new business model—transactional video on demand. In 2012, this was completely new. Closing these contracts required building long-term trust, which involved constant travel to London, Cupertino, Buenos Aires, Mexico City, Miami, and Madrid. Every two months, I had to be in each of these cities. Interesting, isn't it? For the first month, yes, but then this routine triggered a severe depression. In addition to the physical toll of travel and time zone changes, I was leaving behind my daughter, who was just 1 year old. I began shortening the duration of my trips to spend fewer days away extending my workdays abroad- starting with meetings at 7 a.m. and going until 10 p.m. My health couldn't handle it. Apple wasn't the nicest company I've worked for, nor was it where I learned the most. I paid a high price, but looking at the positive side, I was introduced to a digital business, met highly prepared executives, and learned to set boundaries, gained a lot of emotional maturity, and a star on my resume. There is hardly ever an interview during which I'm not asked about my experience at Apple. Usually, I share other stories from my time there, but here I thought this one mattered the most.

I was brought into this group by a friend that I greatly admire, Daniela Mignani. We worked together at Globosat, and she referred me to a position at Oi TV, which was a significant turning point in my career. At Oi, Dani's husband was my direct boss. As a São Paulo native living in Rio de Janeiro, Dani and Volpini welcomed me, and I became so close to their family that I sometimes helped their daughter, Juliana, with her homework. When she grew up and came to study in São Paulo, she stayed at my house until she found an apartment! Once again, for me, it's all about the joy of building connections. I am the mother of a daughter, Vicky, who motivates me to be better every day. As a mother, I always emphasize the importance of taking initiative, autonomy, giving your best, respecting, and helping others. It filled me with joy to see the topic she chose for her school project: Gender and Equality - Women in Business. I hope to see her in this group soon, to share, learn, and teach so that we can spread the message to future generations that "raise and raise others." Here's to a world with more connections and a larger repertoire.

ADRIANA SEIXAS

Marketing, Branding, and Communication Executive specializing in Brand Strategy, focused on improving the reputation of both companies and individuals, promoting trust relationships with all stakeholders, and driving Brand Value.
LinkedIn: www.linkedin.com/in/adrianaseixasbraga

KNOWLEDGE: THE ESSENCE OF MY PURPOSE

THE DAY THAT TRANSFORMED MY LIFE STORY

I was born in São José do Rio Preto, a city in the countryside of São Paulo, and grew up listening to my mother say that "knowledge is a passport to a world of possibilities!" It may sound like a deep belief in noble values, but it's actually a mantra cultivated from significant trauma.

At 20 years old my mother, Cecília, married my father, Murilo, a successful doctor 14 years older than her. Perhaps, out of jealousy for her beaty and intelligence, he convinced her to drop out of college. We were the perfect family of a TV commercial: my brother Ricardo, me as the middle child, the youngest Isabela, and my mother exclusively dedicated herself to motherhood and household routines. She was an excellent hostess, and our home was always full of people, whether during birthday parties, Christmas, Easter, or weekends with friends and family.

When I was 9 years old, my father suffered an aneurysm and passed away. Life seemed to come to a standstill for a week. The house was filled with people. Some adults in the backyard were trying to console us kids, while others in the living room were advising my mother on how to manage the farm, an inheritance left by my father. Due to her limited role as a mother, her lack of practical knowledge was enormous. She didn't even have a bank account—imagine the challenge of running a farm without any knowledge of planting, harvesting, or managing coffee plantation workers!

I don't remember seeing my mother cry. The following week, with immense strength and determination, she hired an agronomist to fill her knowledge gap and took over the farm's management. As if that weren't enough, she found ways to assure us that everything would be alright. We resumed our routine, with my mother continuing to be present in our daily activities, instilling essential values to shape our character, and serving as an example of resilience.

My mother's story shows that we can transform our identity based on the future we want to create. We're not tied to our past personality and behaviors. It reminds us of the importance of taking charge of our lives, knowing our purpose, and preparing for where we want to go. My mother used her purpose as a guiding compass through the storm.

THE VALUE OF KNOWLEDGE

All three of us were excellent students! We even complained at the end of the year about not receiving any gifts, as friends who barely passed were rewarded with the most desired toys of the moment. My mother would always reiterate that it was simply our duty. She not only demanded good grades but also insisted on us doing extracurricular courses such as English, piano, ballet, geometry, writing, and whatever else she could find to complement our school education, preparing us even more for college entrance exams. It was her way of "raising" her children to be better, valuing Knowledge, as she had felt its absence when she had to take the reins of her life, unprepared for such independence.

In our teenage years, she got it into her head that we needed to go on an exchange program to solidify our English skills. It wasn't common for someone from a small town, but being the trailblazer that I am, I jumped at the opportunity. My first plane trip took me to live with a family in the USA for 6 months. I returned convinced that I would study in São Paulo, at the best college for the course I would choose, as a gateway to a world of opportunities!

I was admitted to the business administration program at EAESP-FGV without the need for any preparatory courses. There, I felt like a fish out of water! All the students knew each other from the big schools in São Paulo or the famous preparatory course for FGV's specific entrance exam. In this context, I learned a lesson about my future identity. It was up to me to establish my personal brand through trustworthy relationships so that people would want to be around me.

THE VALUE OF KNOWLEDGE

I graduated and joined C&A's Trainee Program. I worked in retail for a few years until my sister "raised me up" to the challenge of starting a multi-brand women's clothing store in the city of Rio Preto. My sister studied at the São Francisco School of Law at the University of São Paulo and was a master at cultivating trustworthy relationships! With our personalized and welcoming service, there was no competition, and the store was a success, representing coveted brands from São Paulo and Rio de Janeiro.

On a trip to Rio, we met Kao, the brother of a friend from Rio Preto. Mutual interest sparked! A few days later, I heard a message from him on the answering machine and called back his workplace in Rio. I asked for Kao, and they said there was no one by that name. I asked for Carlos, and still nothing. I turned to my sister, who explained to me that his name was Carlos Duilio, and he usually went by just Duilio. Knowing his correct identity, we started dating and have been married for 20 years, always accompanied by confusion about his name.

That same year, we got acquainted with commercial Internet. UOL chat was a big hit. To find a specific page, you would simply search on "Cadê" via Netscape browser. My friend Vivien, who had been working at TecToy since our graduation, excitedly called me to say they would represent one of the largest internet service providers, CompuServe, in Brazil. She explained that they needed someone to handle marketing and customer experience, so she pulled me and "raised" me in the company. It was sensational to witness the beginning of this digital revolution, to learn about the business, and create the brand's communication strategy. Even the slow dial-up internet connection couldn't slow customer's enthusiasm down!

AOL acquired CompuServe in the USA and operations in Brazil were shut down. Before I could look for another job, Kao invited me to live in Venezuela for a year. I didn't think twice; it was an opportunity to learn another language. The fun part was the traditional name confusion. Venezuelans couldn't pronounce Duilio, so there he became Carlos!

THE VALUE OF PURPOSE

I returned to Brazil and soon got an opportunity in the new business area of an electronics industry. One benefit that caught my eye was the company's willingness to sponsor an MBA. I had always planned to pursue a master's degree, and after much negotiation, I secured approval to pursue a Professional Master in Administration (MPA) at EAESP-FGV.

Professor Luiz Carlos de Queirós Cabrera led the Career Management course. Two exercises were assigned. The first was called "Life Story." My text was long, comprehensive, covering my personal life, family, professional and social life, and rich in details about facts, achievements, and events up to the present time. It conveyed the pride and joy I felt for seizing every opportunity life offered. I deeply understood my "past self" and my "present self." The second exercise was a letter to be sent to Professor Cabrera after 10 years, detailing what had occurred during that period. Again, my text was rich in personal, family, and social aspects, but there was very little about my professional future. In other words, I couldn't write about my "future professional self." I realized I needed to shift my focus from defining my identity based on my "current self" to who I aspired to become in the future.

I had a feedback session with Professor Cabrera. He led me through a candid self-awareness exercise that changed my professional life. It was like a therapy session. As I talked, I diagnosed the problem myself: I lacked a purpose! Since purpose isn't something you create but rather emerges from your values, I realized that mine is to use knowledge to strengthen the reputation of companies and individuals, promote trustful relationships with all their stakeholders, and generate Corporate Brand Value and Personal Identity, respectively.

THE VALUE OF REPUTATION

Around this time my friend Vivien from college had taken over as the commercial director of Fleury Laboratory. Most healthcare companies lacked a marketing department because the medical community believed that the discipline was used only by companies with questionable images. Despite this prejudice, I was pulled once again by Vivien and "raised" to the challenge of structuring the marketing and communicatior department and managing Fleury's brand reputation.

I led the rebranding of Fleury Laboratory into Fleury Medicina e Saúde, or Fleury Medicine and Health, earning recognition as the most valuable brand in the complementary healthcare sector, according to a Brand Analytics / Millward Brown survey in 2010. My strong reputation in brand management led me to another healthcare institution, where I created the A.C.Camargo Cancer Center brand to replace the Cancer Hospital brand. The results were significant, with a perception increase from 17% to 26% as the best hospital for cancer treatment and a growth in new patient admissions from 7% to 25% in the first year alone.

Still in the healthcare sector, I had the opportunity to launch the NotreDame Intermédica Group brand. The strategy brought a reputation for quality services with excellent cost-benefit, generating brand value, evidenced by the stock price rising from R$16.50 at the IPO in 2018 to R$66.95 in 2022.

These are three success cases, all from the same sector, but with very different strategies among them. I believe the process starts with a good diagnosis. You need to feel the pulse of the business, know its differentiators, and listen to their stakeholders. You need to invest in values, and, in due time, the brand's purpose will naturally emerge. Only with the brand's identity established can you move on to communicating its positioning and attributes to the market, thus generating reputation gains for the brand.

THE VALUE OF "RAISING"

My Purpose of spreading knowledge also shaped my leadership style. I'm deeply committed to people's development, consistently "raising" women up by empowering them with knowledge, fully aware of its transformative potential in their life stories.

I've been "raised" by wonderful women and have "raised" many others. But my greatest pride is using my Purpose to "raise" my daughter Marina, echoing the legacy I inherited from my mother. Today, she understands the power of knowledge in shaping her life! She's pursuing Electrical and Computer Engineering at USC in Los Angeles and knows how to benefit from both an innovative formal education and relationships with people from different cultures.

Recently, my friend Tina, whom I met during my master's, introduced me to the group "Rise and Raise Others." It's a privilege to be among strong, intelligent, and empathetic women in this support network. It offers an invaluable platform for sharing experiences and knowledge in an environment filled with sisterhood. Once again, I was "raised" by someone I met while studying! And once again, the two values imparted by my family—knowledge and trust—are together, allowing me to exercise my brand identity and my Purpose.

ALINA ASIMINEI

Regional Sector Leader Europa, Middle East, Africa at Kimberly Clark Kimberly–Clark Corporation
LinkedIn: www.linkedin.com/in/alinaasiminei

A JOURNEY OF PASSION, GROWTH, AND RESILIENCE

THE CURIOSITY THAT SPARKED A DREAM

Lesson 1: Nurturing Curiosity to Unleash Boundless Potential
I was born in Iasi, Romania, to a loving middle-class family. Growing up, my parents instilled in me the importance of education and the belief that I could shape my own destiny. However, living under the confines of a closed regime, my heart yearned for exploration and the desire to know the world beyond the borders. Curiosity became my guiding light, igniting a fire within me that knew no bounds.

EMBRACING THE CALL OF THE UNKNOWN

Lesson 2: Embracing the Unfamiliar and Striving for Greatness
When an opportunity to study abroad in Portugal presented itself, I leaped at the chance. Leaving behind everything familiar, I embarked on a journey that forever transformed my life. The world unfolded before my eyes, and I discovered that settling for mediocrity was not an option. I embraced the notion that greatness lies in pushing beyond comfort zones and never ceasing to reach for more.

TRUSTING MY INSTINCTS, EMBRACING CHANGE

Lesson 3: Embracing Change as a Catalyst for Personal Growth
Leaving my hometown of Iasi behind, I arrived in the bustling city of Bucharest, eager to carve my path. Although uncertainties loomed large, I listened to the whispers of my instincts and trusted that I would find my way. Supported by friends, I embraced change as a catalyst for growth, knowing that true transformation occurs outside the confines of familiarity.

HUMILITY AND THE WILLINGNESS TO LEARN

Lesson 4: Embracing Humility and Unleashing the Power of Continuous Learning

To sustain myself in Bucharest, I took on various jobs, including working at McDonald's as a Manager Trainee. With a humble heart, I embraced the opportunity to learn from the ground up. The experience taught me the power of humility, the importance of being open to new experiences, and the tremendous growth that comes from a constant thirst for knowledge.

SEIZING OPPORTUNITIES, REGRETTING NOTHING

Lesson 5: Embracing Opportunities and Living a Life with No Regrets

The chance to work at Nestle in Portugal beckoned, and though it meant leaving the comforts of home, I knew deep within me that saying "yes" to this opportunity was the only path I could take. Regret was a notion I refused to entertain, for I understood that true growth and fulfillment come from seizing every chance that comes our way. K-C Internal Only.

RESILIENCE AND THE POWER OF INDEPENDENCE

Lesson 6: Cultivating Res'lience and Discovering the Strength Within

Living alone in Lisbon, far from the warmth of family and familiar faces, I discovered an inner resilience I never knew existed. Nestle became my foundation, where I built the pillars of responsibility and self-reliance. Each day taught me the value of hard work and the profound satisfaction that comes from creating my own path, both personally and professionally.

TRIUMPHING OVER CHALLENGES IN A NEW LAND

Lesson 7: Resilience, Innovation, and Embracing the Journey

As life led me to Brazil to be with my beloved husband, *Nestle Brazil* became my new canvas for growth. Market challenges and declining market shares greeted me with open arms. However, armed with resilience and unwavering determination, I harnessed the power of innovation. Together with my team, we breathed new life into brands, defied the odds, and witnessed remarkable growth against all odds.

A STRUCTURED APPROACH TO OVERCOMING OBSTACLES

Lesson 8: The Art of Problem-Solving with Clarity and Purpose

At *Philips Brazil*, I faced a fresh challenge: reviving the Domestic Appliance division. Armed with passion and a structured approach, I delved deep into the intricacies of the industry. Every decision made was steeped in rationale, driven by a clear vision of success. It was here that I learned the profound impact that structure and meticulous problem-solving can have on achieving extraordinary outcomes.

THE BLOSSOMING OF THE SELF

Lesson 9: Resilience, Growth, and the Endless Journey Within

In the face of trials and tribulations, I realized that resilience was my greatest ally. Through every hardship, I uncovered hidden strengths and nurtured personal growth. The journey was never easy, but it was through these moments of struggle that I blossomed into a stronger, wiser, and more compassionate individual.

EPILOGUE: EMBRACING LIFE'S TAPESTRY

Lesson 10: The Tapestry of Life and Embracing Every Thread

As I reflect on my journey, I realize that life is an ever-unfolding tapestry. Each chapter, with its triumphs and challenges, has woven a story of passion, growth, and resilience. From the depths of curiosity to the heights of personal and professional achievements, I have learned that embracing the unknown, trusting our instincts, and embracing change are the keys to unlocking our true potential. May my story inspire others to embark on their own remarkable journeys of self-discovery and fu fillment.

ANA CORTAT

VP Brand and Connections Strategy at Soko
email: anacortat@icloud.com / ana.cortat@soko.cx
Instagram: @anacortat / Twitter: @anacortat
LinkedIn: www.linkedin.com/in/ana-cortat-8bb745a/

BETWEEN WORLDS

As I always say, I am a gerund, happening while what came before and after me reveals itself. I like to imagine that, like me, many other women have woken up, and will wake up one day, with a latent desire to look inside, recognize, welcome, and honor everything they carry, both the darkest and the most sacred.

The story I am about to tell here began before I was born, and influenced and continues to influence who I am becoming in all dimensions. The journey to the moment when we are considered to have the right to a seat in the room where the decisions we make influence the lives of thousands of people, is full of invitations to forget our beliefs and where we come from. Regarding this, all I can say at almost 58 years of age and 40 years of profession, can be summed up in one word: resist!

In July 1965, I was born in a small town in the interior of the State of Minas Gerais. Small, but much larger than the town where my maternal great-grandmother was born, and much closer to it than the country from which my paternal great-grandmother's family left to live in Brazil.

Grandma Carlota, my maternal great-grandmother, was born on one of the several coffee farms in the interior of Minas Gerais, in the region near the town of Espera Feliz. She was born under the "Lei do Ventre Livre" (*the Brazilian law that abolished slavery for children born to enslaved women*). A stroke of luck that her sister, Aunt Efigênia, did not have. Aunt Efigênia was born into slavery. Mother Cila, my paternal great-grandmother, was born Tarcila. I hardly knew her, but I've heard that her marriage to my great-grandfather united different European countries. In fact, I have a memory of only one meeting with that woman with very white skin and hair. These two women never met, but the story of prejudice that unfolded from their lives defined my identity, even when I tried to prevent it from existing.

My maternal great-grandmother had several sons and daughters, one of them, my Grandma Olivia, was a strong and sweet woman. Stronger than sweet. She got married when she was less than 15 years old and had her first child before she turned 16. Watching her give orders to the workers on the farm, wring the necks of chickens, dice pigs, turn lard into soap, fix the roof, roast coffee beans, offer her lap when we couldn't sleep, face the people who somehow tried to subdue her or any of us, made me discover at a very early age that there is no limit to what a woman is capable of accomplishing, nor to how pain can transform this capability into a struggle that seems to have no end.

Like Grandma Carlota, Grandma Olivia also never knew who Mother Cila was. They may have seen each other at some point, but I never saw them in the same room, at the same celebration, or on the same street. The racism that almost prevented my parents' marriage made us grow up recognizing and being challenged to choose sides. Grandma Carlota or Mother Cila. Father or Mother. White or Black.

When context somehow force you to choose between sides without which you wouldn't exist, the result can be that you end up not existing anywhere. I grew up without thinking about race, origin, culture, and ancestry. Because of our skin color, my sisters and I didn't seem to have been born of the same father and mother. We knew what made us the same, but we never thought about what made us different. I was the black daughter, but to Grandma Olivia, I was blessed with an undefined brown color, a "perfect nose," and "good hair." Please understand, my grandmother was a great woman, but she carried sufferings she couldn't overcome. To her, whiteness was a way to reduce pain.

> *"Motivated by European ideas of racial purity and bloodline, whiteness was an index of honor and value, entitling individuals to public office, recognition, and wealth. Belonging to a caste had impacts not only on people's civil and religious rights but also determined taxation aspects, impediments to assuming public and religious positions, and restrictions of movement". (WORLD BANK GROUP, 2018)*

The idea that whiteness was an index of honor and value that opened doors and provided conditions denied to the African population and Indigenous people was dominant for a long time in Brazil and throughout Latin America, and still is. Whitening considered black and Indigenous populations as "inferior races" and, therefore, as obstacles to a European standard of development and progress, as projected and desired by a white elite, of development and progress.

> *"The whitening ideologies impacted public policymaking to the point*

of encouraging European immigrants to establish themselves in the continent with the intent of progressively whitening the population. From 1880 to 1930, Argentina, Brazil, Cuba, and Uruguay received over 11 million European immigrants. In 1925, the Uruguayan government proudly announced that the country was at that point 'entirely of European origin' despite its large Afro-descendant population." (WORLD BANK GROUP, 2018)

I was born in the presence of the absence generated by racism, but compared to people who were born without any passing, I remember very few encounters where I was face-to-face with it. When I was 14, I was followed from the school gate all the way home by a group of girls shouting: "Crazy black girl, crazy black girl!", "Who do you think you are, you colored girl?" and other things that, even after so long, I can still hear.

At 25, my boyfriend told me that we could never have children because his mother would not accept a "black grandchild." He said this while I was telling him that I was pregnant. He continued his reasoning by stating that he would personally see to it that I would be nothing or no one if I decided to go through with the pregnancy. Unfortunately, at that moment, I believed that he could destroy me. A few years later, while staying in the same house as a group of friends in Búzios, the son of one of them asked me if I was there to be his nanny. These are stories that I spent a huge part of my life believing that if I didn't tell anyone, they wouldn't exist.

Time went by. Professional success came as a result of many things, including 12-hour workdays in environments where harassment was normalized and a willingness to forgo vacations. With all the bad things that were generated and three burnouts - one of them incapacitating - I needed to look at what I was leaving behind as I charged ahead.

That's how I fell in love with questions. I kept asking myself who was the person that was revealing herself in me, what was mine, what belonged to others, and who I was learning to be. Yes, I always tell my students to fall in love with questions! The passion for finding the answer can make the first thing you find seem like everything you need. Whenever you believe you have found the answer, understand what it means, and formulate a new question. This will generate the necessary friction to keep you moving forward. That's how I kept going.

I participated in my first electoral campaign at the age of 23. After that, I took part in two presidential campaigns and ten state government campaigns, and I took on what I understood to be a board of directors at the age of 27. I left Minas Gerais at the age of 30 and ten years later became vice-president of a multinational company for the first time. During that time, I do not recall being offended or passed over in any aspect that was clearly related to race or color. As my grandmother predicted, her marriage to a Swiss descendant and my mother's marriage to a German descendant had "gifted" me with enough passing that I only had to take care of a few details: I rarely went to places where I had to spend a lot of time in the sun, and I was always "protected from darkening" by sunscreen and by carefully brushing my hair straight at least twice a week. One of the skills in which I excelled, among others, was becoming increasingly white.

Consciously or not, we are part of a social structure that creates notions of belonging based on similarities. For this reason, as Grandma Olivia imagined, my "undefined brownness," my "perfect nose," and my "good hair" allowed me to be included and made me white enough in the white eyes of my reference group.

It took me a long time to pay attention to what it all meant. It took decades before I started researching my own history and realized that the idea of miscegenation as a representation of racial harmony, an expression present in several texts I consulted while trying to understand, reinforced the belief that ethnic-racial relations in Brazil and throughout Latin America did not require attention, recognition, care, and change.

> "The idea of miscegenation continued to associate progress and the future with whiteness, which continued to symbolize modernity and development desired by Latin American societies. Whether consciously or not, theories of racial mixing emphasized the superior status of whiteness over other racial contributions. In this context, attempts to visualize racial differentiation were increasingly seen as contrary to the national discourse of progress and unity and were often characterized as promoting racism." (WORLD BANK GROUP, 2018)

The silence and complicity with the violence generated by racism are not part of a story that I tell believing that it only concerns others. These were also issues that were not on the agenda or seemed relevant to me for a long time as I grew professionally. Until the day I had to explain to the creative vice-president of a large agency that an ad where a black painter applying white paint under his arm to promote the advantages of an odorless paint was racist. That's when I heard him say that my problem with the ad was personal. Finally, after a long time, someone was defining me again by my difference. It was liberating. He was right, it was personal. The ad was never aired, and I never forgot who I am.

I am Ana Cortat. Descendant of great men and women brought by force to be enslaved in Brazil. I grew up under the ideology of whiteness. I was born between worlds, and I will never allow anything or anyone to hijack my right to live the ancestry with which I identify and prevent me from using my place in the world to collaborate so that the history that will be written from here on will take us to a better place than the one we have been in until now.

REFERENCE

World Bank. 2018. *Afrodescendants in Latin America: Toward a Framework of Inclusion.*

ANDRÉA FREIRE HOPPE MARTINS

LinkedIn: www.linkedin.com/in/andreafhmartins

FEMININE POWER IS A WORD

We are living through interesting times. We are protagonists of a movement that is slowly dismantling crystallized ideas in a patriarchal and sexist society. Women who achieve their professional goals and fulfill their desires serve as inspiration to others. They can be and they can do whatever they want and are increasingly numerous. When I see the success of the Stanley brand - my current job is to develop it in various countries - I feel more than pride and motivation to move forward. I feel the power of a story materializing around me. My story. If I said that only the women in my life gave me the impetus and conditions to get where I am today, I would be unfair. Yes, they were very important. But fortunately, the trajectory of a person - in my case, me - is not always as obvious as some soap opera or streaming series scripts. As the youngest daughter, I saw my father die in 1990, at the age of 77, when I counted only 14 years old. The mourning was amplified by my mother's depression, stepmother to my half-brother and half-sisters, almost her age.

I had the privilege of having a brother "ahead of his time", thirty years older. José Luís, married and with children, was a "brother" who took me under his wings like another daughter. Not at all sexist, he saw me with 100% potential to achieve my dreams, seek my happiness and fulfillment.

He passed away years ago, but Zé was a self-made man who taught me the value of work, financial responsibility, and the ability to manage and plan. During school holidays, I "seriously-played" at working in his company or on his farm. He was an entrepreneur who rose high, and helped me after our father's death, encouraging me to seek more and more knowledge and experiences. He funded me as a high school exchange student - which I did in a tiny town in Idaho, United States. I collected experiences, matured, and mastered English.

I chose to study marketing at ESPM, in Brazil, in the early 1990s because it was a new profession that would allow me to create, build, and fly. As we were running out the resources my father had left, I needed to find work to continue paying for my school. I was still a freshman. Given my lack of work experience, the only job I could get was as a salesperson in a clothing store. But the injustices committed by the owners -

which financially harmed me and my colleagues - outraged me. In a short time, I quit. Other employees followed my example and resigned. I think it was at that moment that I saw myself, unintentionally and for the first time, as a leader. However, leaving bad bosses may cleanse the soul, but do not dissolve the bills. I had college to pay for. I needed to enter my field of study as soon as possible: marketing. I got an internship at a small agency. My dedication and my desire to learn were infinite. Result: hired! College guaranteed, paid for, and completed. Phew.

It didn't take long for me to feel the need to improve my education. The idea of spending some time abroad came up. Once again, my brother came into play, agreeing to sponsor a Business Administration program abroad. And I found myself embarking once again to the United States, this time to study in UCBerkeley. 1997 was an intense year. Studies. Internship. Effort. Reward. I was sure it would come. And it did. Upon returning to Brazil, Reckitt, the first multinational I had worked for since 1994, rehired me. At 23, I was promoted to manager, the youngest in the company's history. It was a great moment of satisfaction, both for the journey behind me and for the road ahead of me. Mainly, for being able to support myself financially and help my mother.

I have some quirks, like everyone else. One of them is very dear to me: my endless desire to know more, to learn, and satisfy any curiosity that would make any cat with seven lives or more jealous. Come on, cat. I doubt you're more curious than me!

I've never stopped studying. After my studies in California, I joined leadership programs at Columbia and Stanford, and even a one-year executive program at Yale. I met incredible people, loyal companions, and colleagues who supported me and continue to support me to this day. A group that helps me see and make sense of so much effort that, yes, brings a lot of joy and a sense of being on the right side of life. I've never worked for competing companies and always wanted to add different areas of expertise precisely because I was seeking new knowledge and experiences. I've held positions in marketing, sales, and general management. I've lived in five cities and three countries. I've worked for private and publicly traded companies. Family-owned and professionalized businesses. Brazilian and multinationals. A collection of experiences that shaped me, as well as my passions. I love reading. I love traveling even more so. I love discovering places that open my mind. I take my daughters with me whenever possible. They encourage me, mirror my example, and overflow with pride for my achievements.

My journey arouses interest and provokes recurring questions: how did you plan your career? How did you reach the top? How do you balance career and motherhood? Since I took over as president of Kraft Foods Ecuador at 35, my answer has been repeated. It sounds somewhat surprising, but it is entirely true: I never planned to reach a certain end, I always dedicated myself to today, to surpassing myself, to giving my best. While I did not plan the evolution of my career, I intensely walked paths that led me to ever greater heights. I have always been driven by a huge desire to learn. The desire for more knowledge mixes with a capacity for over-delivering and strong dedication to everything I do.

Without false modesty, I consider this one of my greatest qualities. And to these personality ingredients, I add the support received from people close to me and the ability to seize all the opportunities that appeared. There you have the recipe for my life. But like any good dessert, my recipe includes a special topping: my husband, partner, companion on all journeys. I am with Rodrigo, and he has been with me, for better or for worse, since I was 23 years old. He is proud and supports me in my determined way of being, dedicating my energy and strength to reach the highest possible goals, and this makes him the ideal father to my daughters Victoria and Beatriz, now teenagers.

When Vicky was 4 years old and Bia was 2, I received a challenging invitation with an excellent opportunity for personal and professional growth. At that time, in 2012, we lived in Curitiba. Rodrigo worked for a telecommunications multinational in the commercial area, and I worked for Kraft Foods as Beverage Category Director.

One day, on another ordinary day in the city, with cloudy skies and that typical chill in the South of Brazil, I heard the proposal that would change everything and reward me with unforgettable moments: I was chosen for the position of Business Unit President in Ecuador. Should I accept? Do you know that up and down feeling of a roller coaster? Well, that's how I felt. Butterflies in my stomach mixed with excitement, happiness for the recognition of my work, enticed with the idea of experiencing a unique leadership experience that I judged myself fully capable of facing. But I had to consider my family. It would be a transformation in their lives. It's the kind of decision that should not be made alone. All of us women are strong and capable of doing everything we desire. However, we must never forget that we are humans and not comic book superheroes, although everyday life skews us in that direction.

We decided to go ahead, but not before having many conversations and guarantees of supporting networks. Rodrigo quit his job, where he had been for ten years, and took a sabbatical period to help with the care and education of the girls. The fact is that Ecuador was an intense period. What could have been a common international executive experience, dealing with daily corporate challenges, ended up becoming a special learning experience. Leading the unit during the Cadbury acquisition by Kraft was a kind of "never-planned gift". At home, my husband and daughters were learning another culture, and other languages, accumulating unique experiences and stories. But Ecuador also had a downside. I confess that I didn't think much about sexism, because I never felt less or stopped growing because I am a woman. Until I had to deal with this issue. It was before a meeting of leaders from various industries. I was talking in a group of men when suddenly one of them said, "What did you do to get to this position so young?". I didn't know the guy whose tone was cynical and misogynistic. I felt like a knife was piercing my stomach and was not naive to really understand the intention behind his statement. I pulled all my energy together and replied by asking if he had enough free time to listen to my professional trajectory, which was my way of defending my honor and that of all women who rise through their own and their team's merit. One piece of advice: never leave an idiot without a response.

I was lucky enough to come across other "gifts" on my executive journey, each of them adding immeasurable value to my story. In 2017, already back in Brazil so that I could be with my mother in her last years of life, I was part of the team that presented Camil Alimentos to banks and financial analysts and participated in the IPO (initial public offering) of the company. Two years later, I took over as president of PMI Stanley in Rio de Janeiro. Once again, the family moved to a new city, not without facing resistance from the girls, who were adapted to São Paulo. And now they enjoy, grateful, their Carioca lives. In the new company, I once again received the "gift" that spices up and makes the executive career more flavorful: PMI Worldwide was bought by another American group. I can say that it is much more difficult to be acquired than to acquire, and this was another valuable experience, another floor built in my castle of learning. Don't think it was 100% easy. It's a journey and, as such, there are rocks, holes, and other obstacles. However, it is precisely overcoming each of them that strengthens one's story. It is, in a way, like a hero's journey. It serves for fiction, it serves for reality: from ordinary life, they are called to adventure. They hesitate, find their mentor, accept, cross the unknown, and make allies and enemies. The reward and recognition always come.

I feel immense satisfaction when I see myself today, putting all my experience at the disposal of mentoring projects, alongside NGOs or guiding talents within my own organization. I use my position to encourage diversity in my company. I make it clear that the energy I dedicate to work is generated by a feminine power that sees no limits to gender. I create a culture of equal opportunities. I advocate for open discussion, and flexible ways of working, encourage women to be present at special moments for their children, promote pregnant women or those on maternity leave, and give visibility to their achievements. And the list goes on. In summary: I spare no effort to facilitate the path of women towards fulfillment, doing everything to allow their growth without barriers. For me, this is non-negotiable. If I cannot change the world, I can impact individual lives. I take pleasure in making this difference. I think my motivation, drive, and achievement impulse are innate. I have a strong personality that has benefited from sparks ignited by various people around me. They helped spark a flame of success that I hope never to see extinguished. I want the light of this fire to illuminate the path and the heart of my daughters, so that they can do what they love, so that they do not limit themselves and never subject themselves to expressions like "women cannot." Yes, they can. Everything.

ANDRÉIA BARBOSA SANTAMARIA

Head of Industry CPG - UOL
Instagram: @desantamaria
LinkedIn: www.linkedin.com/in/andreia-barbosa-santamaria-a0192a82

GIVING UP WAS NEVER AN OPTION

WHERE DID I COME FROM?

I was born in the North Zone of São Paulo, in the neighborhood of Vila Nova Cachoeirinha. I am the middle child of Maria de Lourdes da Silva and Severino Barbosa da Silva. My parents always told me that my mother's delivery was not easy. At that time, it was common for women to want a normal natural birth performed at home; however, no one ever counted on the risks, like my case where. I was with the umbilical cord wrapped around my neck. After hours of trying at home, I was born in the maternity ward. My father told us that the doctor asked, "Which one do I save?" And my father logically replied, "Both!" When he saw me, my father fell in love with me.

Little did he know that I had already made a soul pact with my father. I may not have his skin color, but I understood all the pain he endured in our racist society. My father and I had a connection from past lives, and often I was more than just his daughter, resulting in my early maturity as I took care of him, this "negão," from a very young age. Neither I nor my sisters, Adriana and Fabiana, inherited his black skin, but we inherited his courage, generosity, and sensitivity. I attended elementary school in a municipal school. My childhood was very sweet and fun; among various friends, some from the hill and others from the neighborhood where I lived, I discovered myself in living situations that made me reflect on human behavior and society, because there - between school and street games - I noticed the difference in social class. Always very sensitive, I navigated between the two worlds, and all of this only made me certain about my choices in life.

MY UPBRINGING, MY REFERENCES

My school was in front of my godmother Elizabeth's house, a strong woman of German origin who expressed her love through cooking. She also played the role of a grandmother. I was talkative and had a curiosity about the world. I remember from a young age that I had a feeling of "being" someone that my parents and grandfather could be proud of, and along with that feeling, there was also the desire to offer my parents a better life, different from the world that was restricted to the North Zone. Time passed, I grew up and understood many things, including the difficulty that was the biggest and most curious for me: dealing with my father's illness. In my adolescence, I understood that my father suffered from alcoholism, and that was why so many uncertainties surrounded our family. Even when he least believed that he was giving me something, he didn't know how much I was learning and strengthening myself. The disease itself was not the most difficult, but rather all the judgments and prejudices that disadvantaged him in life. As I grew up, I also came to understand my father's illness; alcoholism was something that often made the whole family sick. We couldn't make many plans, and we never knew if we would be okay.

My father was one of the most loving people I have ever met in my life. A man who taught with his gaze, saying "thank you" and "fly far, my girl". When I was still young, he looked at me and searched for something in each person that could nourish me, even without their realizing it. My aunt Fatima was a successful executive; my mother carried strength and courage; my older sister, Adriana, was the intelligent one, full of skills; my godmother had the determination and strength of a German. Each of these women brought something that inspired me and awakened in me the desire to be like them. Could I, Andréia, ever be a courageous, audacious, intelligent, loving, generous woman of success? Living with these women made me grow, with the certainty that the bond of love and reciprocity was the fuel I needed to be.

PROFESSION

Choosing my profession was not an easy task; it seemed that I had no aptitude for anything; no vocational test worked. I think the impostor syndrome started there. It was by elimination that I chose advertising. When I finished my technical course and entered college, my mother was working for an advertiser. Owner of a successful agency "Delta Propaganda," Mr. Carlos Guntovitch told my mother: "Tell your daughter to look for my son and he will find an internship for her." I did my first internship in a marvelous agency, with incredible people. But it ended and college was expensive; I needed to find something paid. So, I became a media assistant at an agency in Santana called R&S Propaganda.

But one beautiful day, reading *Meio&Mensagem*, I came across a news article announcing that a **woman**, Cristina Carvalho Pinto was opening a new advertising agency. I cut out the article and showed it to my mother when I got home; it would be a dream to be able to work there. My mother encouraged me, and I made my resume that night with my sister's eager help. I bet there was nothing more powerful and vibrant on the planet than a mother's words. Then, after three days, Marcia Salgueiro called me asking me to come in for an interview; I couldn't believe it was happening. I joined Full Jazz! There I connected with the world, with people, with my field. I started to develop myself, make friends, and build my career. Cristina Carvalho Pinto is a very admirable woman, and there was another trait that I admired deeply: Her way of speaking with employees, her concern for everyone's health, and at the same time so demanding, creative. I stayed at the agency for three years and then moved on to incredible leaps as a media professional.

Between my 27th and 30th years, I was flying. I got married at 27 and became pregnant at 30 - the greatest joy of my life. But as nothing was easy, during my pregnancy we also discovered the impact my father's health would have on our family, when he was diagnosed with throat cancer. Along with the birth of my daughter, I had to manage the worst feeling of all: "fear." For the first time, I was afraid of losing my greatest friend, but Barbara was our strength; my father knew how important it was for us to go through everything and win together. And we did it! This new phase of my life made me reflect a lot on quality of life, family, work; and many things led me to reflect on the importance of acquiring new knowledge. I began to be bothered by corporate behavior. I noticed that the people who were promoted were mostly men. They stood out and were part of a "clique" that I didn't see any possibility of belonging to, and not just because I am a woman. First, because I didn't imagine acting in that way, and then because some invitations never came. But I didn't give up. I went through several big agencies and enjoyed incredible years and a lot of learning with incredible leadership opportunities. Despite enjoying a certain level of success, I realized that I wanted to change fields and learn new things. Together with my husband, we began to think about the paths we could take. It wasn't an easy decision. I was passionate about the media field in which I worked, but the lack of time with family, the lack of financial advancement, and the lack of vision for professional growth were among the reasons why I decided to change.

I then accepted the invitation of a great friend, Alexandre Barsotti, to work with him at Editora Três. I was hired as a business executive, serving direct clients. I traveled more than 100 km per day interviewing new clients, but I was happy because someone was giving me the opportunity I needed.

THE TURNING POINT WAS NOT EASY

Starting over and seeing that the glamour as a media professional had ended was strange. At that moment, I evaluated my true friends, adjusted my course, and, together with my husband, who has always been my partner and inspiration, began to outline my growth plan.Things started happening. I continued until Barsotti, my director, called me for a conversation. He had a "digital" vacancy because Editora Globo was digitizing; the challenge of this transition was to act simultaneously on all titles as a multi-platform. I thought: Will I be up to this challenge? My digital professional experience until that moment had only been as a media technician inside agencies. I didn't know if I had the skills and techniques to move into sales.

I "turned the key" and started studying digital technology. I had the support of many colleagues and worked there for nine years. I started as a digital executive, reached the position of Manager of Women's and Digital Magazines, led the transformation of Marie Claire magazine, along with a team of five incredible executives, including two of my best friends: Rosa and Alexandra. Years later, I became pregnant with my second child. It was special for the family because during that time I had lost a pregnancy; so, I knew it was a gift that we were again experiencing that emotion. I also encountered again the fear of my father being sick again during my pregnancy. There was no more alcoholism, but his health was very fragile. Gian Luca was born and nine months later, my father passed away. It's amazing how sometimes we have to deal with such contradictory feelings simultaneously. Joy and sadness go hand in hand, and it's up to us to understand the purpose of life. There I discovered a new and different Andreia: a mother, wife, and daughter, with a strength that I couldn't explain. It seemed that nothing else frightened me. I stayed a few more years and my cycle at the digital publisher ended. Now, with two children and advancing in age, new insecurities appeared. Despite feeling more prepared for life, the sense of feeling overlooked was something new and strange to me."

"BUT LIFE GOES ON"

It was now time to explore new horizons. After the publishing house, I went through new opportunities and began to see that life is not just about results and performance. So, I decided to take care of the hardest part of Andréia: knowing how to relate, how to open myself up, without suspicions, without armor, without fear of planning. After about three months, I had the opportunity to go to Disney Company, Radio Disney. The desire to dive into the digital world had brought a certain restlessness;

what I wouldn't imagine is that diving 100% into digital would open up new doors of opportunity and fields of knowledge for me. Five years ago, I was invited to take on the strategic position at UOL (Universo On-Line). I became head of the CPG (Consumer Packaged Goods) segment. Being at UOL is challenging; it's an industry that challenges me daily. I wake up every day with the desire to contribute and learn something.

In this year of 2023, I was able to travel to Austin, Texas and visit SXSW. I never imagined that I could see so many opportunities like I saw at South by Southwest. It were incredible days, a unique experience that I recommend to everyone, a mixture of knowledge along with a lot of gratitude. Do you remember that girl from the ZN movies who wanted to fly? That was the feeling I had. I remember that when I received the proposal from UOL, I said to my directors André Vinicius and Bebeto Pirro: "Why me?" At that moment, I didn't even believe that I should be considered for the position, going to the largest portal in Brazil and leading the CPG category seemed like a dream. But they clearly had a good set of reasons for choosing me.

My husband used to tell me: "Do you still not understand why they chose you?" I immediately started thinking about all the qualities and qualifications that led me to this position. Today, I am certain that all my experiences have brought me to this moment. I have built this journey, and there is still so much more to come. It's amazing how often we doubt our own abilities, knowledge, and power. Today, I know that we can go far beyond what we think is possible and that we don't always have all the answers, but believing in ourselves, preparing, and taking action make all the difference. Seek knowledge, embrace your vulnerabilities, always wish for the best, and be sure that your journey will take you to incredible places. These are the components of success. I am grateful for the incredible women who are with me on this journey, and my family, especially my husband, who supports and endures this crazy life of being an executive, mother, and wife. And of course, to my parents, who always believed in and supported me.

ANDRESSA MARTINS

CEO World Advertising Festival of Gramado. Master and trainer in NLP - Neuro-Linguistic Programming from the Free School affiliated with NLPU - California. Director of ALAP, the Latin American Advertising Association, a nonprofit organization present in over 17 countries in Latin America. Entrepreneur at Just Grass USA.

Instagram: @andressamartins.me
LinkedIn: www.linkedin.com/in/andressanyc

IT IS POSSIBLE WHEN YOU BELIEVE

THE BEGINNING OF MY PROFESSIONAL LIFE.

The beginning of my professional life started early, at 13 years old, my first job was in the accreditation of the Gramado Festival. My uncle, João Firme, founder and ideator of the event, gave me the opportunity to be closer to something that I admired since I was little. I admired my uncle for the work he did, the trips taking the name of the Festival and the agility with which he managed to bring people closer. My mother and my brother worked at events and my father had his own business. At 15 years old, my father lost all his assets, and I had a paid trip to Disney. Arriving in front of the castle, I made a promise to God, Walt, all the Saints I could remember: whatever happened, I would come back there every year. It was at that moment that I began to believe that, if I knew how to dream, I could achieve.

FACING CHALLENGES.

While dealing with the supposed "imposter syndrome," I realized that many women I met during my journey also faced the same dilemma. I always saw this symptom as a result of the sexist culture that subjugates women and makes us incapable or insecure to occupy leadership positions. When my father passed away, I thought I would never be completely happy again. He was the person who encouraged me the most in life. Days after his death, we found a key to the locker where he kept his belongings at the card club he frequented. When I opened the locker, to my surprise, there were newspaper clippings and photos of my travels hanging there. I understood that my place was no longer backstage because the most important person in my life was very proud of me. Two months later, Fabiana Antacli called me and said she would connect me with a wonderful woman who knew Disney like no one else. That's when I received an invitation from Natasha Caiado, from Wish, to take the most incredible trip of my life. In San Francisco, California, on a night when I couldn't sleep, I remembered when my mother made me count sheep. I counted and recounted until I gave up and started to thank.

I said, "gratitude, gratitude, gratitude." That moment was the first time since my father's departure that I felt complete again. It was a very important moment, in which the key turned. the following text: Taking the lead That was a moment to make the most important decisions of my life: accepting the challenge, facing my ghosts, realizing my dream of directing the festival towards a path I always dreamed of; and another one was the choice to get pregnant, on the eve of turning 40 and in a non-conventional marriage. My family background is more conservative, so as expected, both decisions shook me and my family too much. At that moment, several movies of my life were passing through my head: the longing for my father, the promises I made to myself, the struggles I went through working in a male-controlled environment, the desires, the fears, the dreams. All my thoughts led me to that moment in life. And after much feeling and reflection, I decided that from that moment on, I would take care of two children: Helena Maria and the Festival.

THE GRAMADO FESTIVAL: NEW PROJECTS AND IDEAS.

The festival was founded in 1975 and has since been a meeting point for advertising, marketing, and communication professionals. The event is known for being a platform for discussion, presentation of creative and innovative ideas. Many famous advertising campaigns are launched at the Gramado Festival over the years. Under my leadership, I hoped to innovate in this edition. After more than forty years of history, it was as if the festival had a life of its own, with several phases and various significant moments. After a five-year hiatus, the festival and I faced, in 2022, a recovery process that questioned the value of the event. Not only for the public and the advertising market but also in the face of my own ghosts. It was not easy to resume a project the size of the festival, especially with such a traditional and conservative profile. I wondered, "*Does the festival and everything it has to offer still have the same space in the market and in the public's imagination?*" "*Will people still be interested?*" "*Will the changes I want to promote be sustained?*" Several long-time partners of the event were moved by the cause and donated themselves in the most generous way possible. Partners from the past and present, joining a dream that I understood was only mine.

In 2022, at the comeback edition, we talked about how advertising behaves in the digital era. We heard brilliant minds talk about how to build brand narratives, how to offer immersive experiences, and how influencer marketing has been transforming investments in content and media. And it worked! The feedback from the audience and partners was incredible. The proposal to bring back the festival with a new look, following a new editorial line, with a focus on diversity and representation of speakers, was very well received by everyone. It was a confirmation that the path was correct and both me and the festival could hold our heads up high and move forward.

Social Innovation

By 2023, the plan goes beyond, bringing practical knowledge and systemic visions around the creative market, bringing together agencies, professionals, and other diverse players who develop transformative projects aligned with social demands. I want the festival stage to be an amplifier of new voices, new talents. I dream of a more plural, diverse, and - above all - more connected market with the spirit of the current time. Our role will be to teach, inspire, and debate, as that is what drives us. With the resumption, this new hybrid format also came, mixing both in-person and digital experiences. This gave us the possibility to reach many more people, including reaching people with disabilities using inclusive resources.

Project Voices

I am very proud to bring the Project Voices to the festival, which is carried out in partnership with Flagcx (from Martini - an incredible long-time partner of the Festival) and the collective Papel & Caneta (led by André Chaves). It is an initiative that aims to recognize people who are revolutionizing the advertising market with independent and innovative projects, but who still operate on the margins of the mainstream market. This is a project that connects me directly to my own trajectory, because for me, it is as if the festival is doing justice by offering the stage to those who deserve to have their ideas, visions, and voices amplified.

Every year, the Papel & Caneta collective conducts a survey to list more than 30 Brazilians who, both nationally and internationally, have achieved fantastic results with their projects. At the Festival, "Voices" has six categories: New Leaders, Career, Business, Education, Project, and Platform. The jury, made up of 24 professionals, has the task of getting to know the 19 transformation initiatives through an online platform, in which those responsible for the trajectories send five-minute audios. The jury selection process itself involved an act of listening - something that I always lacked during the period when I worked behind the scenes.

Digital Innovation

The post-pandemic world is constantly changing, and people are still adapting to the "distance" format for various activities, such as work, study, and content consumption. The advertising market and, consequently, the Gramado Festival, have also followed these changes, expanding the possibilities of format and opening up to new platforms, such as Meta, Yahoo!, and TikTok, in addition to traditional ones, such as TV and radio. And to think that back then, when I was the young dreamer behind the ticket booth, we didn't even dream of these forms of interaction with the public. It was much more difficult. I believe that the festival's main focus has always been quality content, and we have been able to innovate in various ways. This allowed the festival to show itself even more comprehensive, reaching an even larger audience. One of the most interesting themes addressed in such a special edition was the new profession that emerged in the era of social media: the digital influencer. This profession is gaining more space and prominence in the advertising industry. During the festival, it was discussed how brands are increasingly seeking to approach their target audience through the hiring of digital influencers, who are responsible for creating content that generates engagement. Unlike traditional advertising, the relationship between brand, influencer, and customer is closer and more pleasant, like a conversation between friends.

Conclusion

Taking on leadership and facing challenges are important parts of my professional journey. Although I faced imposter syndrome and prejudice for being a woman and part of the LGBTQIA+ community, I persisted and succeeded in leading the Gramado World Advertising Festival. I am sharing my story to serve as inspiration or encouragement for those who are starting their careers and dealing with similar challenges. Today, I see that my ideas are still alive, make sense, and now I can execute them with new connections and partnerships that believe in me and propel me forward. I had the support of an incredible human being, a mother, woman, warrior, Bianca Andrade (Boca Rosa), when she accepted to go on stage with me. Being with her, I could understand why she shines;

looking at the admiration of her team, the way their eyes shone when they looked at her said a lot about the person she is.

And it is this human being, Bianca, who makes me feel good when I am near. The closing of an event with a panel of women in leadership was extremely significant to me as well. First, because I mediated this panel and it ended up becoming a symbolic way of concluding this passage of the "baton" to my hands. And second, because I went up on stage pregnant, taking care of my daughter, Helena Maria, and concluding an important cycle of a new phase of my other "child", the festival. All of this, in the presence of women whom I admire, respect, and am inspired by. Therefore, I am immensely grateful to Manzar Feres, general director - integrated business in advertising at Globo, who was my first "yes", who believed in this symbolic closure that the panel represented. I also thank Fátima Pissarra from Mynd, Manuela Costa from Vila da Mônica, Rachel Maia, and finally, Natasha Caiado from Wish, who also participated and helped make that moment magical in the history of the festival. It is a magical moment in my life as well. My sincerest gratitude to you all. After the closing of this panel, I was invited by Natasha to join the group of women "One climbs and pulls the other up". In this group, I feel welcomed, respected, and encouraged to achieve all my personal and professional dreams. At this moment, I am crossing a new cycle of affirmation, expansion, and renewal of strength. I believe in better days, both for me and for Helena Maria, and obviously for the festival. I am deeply grateful for the opportunity to share this story with you and sincerely thank you for your unconditional support. Just as Chris Gardner speaks in his movie "The Pursuit of Happyness": "This part of my life, this little part, is called happiness".

ARIANE SANTOS

Passionate about a better world, Administrator, designer, circular economy specialist, founder, and CEO of Badu Design, a socio-environmental business, an initiative with the purpose of reconnecting people through circular design.
Instagram: @badudesign
LinkedIn: www.linkedin.com/in/arianersantos

REDEFINING FOR TRANSFORMATION

How many times have you felt the urge to start over? And how many times have you been pushed out of your comfort zone and had to change course in the surprises and unpredictability of life?

No matter how challenging it is to start over or rise when life throws you a curveball, there's something precious to learn, observe, and emerge stronger. Without romanticizing suffering and new beginnings, but understanding that we have cycles that allow us to experience these challenges and emerge with a broader perspective.

In this chapter, I will share my experiences and the things I've observed and learned while on my journey. Beyond the names of the companies I've worked for and the positions I've held, I've decided to bring forth the essence of my life, what makes sense to me, and what might somehow inspire something in you.

But first, let me introduce myself better. I'm Ariane, the daughter of Teresinha from Pernambuco and Geraldo from Minas Gerais. I was born in Curitiba, where they met and settled. I'm grateful to have two sisters, Viviane and Elaine, who made my childhood happier and who have always been by my side. I also had the great joy of having fantastic grandparents. I was lucky to be born into a family full of love and affection. Despite the family's modest means and various vulnerabilities, love and the guidance to study were never lacking. I was taught values like honesty, integrity, respect, and others that have guided my journey.

My parents amicably separated when I was three years old, and my father was always present in our lives. I grew up in a home with four women, and the power and energy of femininity reigned in that house. My mother, my queen, was an example of courage and resilience, and I deeply admire everything she went through to raise us. I learned to be resourceful, to be more creative in the face of adversity, and to take on responsibility from an early age.

I've always enjoyed reading because I loved living the stories I read. In my adolescence, I read "Pollyanna girl and young woman," and from that moment on, I understood that everything had a positive side, and I started playing the glad game. Whenever there was a lack of something or bad situations, it was because something good would follow. I grew up with a positive outlook, but later, I discovered that the glad game didn't always work, and I was masking my pains, sufferings, feelings, and avoiding reality. I became aware, awakened, but I continued with a positive mindset.

I started working at the age of 14 and attended school in the evenings because it was an opportunity to change my perspective and progress. I realized that if I wanted something, I had to go after it, and life became a race. They used to say I was like a live wire, always getting involved in every opportunity that came my way.

In every company I worked for, I dedicated myself and quickly stood out, advancing to better positions. I began studying Business Administration at a private university, but after two years, I could no longer afford it, and I had to drop out and start over. I studied on my own at home and received support from a program for Black individuals, which helped me get into the Federal University of Paraná to study business administration. It was a significart achievement after the disappointment of not being able to continue my education at the previous college due to financial constraints. But the Federal University was incredible and highly competitive. It was a big win.

Over time, I worked for various companies, eventually becoming the Executive Director of an international entrepreneurial education organization, and I was establishing myself with everything going well in life.

I had the opportunity to study in various organizations, often as a scholarship recipient, and met incredible people on my professional journey who allowed me to travel to various cities, bringing significant lessons. Some angels always appeared on my path.

I took various courses, and one of them was training with Humberto Maturana and Ximena Dávila - Cultural Biology, discussing love in organizations. It left a profound impact on my life, particularly with a seemingly simple question: What do you want to preserve in your life? And what no longer makes sense? It was intense, and it led to several twists and choices after that question.

One of those changes and decisions came from an invitation from a friend and colleague to start a business, and I accepted the challenge.

I left the secure job, and just when I thought I was on the right path, she gave up, and once again, I had to start over and postpone the possibility of entrepreneurship.

I went to work for another company in the field of projects and marketing, developing pattern designs since I had knowledge from the design course I took while taking on part-time jobs and having empty time slots.

As I began to find balance, my grandmother, who had shown me the best of the world, experienced health issues. She became bedridden, had to amputate her leg, lost her vision due to diabetes, and suffered a stroke. It was time to stop everything and take care of her.

Two years of care followed, and when she passed away, I fell into a deep depression and nearly attempted suicide. I shared this story in a TEDx talk years later. It was the first time my family and everyone learned about this, and it was important to talk about it to heal from that phase. To this day, I receive messages from people who identified with this situation and felt more open to discussing personal mental health and mental health within organizations.

After the suicide attempt, I needed to reconnect and decide what I would do from then on. I decided to work on something that made more sense given everything I had experienced so far. I realized that I had spent years copying other people's patterns and not recognizing my authenticity. This phase of reconnection and deep self-discovery was essential for taking the next steps.

I rekindled my desire to become an entrepreneur, and at that moment, all I had was $30. I used that money to start Badu Design, making hand-stitched artisanal notebooks in my "quartellie," a combination of a bedroom and studio. It was a way to start something, and it was therapeutic. Despite everyone thinking it was crazy, after so much effort and study, to stay in my room producing, at that moment, it was time to reconnect, and I knew there was something more significant in everything I was going through.

I persevered and discovered more and more possibilities in this new work format. I remembered all the women I had encountered in hospitals who had no job opportunities. After all, those who care are often not cared for, and the majority are women taking on the role of caregivers. I started to pursue entrepreneurship in this cycle of vulnerability but dreaming big.

I began teaching the women in my community to create various items with fabric. Then, a neighbor brought a bag of fabric scraps that the seamstress discarded every week, and they were beautiful and could be used for many things. Curious, I thought: if the seamstress throws away such a large quantity, how much do textile companies discard? I discovered that it's 170,000 tons of textile waste and over 39 million tons of various waste materials. From that moment on, I decided to use only waste materials.

The business progressed, and while it faced setbacks, I picked myself up. We transformed into a socio-environmental impact business that redefines industrial waste, not just fabric but also wood, iron, plastic, and other materials discarded by the industry into design products, in line with companies' ESG (Environmental, Social, and Governance) actions, with a focus on circularity.

Today, Badu trains women in social vulnerability in circular design. They go through a socio-emotional development phase, have the opportunity to develop, learn a profession in upcycling, and become business partners of Badu Design. They are environmental innovators, creative individuals who, at the bottom of the pyramid, are redefining material waste and their lives.

Initially, there were three women participating, then ten women, and now we have a network of over 1,500 women spread across four cities in Brazil producing circular designs, creating sustainable art and fashion. Badu Design was born to be great and will continue to grow to increase its social, environmental, and economic impact. Soon, we will be present in all states in Brazil and abroad.

We have been featured in various media outlets and received awards from Natura, Aliança Empreendedora, Unilever, Instituto Legado, magazines, and even from the UN as Climate Champions due to the importance of the climate emergency and issues of justice and environmental racism. We produce for major companies and have gained recognition in the market. We are redefining perspectives and showing that at the bottom of the pyramid, there are many powerful women reinventing themselves and contributing to these much-needed changes.

I've lived intensely in the past ten years, breaking cycles of scarcity and moving towards abundance and prosperity that we all deserve. We are in a harvesting phase, reaping what we sowed with love, hard work, and dedication.

Many women who were once seen as worthless, much like the discarded materials we transform, have defied the statistics and are changing their paths because they reconnected and discovered their potentials. No one empowers anyone; we reconnect with our essence, knowledge, and with support and opportunities, we evolve. Through collaboration and a support network, we strengthen ourselves.

I learn from them every day and understand the importance and necessity of us all arriving together, breaking the patterns of society that women face. When we talk about women in social vulnerability, it only exacerbates the layers of inequality to overcome. It will only make sense if all have opportunities and conditions to arrive together. That's why Badu exists, and I am dedicated to this purpose.

We are not all the same; we need more equity, emphasizing the importance of diversity and lifting each other up. I am a Black woman and have experienced various forms of violence due to structural racism, and I still deal with it daily. But I don't let it pass, as I know who I am. Our ancestors were kings and queens, not slaves; they were cruelly enslaved. Let's break the bubbles, acknowledge our privileges, and create opportunities to reduce inequality and help all women achieve their goals.

I was lifted up by Cris Pereira Heal, who has supported my dreams and purpose at Badu. I deeply admire her and other women in this network. It was one of the gifts that entrepreneurship brought me, among many people who were angels at the right time in my journey. I thank God for love and care at all times and for the beautiful family that encouraged me every step of the way.

To all of you:
May there be love to start over, as the song says;
May we redefine our limiting beliefs;
May we have the courage to transform what doesn't make sense;
May we understand our worth and that we are part of a whole, despite our differences and stages of awareness;
May our loving essence be expanded, and may every woman never forget the power she possesses.

Together, we transform!

CAMILA GUARDIA SERRANO

Innovation executive with expertise in business development, digital and cultural transformation
E-mail: camilaguardiaserrano@gmail.com
Instagram: @camilaguardia
LinkedIn: www.linkedin.com/in/camilaguardiaserrano

DOORS ARE ALWAYS OPENING, CAN YOU ACKNOWLEDGE OPPORTUNITIES?

Being a 42-year-old woman with a considerable track record in product innovation, digital products, and the business development market means dealing with convoluted thinking almost every day. If I said that I planned to be in this area, that I prepared to work in one of the most interesting and well-paid scenarios of all time, it would be fiction.

The truth is that reality surpasses fiction. If you think of moments of tension, twists and turns, heroes, or rather, heroines, reality tends to be better. My biography is full of great women. Women who pulled me up in dramatic and decisive moments. They still encourage and inspire me to this day. Throughout my history, I have also been pulled up by Vinicius, my only brother, who always cared about broadening my worldview.

My professional career has given me the chance to experience a large range of business areas and different corporate mindsets. During these years as an innovation executive, I achieved a strong expertise in digital products, business development, and cultural transformation. Working in Technology, Airlines, Travel and Loyalty markets industries, I could play inspiring roles for companies such as IBM, EDS, LATAM, Multiplus, Livelo and most recently as Head of Innovation at Smiles. Currently, I act as Head of Business Development at Telostot, serving as innovation advisor, mentor, change agent, and digital transformation enabler.

My curiosity and hands-on approach to life has been my pattern since I was a child. I grew up in the midst of two very different families. On my mother's side, a traditional profile of Spanish immigrants. On my father's side, a bohemian family that used to host parties with live music in my grandparents' backyard, crowded with all kinds of people. There were four of us: my father, my mother, and my older brother. We lived in a middle-class neighborhood in the city of São José dos Campos/SP.

When I was nine years old, my father was unemployed for at least five years, and our financial situation changed drastically. As I child I went through long critical moments. My mother, who always worked as a homemaker, played a fundamental role in managing the home so that we lacked nothing. We were the classic example of the Economy of Love, a term coined by economist Hazel Henderson to refer to a type of work that is not measured in the financial parameters that rule the economy – a function that is often invisible. During this time of economic challenge, we learned to maintain a light and fun disposition while we made chocolates to sell in our neighborhood. I was in charge of sales in the condo. At the time, my brother also worked outside the home, and together we were able to bring some money home. That feeling was pretty cool.

I learned early the – work-effort-reward paradigm, and it has shaped the person I am today. At 14, I got a temporary job at the mall as a saleswoman. I had no idea at the time that I would gain skills like enchanting customers. I stayed there until I was 17, when I was already a sub-manager in a clothing store. All I wanted was to study, learn languages, and explore the world. My dream was to do an exchange program. During that period, my grandmother Didi, knowing about this dream, sponsored my English course.

So I went away to Topeka, the capital of Kansas, for my first international trip. I attended my last year of high school there. I remember the feeling of getting to know a first-class school. For someone who had studied in public school all her life, it was indescribable. An enchanted world.

LIFE WOULD NEVER BE THE SAME

For someone who always enjoyed having freedom, moving to a bigger city was a one-way street. When I returned to Brazil, six months later, I lived in São Paulo. There were no family or friends. It was a new beginning. But autonomy is something that, once we experience it, we are never willing to give it up.

I passed the admission test for Tourism College and got a job in a software factory as an administrative assistant. I was curious, asking and studying on my own. They offered me a programming language course, and before I knew it, I was developing software. Upon realizing that I was in a promising field, I transferred my position to the Information Systems Management degree. It was like, almost unintentionally, that I entered the technology field – a field that opens doors, opens minds, and provides access to the job market. I had no idea what I was getting into. I improved myself and became an Oracle developer.

I practiced skills that are still relevant today, when it comes to making data-driven decisions. The evolution of my career went through business analyst, support manager, operations, project manager, and business consultant. One characteristic of mine that permeates this entire story is restlessness. I had an enormous curiosity to understand the real needs of the client, to have empathy. I wanted -- and still want -- to mobilize people towards a common goal in order to attain great achievements.

I graduated with some specializations, and I married a man a few years older than I. Together we had two children, Pedro and João, my great loves. After a while, I realized that my husband and I were very different. I wanted to conquer the world and grow. But I felt diminished, censored. My career continued without major advances, like a car driving with the handbrake on.

Nobody builds a family thinking it might end. But when being in a relationship triggers panic attacks, anxiety attacks, and other threats to your health, it's time to abort the mission. In the middle of this realization, I received a dream job proposal that would be a leap in my career. But I was fragile and sick, so I declined the offer.

I am not able to talk about my life without talking about my friends. At that time, it was essential to have some very important people for me: Marcela, Maisa, and Michele, among others, strong and independent women. I am very happy to be able to count on a support network. They are the family I built away from my home city, a network of strong affections.

It was with the help of these great partners that I managed to find my balance again and to get out of that relationship that had no longer made sense for a very long time ago. Today, I say with all certainty: never forsake your friends. Husbands, boyfriends, and jobs sometimes come and go. Friends are forever.

The end of my marriage came in 2018. At the time, I had led a project for the first loyalty company chatbot in Brazil, based on artificial intelligence. I was invited to participate in an annual conference held by Facebook in Silicon Valley. When boarding the plane to come back to Brazil, infected by that interesting universe, I was certain that my marriage was coming to an end.

Trips always have a life-changing tone for me. They open horizons and make me reflect. It was challenging to reorganize my entire life while ensuring that my children were well. But I succeeded. And I rediscovered the Camila I knew.

BACK TO THE GAME

With my personal issues on track, I came back with full force. It was as if I were making up for lost time. I led large and innovative projects for loyalty programs, conceiving new programs for low-income clients, AI-based gamification, wallets with instant payments, travel planning, and team restructuring. Always applying methodologies that best-suited the rapidly changing economic outlook.

I became a person passionate about exploring new opportunities and finding non-obvious paths. At that time, I was responsible at my company for digital transformation strategic planning. Then Camilla, a namesake colleague who worked as an Innovation Manager, opened the door for me to move into the Innovation Lab. To put it simply, it's one of the best places to be, where we create new solutions, business models, and test partnerships based on customer needs. We can experiment, make mistakes, and learn again by launching new products and services in the market.

Camilla taught me the value of authenticity. The importance of being who you are, no matter where you are. It's a huge paradigm shift when you think about the corporate environment. I recognized qualities that I had not appropriated, such as being resilient, a team player, a pollinator, and a great manager. It was so liberating to assimilate all this! I began to trust myself more and was able to deliver major projects. The result of this part of the story is that I became the head of innovation. I did it!

In the innovation field, I could compile my knowledge in a simple way. I say that I help people bring ideas to life, understand innovation in a practical way, and connect with others. I like to contribute to opportunities for impactful, scalable, technology-based business development that generates value and makes a difference.

In the same year, I was invited to lead the gender equity group in the company, an opportunity to share a bit of my story and build initiatives to shed light on the relevance of the topic. We still have only a few women in technology careers in high leadership positions. That is not the focus of the narrative here, but I have experienced harassment and seen many male colleagues promoted before women who were quite ready for the promotion. To achieve something, it still seems that we women have to prove much more than men.

Lifelong learning – anything, anyway – is one of the points I consider fundamental for one to keep growing. Remembering my story, I see that the desire to learn something new has always been crucial for me to have the chance to develop myself and become a successful woman. Learning, learning, learning. I do this by venturing into fast-paced courses to update my skills, participating in major conferences and festivals, being active in communities, being close to people who inspire and teach me, and being connected.

SO, I BECAME WHO I ALWAYS WAS

Today, I work as a mentor for people, innovation advisor, and with initiatives related to entrepreneurship, digital transformation, strategy, development of new businesses, and digital products. I am at my best when I am cultivating what will be the next chapter of my professional life. At the same time, I am a dedicated and loving mother who has fun with my boys; and together we give thanks and pray every night before going to sleep. I am the same Camila that I always was, free, restless to learn, and motivated to knit together new knowledges and insights to create something that really improves people's lives. This is still what excites me the most. Untying a knot. Solving a puzzle. Positively impacting. Leaving a legacy.

You cannot build something true if you are not authentic. When people ask me if working with innovation means doing difficult things, I say that innovating is solving a problem in a simple way, and that technology is just one of the enablers for all of this. It allows for scale. The continual challenge is the ability to understand people, to have the sensitivity to understand different realities, to connect people to solve complex problems.

If I could give you one last piece of advice, it took me years to understand this, it is not to wait for external recognition to be sure of your ability. Validation from the outside may never happen. Not the way you imagine. If it happens, it will have a fleeting impact -- an effect that will end quickly. External approval is never ultimately satisfying. Self-confidence is like a little plant: you have to take care of it every day; it takes time to get strong; and it is subject to inclement weather. But you are solely responsible for it.

It may sound a bit cliché – clichés serve a purpose, nonetheless – but never let anyone diminish or disrespect you. Never stop doing something because a negative comment or evaluation has shaken your confidence. I know it's complicated to preserve this in our ultra-connected world, where everyone talks nonstop, and we are more exposed than ever. If, even so, one day you feel lost, wanting to give up, do something simple: call someone who will encourage you and lift you up!

CARLA RIGHI

Integrative Nutrition Health Coach
E-mail: health.coach@carlarighi.com
Website: www.carlarighi.com
Instagram: @carlarighicoach
LinkedIn: www.linkedin.com/in/carla-righi-93b26950

THE UNIVERSE ALWAYS CALLS US TO OUR PURPOSE. IN ONE WAY OR ANOTHER, WE ALWAYS BUMP INTO IT

A busy life. Plans, goals, and recognition. Little time to take care of oneself. Until the bill comes due, and your purpose screams in your face.

A lawyer with a specialization in Business Administration, with experience in large banks and the executive aviation market, Carla Righi was not afraid to reinvent herself as she matured into womanhood in order to pursue her great passion since adolescence, integrative nutrition. A graduate from The Institute for Integrative Nutrition in New York with specializations in Hormone Health, Gut Health, and Emotional Eating Psychology, she is a coach of Integrative Functional Nutrition and, through her individual and group coaching programs, has helped hundreds of women around the world to navigate the hormonal, gastrointestinal, and physical changes that begin after the age of 35, extending beyond through menopause.

I am a Brazilian living in Silicon Valley, California, married to Edu, mother of Lucas and Gabriel, a lawyer with a specialization in Business Administration by education, but after two big "calls from the Universe," I decided to leave an extremely promising career in the corporate world and follow my great passion, Integrative Nutrition.

I feel it to be important for me to talk about one of the most relevant points in my personality: my anxiety and my perfectionist tendency. Since I was little, I have always felt a great need to take care of everything and everyone, trying as much as possible to minimize any possibility of error.

This strong expectation has always been internal and not external. I never felt directly pressured by my parents in this sense. Of course, I noticed how much I made them proud with every top grade, or every time I stood out in something. This sense of well-being resulting from external approval grew and grew inside me with each new situation in my childhood and adolescence, extremely critical periods in the formation of our personality. The big problem is that this feeling of well-being from external praise was addicting me. Without my being aware, it was generating an unconscious dependence.

Time went by. I grew up, matured, and learned the hard and painful way about the impossibility of controlling every situation in our lives, no matter how much effort and energy we put into minimizing our chances of error. After all, for those with a perfectionist tendency, dealing with mistakes and failures is not a simple matter: self-criticism is so sharp and exaggerated that it hurts much more than necessary.

I begin by confessing that my professional life had a frustrating beginning. In other words, even though I had a strong desire to study nutrition, I ended up following my father's advice (with all his good intentions at the time) and studying law, since "Nutrition doesn't make money, daughter. You write and speak very well. Study law and you will have a much better future."

After graduating from law school and passing the Brazilian Bar Exam, I even worked in the legal field for a while, but soon felt that the formalistic and bureaucratic reality of the Brazilian judicial system left me extremely frustrated. I knew that I definitely did not want to pursue that professional path. Following that, I pursued a specialization in Business Administration and followed my professional path in the corporate world, working for large banks and in the Executive Aviation market.

During my career in the corporate world, I admit that I enjoyed a high level of success, considering my age -- the number of promotions I received, and the salary I earned. However, in terms of the professional routine, the story repeated itself for the vast majority of us women in the corporate market: a lot of stress, deadlines, goals, endless work hours, constant national and international trips, and completely unregulated eating habits (often I would go without eating all day without realizing it), and exercise routines of this type: "If I have time, I'll do it; if not, it'll have to wait until tomorrow."

It was during this time that I began to feel the first direct impact that stress can cause to our body physiologically. At age 26, I suffered from strong migraine headaches and paralyzing abdominal pains due to an irritable bowel syndrome that doctors only managed to diagnose and treat after more than a year of chronic suffering. At that time, this syndrome was not well-known, and the remedies were extremely inefficient.

In fact, 20 years ago, no one talked about irritable bowel syndrome, much less burnout. It was during this time that I had my first wake-up call. Debilitating headaches (which even caused me temporary speech paralysis) and abdominal cramps that made me lie on the office bathroom floor every day. At that time, my body was literally screaming at me: "Carla, you must stop right here because I'm already reaching my limit, and you will suffer increasingly worse consequences."

But, driven by the perfectionist mindset of someone who needed to prove themselves to the world, I made adjustments to my diet through trial and error (and without any support, since no nutritional studies were directed at my syndrome at that time), and I continued with my busy life. After all, like most executive women, I didn't "have time to investigate more deeply" this connection between our mind (stress and perfectionism) and the effects on our body.

However, with the birth of my first child, I received my second wake-up call.

Around six months old, my child began to experience health problems without any specific cause or diagnosis. It was as if his immune system was not responding correctly to internal pathogen stimuli. Any small initial trigger, like a common childhood illness, would evolve extremely rapidly in a matter of one or two days into a complicated health crisis. In addition to this, he had very strong respiratory reactions every time he consumed any food with cow's milk protein. It was as if he had micro-bleeding in his lungs when he ingested milk or dairy products. I really lost count of how many times I had to rush my son to the hospital for emergency admissions, when after 3 days a common cold became serious pneumonia that was compromising part of his lung. Or when, after a brief bout of common childhood diarrhea, he was rushed to the hospital and, after three days, we discovered that a bacteria had settled in one of his kidneys and permanently damaged 30% of its function.

ALL available immunological tests at the time, both in Brazil and abroad, came back negative. None of the doctors (many of them renowned) were able to come to any conclusion about my son's problem. Therefore, when my son was six months old, I resigned from my super promising career as the only female sales manager of executive jets in Brazil and began to take care of my son full-time, accompanying him in his comings and goings to the hospital.

It was during this time that I again delved into the world of nutrition, in order to try to find alternative paths to help my son, who, by this time, unfortunately was taking more than 10 different medications in a single day. I can say with absolute certainty that the first five years of my son's life were the most difficult of my entire life. But, on the other hand, I can also say that all that anguish and suffering made me a stronger and more mature person. I don't mean that I feel "stronger" only in the sense of being more ready to face difficult moments, but rather because of that extreme situation I experienced, "almost losing" a child, made me awaken to the importance of consciously experiencing each and every present moment.

The biggest lesson I learned from this phase was that the small gifts of our daily lives are daily presents that we receive from God, and that each gift should be consciously appreciated -- as we do not know what tomorrow will bring. But as you know, our lives change and bring us new challenges with the potential to make everything more "fun."

Eventually, everything seemed to be more peaceful regarding my son's health, when, at around seven years of age, he began to present more normal immune responses. I had already resumed my professional life when the opportunity arose through my husband's work for us to move to the United States. Once again, a perfectionist to the core of my being, here I was, trying to organize all the change and adaptation for myself, my husband, and my children in another country in a way that I "illusorily" thought could be "perfect" -- if only I could sort out in advance all the details.

We arrived in the United States in 2017, I was 40 years old at the time. In other words, far from being a little girl, I possessed some knowledge about myself and how stress could affect my body and my health. However, even so, with all the anxiety generated by the change, by the adaptation of the children to the new culture, the natural frustration with the language, the longing for family and friends, and the lack of domestic support, I again entered a spiral of stress, with effects on my body, but this time with the aggravating factors of my age and my hormones. The hard reality is that when I entered this new chapter in my life, my body again began to "somatize" (reflect in my whole body) my stress. The symptoms came this time in the form of depression and anxiety, which manifested themselves through an extremely troubled relationship with food.

Slowly, but with ever-increasing clarity, it all started to make sense. All the health problems that I faced, both mine and my son's, made me see something that seemed to be "screaming" in front of me for many years without my understanding. This was the moment when I should start from scratch and study what had always been my great passion, but which due to internal pressures and a huge need to meet others' expectations, I had decided not to pursue, namely, nutrition. It was from there that I started studying at the most well-recognized integrative Functional Nutrition School in the United States, delving deeply into the connection between food and our metabolism, hormones, immunity, gut, and emotions.

Today, I see myself in a much deeper way, both physically and emotionally. I understand that everything I went through was necessary in order for me to help other women with the true empathy of someone who has already experienced health problems like theirs, not just someone who has mastered technical knowledge about them from a stance of pure objectivity.

I must confess that I feel truly privileged. Not because of my position or my professional status, but because I have the privilege of working in a field about which I am extremely passionate, one that allows me to help other women in an integral way, either through their physical health or their emotional health. More than a job, I feel that this path, literally built from the personal health challenges I faced, has truly become my life mission.

Today, as an Integrative Nutrition Health Coach, I have helped hundreds of women around the world deal with the physical, hormonal, gastrointestinal, and emotional changes that come "without asking permission" along with our physical maturity. With a heart full of pride, I can say in all honesty that my greatest learning has been that it is never too late to listen to the calls of the Universe and to seek our true purposes in life, even if, to find them, we have to break our own preconceptions and reinvent ourselves from the ground up.

CAROLINA TUTTOILMONDO

Ad Sales Director - Digital Business Development
LinkedIn: www.linkedin.com/in/carol-tuttoilmondo/

LIFE WAVES

I am Paula Carolina Sanghikian Tuttoilmondo, better known as Carol Tuttoilmondo, descended from Armenians and Italians, the fruit of the union between a lawyer and an engineer.

I grew up in an eclectic, diverse, cheerful and thought-provoking environment. My mother organized dinners at home, attended by businessmen, artists, journalists like Helena Silveira and her brother Miroel Silveira, theater director and critic and my parents' cupid, in addition to the stylist and great family friend Roberto Issa. My parents' marriage, my birth and other events appeared in society columns, in addition to some interviews with my mother that were also published at the time by Folha de São Paulo newspaper.

I grew up surrounded by four great women:

- my mother Marlene, as beautiful as a Hollywood actress, taught me that our greatest value is not in appearance but in who we are, a lawyer who has always been empowered and obstinate;

- my godmother Julieta, a politicized, articulate woman, a great hostess who organized dinners at her house to receive heads of state and the Armenian church;

- my paternal grandmother Norma, a great matriarch and the foundation of the family, extremely spiritual, personification of love and a very good cook, married to my grandfather Adolpho, a business administrator who loved philosophy, a persistent reader in the search for the meaning of our existence;

- my maternal grandmother Ascanouch, stylist and very daring for the time, feminist and against arranged marriages, but who ended up not resisting the charm and charisma of my grandfather Samuel, a tenor and great shoes negotiator.

All very different, but strong women, with a lot of personality and inspiring, each in their own way.

But it wasn't just them, my biggest driver has always been my father Ciro, an example of ethics and character, known in college as a "diplomat" for his gifts in mediating and resolving conflicts, the truest and kindest person I know. While part of

The side text: REAL LIFE STORIES FROM INSPIRING WOMEN

the Armenian family worried about predicting who I would marry when I grew up, he said I should marry whoever I wanted since he raised me to be independent. I would be what I dreamed of. And so, it was...

PROFESSIONAL CHALLENGES AND ACHIEVEMENTS

I am a lawyer turned publicist. For the last 20 years I have been working with digital media in companies such as TV Globo, Estadão, Telefonica, Record TV, Grupo JP and startups defining Multiplatform business strategies.

I started at Globo in 2004, at the hands of a woman who believed in me. Even having experience only in the world of Law, Sandra Magalhaes saw something in my profile that made her believe in my potential, opened up a new and completely different world for me. The atmosphere at Globo.com was that of a startup, all very young, creative and full of energy, leading the beginning of the digital media era. Little did we both know where this was all going to lead, but she had put me on the path to something that became my passion and life's mission.

After 3 years as an account manager at Globo.com, another woman was responsible for my change. Isabel Borba, director of Estadão, who in 2007 gave me my first opportunity in the commercial area, to be one of the three commercial executives responsible for launching Limão, the first Brazilian social network. And it was at Estadão that I developed my career, starting as a salesperson and leaving as a director. There were 8 years of challenges, we experienced the reflections and impacts cf digital on the business of major newspapers, we launched new products, I created the Branded Content area and structured the programmatic media. In the group, I led many daring projects, such as the first newspaper in the world to deliver a cover with a touchscreen to their subscribers in the launch of a Fiat car. This campaign integrated several media platforms and ended its delivery with an activation in the Cannes Festival.

After 8 years I accepted Portal Terra's proposal to lead their commercial area, but a few months later came a big cut, they ended up with the entire editorial and production team. This situation would make many give up, but my profile has always been to find ways and that is how I created one of the main content strategy partnership contracts with Estadão, which took over the portal's editorial management. I also structured projects such as the Salvador Carnival and music events with online transmission and content production, without ever having produced an event before. I remember getting on a plane, negotiating with Salvador City Hall to broadcast the carnival, finding the box, the presenter and everything else that was necessary to put the project on its feet. When I returned, many Terra employees thanked me with teary eyes, because seeing our project realized

73

brought hope and inspiration to a company that was preparing to close and that, because of a stubborn leader and a competent team that believed and carried out, we delivered creative cases and we carried out large projects in 3 years, all with high profitability.

In 2018, TV Record called me to restructure the entire Multiplatform area that was falling revenues in the last 4 years. In 3 years, we reversed the situation, tripled revenues, and prepared the company for the future integration of TV with the broadcaster's multiplatform products. All this was only possible because, once again, I had a wonderful team and a great partner at my side, the Director of Operations Claudia Caliente. Our constructive collaboration at work extrapolated to life and today she is my friend and my daughter's godmother.

I am also proud of having been the gateway to the digital media market for great women who had experience in traditional media, such as Marcelle Azevedo, who I got from Radio Eldorado and Andrea Santamaria (co-author of the book), who I got from Publisher Globo. Both excellent professionals who were part of my team and who built an impeccable career in our advertising market.

I was also lucky to have many other great women on my team, such as Lívia Montemor, my BI head at the time (also co-author of the book), an expert in data and digital mkt, in addition to having inspired Sue Ellen Durães and Laita Laguna, my commercial directors, both creators of content projects involving major brands and special women.

I became a specialist in building teams suited to each challenge. Over the last 15 years, I have led 165 people in different teams and areas, such as sales, operations, planning, programmatic media, content partnerships, product, BI and MKT throughout the national territory and LATAM.

I was successful in my projects with and through the people who worked with me, I always liked to lead with respect, empowering and preparing the team for challenges.

They said I could accomplish the impossible. Inspiring and transforming lives through my work is what always moved me, results and money were consequences.

The challenges were countless, in most of the companies I worked for I suffered moral harassment, I was confronted and harassed by men who had been there for years, always doing everything the same way and who were bothered by our arrival, for the simple fact that we changed the standard and accomplished great things. Our competence was an "aggression."

Despite everything, I never let myself down, I did not allow myself to be distracted by attacks, my focus was to inspire and achieve.

Professional Challenges and Achievements

But it wasn't just professional challenges, life tested me in different ways. At age 39 I had thyroid cancer, cured myself and decided to change my life. After 12 years, I separated from the father of my first child, leaving in search of self-knowledge to reconnect with myself. I fell in love a few times and had my second daughter as a result of a quick but extremely harmful, abusive, and psychologically violent relationship. I never imagined it was possible for a leader, well-resolved and independent woman to become a victim of something like this, but we are all human and vulnerable.

At 3 months of my second pregnancy, I received a diagnosis with a high percentage of chances of an anomaly in the baby. It was in shock, but deep inside I did not believe it was real. Contrary to the suggestion of doctors, I even refused the possibility of an abortion, it was life, a blessing, there was hope and a lot of love involved. I believed that if God put me in that situation, it was to learn something and not run away. I would love and take care of my daughter, however she had to come. I got attached to God, prayed and I am sure that if she had any illness, Faith healed her. Because with Faith we are capable of anything! All subsequent tests were negative. My daughter was born beautiful, healthy, and perfect.

One day a friend told me that life is not something linear, in fact we live in waves, sometimes we are up, sometimes down, but the most important thing is at the moment of downfall not to identify ourselves with that, with the guilt or failure. It is just transient situations, none of that changes who you really are in essence.

Restarts

I started and started again many times, I had to rebuild myself a few times after a few falls. I got discouraged at times, but I never gave up, I never lost faith and the certainty that everything comes for a reason, which is our evolution. Our tears today are preparing us to reap great fruits tomorrow.

When I look back, every time I achieved something of value, I had to step out of my comfort zone and take risks. I took risks in my personal and professional life, sometimes I failed, but mistakes are part of our trajectory and they are great teachers. Through them I became who I am, in addition, they brought me empathy.

In the most difficult moments, professionals like Lívia Zillio and Raquel Laham pulled me along, as well as the wonderful yoga teacher Erica Piza de Toledo, all of whom are now great friends.

I am also a father and mother, one hundred percent financially responsible, like many women in Brazil from different social classes and I felt firsthand what it is like to lose your job and have to deal with the fear of not being able to cope with all the responsibilities and commitments with your family.

It does not matter the size of the cross you carry, your will to achieve, aligned with your values and who you are, added to the people who will appear on your path, it will make you get there.

RISE AND RAISE OTHERS

I fight not only for my space or for my daughter, but for all of us, believing that together we can break down stones and obstacles, opening more peaceful paths for the next generations and being an example of patience and resilience, since there will always be a way.

I felt honored to be part of this project because I believe that by sharing our experiences, we can inspire or give strength to those who somehow identify with our history. If we can transform one life, it is already worth it.

And what more do I want?

Get involved, more and more, in projects aligned with my values.

Motherhood taught me resilience. Life taught me the strength of overcoming. And my own results prove that women have a lot of space to conquer and lead. I am involved in the women's cause, to help create an ecosystem to promote equality in business, inspire new leaders and share experiences.

Today I am part of AngelUs, a platform that connects women for professional growth, designed by Claudia Colaferro. I am also proud to be a mentor at Soulcode, whose purpose is to transform lives through free technological training and employability, a project by the inspiring Carmela Borst. Both great women and leaders who are also part of this important Rise and Raise Others project.

I cannot fail to thank my dear friend Eliana Cassandre who pulled me into this beautiful project created by Natasha de Caiado and her superpowers of realization and transformation.

We are more male than most men.
Rita Lee

CAROLINA DOSTAL

Founding partner at OitentaIN (www.carolinadostal.com.br)
Linkedin Advisor for C-Level Executives , Angel Investor, B2B Marketing Professor,
ABRH Director, Personal Branding and Mentor
Instagram: @caroldostallinkedin
LinkedIn: www.linkedin.com/in/especialistalinkedin

FROM PERSONAL LIFE TO PROFESSIONAL ASCENSION BUILDING A DIGITAL LEGACY OF EMPOWERMENT, POSITIVE IMPACT, AND INSPIRING TRANSFORMATION

I have always believed that we all have a life purpose. Mine is to empower professionals, showing them the enormous power that they possess and how social networks are fundamental today. Brazil is known for its diversity, and my personal story reflects this cultural richness. Daughter of an immigrant from the former Czechoslovakia and a Brazilian mother, I always knew that my trajectory would be unusual. I was different because I had a half-sister who didn't speak my language, a father who was Czech-German who, from time to time, spoke in a complicated way, traveling the world and bringing me exotic things as gifts. From clothes that completely escaped the standard of Brazilian children in the 1980s, as well as flashy books and school materials. At that time, the import market in Brazil was limited, and it was difficult to have so much variety.

Living with my half-sister and my Czech-German father also taught me the importance of communication. Dealing with the language barriers between us made me realize how fundamental it is to be able to express oneself and understand others, especially in different cultural contexts. This skill has proven valuable throughout my life, both in personal and professional situations. From the age of 11 I was often sent on my own to study abroad. I remember the tightness in my chest, the insecurity, and the fear I felt. First, I went to study in Germany, at a school that was mostly attended by Europeans. At that moment, I felt the weight of being a foreigner. I was the only South American in the school. In the first few days, I was annoyed by the stupid questions they asked me: if I lived with snakes and monkeys, if I had a TV, etc. I prefer not to go into details . . . .

At 12 years old, I went alone once again, this time to the United States, to a

REAL LIFE STORIES FROM INSPIRING WOMEN

city called Winston Salem, in North Carolina. There, I was able to improve my English and make very different friends. I stayed with a European family who had just lost their daughter to a rare disease. Amidst their pain, I was able to bring a lot of Brazilian love to them, and I am sure I helped in their grieving process. It was a beautiful experience! This cultural diversity and exposure to different languages and traditions from an early age provided me with a broader view of the world and helped me develop skills of adaptation and communication.

I grew up in an environment full of challenges and learning experiences, but I was also a victim of a sexist society. My mother, despite considering herself modern and progressive, ended up teaching me misconceptions about emotional relationships and the role of women in society. This led me to see men as enemies, devoid of feelings. However, life surprised me, and I became a single mother of a wonderful boy. This experience completely changed my perspective on men -- showing me that men, like women, have feelings. The arrival of my son gave me the strength to discover who I really was and reinvent myself in the face of adversity. Gradually, I matured and built my own life story, full of achievements and discoveries. I graduated in Business Administration and obtained a postgraduate degree in Service Marketing from FAAP, as well as specializations in Digital Marketing from CommSchool and Entrepreneurship and Negotiation Techniques from FGV."

That's where I found my true passion: helping professionals stand out in the digital world and build a strong digital authority for the future of work. I founded Carolina Dostal LinkedIn Advisory, a company specialized in developing and remodeling LinkedIn profiles for professionals in various sectors and became a regional director of the Brazilian Association of Human Resources (ABRH). I have always believed that each person possesses immense power within themselves and that social networks play a fundamental role in today's society. The internet has revolutionized the way we connect with people around the world and how we build relationships and businesses that were previously unimaginable.

In this context, the development of a personal brand has become essential for our professional projection and differentiation in the midst of competition. I believe that each of us has something unique to offer, and it is through sharing these qualities that we can build a digital legacy that reflects our best version. For this reason, I started giving lectures and workshops highlighting the importance of image for a professional's reputation, and LinkedIn as a networking and content tool in the digital age. With this work, I have approached many admirable leaders and increasingly believe that contact with the digital world is essential to leverage one's career. I also believe that LinkedIn is one of the most important tools for this. Please allow me to share an interesting fact with you, especially for those who are afraid of public speaking.

The first lecture I gave could have been more peaceful... but it wasn't! I gave a lecture to 900 people. I had no idea about communication techniques, tone of voice, stage positioning... nothing! I swear that this scared me a lot. However, I soon remembered my mother's voice saying that no one is better than anyone e se and that shame can come from extreme vanity. So, I learned that I don't need to be the best, I need to prepare myself, but above all, I need to be myself. That's the secret. Often, when we want to impact more people, we have to be channels of communication to the world and vanity has no place there. Generosity in sharing expands in such a way that it overrides vanity like a three-million-ton truck.

One day, during a visit to the LinkedIn office, I learned from a great friend the concept of "thought leadership," which has since become an integral part of my work. This concept made my eyes truly shine! I thought: the C-levels I work with, for the most part, don't just want visibility, but to build a better future. From there, I started helping them become digital and life influencers. A thought leader spreads ideas that demonstrate their experience, competence, and knowledge in a particular subject, becoming a point of reference and ultimate authority in that sector. Thought leadership is a privileged place of speech and listening in the market, through which the leader guides and develops a positive reputation, becoming an increasingly respected reference in their area. I teach them that a thought leader can speak to topics that have already been addressed, but with the difference of doing so from their own perspective and repertoire of knowledge – all the while legitimately respecting other's beliefs.

One becomes a safe channel to support others in the process of being authentic. To take control of their own career and professional life! Through my work, I realized that it is crucial to present our qualities to the world. And this certainly is not just about financial gain. I learned from Edu Lyra (a respectful social entrepreneur in Brazil) that not everything is about money. "If you work only for money, you are poor in spirit. It is necessary to seek purpose and meaning in everything we do."

I believe that building a digital legacy is essential. We are responsible for feeding generative artificial intelligence with information all the time. This is because we live in an era where artificial intelligence (AI) is increasingly present in our lives, and it is crucial that we feed the internet with information that contains our best vision. By doing so, we are contributing to this gigantic database having positive inputs to generate knowledge and wisdom from our "inspiring leader" thinking. Inspiring generations to unite efforts to create an extraordinary world, where everyone can flourish. Our digital legacy should be a source of pride for future generations and contribute to the knowledge and wisdom they will inherit.

When your grandchildren search for you on the internet, what will they think about you? I leave this important reflection here!

REAL LIFE STORIES FROM INSPIRING WOMEN

REFERENCES

SCHOOLEY, S. What Is Thought Leadership, and Why Does It Matter? BND. Available at: https://www.businessnewsdaily.com/9253-thought-leadership.html. Accessed on: April 12, 2023.

THOUGHT leader. Cambridge Dictionary. Available at: https://dictionary.cambridge.org/pt/dicionario/ingles/thought-leader. Accessed on: April 12, 2023.

CAROLINA NUCCI NISHIYAMAMOTO

Co-Founder Women in Business | CMO & Partner Marketing de Gentileza | TEDx Speaker | Columnist and Knowledge Expert @Startse I journalist, engineer, marketer, saleswoman, entrepreneur and proud mother
Instagram: @carolina.nucci
LinkedIn: www.linkedin.com/in/carolinanucci

WHERE DO YOU GET THE STRENGTH (AND COURAGE) TO TAKE THE NEXT STEP?

As an Asian kid, I learned that speed was a measure of success. I was taught early on that success only comes to the person who runs faster, arrives first, does better, takes one step after another without looking back.

So there was no other way but to run. And I ran.

I ran to get the best grades in school.

I ran to get my first job at 16.

I ran to study in the best colleges.

I ran to get great jobs at great companies.

I ran to make the boldest career changes - from journalism to engineering, from engineering to marketing, from marketing to sales, and then marketing again, from B2C to B2B, from multinationals to startups, from startups to entrepreneurship, and so on.

I ran to get promoted, to get recognized, to always get that something more.

I ran to get bigger, bolder, better and a badass - whatever that means.

Running, for me, was a validation that I was on the right path - even though, ironically, as I was always in such a hurry, I wasn't paying that much attention to the righteousness of my path choices. The very act of running gave me momentum to keep on running.

Don't pay attention to distractions, run over obstacles, ride your feelings wearing a mask. Focus on looking forward to new goals, objectives, achievements...

With each acceleration, my head became further away from the present and more focused on the future, in a way that happiness always seemed to be 5 steps ahead - or more.

But then... I became a mother.

My Olivia came and, overnight, I found myself in the present for the first time. With her, I wanted to follow every step she took, metaphorical or not.

But, as she was born in no rush, I realized that I was the one who was at the wrong pace.

Happiness was no longer 5 or 10 steps away. It was here and now, and if I continued running, I would just run farther away from it.

On the other hand, I didn't want to stop - and I didn't. I wanted to keep moving, just not the way it was before, running like crazy. From that moment on, each step started to matter more, the act of moving gained another meaning, because not only I wasn't walking alone, but I had someone by my side learning to walk with me. A girl, like me.

Also, if I ran too fast, not only would I not see my little one grow, I would also teach her that the only way to be happy... is to run like I ran - which, as I now know, is very far from being true.

I never imagined that being an example to someone else would motivate me to relearn how to move. That's when, all of the sudden, the weight of that responsibility kicked in.

After running so much, I hadn't even realized that the road I was running on, as an asian woman, was full of rocks, holes and puddles. I was always so desperate to move forward that I hadn't realized that one of the reasons I felt I had to run like that was because there were others running smoothly and faster in their scooters and bikes, not nearly as tired and broke as I was. And worse: by doing that, I also wasn't paying attention to others who had even more difficulties than me along the way.

I spent years ignoring those differences, being stupidly proud of running like crazy without the same resources. My body was so heated and my head was so busy that I didn't see the prison I was in.

However, changing paths seemed much more challenging now. Even if the idea of change and being free looked promising and hopeful, for the first time, I felt a huge fear of falling.It seemed that the risk and the size of the fall became greater.

What if I trip and fall? What if the new path is worse than the one I'm on?

If I make a mistake, what will people think of me?

Isn't it better to slow down and stay on the same road I know so well?

It's what I now call the prison dilemma. Should I stay on the path that I am familiar with, even though it's not what I want anymore? Or should I risk it all to test a new road, even though I don't know what it looks like or even if there's room for me?

At first, the fear won and I insisted on that well known path, thinking I could somehow change it from within - which obviously didn't work. That newly found self awareness kept screaming in my head until I **understood that fear and accommodation, in themselves, were not good incentives for any next step, nor even good examples to give to anyone, much less my daughter.**

So, without losing my rhythm, I looked around until I found a new road that suited me better. Finally, I was drawn to a direction that seemed to have more life and color, but still had a lot of space to build or improve the pathway further ahead. I immediately thought to myself: this is where I can move and also be part of creating a different road, without those hidden holes and dirt, more clear, with the right signs. A road to which my daughter can be happy to go one day.

For a long time, I felt like every step I took was worth it. I felt like I was finally myself, without the never-ending rush and without the masks from a while ago. Being myself actually enabled me to connect and collaboratively build each brick of inspiring new roads. As we built, there was more room for people to join us.

To my surprise, what started as an invitation for amazing people to help me create something new from scratch turned into incredible moments walking alongside them in those brand new roads we built together. Some have been with me until now, others have continued building their own new paths, but still keeping in touch sending messages to talk about each new step and share the challenging and happy moments along each road. Looking back, these people made it all worth it.

It was quite a road. The first one I actually built to walk in, with everything good I had to offer.

Maybe that's why it took me a while to realize... When I fell face down on the ground.

At first, I didn't understand how, much less why, I fell. Did I trip? Did someone push me? But the why wasn't important: **In 38 years, that was the first time that I stopped moving**.

After running for so long, the fall hurt me more than if I had stopped gradually. Also, as I thought I was finally on the right track, the size of the fall felt bigger, unexpected. The heat of the body gave way to a different, deep physical and emotional pain.

Physical pain has been part of my life since my teenage years. But only 3 years ago I discovered it was all due to a degenerative disease in my spinal cord that affected me with loss of sensitivity in parts of the body (making me more prone to burns and falls) and terrible chronic pain (kidney stones pain level, only continuous and throughout the body). It's an invisible disability that few people understand. I only understood it recently myself - and accepting that I am a person with a disability was a crucial step to face it head on.

Over the past 3 years, this unbearable pain has limited my life exponentially. My routine includes 9 strong medications, physiotherapy, treatments and surgeries to relieve the pain. As my doctor says: "Every day, you have to find the strength to overcome the pain and move on, otherwise your body will always prefer to stay in bed". Well... Now that I stopped, it was like my daily strength to get up was gone and I was ready to give in to the physical pain.

But mostly, what knocked me down was the emotional pain. It wasn't about losing the road I loved. It was mostly about the people that were on the journey and built it all with me. For me, it meant something. But they moved to a new road I couldn't recognize anymore, without looking back. While on the ground, I could see the cracks and mistakes hidden behind the flowers and disguised with colorful paint. The connection was gone and I felt like I wasn't enough anymore. For a moment, I thought: should I have given in to them? Should I have put the mask back on just to keep on moving? Was it all worth something?

Then the fall felt like rejection, like being out of league. Stopping felt like failing - myself, the people around me, my daughter... As I was down, I gave in to the pain and sadness and stayed down.

Out of the road, lots of loved ones were actually yelling for me to stand up. You're amazing, you'll figure something out, you know how to start over. We're here for you. We trust you. Stand up!

However, when we stop and the heat is gone, it's easy to embrace your worst deepest fears and stay comfortably down. They don't really know me. I'm an impostor who doesn't know what she's talking about. What did I accomplish, really? People must be laughing at me. What the hell am I going to do? Is it all worth it? For what? For who?

"For who". I spent weeks laid down in pain in my bed, without energy to even play with my daughter. On a Sunday, before lunch, Olivia came close to me, angry, looked me in the eye and said: **Mom, will you ever get up again?**

Yes, I will, Oli, I'll start right now. And that was the turning point.

Obviously, it wasn't like magic, but it was the sparkle I needed to remember why I started even questioning my way of running like crazy and why I should be moving in the first place.

From that moment on, I started to think forward again. Just because I fell once it doesn't mean I'll never be able to accomplish anything ever again. It's not because previous pathways didn't work that all other roads are doomed forever.

I still believe in a lot of great things some may find naive - but I don't. I believe in the power to build great new pathways alongside great people. I believe we can even the field so more and more people have the same level of opportunities. I still believe that it's possible to break bad patterns as we build new powerful ones.

With that in mind, I changed and I started over, again. Now, as an entrepreneur working in 2 great projects involving human-centered businesses and gender equality. It's a new change and a new pathway, the latest one I wanted to share here.

First of all, despite all the pain from the fall, it was actually very important to stop for a moment. For a moment, stopping is good. It shouldn't be judged as a character flaw or something to be ashamed of. It's a time to reflect, pick up the broken pieces, put them back together and decide next steps.

However, stopping for a long time is the utmost comfort zone. When we're standing still, we're less likely to fall and get hurt again. It's safe. But it also doesn't get any better than that.

In order to get the good things we want in life, one way or another, we have to move towards **something we believe in**. The problem is that the act of moving, in itself, involves risks.

If I stay still, I don't run any risk of falling. On the other hand, between my current place and the next step, there is always a moment of imbalance. With one foot in the past and the other moving towards an uncertain future, there is a moment of instability. There's a risk of falling in each step we take.

When we're moving at a stable pace in the same direction, we don't even notice these micro seconds of uncertainty during each step. The fear of the next step only becomes relevant when we stop or when we decide to change directions. It's the change that makes the next step harder and, if we let it, the fear takes place and we stay still.

In order to overcome the fear and get the strength and courage to take the next step, these are the powerful sources of energy that make me move forward.

The first is the source that grows stronger at each step: **our experience**. Just because I've changed a lot of times doesn't mean I always have to start from scratch: every new step we take gives us strength for the steps that come next.

The second is one we can redirect: **our fear**. We give so much power to our fears, so why not redirect that energy to something worthwhile?

Which brings us to the third source, the one I've covered most here and gives us direction when we're lost: **our purpose, our why**. To do this, we just need to find it. For me, it's still my daughter, my most powerful source of energy to keep going.

Have you found yours? **Why do you move?**

CHRIS AYROSA

Founder of Ayrosa & Co, event experience designer, scenographer
Instagram: @chrisayrosa
LinkedIn: www.linkedin.com/in/chris-ayrosa-97044549

A CREATIVE JOURNEY OF MISTAKES, LEARNINGS, COURAGE, AND, ALWAYS, PLENTY OF BEAUTY

It wasn't easy to choose a path to tell my story. I never wanted to write a book or anything similar because, truthfully, I have always been meticulous and unable to consider a text ready, finalized, perfect. The phrase "nothing is good enough that it can't be improved" has always been with me, shaping the professional I have become—a designer of experiences, a facilitator of meaningful encounters, someone deeply passionate about beauty in all its forms. Looking back, I realize that this belief in continuous improvement never paralyzed me; instead, it propelled me to strive for better, to keep improving—myself and the people who joined me on this journey. In my more than 40-year-long adventure in my profession, it was not my achievements but my mistakes that ultimately brought me here.

I am a historian, and early on, I felt in love with the ability to connect facts and data, weaving them together to make sense of time. Guided by my attraction to beauty and empowered by the creative freedom instilled by my father, I ventured down paths I never planned but which took on profound meaning when I reflect upon them. First and foremost, I must acknowledge the immense privilege I have enjoyed throughout my life. The privilege to make my own choices, to work in a field I love, to form professional partnerships with individuals and companies in the luxury segment—though it comes with its own unique demands and idiosyncrasies, it also allows for great heights to be reached. I soared high because life granted me that possibility, but also by choice— not everyone takes advantage of the chances life offers.

I have learned early on about the power of bringing to life the ideas born from my own imagination, without fear of making mistakes. I have five siblings—two brothers and three sisters—and I am the proud mother of two daughters. I have been inspired by both men and women throughout my journey. One of the first influential women in my life was my maternal grandmother, Maria Antonieta Medeiros.. She was a woman ahead of her time, a true visionary. She created the "Sanitas Institute" in the heart of São Paulo—a spa that introduced innovations such as Pilates and healthy food menus. She possessed remarkable erudition, captivated with her intriguing nature, and had an uncanny ability to understand people. Another woman who continues to have a profound impact on my life is Maria Regina—Mrs. Régis, my mother-in-law of 50 years. I first met her at the age of 16 when I started dating her son, Alcides Ayrosa, who eventually became my lifelong partner. To this day, Mrs. Régis remains my closest friend, even at the age of 95. They had a country house where she would create beautifully set tables for meals—always thematic and elaborately designed. I found her work fascinating and eagerly assisted with the arrangements. These experiences instilled in me a deep appreciation for the ability of meals, tables, and even environments to bring people together, evoking unique and emotional experiences. However, I must confess that my father was possibly the most significant inspiration in my life. He was a humble man who possessed a remarkable business acumen. While accomplishing extraordinary feats, he also dedicated himself to organizing the June festivals at Our Lady of Fátima Church near our home, with the aim of supporting the local community.

It was my father who let go of the desire to see me pursue a career in medicine and allowed me to choose my own path. I had aspirations of becoming a nun and was fascinated by archaeology, but at the age of 17, during the dictatorship era, I enrolled in History at the University of São Paulo (USP). But teaching was not my goal; I wanted something more dynamic and engaging. At that time, I didn't have the connection with art that I would develop later in life. I worked at a 17th-century Renaissance desk, sometimes in front of sculptures by Degas, other times with collections from Mesopotamia. One time, my friend Claudia and I received an invitation – I would say more like a summons - from Professor Bardi to have lunch with him and Umberto Eco. I remember panic setting in when we realized we barely remembered anything from the lectures on optics and semiotics in college. And I remember Claudia reassuring me by saying, "Let's just listen..." And that's what we did: even without fully understanding the conversation in Italian, we left proud to have participated in such an important event. It was an experience I carried with me for a long time, and it's just one example of the many incredible things that happened in our lives at that time. I was passionate about what I was doing, but then another huge door opened. My father worked with Holstein cattle, and my brother, Luciano Cury, started breeding Arabian horses (he later became one of the largest breeders in the world). I started attending auctions and exhibitions in places that were quite rudimentary at the time: we sat on circus bleachers under canvas where the animals were displayed. These were events attended by big businessmen, and that's how it worked. One beautiful day, we went to an event in one of the biggest Expo houses in SP that had been "arranged" for the 50th anniversary of Holstein cattle in Brazil. I was enchanted by the setup, which was actually quite simple, with fabric coverings and wedding benches, but I remember hearing from my brother's girlfriend, Adélia – the daughter of a prominent Arabian horse breeder – that in the United States, animal exhibitions and auctions were always presented better. She suggested that I start doing that in Brazil. At that moment, I thought: I want to do this with my life!

And that's how my career as a set designer was born. At that same event, I approached the Secretary of Agriculture, who was a friend of my father, and asked him to give me the contacts of all the presidents of Horse Associations that would participate in Expande, an exhibition of all animal breeds that would take place in two months in São Paulo. I explained that I wanted to make the exhibition space more pleasant, with tables where people could have a drink, and I remember the Secretary's look of disbelief. In front of him, I called the president of the Lusitano Horse Association, introduced myself, explained the project, and all I remember asking was: "Trust me." And so it was.

In this frenetic pace of work, and having contact with many different people all the time, I was very afraid of being mistaken for an opportunist, and I wanted my (good) work to always stand out beyond any other attribute. That's why I got used to having meals in hotel rooms, never in restaurants, so as not to appear "available." I never told anyone about this. I preserved myself, and it worked. I managed to go through all these years without ever being harassed or experiencing any uncomfortable situations. It's also interesting to remember how resourceful I had to be to train a workforce because there were no people available to perform the services I needed. There was a lot of prejudice surrounding working with animals. I remember myself inviting people who were unloading trucks to help me with cleaning and organizing the stages, taking the animals out of the stables I set up, dismantling the stages, and sanitizing them so that there would be no residue left in the venue. These people started working with me at all events, and some of them turned it into a business and expanded it throughout Brazil. I was very lucky; I met really nice people, and I spent at least 30 years working with this all over Brazil. Today, I'm not ashamed to say that I was indeed the person who understood the most about livestock fairs and exhibitions and other animal breeds, mainly because of the ability to bring people who did it with love closer. The purely mercantile approach didn't work, and whether it's events with animals or products, the goal is always the same: to build an emotional framework around what needs to be celebrated. I brought Denise, for example, a woman who worked with her husband in a flower stand, closer to me; she started making flower arrangements for the events. Like me, she never said no: she always found a way to solve any problem that arose. I taught, but I also learned a lot from people like her. And I don't "brag" about any achievement because I have always had the humility to recognize that I had and have the privilege of using my clients' money – usually luxury brands – to realize so many incredible projects.

I went through difficult phases; I faced an autoimmune disease that caused me to gain a lot of weight and make complicated choices, such as being one of the first people in Brazil to undergo bariatric surgery. I paid and still pay a high price for it (but that's another story that maybe I'll detail another time). I have always been vain, and I faced these different phases believing unconditionally in the beauty that I carried within me. It's curious to look back and reflect on the origin of this attraction to beauty, to organized and visually pleasing things, and the desire to create parties around a theme. I often think of the June festivals at Our Lady of Fátima Church organized by my father and the joyful feeling they brought me, even as a young child. I was fortunate to have a family that loved to celebrate life – and I also remember my mother, who loved carnival, throwing big carnival parties at home. Those were moments that shaped me as a person. At 67 years old, after 42 years in my profession organizing so many unforgettable events worldwide, I am still active, with energy for much more, and with a desire to create events with joy, simplicity, humanity, and purpose. I'm a fan of new beginnings, and my life is full of them; it's worth mentioning that I am going through one right now with the man of my life, with whom I was married for 45 years and from whom I separated because we were not happy. We started dating again during the pandemic, reaching a total of 50 years together.

By now, each of us have our own home, and I understand our limits and affinities better. I have learned a lot, sometimes the hard way, about respect. But luckily, there is time to help us mature emotionally – and to give us second, third, new chances to start over. Alcides is one of the great men I have worked with – who has always been by my side, whether in my company or taking care of our daughters while I spent 15, 20 days traveling across Brazil. While I silently cried during takeoff, missing my daughters. In this journey, I have also brought many powerful women close to me, and I am proud to say that two of them are my daughters: Carol worked with me for 25 years, and Ju, for 7. Like me, they found open windows and leaped through them. They are brilliant women who have found their own paths and replenish my youthfulness. They have also made me a grandmother, one of the greatest discoveries of my life: I discovered a love in João and Maria, my grandchildren (Carol's children), that I didn't even know I was capable of giving. It has restored me as a human being and leads me to play with them as if time had never passed, or rather: as if there was no time, as if time was a suspended abstraction in the air.

This year, I gathered the courage to attend SXSW for the first time; I must say it was challenging but very good. I now feel stronger, and that makes me get up in the morning and explore new paths every day. To create beautiful things makes me feel alive. I am very proud to have come this far with the precious help of many people who have "raised" me, as the title of this book says, but raising someone is meaningless if that person doesn't extend their hand to you.

CILA SCHULMAN

CEO of Ideia Opinion Research Institute
E-mail: cila.schulman@ideiausa.com
Instagram: @cilaschulman
LinkedIn: www.linkedin.com/in/cilaschulman

ALL THE TIME IN THE WORLD

Just like with the same-hour phenomenon, such as 11:11 or 22:22, there is a belief that when a person looks at the clock and the digits of that time appear in reverse, it is a sign that something is going to happen. You can even find this on Google.

When I started working at a newspaper as a reporter in 1978, there was no Google, no cell phones, and no online dictionaries. There were LED clocks that displayed same or reverse hour digits. I was 16 years old. Today, I'm 61 and I'm having a conversation with ChatGPT while visualizing the numbers 61:16 in my mind. Could it be a sign that something is about to happen?

In reality, of course, things happen all the time. "Oh... so you're 61!" I hear that quite a lot, just like I used to hear that it was impossible for me to be 16 years old and be in charge of the politics section of a daily newspaper. It was possible because I was fortunate enough to be mentored by a journalism genius named Reynaldo Jardim (who created the "Caderno B" of Jornal do Brasil, another great newspaper that no longer exists) and he decided to trust me. As the meme says, Jardim wasn't just crazy, he was nuts.

Just like him, I wasn't just crazy, I was nuts. Underage, I needed authorization from the court to work at O Globo newspaper in Rio. Crazy, and still underage, I got slapped by a military officer when I tried to get a statement from General Figueiredo, the president of Brazil during the reopening era. I risked my life when I wrote about soybean smuggling in Paraguay, and I faced difficulties when I revealed the first camps of the Landless Workers' Movement in the Southwest of Paraná.

At 18 years old, I got married with a guest list of 1,200 and moved to Brussels. The marriage, seemingly a natural destination for a well-bred girl like me, didn't flourish.

I was 21 when, back in Brazil and on my new path, I reported on the first major rally for Diretas Já (Direct Elections Now); soon after, I covered the campaign and final days of Tancredo Neves. To this day, I still can't listen to "Coração de Estudante," the soundtrack of that democratic tragedy which I witnessed as a young reporter.

At 24, I was invited by Veja to moved to Brasília, where I witnessed the Plenary session of the Constituent Assembly. I was promoted to assistant editor of international affairs, and had big plans to become a foreign correspondent. At 26, despite the promise of a branch in Milan, I ended my early career in journalism and ventured into entrepreneurship. I specialized in Corporate Communication and opened a press office. My first client was a political candidate. We won the election, and that became my profession, coordinating election campaigns and advising governments.

At 31, I became the Municipal Secretary of Communication, and at 33, the State Secretary. Both experiences taught me a lot about public policy and gave me a unique insight into the joys and challenges of being in government, which one can only learn by being on the other side of the counter. At the age of 35 I became a mother. Ten months later, I lost Geraldo, the father of my child, to liver cancer.

I was the vice president of one of the largest advertising agencies in the country, overseeing teams in more than a dozen states. At the end of that period, I think I experienced a burnout, although it didn't have a name back then.

In search of an escape from the series of difficulties that came with Geraldo's death, I found the most obvious one, the airport. At 37 years old, I moved to DC to study at the Graduate School of Political Management at George Washington University. This experience not only strengthened me emotionally but also forever changed my perspective on strategic planning and campaigns, opening up a universe of contacts and opportunities for me.

The decision to be part of a world as male-dominated as politics was not a calculated one. I didn't even imagine the magnitude of the challenge. Contributing to this recklessness was the fact that I came from a place of immense privilege. I was born into a white family with more money, power, and access than most. My father was the president of state-owned companies, the third-largest private bank in the country, and the Brazilian Federation of Banks. My mother ventured into the fashion business when women of her generation were meant to be housewives. I was raised with travel, books, languages, home lunches with government ministers, Fiorucci dresses, and Cartier watches.

Because of where I came from, I felt protected. What a foolish notion. I was harassed, undermined, disrespected, hurt without a second thought. Having experienced that makes me reflect on how infinitely more difficult it was and still is for women without the privileges I had. In my case, we shouldn't generalize. After all, I entered many doors because I had the key. But I quickly understood that opening the door didn't mean being welcomed in the room. Often, it was quite the opposite. Initially, people assumed I lacked competence. A recommendation letter from Jardim to the Marinho family, owners of the biggest media conglomerate in Brazil, summarized the common perception: "When she entered the newsroom, I was skeptical. She seemed like a spoiled rich girl! Only later did I discover how talented she was". Ultimately, the strong letter of recommendation won the day for me, but I must also acknowledge the high degree of resentment my presence in that room caused.

Being tall, slim, and educated both helped and hindered me. Just the other day, after watching an interview of mine on the political landscape, someone wrote on social media that with the amount of time I would spend taking care of my "mane" [sic.], I wouldn't have time to cultivate my mind. "There can't be anything in her head," they concluded, perpetuating the deeply ingrained belief that a well-groomed and well-dressed woman cannot be intelligent.

In journalism, I faced prejudice for being different. Not necessarily just for being a woman. When I arrived, there were already plenty of strong and brilliant female reporters. I was quickly welcomed and became part of the gang of girls. I was unfamiliar with the word "sorority," but I know that I fully experienced it in the 1980s in every media outlet I worked for. Throughout my life, I have made and continue to make great friends – both female and male – in journalism, an inclusive team-based profession.

However, embracing femininity in a male-dominated and sexist world like politics and finance was, and still is, a challenge on a different level. In my mind, I didn't need to be a man, but I needed to act like one in order to compete on equal terms with them. Being a woman cannot be allowed to be an obstacle, I thought. Mundane examples, like going out for dinner, were a source of risk and gossip. I firmly believed that there was nothing wrong with going alone with a client to a restaurant. It was obviously just an opportunity to exchange information, as men do every night in Brasília or São Paulo. Of course, countless times I became the subject of other people's fantasies, attributing to me affairs I never had. In fact, I never had a single one – *ça vas sans dire*. ("It goes without saying," in French.)

Acting in a spirit of camaraderie, of being "one of the guys" in my professional interactions put me in risky situations more than once. It was not uncommon for a colleague, after a glass of wine, to attempt to touch my leg. And it didn't even require alcohol, that kind of proximity occurred also after a lukewarm coffee, when the waiter left the room. My reaction was always the same. I would burst into loud and pathetic laughter. That ridiculous laugh had the power to disarm the guy, and it invariably worked. Looking back, with the awareness I have today, I know that I was only able to escape because I had financial security and a prestigious surname. Being well-compensated has always been part of my professional value, but it was not a matter of survival. Today, I also understand the magnitude of the violence that I and other women have endured, without realizing how wrong it was.

I ran memorable campaigns and fueled myself with every drop of adrenaline that only an election can offer. It's an activity that manages to be more exciting than the deadline at a newspaper. Joining a campaign is like going to war, except, among the dead and wounded, everyone survives. Well, not always. Defeat tastes bitter, takes a long time to heal, and destroys friendships. I formed strong and lifelong relationships during political campaigns. I enjoyed every victory, but I was also blamed, attacked, and "canceled" by competitors – the term didn't exist then, but the feeling did. It was never easy to be one of the few women in a position of power.

In 2009, shortly after Obama revolutionized the use of social media in his presidential campaign, I was hired by a major political party to structure everything related to the web in preparation for the upcoming presidential election in Brazil. During the 2010 campaign, I led a Twitter strategy, a social media platform that politicians had rarely used, and it received great recognition. In 2013, leveraging my crisis management skills developed over the previous years in politics, I became part of the core team in one of the biggest corporate disputes in the history of the country, working for businessman Abílio Diniz. It was another extraordinary professional experience. I was 51 years old and felt fulfilled.

Only two years later, when I entered menopause, it felt like my life was falling apart. I would cry all the time. I started hormone replacement therapy, and the crying stopped. The process of perimenopause was painful and affected my self-esteem. It took me years to find the right treatment. It was a challenging journey to reconnect with my body, mental health, and energy levels.

While I felt physically terrible, on the professional side, once the tears ceased, my career continued to thrive. In 2016, I became a partner and vice president of IDEIA Instituto de Pesquisa. Today, I am the CEO of the company, working with people who I admire and trust, and doing what I love and know: public opinion, innovation, strategy, consulting, impact, crisis management, and public policy.

Some time ago, in addition to discussing politics, I decided to talk about menopause on my Instagram profile. With every post, I realize how much of a taboo this topic is. It's as if by not talking about it, we try to avoid going through this phase of life. If aging is a sensitive issue, I am here to disrupt, because I firmly believe that we need to talk about it so that both men and women can understand this process. After all, if an informed woman like me went through so many challenges during perimenopause, what about the majority of the population who have zero access to the needed help and support systems? What public policies are being discussed in this regard? How much workforce do we lose by not addressing this issue, with a population that is increasingly female and aging? That's why I speak up.

At 61 years old, I don't seek the body of a 40-year-old or the skin of a 50-year-old, but I feel comfortable with what I have. That certainly makes me more beautiful and interesting. At 61, I rededicated myself to everything that is innovative in my field. I am the CEO of a research institute that uses the most current innovations for data mining and technology. During elections, we help financial markets understand the political landscape and make better decisions for their clients. I am a partner in a monitoring tool, V-tracker, which combats fake news, one of the plagues of our era. And I am a part of Pinion, a for-profit software application that has over 3.5 million registered users who perform social and environmental impact missions. I am a fan of the idea of microtask remuneration from Pinion, especially in a world that will be displacing thousands of people per second with the advancement of artificial intelligence.

My greatest contribution to the world is, undoubtedly, my son, who is also my partner on an Instagram profile where we produce exclusive content about politics and lessons for a crisis-ridden world. In a few months, Felipe and I will be 62:26 together. When that day comes, I believe that something good will happen.

CINARA BASTOS

Founding at Lumin'área Brasil Psychotherapist, mentor, teacher, writer, and metaconsciousness researcher.
Instagram: @cinarabastos
Youtube: @luminareabrasil
LinkedIn: www.linkedin.com/in/cinarabastos

LIFE PULLS US

More than half a century ago, in a house located in a very small country town in Brazil... The most experienced doctor in the field looks deeply into my mom's eyes, saying: "Your baby is in a very bad position, with the umbilical cord wrapped around its neck. It will be a risky delivery. I cannot give you any hope." Imagine this moment when a 23-year-old young woman, who had already been facing so much unbearable suffering, received these words. Full of courage and fear, she traveled on precarious roads in order to be by her mother's side and either facing the risk of losing her baby, or dying during delivery. The day was Holy Friday the 13th, 1968. There was a full moon filling the Easter sky. It was a blessing date, as suddenly the miracle happened: the water broke and there was barely time to get to the maternity ward; the baby who had been given up for dead weeks before, now arrived fully on her own... sliding in a hurry into the hands of the midwife to reach the arms of the wisest and most loving grandmother that Garça City could ever know, Dona Dirce Schiante Zago. That baby was me. Now, as I write these lines, the little girl who was born despite the worst projections is turning 55 – exactly on the Easter week! Looking back in history, I see many moments in my life when I was "hanging by a thread" but saved by grace, as a symbolic echo of my birth.

SELF INQUIRY FROM CHILDHOOD

Every healthy child loves to ask questions, even if the questions are inconvenient. I did that a lot, and I remember this one: *If life is already so difficult out there, why do adults insist on creating problems when they get home?* I was left without an answer. And between the ages of seven and eight, questions of a different order began to intrigue me. I loved to paint, run, and play, but I wouldn't give up my time in silence. I used to sit on the doorstep of the room that faced our garden. It was my oasis. While I observed everything, I felt the flamboyant blooming flowers in shades of orange, the ants working hard, the lightness of a flycatcher's flight, and the movement of the rare clouds floating below the blue sky; and I wondered things like: *What exists beyond what I can see? What force makes the birds' wings beat, that moves the wind and everything else that exists in the world? What is God really like? Why was I born?* I was releasing these questions to the wind without expecting answers (and didn't even know yet that this was a form of meditation). I just remained in silence, feeling and contemplating. Suddenly, something very magical happened. It was as if I had been pulled into another dimension without leaving my place. I was taken up into an indescribable state. I looked at my little hands, arms, feet, and in that moment, I understood that I was not just a physical body! It was as if the notion of "I" had given way to a more real and intangible understanding of the substance of life, where atoms were visible. There I began to understand that nothing that exists in the physical world can really be separated from the WHOLE. That moment was like an epiphany. The most real sense of reality I had ever experienced. However, as a child, I lacked the vocabulary and courage to tell anyone about it. And the search for belonging made me keep this moment of realization a secret. I was afraid of being judged "crazy", and preferred to resist the impulse to share this experience that must have lasted only a few seconds but seemed like an eternity . . . a place out of time. Today, I see how everything connects. That was the first tug of life awakening in me, which sparked the interest to explore the subtle nuances of reality. And as my biography unfolds, the mosaic of circumstances full of signs and omens that forms the incredible *hologram of life* became gradually clearer. Observing it with openness and curiosity lead to understanding the "whys" of our history, and how to occupy our place in the world.

THE SCHOOL OF LIFE: FACTS PULL US TOWARDS FREEDOM

I grew up in a conflicted environment, where freedom was a distant dream. Life conditions required from me daily doses of resilience in order to emotionally survive. Just by being born as a girl I was deprived of some fundamental rights, turning aspects of my life into a grueling battle. My main goal was to walk on my own pace into the future on my own choice. Yet, amidst these challenges, I learned invaluable lessons about the power within—the first muscle I had to develop in order to forge my own path with dignity and, some degree of autonomy. This was pretty clear to me.

Driven by a burning desire for being free to seek personal development, I took the courageous step of leaving home and pursuing my studies in the bustling city of São Paulo, by my own. In doing so at my 16th, I confronted not only basic deprivations and deep-seated fears, but also abusive situations that threatened to crush my spirit.

I found myself facing many adversities alone, but that solitude served as a catalyst for my personal growth and nurtured my faith. At the age of 21, I gathered the courage to launch my first business - an endeavor undertaken with no resources, assistance, or any sense of financial stability, all amidst Brazil's most tumultuous economic era. It was the worse time of chaos and uncertainty, but I refused to let external circumstances dictate my destiny. Yet, just as success seemed within reach, a devastating robbery shattered everything I had painstakingly built, leaving me with nothing except the light of my professional credibility which was built along years with profound devotion to work. It was a lesson discerning about the transient nature of material possessions and the intrinsic light of intangible values that propel us to move forward.

Untying knots and passionately opening paths are part of the innate existential program of somebody born in under an Arian sign. Still, in terms of health and longevity, there must be a natural sense of limit even for the commitments we adopt in surviving. That was a learning from my first experience with burnout at the age of 26. I was already working non-stop in order to support my business in unbelievable adverse conditions. The lesson this "burnout experience" taught me was learning to identify and respect the limits of the body, instead of making continual demands on it, as if human organism were an unstoppable machine.

Some resets happen repeatedly in our lives till we *get the message*. When, for example, the dream of settling my future in California was finally coming true in the year 2000, it was interrupted by an accident that almost made me permanently disabled physically. Yet, after enduring two arduous years of surgeries, rehabilitation, and intensive therapy, I understood that the pursuit of growth and self-discovery requires a complete openness to the human experience itself, including the emotions and vulnerabilities we fear to face along the way.

During my childhood, crying or displaying any form of weakness was forbidden at home, as if emotions were a problem rather than an essential part of human spirit. Our culture, mainly in the business realm, still lacks space for recognizing and acknowledging emoticons properly. Over the decades, working with diverse companies and individuals, it was sad to witness exceptional professionals, visionary entrepreneurs, and relentless high achievers falling ill and losing themselves in the void. Inside and outside multinational corporations, I observed countless cases where people of all ages were robbed of the joy of their achievements due to their habit of neglecting their emotions and disregarding signs their bodies were sending them. They persisted in dysfunctionalities that took a toll on their physical well-being, relationships, and even their sanity. It became evident that the fast-paced and automatic mode of anxious daily routines could easily lead to a state of self-abandonment, trapping us in incapacitating depression - a fate none of us desire.

Regardless of age, we tend to fall as victim of an insatiable quest for "results at any cost", without balancing our potential to grow with our integral health. I, too, found myself ensnared by this trap on several occasions throughout decades of work, paying a hefty toll for it. The true price became more evident when I unexpectedly entered a menopause, taking me to navigate unknowing territories of my body's chemistry and challenges that came with it. This period coincided with a career transition, a family crisis, deep heartbreak, and the burden of coping with five losses in a mere year. Yet, once again, grace intervened, offering redemption from my own self-negligence through meditation, conscious studies, and the pursuit of discernment. In those moments I discovered the luminous power of life purpose. Grace, in its many forms, is always present.

The Gift of Human Awareness

In the school of living I see life unfolding as a complex mosaic of experiences, where spirituality functions as the glue that binds each fragment into a coherent and mysterious whole in which we are breathing. Observe this happening in daily routine, despite all the challenges or dramatic facts that are produced by our human blindness. We may realize that we not need religious standards to deal with our complexities, but we do need essential spirituality to be able to edify ourselves from the inside out, consistently. I learned that this is the highest subtle empowerment which enables us to transcend any adversity, finding more profound meaning in every challenge we encounter on our evolutionary path. We are a living process happening in each "right now" with a sufficient intelligence to recognize that our vulnerability may be a master that stimulates our potential for growth. In many ways, this teaches us to appreciate the significance of self-reflection and self-awareness along life, and how these elements are vital for us to truly thrive.

In 2012, in an ICU, I experienced the special blessing that many call as an NDE – a Near-Death Experience. How was it? After being taken to a place of FULL LIGHT (where the feeling was of total completeness, peace and infinit joy) I was literally pulled back to inhabit my physical body. It was as if, suddenly, that dimension (of infinite freedom and fullness) had been shrunk and sucked into a body, entering from the very top of my head moving towards the feet. Impossible to forget the deep sensations of that moment! There was no "I" in this experience whatsoever. It was simply a flow of higher energy, a living consciousness. By 'coming back' to the tangible world fully conscious of what I experienced, changed everything!! Just to experience this moment, it would have been worth being born! It was like attaining a level of awareness that unveils the very essence of our soul, showing us what we are truly made of. No social or professional title, no award, no other type of power . . . nothing could be more precious than this very present moment. c In fact, there is no human language nor vocabulary to describe the magnitude of this "*INPERIENCE*" in the ICU. During its unfolding, it was clear that we are actually a singular part of an INFINITE INTELLIGENCE - AN ETERNAL AND INDIVISIBLE WHOLE. The feeling is that I've been in a "state" where consciousness overflows the limits of any reason, where everything that is actually IS moving LIGHT!!

Life is a dance between the infinite and the limited time lapse in which we can evolve. We are the dancers responsible for shaping our own steps... By embracing the journey with a free spirit and nurturing the inner flame that propels us, we discover what it means to be fully alive. So, it's time to remember that **NO ONE WILL DO FOR US WHAT ONLY WE CAN DO FOR OURSELVES.** May each of us find the courage to explore the unknown, the self-love to care for ourselves, and the wisdom to dance in harmony with the eternal melody of existence. This is what pulls and open space for us to pull others as well. Let's embrace and amplify this luminous process together!

CLAUDIA COLAFERRO

Former C Level executive and actual Founder, CEO and investor of AngelUs Network - a digital platform with almost 300 recognized women helping others to succeed.
Website: www.angelus.network/
LinkedIn: www.linkedin.com/in/claudiacolaferro

INFINITE POSSIBILITIES: MATURITY WITH PURPOSE

My story begins in the city of Itapetininga, in the interior of São Paulo, a peaceful place where almost all my relatives still live. I come from a matriarchal family in its fourth generation, and my mother was the first person in the family to attend university. Both my parents come from simple, religious families, and education was able to open possibilities and dreams. I grew up with autonomy, a lot of freedom and responsibility given by my parents.

There was a requirement from my parents about what or where to study. But their expectation was always that everyone would have a degree. My choices in the entrance exam were very broad. They ranged from mathematics, computer science, business administration, and medicine. I was approved in my first entrance exam for Business Administration as the best option at the university at the time and the only one I applied for, however, in a private school. At that time, we went through a bankruptcy process in the family, and we did not have the financial means to pay for my education or even pay for my housing in the city of São Paulo, where I would have to move and live. I must go for scholarship (80% of the course to pay for after my graduation). Life in the big city was expensive and tough for me. I lived in a shared apartment with other students to reduce costs for everyone. One of the biggest lessons about respecting others came from that time.

I started working in the afternoons and evenings to help with the cost of living in the capital. I work as 'au pairs', caregivers for children, or babysitters for a little French boy, Florian, for my first three years as student. And at night, I gave extra classes to high school students who needed extra lessons in some specific subjects. What I can say about this time is unlike the happy memories of my friends who enjoyed their time at laughing, drinking beer, and playing with each other at the college, I don't miss that time so much.

In my last year of college, I had to start an internship in companies, which was required for my degree, and I went to work in the marketing department at a bank. From this experience, I knew that I wanted to be part of the area that is the strategic focus for the company. After that I've started working for Natura, a Brazilian beauty door to door company, but that didn't stop me from participating in the largest trainee selection program at *Gessy Lever*, now *Unilever* just 6 months after starting the job because the company was recognized as a reference in marketing and so it was. I stayed there for almost ten years. Unilever was really a school and offered me very different opportunities, which helped me to form my baggage of experiences and learnings that still structure me for the challenges today. Since I entered college, I knew that the executive world was what I wanted. I set clear goals for my career, positions to which I would have to ascend, and the ideal times to achieve them, if I really wanted to become a company president.

After my first 2 years as trainee at *Unilever* I received my first expatriation proposal to move to Santiago, Chile, to work at *Malloa*, a leader in food in that country and a recently acquired operation. One of the first experiences in which I experienced the difference between being a woman in the business world compared to my male colleagues occurred at that opportunity. I was the first woman to receive an expatriation offer in Latin America. Normally, for executives, the package includes housing and other benefits to all family members. When I officially received my contract, the benefits came only for me. It was my first negotiation for equity in the business world that I remember. After almost 2 years in Chile, I decided to return to Brazil where my first child was born. On my return I was transferred to manage the Dove brand for the entire Latin region, because of my previous experience in Spanish culture. *Unilever* has my utmost respect. It was there that I had my best bosses – always male. The two best bosses, who influenced me both technically and in leadership, were from this company.

After almost ten years, I received the opportunity for a director position at Coca-Cola, based in Rio de Janeiro, and decided to leave *Unilever*. It was an unmissable opportunity for the whole family, and Fabio, my husband, also managed to move there for a work opportunity. Taking care of one of the most iconic brands in the world, combined with North American culture, but with local implementation by local bottlers, at the time the 15 most influential families in their states, seemed very interesting to me. And so, it was. The period of almost six years in the company brought me many colleagues who became friends and many incredible projects that I am proud to have participated in. At Coca-Cola, I achieved a hierarchical position that I was seeking and had in my plans. This time was one of great exposure and autonomy. We did promotions with Avon, we created an event calendar to reconnect with young people with the biggest Rock concert in the country - Rock in Rio and also, we implemented two World Cups with a contract negotiated directly with Pelé, when we recovered all his personal awards, images, and moments to set up the Pelé Museum. Many activities that were created under my management were implemented for many years after my leave. After years in the position of director, the next step would be the vice presidency, but I would need to leave the country and it would not be possible for family reasons.

That was when I went for another experience, now in the world of technology, more precisely in the world of cell phones. Motorola was my third experience as an executive.At the time, Motorola was considered by the market to be the most innovative device and technology was a huge learning that I needed to acquire and decode for myself and for users. Working for technology and delivery service for the first time was challenging, but the learning from partnerships at Coca-Cola taught me a lot about collaborative work. We obtained several profitable partnerships despite of mostly men always in the room at the world of technology.

After two years at Motorola, I've decided to give a boost to my marketing knowledge. I thought I should delve deeper and better understand how decisions were made by consumers. I decided to enroll in the master's program studying neuroscience at Economics and Business campus, where I concluded with a study on Neuromarketing and its contributions to understanding the consumer. My thesis has accumulated almost 10,000 visits to the USP website, which leaves me quite satisfied with the usefulness that my research product has brought to people who want to start in the field.During my master's degree, I was invited to be the vice-president of Philips and to be part of a board for their three divisions, each with its own individual goal. This journey lasted two years, when I received a very special invitation to join a newly formed group, *Dentsu international*, in a project to set up a network of digital agencies in Latin America, focused on bringing to life an ecosystem of innovation through the acquisition of startups.

My path as CEO had arrived, and I believe it was my greatest experience of intrapreneurship. We acquired in Latin America almost fifteen companies in seven years, building an innovative and complete network of digital services, present from Argentina to Mexico. *Dentsu* was my home for the past ten years and where I explored the world entrepreneurship, including understanding the barriers to female founders and their needs to dream big. They have lots of challenges: in conceiving the idea of their businesses, in the technical knowledge necessary to structure the product, in all the bureaucracy needed to start a business as well as in financial funds to make it happen. In addition to that there is a lack of examples of other women who have undertaken and succeeded on their projects to serve as inspiration for others. The program served as inspiration and guide for what I would develop years later.

After the successful implementation of the structure in the Latin region, I was invited to join the leadership team in the United States, taking my whole family who also made plans for this country. I lived for four years on American soil and learned a lot about leadership in general, as I was now part of the board of the world's largest operation of the group. A world made by entrepreneurs, mostly acquired companies led by men, coming from 27 acquisitions in the country. However, it was the lives of female employees, especially in the agency world, where I saw firsthand what happened to them in companies. They gave up on continuing their careers as soon as they decided to get married or have children. Inspired by the American value of equality, where everyone should have same rights in the business world I made a speech at TED-type event called *DisruptHR*, where I expressed my point of view on possible solutions if women wanting to lead their careers towards what they deserve. There, in February 2020, the idea of launching *AngelUs* was born - a company that I founded and debuted as an entrepreneur.

AngelUs was conceived as a network of women recognized in various fields, who prepare others for leadership in a digital environment, ideally designed to prepare any women to face their professional stage: beginning it, changing it paths, or even reinventing themselves to a new one. We plan to help as a network force the main problems a women face: not knowing what they want to do or what they are capable of, or even their limitations and dreams; the elaboration of a plan to put their project and deadlines into practice; or even where to seek help; showing examples of others women's to serve as inspiration. We conceived a "factory of women leaders," in a progressive process, with three phases : 1)a self-knowledge process to help them understand what they want to do with the strength; 2)a customized plan of activities that they should perform so that the project can be put into practice; and 3)a network of more than 250 women who will help them in each of the tasks, offering knowledge, experience, training, or even services so that the project or career evolves according to the plan in time. Thus, in the same place, we can support women throughout their trajectory, building autonomy of learning and monitoring by others who have already made it.

As the sole investor, I suffer from the pains of entrepreneurship. I have many doubts about which direction to take in areas that are not my strengths, which made me investigate the world of Venture Capital, companies that provide capital and often help structure the business. It is where I found a world even more male-dominated than I was used to in my previous experience. I believe that, because it is still in its early stages, the world of startups still has a masculine culture on ways to operate the business. But I am confident that I am living on my purpose now, at a moment in life where my gravitas can impact people, which moves me. When I help a woman, I understand that I can open paths, inspire, and really support her. And then, at that moment, all doubts disappear!

I think it's important to highlight the role of my partner in all the professional journeys I've decided to face. I believe I found my "trampoline man". Despite having a role as the organizer of my home and being a (happy) mother to Carolina and Henrique, I always knew that perfection was not what I was seeking and that I needed, and I still need help. And that's where the role of the trampoline companion comes in. The one who catapults you up, helping, supporting, sharing, and adding his vision. I always say that you must be careful with the anchor ones. Those people who pull you down. Who anchors and leaves you static with the false sense of security in a world that is constantly changing. So, having clarity about what you want for life may help you choose the right ones around you.

Looking back, I feel like I am where I wanted to be. I am comfortable in my own skin, but I still have a lot to accomplish. For myself, for my family, and for all the women I dedicate myself to help at *AngelUs* in what they deserved to become. Let's #empowerwomen aka #mulherar?

CLAUDIA FURINI

Woman, mother, wife, advertiser, and Director of Marketing, UX, and Sustainability at Banco BV since 2017. Claudia's journey from teenage parenthood to corporate leadership showcases resilience and a mission to inspire other women.
Email: claufurini@gmail.com
Instagram: @cfurini
LinkedIn: www.linkedin.com/in/claudiafurini

THE PERFECTLY IMPERFECT EXECUTIVE.

A story of overcoming obstacles, and genuine authenticity. A teenage mother navigated challenges to emerge as a successful leader, defying norms and accepting her flaws. This journey underscores that the quest for perfection is an illusion; true fulfillment comes from accepting oneself, cherishing achievements, and acknowledging vulnerabilities. It's about liberating oneself from societal expectations and embracing one's unique imperfections.

HEY MOM, I'M PREGNANT!

The word "perfection" has always been a persistent echo in my ears. From my earliest memories as a child, I was shaped to chase excellence, to stand out in any challenge I faced. Society, with its often-unattainable standards, didn't only influence my wardrobe choices, but also shaped the way I thought, my actions, and even my deepest dreams. The pressure was omnipresent, in every corner, in every glance, in every whispered word. Society set strict standards of beauty, behavior, and achievement to which I felt compelled to conform. And, just like countless other women, for years on end, I struggled to fit in, to be accepted, to meet these demands which were often stifling.

However, like a river that changes course after a powerful storm, life presented me with an unexpected turn. At 16, I discovered I was pregnant with twins. This new chapter in my life, filled with twists and overwhelming emotions, plunged me into a sea of responsibilities I never imagined facing so soon. While my friends were planning their graduation parties, discussing dream trips, and preparing for college entrance exams, I found myself amidst medical appointments, ultrasound scans, and the eager anticipation of welcoming two new souls into the world. They dreamt of their academic and professional futures, while I was adjusting to the reality of being a young mother, trying to balance the demands of motherhood with my own dreams and aspirations.

Becoming a mother in my teenage years wasn't just a physical transformation, but also a profound spiritual and emotional metamorphosis. I faced towering challenges, but in return, I discovered within me a resilience and determination I never knew I possessed. Faced with disapproving glances and whispered criticisms, I drew strength from the love for my children and the belief that I could overcome any adversity. I chose not just to confront the stigmas of early motherhood, but to use them as fuel to break barriers and achieve my goals. Every decision, every step, every sacrifice was made with the well-being of my children and my own growth in mind. I was aware of the forthcoming challenges, but I was determined to show myself and the world that youth and motherhood could walk side by side, motivating me to always seek the very best.

Learning to Cope with Burnout and Embracing Imperfection

My professional journey began without grand ambitions or dreams. At that time, all I desired was a steady paycheck, health insurance, and childcare support for my boys. However, the universe, with its unexpected twists, had different plans for me. With resilience, determination, and the unwavering support of my family, I managed to complete my education and embark on a professional career that initially seemed far from my reality.

I often say that I can't discuss my career without mentioning my children. For me, it has always been a challenge to balance the demands of motherhood with workplace responsibilities. I married a wonderful man whom I met at work. Together, we became a formidable team, sharing life's challenges. With him, I had two more children, and the pressure to be the perfect mother, the perfect wife, and the perfect professional kept escalating with every step. Starting as a Telemarketing Operator, with perseverance and dedication, I rose to the position of Marketing Director in a major Financial Institution. The hitch was, along this journey, I constantly pushed myself to meet every expectation, chasing a form of perfection that I began to realize might be unattainable.

That's when my body began to signal exhaustion. The stress piled up, sleepless nights became frequent, and weekends, which should have been moments of relaxation, were consumed by worries and pending tasks. I kept myself perpetually busy, racing from one commitment to another, ignoring the limits of my body and mind. Until one day, the inevitable happened: I suffered a burnout.

The burnout was a moment of collapse, a turning point that forced me to confront reality and acknowledge my limitations. It was a painful journey, yet transformative. I realized the perfection I so ardently sought was elusive and unattainable. I understood that I couldn't do everything, and it was okay to admit my weaknesses. It was a valuable lesson in self-acceptance, self-compassion, and the importance of self-care. I learned the significance of listening to our bodies, respecting our boundaries, and recognizing that being human inherently means being imperfect. And in that imperfection, I found the true essence of life

SETTING PRIORITIES AND BUILDING A SUPPORT NETWORK. PULL ME UP! I'LL PULL YOU TOO!

Setting Priorities and Building a Support Network: Pull Me Up! I'll Pull You!

It took an extensive process of self-awareness and acceptance to realize that I was imperfectly perfect. Accepting my flaws, recognizing my boundaries, and forgiving myself for not always achieving perfection were vital steps in this journey. Motherhood and my professional life didn't need to be a competition but an opportunity for growth and learning.

From that transformative moment, I began to reevaluate my relationship with work and motherhood. Society often bombards us with images of superwomen, those who seem to balance everything effortlessly. However, the truth is, each of us faces our own unique challenges and battles. I had to understand that sometimes, the relentless pursuit of perfection could lead me down a path of dissatisfaction and stress. I recognized the need to craft a narrative anchored in authenticity, balance, and acceptance.

Endless afternoons at the office, weekends filled with chores, and moments missed with my family began to weigh on me. After all, I didn't need to be a superwoman juggling everything; I needed to be a real woman with dreams, desires, and limitations. Acknowledging my weaknesses and limits became a crucial step in this healing process. Self-awareness emerged as an indispensable tool, helping me pinpoint what truly mattered in my life and what was merely the result of external pressures.

With this newfound understanding, I started setting clearer boundaries at work, dedicating quality time to my family, and seeking activities that brought me genuine joy and satisfaction. I rediscovered old hobbies, like reading and dancing, and began to cherish moments of relaxation and disconnection more than ever.

However, it wasn't always smooth sailing. At times, I felt overwhelmed, struggling to find balance amid the numerous demands of my life. That's when the importance of establishing and maintaining a solid support network became evident. Connecting with other women, who shared similar experiences, was rejuvenating. Together, we laughed, cried, exchanged advice, and uplifted each other.

This community became a fundamental pillar in my life, offering support, understanding, and above all, reminding me that I wasn't alone in this journey. This support extended beyond friends and family to support groups, therapists, and coaches who assisted me through the challenges of motherhood and career.

My career and motherhood story are a journey of continuous learning. From the first steps in this adventure, every experience has shaped me, every challenge fortified me, and every triumph nourished my spirit. While I still face obstacles and moments of doubt, I now understand that I don't need to be perfect to succeed. True fulfillment lies in embracing my authenticity, accepting my imperfections, and seeking a balanced life where I can be the mother, the professional, and the woman I I WANT to be.

Today, I embrace my imperfection and move forward, learning from my mistakes, celebrating my achievements, and building an authentic life. Motherhood and career are not obstacles, but opportunities to grow, evolve, and inspire other women to embrace their limitations and find their unique path to happiness. Every step, every decision, every tear and laughter are part of the mosaic of my life, and it is this tapestry that makes me who I am. Life presents us with countless challenges, but also gifts us with moments of pure joy and fulfillment. Amidst it all, I continue to seek balance, striving to be the best version of myself while nourishing my soul with the little pleasures and the great victories.

On this journey, I hope to inspire other women to find their own voice, challenge conventions, and embrace their stories with love, acceptance, and courage. Because in the end, it is our self-love and authenticity that guide us to true happiness. And I continue, whether confident or vulnerable, knowing that my story is unique and valuable, exactly the way I am: **imperfectly perfect.**

CRISTIANE PEREIRA HEAL

Partner at Proa.cc Brand-shaping Studio. Sustainability and Impact Strategist at Batux Live Marketing. Board Member at Badu Design Circular, a socio-environmental business.
Website: www.proa.cc
LinkedIn: www.linkedin.com/in/crispereiraheal

"BECOMING OUR TRUE SELVES."

I was born and raised in a modest family in the city of São Paulo, where I learned from an early age the importance of the values instilled by my father and the determination of my mother to chase her dreams.

My mother spent a significant part of her adolescence assisting my grandmother in taking care of her siblings, while my father, at the age of 13, questioned his submissive and vulnerable situation in Minas Gerais and decided to leave home. He understood very early on that the local culture of "kissing the hands" of priests and influential people in the São João Del Rey region in the state of Minas Gerais would not lead him anywhere. From a young age, he realized that he wouldn't be the one determining the next steps in his future, and that others would do it for him. Unfortunately, he witnessed the real-life story of his godmother, who lived a life enslaved in the kitchen of one of those deemed important in the town. He found the courage, persuaded my grandparents, and they moved to São Paulo with the whole family. He met my mother, and that's where a new chapter in a story where they would be the protagonists began.

My father and mother, Mr. Pereira and Mrs. Cleusa, formed an unbeatable duo, incorporating strength and love in raising four children. My father arrived in São Paulo as a construction worker, had the opportunity to study at Liceu Coração de Jesus College after winning a scholarship, got married, and graduated with two higher education degrees. My mother embarked on a challenging journey of complete dedication to the family and the education of her children. They faced many hardships together, including losing everything when a nearby dam's floodgates were opened following heavy rain that resulted in flooding of their first home, forcing them to start from scratch.

My three siblings and I grew up hearing these stories of determination, courage, responsibility, and resilience, with a positive outlook on life and the belief that life's obstacles could be overcome with knowledge and hard work.

These life examples shaped my character and paved the path I chose for myself. I always enjoyed studying and easily adapted to the school environment. My father secured a stable job at the multinational, ICI Brazil, within the company's internal communication department. My older brother successfully sold advertising space in the yellow pages phone directory in Sao Paulo. I remember the day he brought home a copy of Meio & Mensagem, a trade journal for the local advertising industry that, in that issue, featured Washington Olivetto, one of Brazil's most famous advertising executives. The story of Washington Olivetto's professional trajectory and success inspired me, sparked an interest in the communication industry, and quickly became a passion.

This new interest then led to me setting an academic goal: to study Communication and Media at the Fundação Armando Álvares Penteado (FAAP) University, with the end objective to work in an advertising agency, and, perhaps one day, work with Washington Olivetto.

When I entered university, I felt a mix of excitement and gratitude. FAAP University was always my dream college, and at the same time I had also passed a trainee selection process to enter MPM Publicidade, the largest advertising agency in Brazil. However, the first day of this new life was a reality check. Upon entering the agency, I noticed the social class differences that separated me from the people working around me. That moment highlighted the discrepancy between the working-class eastern suburbs where I lived, and the privileges concentrated in the rich southern suburbs of São Paulo. The shock was twofold because I started working at the agency on the same day as my first class at the private FAAP University.

The distance of my work commute was an obstacle I faced every day. I depended on a bus line, and then the subway. Most days I would spend 4 hours commuting to and from work/university. Initially, the trainee salary I received was exactly the amount of my FAAP University tuition fees. Over time and with good grades, I obtained a partial scholarship that enabled me to buy books and materials for my studies.

I felt the pressure to adapt and fit into those environments. I ended up trying to become a copy of the upper-class people around me, losing my identity. I felt obliged to change my appearance, way of speaking, dress sense, and even my personal tastes and preferences.

I was learning a lot and was completely amazed by everything that was new to me, filled with enriching references. However, this change distanced me from the people who were part of my history. It affected some of my relationships, and I almost lost valuable friendships. It was a radical and strange change from what I used to be.

Many years passed, along with increasingly more senior jobs at various advertising agencies, and I found myself increasingly distant from the real me. I didn't know it at the time, but this distancing prevented me from being fully present at work or even socially. I didn't feel capable of contributing in the best way to discussions; I believed I could offer more if I had space to include my beliefs and differences. However, I couldn't see an opportunity to express my most genuine opinions without feeling like I was exposing myself too much. I wanted to better assert myself but couldn't find a way to do so.

At the same time, that moment was one of affirmation for the professional I was becoming, so I didn't entertain the emerging perceptions, promptly dismissing them.

With time came promotions, new positions, and responsibilities. The differences continued to raise doubts in myself regarding my position and competence. I began to grapple with imposter syndrome and still felt isolated.

I faced the common challenges and barriers in the corporate world, especially for women in leadership positions: disappointments, competition, wage inequality, interruptions, and the appropriation of my ideas. Among my male colleagues, I was always the last to be promoted. It was common to look at the organizational chart and see these male colleagues doing the same or less responsible work with higher job titles than mine.

Observing other women fighting for their spaces made me realize how distracted I had been, not noticing the paradox I was in: distant from my true essence and desiring to please others. This only heightened my perception that I wouldn't be able to confidently fulfil my leadership role.

In my personal life, a revolution was also on the horizon. I had a high-risk twin pregnancy. My daughters Clara and Luísa were born extremely premature, at 28 weeks of gestation. Luísa passed away four days after birth while Clara fought in the hospital ICU for 4 months until finally being released from hospital. Dealing with this loss created a new meaning for me. Everything I had believed to be important became secondary in the face of the pain and emotions that overwhelmed me. I needed to withdraw to gather strength from my family and my husband.

At work, I had to rely on people's empathy and, most importantly, the trust and support of the team I led.

I realized I could embrace vulnerability, and that, in addition to bringing me closer to the team, it positively impacted the world I wanted to see emerge: one that was less toxic and where people could have space to express their values and contribute their best.

Starting the transformation wasn't easy because my achievements made people who wanted to maintain their positions of power uncomfortable. I felt that my authentic self was starting to bother them.

I found inspiration in the words of Brené Brown, a researcher and author, who believes that authenticity is the key to a fulfilling life. According to Brown, authenticity involves the courage to be who we really are, even if it means facing vulnerabilities and uncertainties. She believes that authenticity is a practice, a conscious choice we must make every day. Based on this perspective, I realized that embracing my authenticity was not only important for me but also for my professional journey. It was necessary to find a balance between who I was and the cultures surrounding me.

I began to realize I wasn't alone. Besides my friends, whom I consider sisters, and my mentors, who were by my side, I encountered incredible women like Nathalie Trutmann, a writer and tireless dreamer, to whom I am grateful for giving me the opportunity to share my story in this book when she "pulled" me into this group of powerful women.

I sought to enhance my education, studying innovation and facilitation strategies at Hyper Island. I graduated and obtained a Corporate Board Member certification from IBGC. Additionally, I earned executive education certifications in Sustainable Business Strategy from Harvard Business School and Cambridge Judge Business School, deepening my knowledge of Circular Economy.

During meetings promoted by IBGC, I met Ariane Santos, the founder of Badu Design Circular. This connection allowed me to apply my knowledge as a board member, expanding my understanding of socio-environmental businesses and their positive social impact. I made space for my passion for sustainability and ESG (environmental, social, and governance) initiatives, recognizing the value of diversity as a fundamental ingredient for innovation.

With this new experience, combined with all my professional experience in advertising agencies - MPM, J.W.Thompson, W/Brasil (yes, I worked with Washington Olivetto), Almap/BBDO, DM9DDB, and FCB - I became a partner at PROA.cc, an independent innovation studio that believes in collaborative work driven by the power of brands and design. I serve as a board member and am responsible for Sustainable Business and Impact strategies at Batux, an innovation agency in promotion.

The journey to my authenticity has been a challenging and transformative process. Through it, I learned to value my voice and perspectives, even when it meant facing resistance and others' expectations. I discovered an inner strength that propelled me to achieve new professional heights, establish new relationships, and rekindle surprising connections from the past, such as my relationship with my mother, who now holds a special place in my life. She helped me understand my maternal and feminine self. At this moment, I can make space to express the beauty of my origin, my strength, and everything I truly believe in.

My story is just one among many lived by women in search of their authenticity. Each of these stories, shared and unfolded, serves as inspiration for other women who want to become the protagonists of their lives. By sharing our experiences, we encourage each other to become empowered and fulfilled in our journeys. As Halla Tómasdóttir, an Icelandic executive and influencer in the development of more inclusive businesses, says: "What we see, we can become."

May these stories be a source of inspiration and encouragement for all women who are seeking their places, being themselves, moving forward without ever losing sight of where they came from.

DANIELA MIGNANI

Senior Executive, C-Level, Mentor - Brazil Former General Director at Globo - Pay TV Business Unit
Instagram: @dani_mig
LinkedIn: www.linkedin.com/in/danielamignani

There are those who say that more important than what we were is what we are today and can be. Movement and openness to change are my engine, especially now in a time of professional transition. A 31-year career has gone by, starting in the financial market – Banco Nacional; retail – Multiplan Group; media - Grupo Globo.

A trajectory that was based on building great brands and products, until it expanded into business management. And it wouldn't have been possible if I wasn't surrounded by people and professionals who supported me and showed me the way.

Lifelong learning. Nonstop courses. It has been a rich and surprising learning journey. I was acknowledged as a media professional by Meio & Mensagem, I won Caboré Award as a Professional in TV and Women to Watch in Brazil. I was a judge on three International Emmys, a member of the UN Women Impulse Committee in Brazil, and I worked voluntarily at Junior Achievement RJ, supporting the entrepreneurial agenda in public schools.

My treasures, loves and guides on this long journey are my partner José Luis Volpini - for 29 years - and Juliana, my long-awaited daughter - for 27. I could not be luckier.

An orchid on my way

My surfer appearance didn't make it easy to find my first internship. Very Long blonde hair, suntanned and face always peeling from so much sun. Times of moisturizer for sunburn, due to inexistency of sunscreen. The Jornal do Brasil was the largest printed newspaper in Brazil at that time, and that was my target. I applied for a position, passed the curriculum screening phase, and went happily to my first interview. The marketing manager was a super busy and well-known professional, and led the Sunday Magazine, a reference. I met my future coordinator, and we started talking. I was analyzed from head to toe, and not taken seriously. In the end, passing through the corridor that led to the manager's office, a series of Margaret Mee watercolors made me react to their beauty and say:

— "Wow, these Margaret Mee orchids are so beautiful. The manager immediately left the room and asked me:"

— "Do you know who she is, and are you familiar with her work?"
—Yes. I spoke a few things about English botany and heard: "You're hired."

Upon returning on the agreed date to start my internship, I was greeted with this comment:

— "You're here because of her, not because of me. You weren't my choice." I asked for the reason, but she didn't give me anything substantial. That stayed in my head, and I couldn't rest until she revealed why. After two weeks, we were closer and I had shown some dedication, she felt comfortable enough to tell me that my appearance didn't inspire credibility.

An incredible experience with a woman who believed in me from the start, based on the content I could offer and without looking at my appearance, and another woman who saw me in the opposite way, but had the greatness to recognize it. It's worth saying that we became best friends and supported each other for the following year. With this episode, at 17 years old, I began a reflection that still shakes my head today, about the complex relationships that we women can have with each other. Structural and cultural legacies, and the certainty that someone benefits from maintaining conflicted relationships. Thankfully, for two decades, this context has been changing every day towards support, impetus to occupy greater public and private spaces, and increasingly sharing with men.

Thus, we are advancing in a beautiful way and with a unity never seen before. More than ever, we are educating and accepting ourselves, reviewing our models, and exercising the daily habit of pulling each other up. Volume 1 and now Volume 2 of this book are one of the concrete proofs that it is working. Fantastic stories with very diverse perspectives. The certainty that volumes 3, 4, 5 are just around the corner.

HEFORSHE & SHEFORSHE

As I reflect on my journey, I have to value men who have been a part of my career. Particularly, except for a few months over these 31 years, all of my bosses have been men. Conrado, Jorge, Guilherme, Bocayuva, Paulo, Wilson, Alberto, another Paulo, Erick. They have always listened to me attentively, considered my thoughts and contributions, and also had open ears to my objections. It's kind of crazy to say this today, but looking back,

I decided at a very young age to build a career. Driven by the idea of being absolutely independent, I created internal tools to deal with this male-dominated world; after all, they occupied the desired positions. I had an extraordinary experience and learning with all of them, and I grew with the leadership of each one of them. Sexism? Many times. But nothing that a good conversation couldn't solve. I always had internal strength to establish this dialogue. On the other hand, my only female boss, for a very short period of time, was also of absolute importance. Leticia, who had a remarkable history in Brazilian TV. We worked together on a beautiful rebranding project of a lifestyle tv channel. She trusted me to lead the channel when she accepted another challenge. A huge path opened up, being a personal and professional turning point.

And as I sat in a chair with broader decision-making power, my choices were mostly to be close to them. Mostly female teams marked my journey. It wasn't always simple and smooth, highs and lows, tears, and laughter, but my inner conviction is that if we don't occupy spaces, we don't develop and improve ourselves in all dimensions. And I affirm: the deepest and most rewarding learnings were with them. I want to pave easier paths for my daughter, niece, and all, but I prefer to act without the idea of exclusion, because we know this place well and it's not comfortable at all. I extol our union as the best solution for creating measures oriented towards parity. It may seem contradictory, but I truly believe that this is the most loving and lasting way.

Humor works, and we should use it even more.

I have very pleasant stories about Globo, and this one is from a lifestyle channel focused on a female audience at that time, and one of the channels under my general management. The editorial territories were Food - Home - Dialogue. It was a channel that explored feminine energy, but far from being a channel for women. When presenting a new positioning to the mostly male executive committee, we used astrology. The point here was to inform that all human beings had masculine and feminine energy, regardless of their gender. What defines us is a set of characteristics and attributes that bring us closer to the female or male. Box1824, with Paula Englert at the forefront, and my great ally in incredible projects, had this idea; She brought in Edu Conte, an astrologer, and together with the commissions members' assistants, we gathered the day and time of birth of each one, and bingo. Before the presentation, each one received their astrological chart with the grading of their energies; we broke the ice, they were entertained with the information, and at that point, we had already managed to bring the idea we wanted. They loved it, and it was very fun. All approved with flying colors.

At that moment, we could no longer talk about a channel aimed at women, as that was a reductionist, out-of-date, and inappropriate concept. It was never easy to bypass a male board with the content we had at hand. Sports, journalism, music, and humor were more engaging and universal than gastronomy, decoration, women's debates, and documentaries that shed light on new societal behaviors. I learned that using humor and creativity to catch attention - even in more formal corporate circumstances - worked very well. In our presentations, it was five other female managers and I; there was always something happening. A super video or an unusual edition, a more provocative visual program, a slide out of context, and so on. We surpassed ourselves. Together, we built a great case of content, marketing, cast, revenue, and segmented audience. All goals achieved every year, and my boss and CEO Alberto's unrestricted trust. A successful union between men and women.

The longevity revolution

With care and some luck, we are walking towards finitude around our 95 years. We have left behind the industrial period, when our body was utilitarian, and we died earlier. Life was divided into playing - studying - working - resting. All well marked chronologically. Today we face the exponential revolution of information, in which we produce symbols, aesthetics, ethics, and services. We will have to play, study, work, and rest simultaneously in our long existence. A carousel of increasingly faster transformations that will require us to develop a set of skills that accompany the spirit of the times. We will have a portfolio of careers, and this may seem scary, challenging yes, but very promising. When faced with changes in myself and my professional life, at 50 years old, finishing a cycle that was beyond victorious, the only certainty is that I will start a new phase the size of the one I have already lived. It is a portal of possibilities that opens up to reach 95 exploring many of the paths that the world presents us. I always think about life concessions: we lose our youth, but we become interesting and experienced. And that is a breathtaking beauty. And we still have maturity in our favor, which will help us no longer just meet the expectations of others.

"One of the friends from my previous job at Globo, Thais Chede pulled me into this group. I pulled Adriana Alcântara, another friend that Globo gave me, and I'm also being pulled by her in this new phase. Lucia, Andrea, and Leticia pulled me. One day I pulled Mari, Fabi, Flávia, Carol, Steph, Bel, Andrea, Beth, Astrid, Sabrina, Fernanda, and many, many others. And all of them pulled me to a place of great evolution. And the dance goes on.

Life is not just about working. You have to leave a good chapter for the craziness that everyone has. JOSÉ MUJICA."

DANI RESTUM

Co-founder Polo Wear (@polowear / polowear.com.br)
Founder and CEO Secrets Lounge (@secretsloungeofficial / secretsloungeofficial.com.br)
Instagram: @danirestum

WAIVERS AND CHOICES – LIVE YOUR DREAM !

I am the product of a mix of cultures – a Ceará-born soul with a Lebanese spice; my maternal grandparents, my mother and her siblings were born and lived in the backlands and did not have the privileges and opportunities that my parents gave me. I am grateful to have strong women in my maternal family as determined caregivers who boldly overcame difficulties and obstacles.

My aunts call themselves "The Three Marys". They represent more than a constellation for me, they are wolves who taught me to behave like a wolf.

My paternal grandfather, Khalil, was born in Chadra, Lebanon. At the age of 17, he came by ship with about 1,500 Italians and only three Lebanese, aiming at trying the luck he did not have in his homeland. It took him thirty days to reach the port of Santos.

I was born on June 17, 1985, in Campinas, São Paulo. My mother was then 22 and my father was going to turn 23 in August - young and bursting with life, they gave me life.

And guess where my talent for fashion comes from, or rather, who was the precursor? My grandfather Khalil, who started early as a peddler knocking on doors to sell clothes, saved his money and opened his first store, which my father used as a playground. Instead of playing on the streets with his friends, he enjoyed setting up the store window, serving customers and standing at the cash register. This legacy passed from father to son and eventually from father to daughter. I still remember the blast I had during school vacations, when my father used to take me to the store to help setting up gift boxes – I just loved it. It was aa joy seeing people happy when they acquired a garment that accentuated their beauty. I was only ten years old, but that time shaped me because I always knew that was what I wanted for my life!

When I was a freshman in Fashion studies at FAAP (Armando Álvares Penteado Foundation), I learned through a classmate an internship was available in the style department of Planet Girls - one of the brands in my family's holding - and I wanted to apply.

Although my family connections guaranteed me the internship, I wanted to go through the process and earn the opportunity like any other fashion student. I got the job and learned very much alongside my father and Adriana, my stepmother and founder of the Planet Girls brand. It was a big challenge, but it was my foundation for the flight I would soon take. I was at the peak of this brand - a phenomenon, a desire, and a reference for Brazilian women's jeans. From an intern in my freshman year of college, I was promoted to assistant in 2003, then to stylist, until I finally reached the position of coordinator. In 2006, I was ready to leave for a fashion specialization course in Melbourne, Australia, when Adri offered me the opportunity to stay in Brazil and participate in SPFW BUSINESS - São Paulo Fashion Week Business. It was a tempting offer that I accepted, and I spent three more years in the world of the stars with Planet Girls.

In 2009, I realized there was no way for me to grow in the area I was in, so I talked to my father about my desire for something new and challenging. My father, quite calmly and strategically, suggested that I take on a new brand that he had registered and wanted to launch. Since I love challenges, I decided to get involved with the new venture. I left the world of stars, glamor and glitz and turned to the universe of horses, initially aimed at men, with an elegant, sporty, and casual touch.

"That was everything I needed, and that's where I totally found myself because everything was new. I had the pleasure of bringing my vision and values to the brand, seeing Polo Wear grow and become the biggest brand in the group. Working with my father, and supporter, who as the brand founder handed me his dream and brought us closer to our essence. As the co-founder, I see the brand as my child, and watching every stage and step taken fills me with pride.

At the end of 2009, I finished my cycle at Planet and at the beginning of 2010 I took over the management of Polo. My personal life was as fast and overwhelming as my professional life, which went from first kissing in May 2009, to living together in mid-July, hearing the marriage proposal in October, and formalizing the engagement in November.

The year 2010 was intense and flew by: the birth of Polo Wear, the preparations for my wedding, the construction of our house and my marriage on November 12, 2010, when I was 25.

Polo Wear gained notoriety and my father sees enormous potential in my life partner to help us in the company. In 2012, he asks him to take over the logistics division, which at that time needed commitment and development.

In the same year, I introduce the women's line to the brand, which until then had been focused only on men. I see this opportunity because, based on consumer information, we know that 65% of purchases are made by women, and I see that we have a hook and upper hand to attract these customers.

When in 2014, pregnant with Valentin, I came across this universe of motherhood, I realized how much the Brazilian market was missing in children's fashion, and during the World Cup in Brazil I launched the brand's baby and children's line."

THE MAJOR TURNAROUND

These were years of growth and opening of the brand's stores; and in 2016, shortly after the birth of Mariah, my youngest daughter, the desire to create my own brand became latent: Secrets Lounge was born out of a desire to bring intimacy and empower women from the inside out. I sketched it out with my team at the time and presented it to my husband and to my father, my manager and boss at the company. They both loved the idea, but since Polo Wear was only six years old, they did not find it interesting for me to dedicate myself to a new brand, when Polo still had so much to grow, perform, and accomplish. And as always, I put my desires and dreams on hold to strengthen and obey other people's will.

At the end of 2018, my husband accepted a tempting job offer from another company and his last month with the group was January 2019.

When I came back from vacation with my children, a relative of my husband called me, opened my eyes, and made me aware of his suspicion my husband was cheating on me; it was March 11, 2019. On that same day, I asked him to come home early from work so we could talk. When I asked him whether he was cheating on me, he looked me in the eye and replied, "Are you crazy? I can't manage one, let alone two."

In the early hours of March 14, after praying to God to protect my family and show me what I needed to see, a command crossed my mind: "Take his phone!" When I unlocked it, I had the adultery evidence. My world collapsed, my hands shook, and I felt lost. That same day we had a talk, and I asked him to leave the house.

After that, I gave him two more chances for our marriage, but I found out he was still having an affair - on July 5, I put an end to it.

We met at the mediation hearing on November 11, 2019, one day before our ninth wedding anniversary. As my attorney says, I came in as a lioness and left as a kitten.

"He was about 15 kilos lighter - a clear sign he was suffering. There, in front of the mediator, the lawyers, and the notary clerk, he asked me to forgive him, to shake his hand, and then to hug him.

I LEFT FEELING AWKWARD, NOT KNOWING EXACTLY WHAT TO DO.

What I take away from my journey is to seek for self-knowledge, financial security and stability, emotional independence, and most importantly, to base, solidify, and root your life in the words of our Creator. He has the answers to everything. He is the best direction to follow. Through His actions, we can gain clarity, create the intimacy necessary to listen to His commands, follow our intuition and know how to say no.

I have childhood traumas I thought I had buried, but I figured that if the healing is not complete, they come back repeatedly until you understand that if you do not deal with them and acknowledge them, they can resurface.

Standing between the two men who were points of reference in my life put me in an unfair position, because to this day I have unanswered questions, and both betrayed my trust - one when I was only five, and the other by committing adultery and engaging in a power struggle in the middle of our separation; it was never about them, though - it has always been about me. Through their lives, through their choices, I have understood and now I am crossing the healing process. When our eyes and ears are open and our mouths do not close or accept the situation, the line is set, and our freedom is given to us by right - a right I have conquered and have been increasingly conquering every day.

I have always wondered whether it would be beneficial to reveal all of that as it involves my family, but as the very title says, "Waivers and Choices". For a long time, I renounced myself in order to fit in, and just like me, the people herein mentioned have made their choices. I am not here to judge, only to help others through my experience to awaken and connect with their essence.

Do not allow your boundaries to be crossed and strengthen your strengths. What has hurt me the most has also strengthened me. You find here a true story, snippets of my life, through which, other women can be touched, identify with, seek help, or serve as a wake-up call for our daughters, family, and friends.

And the final outcome of this troubled 2019 year was that I reconciled with my husband after the mediation hearing, which my family disapproved of and led me to split from my passion, Polo. It was painful and traumatic, but today I understand their point-of-view. They wanted to protect me and made me choose between my job or another chance to my family - I know I could not have both. Following my heart and unaware of my emotional codependency on my husband, I gave up everything I had achieved professionally to dedicate myself to my family. And that is how I was able to fulfill my Secrets Lounge dream.

A brand to call my own.

"Secrets Lounge" goes far beyond a dream, a brand. It showed and shows me every day the links and connections that open up between my personal life and my professional life. Unconsciously, I chose a padlock as the logo to represent the brand. At first, the idea of keeping your secrets, something mysterious, intimate, and deep comes to mind. I realize this padlock, in fact, represented the imprisonment of my fitting into someone else's life without actually having the freedom we all deserve.

I chose intimate apparel without ever having had any real contact with or experience in this field. I have always been involved with the fashion world, but in the casual fashion segment. These are different and specific universes. When I put forward this challenging desire, I see that I needed this intimate contact in my professional life to understand that we are only truly well when our interior is at peace, healed, wounds treated and closed, stainless, guiltless, painless. And is that possible? After all, we all face pain wounds - no one has a perfect life, but we all live in search of it. No wonder I am on the second volume and wrote the chapter of my story during Easter break.

We are temples of God and are made up of body, mind, and spirit.

«I am the vine; you are the branches. If you remain in me and I in you, you will bear much fruit; apart from me you can do nothing» (John 15:5)
top this fear of losing people and understand that you are too a big loss.
Maybe "forever" is about memories and not people.
You must want to spend the rest of your life first and foremost with yourself.
You are strong enough to start over.
Do not see yourself through the eyes of others.
Do not feel guilty about doing what is best for you.
It will hurt today and for a few more days until it means nothing.
One excellent choice for eternity makes up for thousands of wrong choices on Earth.
It is your choice.
I hope you do not have to admire from afar what you had so close.

DANIELA DE LUCA

Founding partner at Tuc Glasses (@tuc.glasses | tucglasses.com)
Founder Rise and Raise Others
Strategic business consultant, mentor, investor
Instagram: @danidelucabrandao
LinkedIn: www.linkedin.com/in/danieladelucabrandao

BUILDING A STORY

It was early 1981. I was 6 years old, attending the first day of school at Colégio Santa Cruz. The teacher seated a blonde little girl, who I thought was so beautiful, named Fernanda, next to me. Fê and I quickly became best friends, inseparable. I was shy, and she was outgoing, and it worked very well. Besides school, we spent weekends together, either at my house or hers. It didn't take long for our mothers to become friends too, and so we continued for years. Until life slowly drifted us apart, each of us went to different colleges and pursued different careers. I became an engineer and she was a publicist. We made new friends, got married, and had children. We only met sporadically.

Forty years later, in July 2021, still living in a time of uncertainties and challenges due to the COVID-19 pandemic, Fê was starting her own business, after ending a previous partnership. I had ended my partnership with Grupo Capim Santo (food & beverage) two years earlier, just before the start of the pandemic, and was well aware of the challenges of running a company. I really wanted her new project to succeed, so I offered help in building her Business Plan and some control spreadsheets so she could move forward on a strong footing. During our conversations, she mentioned how much she would like to have her own eyewear brand and gave me twenty compelling arguments as to why it would be a success. Three months later, we opened our company, creating our brand, TUC GLASSES (@tuc.glasses | www.tucglasses.com), and starting to build a new story together. I decided to tell this story here because it's a real-life example of a project that began with the "Rise and Raise Others" attitude from both of us. Truly. No hidden agendas.

Creating a brand and a company can be an exciting and challenging process. In this article, I will share how we got here and where we are heading, the obstacles Brazil imposes on entrepreneurs, how to build a healthy partnership, how previous professional experiences, both good and not-so-good, contribute to this construction, and how we are working to make it a success.

The initial proposal was quite ambitious: to create an eyewear brand that combined international quality with Brazilian essence, conveying joy and good vibes. Our goal was to offer a product with a modern design, but at affordable prices. The idea was to capture the spirit of a cheerful, vibrant, and colorful country without sacrificing the sophistication and style of international eyewear brands.

The first step was to define the essence of the brand and our purpose. Our brand was created with a strong socio-environmental pillar, as we believe in the power of collective action and that everyone should give back to the planet some of what it gives us every day. Our inspiration was the Amazon Rainforest, and our commitment is to support institutions that promote the planting of native trees in reforestation areas. Through our glasses, we want to attract the attention of the whole world to important and urgent issues and, in partnership with other brands, create capsule collections that generate funds for their respective projects, such as the collaboration we did with Onçafari Association, with part of the income reverted to support the preservation of jaguars in the Pantanal (an area in Brazil).

Then it was time to choose a name. The brand needed to be registered with INPI, a Brazilian institute to protect trademarks and intellectual property and have an available domain on the internet and Instagram. Also, it should also be a catchy, short, and easy-to-remember name. With so many required attributes, creating our decision matrix was just the first step. Name ideas were featured horizontally, prerequisites vertically, and off we went. Our name, TUC, was chosen with great care and affection. It is the name of our character, a friendly, modern, and elegant toucan with fine features.

The glasses we wanted needed to be imported, and the challenges here were enormous. Finding suppliers, learning to communicate with them, working in multiple time zones, designing products, understanding the fine print, learning the import process, and especially adjusting to the outrageous import costs in Brazil. Yes, entrepreneurship in Brazil is a daily exercise in resilience and patience and requires an extra dose of determination (and a strong stomach).

Working with Fernanda has been an incredible experience. We have complementary skills, but the same values and principles, which makes all the difference in the daily management of the partnership. Also, we have a clear vision of what we want to achieve and are committed to success. Our story is just beginning, but we already have a lot to celebrate. With each milestone conquered, we feel the excitement of building something unique and special.

INITIAL OBSTACLES: A WOMAN'S JOURNEY IN A MALEDOMINATED ENVIRONMENT

Ever since I was a little girl, I never knew exactly what I wanted to be when I grew up. Maybe I still don't know. For years I was ashamed to admit that, but today I know that most people don't know, and that's okay. The day I ended high school came, and there was no more running away. So, I decided to apply for Industrial Engineering in Polytechnic School, in the University of São Paulo, and a few months later, I started the course with 16 other women, among 80 men in the classroom. It was better than in my friend Karine's Mechatronics Engineering class, where she was the only girl. During the five years of college, I confess that I don't remember experiencing sexism. We were all equal, after all, the exams were the same for everyone, and the evaluation criteria were purely technical. I soon became involved in the Athletic Association, first as a director and later as President, succeeding another woman, Marcinha, and becoming the 3rd female President of the Association in the 39 years of its existence. The sports crowd is always the coolest. At least I think so. Being a woman didn't prevent us from leading the Athletic Association of a school with 5,000 students, of whom perhaps less than 10% were women at the time. And by doing so, shaping myself in a male environment, and believing it was all okay, I started my career entering the financial market thinking I was very well prepared.

I won't go into details here, but I want to say that it wasn't all okay. And at the time, I didn't realize it because no one talked about these issues. I wore a dress suit with my hair tied back and fake glasses when I visited male clients (yes, all the CFOs of client companies were men). I was called into meetings with my boss in a private room to be invited to dinner (yes, the boss was married), I was never invited to department events. After all, my colleagues didn't want my having contact with their wives (yes, I knew too much and saw too much), and I had my annual bonus slashed when I refused to go out with my boss. Even without embarking on that adventure, I still heard daily that "women only come to work at an investment bank to find a rich husband." It's worth noting that bonuses in investment banks are the main part of annual total compensation. Long story short, sparing my readers from more sordid details, but enough to say that it didn't work out; and I left swearing I would only return to the market after getting married. I then plunged into a four-year sabbatical, trying to understand why that super smart, powerful, well-educated, athletic, and well-adjusted girl didn't make it. Since in a bank our value is measured in money, the message had been delivered. They made me believe I wasn't good enough. And it's crazy how things weren't clear at the time as they are today. At least not for me.

And then I met Fábio, my husband of 17 years now, who insisted I should return to the market, saying it was a waste of talent. He always admired me, encouraged me, and was up for all my "craziness." Thank you, Fábio, for getting me back on track and making me believe in myself again. Of course, I am good enough, or even better! I know that now.

I never victimized myself and never told these stories in public until now, 20 years later, when I found in this book the right place and time.

LEARNING TO BE AN ENTREPRENEUR: OVERCOMING DIFFICULITES AND DEVELOPING THE NECESSARY CHARACTERISTICS FOR SUCECESS

Entrepreneurship in Brazil is a real battlefield. It's no secret that about 50% of companies close their doors before completing 4 years of activity, according to the Brazilian Statistics Institute (IBGE). Difficulties abound, from excessive bureaucracy to a lack of tax incentives, high tax burdens, economic instability, and high administrative complexity. However, for those willing to overcome these obstacles, entrepreneurship can be a great opportunity for personal and professional fulfillment. In our first months of activity, our cargo got stuck at federal customs for almost a month due to a strike. Supplier paid, import taxes paid (which doubles the product cost), and cargo stuck. Rent due, employees to be paid, customers waiting for products, and the customs department sitting on the process. There's nothing that can be done. In Brazil, the entrepreneur is last in line. The only right we have is to sit down, take some anxiety pill, invest more capital in the company, try to believe, and wait.

Generally, entrepreneurs are creative, visionary, determined, and persistent people. They can see opportunities where most people only see problems, and they don't let obstacles deter them. But the most important thing is to have a lot of discipline and resilience, especially for women entrepreneurs. Entrepreneurship is hard work and requires a lot of dedication and effort. Another thing I learned over time is to seek the right help, and that asking for help is not a sign of weakness, but a sign of intelligence. My professional career has taught me to be more of a generalist than a specialist. I have worked in various fields and acquired a broad and varied knowledge, and this has helped me a lot.

Finally, I believe that the key to success is to stay focused. It's easy to get lost in operational work, to be carried away by day-to-day demands and emergencies, and to forget to plan for the long term and set clear goals. We must always be attentive to strategic planning, setting goals and monitoring performance indicators, to ensure that the company is always on the right track and at the right pace. As I always say: "Without discipline, a dream is just a dream."

Entrepreneurship is not easy, but it can be very rewarding. And it's essential to have the humility to recognize that you'll need help. But it is possible to overcome obstacles and turn an idea into a successful business. For those thinking of starting a business, I say: follow your heart, work hard, and never give up! Success is out there, waiting for you!

I dedicate this chapter to my daughter, Maria Alice, who inspires me every day, who shows me the sweet side of life, who is my greatest gift and the greatest achievement of my life. For her, I want to change the world. I love you so much!

DENISE BARBOSA

Intl Trade Advisor- USA Consulate/ Brazil
LinkedIn: www.linkedin.com/in/denise-barbosa-mba-b2469525

Pleased to meet you! I am Denise de Fatima Barbosa, the result of a promise and a lot of love. My name carries the strength of the ardent desire of my father, Luiz, who was anxiously awaiting the birth of a son.

After losing his first child, he went to Fatima in Portugal to ask that my arrival would be one of great health. As a result of this promise, I was born on the day of the final match of the São Paulo x Corinthians soccer championship in December, a long-awaited granddaughter. I grew up under the protection and affection of my parents, who dedicated themselves tirelessly to providing me with a better life. The victory of the team of my heart, and my birth already demonstrate my father's passion for soccer. Very typical of Brazilian patriarchs who have soccer as something of extreme importance.

I come from a large family with many uncles and cousins. My paternal grandfather, the son of slaves, opened the way for the generations of our family to study, by valuing education and becoming an example of overcoming and strength.

This heritage encouraged me to seek a better future and overcome all the challenges that would come my way. As a child I remember my mother being part of the book club, and I was always encouraged to read. We always had to be the best in class, we were only allowed to get a 9 or 10, an example of education. Or a notebook as a gift to write in and remember everything I did wrong for not getting the highest grade.

Thanks to the professional ascension of my father, a VASP (São Paulo Airlines) employee, I had access to a quality and privileged education. From an early age, I learned about the importance of multiculturalism. My father traveled frequently, and I absorbed this global perspective.

I got to know many places, which showed me the diversity of cultures, customs, and traditions. An experience that allowed me to expand my knowledge and understanding of the world we live in. With this background, I grew up determined to be someone in life, as my father always encouraged me. Although I didn't face prejudice inside the school, thanks to my father's protection, I did experience marked situations of discrimination outside of it.

In one episode that I will never forget, a friend invited me to do a school assignment, but I was prevented from entering her house because of the color of my skin. This painful incident made me realize how much prejudice was still present in society, and how I would have to fight to overcome it.

Despite adversity, the self-esteem worked by my parents kept me firmly on my path. They always taught me that, even in the face of difficulties, I had the capacity to overcome them and succeed in life. My father's challenge at the end of high school that I should either get into USP, the University of São Paulo, or finance my own studies was a turning point in my life. Although I did not get a place at USP, my indomitable spirit did not allow me to give up. My determination and passion for knowledge led me to Mackenzie Presbyterian University where I studied Foreign Trade. This achievement was followed by an internship in a newspaper, I moved on and have always sought even greater opportunities to develop professionally.

My journey is a testimony of courage, perseverance, and belief in the unlimited potential of each person. Born and raised on the outskirts of São Paulo, I faced many obstacles, but always had the unwavering will to transcend my circumstances. A seed of self-esteem and resilience was planted in me by my parents. From an incredibly early age, they taught me to believe in myself and to never allow circumstances to determine my ability.

As time went by, my career progressed and flourished. I started my path in the visa industry of the United States government. My dedication and commitment allowed me to quickly climb the professional ladder, first as an events coordinator at the U.S. Department of Commerce and later as a market development specialist. Motivated by the desire to acquire even more knowledge, I continued my studies with an MBA in International Relations at FGV and MIT, where I also studied Innovation and Leadership.

Over the years I had the opportunity to collaborate with influential men, learn from their experiences and skills, and apply them to my personal and professional growth. However, my path has also been marked by numerous challenges and adversities. Events such as harassment, prejudice, and "mansplaining" made me realize the importance of being a strong and independent woman. My commitment to excellence led me to work three times as hard to show that a woman, specifically a Black woman, could excel and succeed in a competitive work environment. This is a legacy I leave for all women who aspire to succeed.

I was lucky to have sisters that life gave me, who supported me in difficult moments. When my father was diagnosed with Alzheimer's, a disease that worsened during the pandemic, I was by his side, caring for him. I stayed by his side during all his hospitalizations, doing my best to make sure he had the best care possible and never felt alone. I was with him to the very end, supporting him during a time of deep pain and sadness.

At the same time, I was also fulfilling my professional responsibilities. I faced a variety of challenges, from organizing events to introduce imported products in the Brazilian market to organizing panel discussions with CEOs to reflect on the lessons learned during the pandemic. During this period, I had the opportunity to interact with the CEO of IBM, who was a source of inspiration to me. Her insights into the power of resilience, the importance of versatility, and the need for self-confidence motivated me to persevere despite adversity.

I was introduced to C-101, board member course for black women, by Patricia Molino and discovered a universe of Black female executives willing to change our history of injustices. They tirelessly advocate for the need to increase the representation of Black leaders in decision-making positions. This discovery gave me a feeling of belonging and made me believe that I was not alone in this fight. They inspired me to believe that we can build a more equal world, and I hope to keep the doors open for the next generations.

My journey would not be complete without mentioning my personal mission and passion: promoting gender equality. I am strongly committed to the cause of gender equality, and women have the power to build a better world for companies, institutions, NGOs, hospitals, and most importantly, to help men live a better life. Based on my personal experience, I understand that the fight for gender equality is not only a women's fight, but a fight for all humanity. Today as an administrative councilor I have not given up my goals, I have not stopped shining. I am opening doors, and I hope to keep them open, for all women of the next generations, to be protagonists conquering space to build a better world. Women need to think of ways to keep and encourage other women in the labor market, and always believe in education, and the importance of equal opportunities as a strategy to actively participate in building innovative environments.

The feminist movement plays a crucial role in promoting gender equality. According to the UN, as we move from the Millennium Development Goals to the Post-2015 Sustainable Development Agenda, we have a unique opportunity to transform the dialogue on women's rights and accelerate progress towards achieving gender equality. Some movements supported by UN Women have the opportunity to accelerate progress toward gender equality through four main means: generating solidarity, engaging men, engaging youth, and making space for women's and girls' leadership. The movements encourage men to identify with gender equality issues, recognizing the critical role they can play in ending the inequality faced by women and girls around the world, both in their own lives and at more structural levels in their communities.

Gender equality is not just a women's issue, it is a human rights issue that affects all of us - women and girls, men, and boys. We can all benefit from gender equality in our daily lives: socially, politically, and economically. When women are empowered, all of humanity benefits. Gender equality frees not only women, but also men, from social roles determined by gender stereotypes.

Today, as an international trade advisor, I have not given up on my dreams and continue to defend women's rights, inspiring the next generation to break barriers and believe in themselves. I am committed to creating a better world for all of us, with equality, justice, and love. This is the legacy I wish to leave.

I would like to thank the sisters that life gave me, Karina Diniz, Eliane Prado, Juliana Martins, Kyoko Shiraishi, Tran Uyen, Roberta Suplicy, Carolina Dostal, Fafa Monteiro, Vanessa Pinsky, Angela Turin, and Gertha Traven. For countless reasons, they all supported me and were part of this amazing chapter in my story.

Reference: http://www.onumulheres.org.br/elesporelas/movimentogloba/ accessed on May 20, 2023

DILMA CAMPOS

CEO Nossa Praia, Head of ESG at BPartners.co., board member, mentor, TEDx Speaker and Helena Souza Campos's mother
E-mail: dilma.campos@nossapraia.ag
Instagram: @dilmasouzacampos
LinkedIn: www.linkedin.com/in/dilmasouzacampos

My mother, Maria Helena, taught me from a very early age to always face adversity in a positive way and to never give up on my dreams. While my father worked as a self-employed salesman, she was the one who managed the home, taking care of my brothers and I, managing the money for the purchases of the house and organizing the family schedule. If we wished for something and our economic situation did not allow us to fulfill it immediately, there she was encouraging us to achieve our goal, with a lot of persistence and flexibility.

Still very young, I entered the world of dance, first studying classic ballet. Already at that time I received the first impressions from the world that, as a black woman, I would always have to be much better than the others to stand out. In all dance company auditions I participated, I was never called, although white girls who were two technical levels below me made it. Some teachers then recommended me modern ballet, where black dancers already had some prominence. At the time, neither I nor my family had enough racial literacy to understand structural racism.

When I was 8 years old, I left public school, because my brothers had won a scholarship at the Anglo Latino school, one of the most traditional and demanding schools at the time. We were the only black children in the school. While my brothers stood out among the student body for playing football very well – everyone wanted them on their team – I was never invited to my classmates' birthday parties. If the environment there was one of veiled racism and exclusion, I could fulfill myself through dance.

It was dance that offered me the invitation to participate in the children's television show *O Castelo Rá-tim-bum, (The Ra-tim-bum Castle – a children's program on TV)* in which I played one of the *Patativas (a little bird)*. All this experience was essential to my future work as artistic director and in the production of events.

I married Swami when I was 19 and when I turned 22, I decided to invest in a higher education degree and ended up choosing Dentistry, following in one of my brothers' footsteps, who was a dentist and a professor at the university where I was awarded a partial scholarship. I completed the course and actually worked for one year in the trade, even specializing in periodontics. But even this degree and the work in the field of dentistry, which could mean a new professional track, only confirmed my option for the initial trail.

Then I continued to gain positions in large agencies, taking on several posts, over a 12-year history in the corporate market. In fact, the amazing artistic director Fernanda Abujamra was the first to believe in my potential and give me an opportunity as an assistant director at an agency.

My artistic experience was an advantage in this market, since events were becoming increasingly multimedia, and technology enabled staging shows where creativity could express itself in full force. In meetings with clients, I quickly absorbed the demand, understood the strategic positioning, and delivered the results. This upward trajectory led me to the position of Production Director in a large group, where I was the only black leader.

CHANGE OF COURSE

Despite having reached an important position, several signs of inadequacy began to appear. First, when I started to see that white colleagues continued to achieve higher positions in the group, while I was still a director. Then, when I discovered that my salary was lower than that of other white professionals in the same position as mine. So, I decided to invest again in my training and applied for the MBA of FGV-SP (Fundação Getúlio Vargas in São Paulo), at the time one of the most demanding selection processes to enter a teaching institution.

When uncertainty about my entry into this institution struck, I consulted with Flavia Faugeres, an executive in a large company. When I opened up my fears to her, the answer was overwhelming: "Of course you will be accepted! Enroll!". Her words were crucial for me to move forward in the process and, of course, to enter and complete this training. Today, Flávia is CEO and one of the founders of Learn to Fly, a platform for personal and professional development and the development of social and emotional skills for organizations. At that time my daughter Helena had already been born and I was looking at what her future would be like.

Now that I had an MBA degree, I delivered and met all targets and yet, I was the target of prejudice from my team. Countless times I was the defeated vote in internal discussions. Until I experienced a situation in which I had been evaluated and prepared to climb up in positions, everything was set for the promotion, and my boss ended up bringing in another professional, a man, to the position, without even telling me about the decision – I only found out by a friend from another agency.

Today, I still try to see the positive side of all these adversities that led me to change the course of my career and to decide to become an entrepreneur in 2008.

ESG BEST PRACTICES IN ACTION

Outra Praia was growing and consolidating itself; though small, my agency offered unique, strategic actions, always emphasizing sustainability and inclusion.

In planning for customers, I always suggested something new, such as recycling the tarps of the event and producing grocery bags with the material, to be distributed to the company's employees. The investment was minimal (less than one thousand Brazilian reais), generated income for an NGO of seamstresses who made the product, and on top of it, positively surprised employees. On many occasions, my excitement in selling the action was such that customers ended up approving the proposal.

Actions were not restricted to the environmental impact of the event. Gradually, I brought proposals for inclusion and diversity to the table. In events that offer alcoholic beverages, we created a risk protocol against violence to women. The entire team is trained in protocol to know how to act in such situations. We put stickers in the ladies' bathroom, alerting that if a woman is being harassed, she can go to the bar and order the drink La Penha, or another name defined in advance. This request initiates the protocol, a security comes to escort and protect the woman from the harasser and to conduct the case in the way she feels most welcome.

In the men's bathrooms, we put up a sign on the door with the following words: "If you identify yourself as a man, then your bathroom is this one." We took out the urinals, so trans men could also use that space. If there is a music show, we include an interpreter for Libras, the Brazilian Sign Language, or audio description for individuals with visual impairment.

A TOUGH DECISION THAT SAVED MY BUSINESS

The year 2015, with the severe Brazilian economic crisis, was the beginning of a period of hard tests for Outra Praia, a crisis that reached its peak in 2016. At that time, an old client, Ana Fontes, founder of the Entrepreneurial Women Network, an institution that fosters female leadership in entrepreneurship, called me to give a lecture. She also nominated me for *EY Winning Women 2016* mentoring program. Little did she know that this meeting allowed me to access other extraordinary women, who literally showed me the direction to save my business.

My mentors, Chieko Aoki (founder and president of the Blue Tree Hotels network) and Bel Humberg (co-founder of OQVestir and Board Member), proposed that I should abandon my main client, because their payment policy to suppliers made the cash flow of a small business impossible and would lead me to bankruptcy in a few months.

Though tough, their advice was vital for the business' revival. Little by little, new customers were emerging, and the company returned to level again. Chieko's and Bel's mentoring and the exchange of learnings with my program facilitator – Cristiane Hilário, and other mentors such as Fátima Zorzato, Sonia Hess, and Júnia Nogueira de Sá – were decisive to understand the most important lesson I learned from this period.

To err is something natural to every entrepreneur, it is part of the process. When it happens, the most important thing is to recognize the mistake, learn from it, and plot a new exit route. The faster you do this, the better.

In 2016 I was invited to be a speaker at Google Women Will, a program aimed at entrepreneur women. By telling the story of my life and resilience to so many women (whose highlight is the sentence, "Never give up!"), I not only rescued the strength to retake the reins of my business, but I believe I inspired many to transform their lives. At least those were the numerous testimonials I received from entrepreneur women from various regions of Brazil who attended my lecture. I am very grateful to have impacted so many women, passing on a little of the knowledge I learned throughout my journey.

During the pandemic, in 2020, I was invited to participate in the first class of Councilor 101 (or C101, as it is known), a program supported by WCD (Women Corporate Directors), KPMG and created by a group of women, which encourages the participation of black female executives in advisory boards. At the time, I was already a board member at AMPRO (Promotional Marketing Association), after C101, I was invited to be a Board Member of the São Paulo Dance Company, Solum Capital, resource manager focused on the alternative investment market, and São Judas University. New professional tracks opened up for me.

At the end of 2022, I decided to sell part of *Outra Praia*, which became *Nossa Praia*, by joining *B&Partners.co. Network* and taking over the position *Head of ESG*, at the invitation of CEO Bazinho Ferraz. My mission is to plan and implement the strategies of all Group companies around environmental, social, and governance agendas.

In addition to implementing the group's ESG best practices, there is enormous potential to extend this message to all the partners and customers we relate to. This multiplier power is something that motivates me every day, because, although the ESG agenda has advanced in society and in organizations, I believe there is still a lot of room to increase this awareness. Not only in companies, but also throughout the ecosystem supply chain and, in particular, in their temporary ecosystems, namely, the events.

Looking back today, I see that every detail of my path has forged the tools that led me to be here today. The experiences of exclusion made me value even more the importance of diversity, inclusion, and collaboration in professional environments. Environmental disasters are warning us all the time that we need to learn to do business under other assumptions, so that we can build viable businesses on a more sustainable basis.

As Head of ESG at *B&Partners.co*, I am very much fulfilled in being able to disseminate the values in which I believe, and as CEO of *Nossa Praia*, I want to impact businesses and brands at levels of excellence in good environmental, social, and governance practices, which will be essential for our future as a society.

DUDA ALCÂNTARA

Builder of bridges and houses. Multi stakeholder articulator, social entrepreneur, political advisor, president of Vivenda Institute to address the housing deficit and Brazil co-chair of Nexus Global network.
Instagram: @dudaalcantarasp
Website: www.dudaalcantara.com.br
LinkedIn: www.linkedin.com/in/dudaalcantara

RESTLESSNESS AS FUEL FOR FLASHLIGHTS

My story is about restlessness, about someone with a deep thirst fcr life, a desire to do more for the world, to leave it a better place than when I arrived. As long as I can remember, I have been involved in social actions. Projects with the homeless population, women victims of violence, several with children, some with refugees. I have taught English, renovated and built houses, collected donations for victims of climate disasters, served as a meditation instructor in communities, and organized socio-cultural events. I used to ask for food and clothing donations at my birthday parties. I also led an international network of philanthropists and social impact projects for several years, which gave me the opportunity to meet Malala this year.

Today I have a much more critical view of social projects and the real impact they have on the supposed beneficiaries. I say "supposed" because I feel that we gain more in these actions than the people for whom we do them.

It was also common for me to join a project to contribute in some way, and in the end, I embraced it so wholeheartedly that I found myself in a leadership role. That's what happened, for example, when I was in college and started organizing off-campus classes, trips, events, and protests, and I became the president of the Academic Directory with the platform "Connection" - a word that has always been strong in my life.

Around the age of 17, I was at a spiritual center during a vacation with my mother - a woman who I also never saw saying no a request for help - when something that would impact me greatly happened. The person in charge of the center asked for help for a family that was going to be evicted and needed to visit shelters to find a place to stay. A whole family with three children. We took the father and the two youngest children, ages 7 and 10, and went searching for a new home. Until we reached the first address, I still hadn't fully understood what it meant.The place was clean, with communal dormitories and bathrooms. At the reception, I saw a man sitting in front of a small television watching a video tutorial on "how to approach people on the street to ask for money." I was very impressed with everything. There were no vacancies at the first shelter, but we managed to find space at the second one. The next thing we had to do was go back to the house to grab their belongings. It was a one room apartment, of about 15 square meters, where a whole family of five people lived. At the end of that day, my mother and I returned to our home without exchanging a word.

This episode was not only the moment when the word "privilege" took on a new meaning for me, but it was also defining, it was how "housing" entered my life. With the question "why did I have a home and these people didn't?" echoing in my head, I started researching the subject, applied, and received a magazine from Habitat For Humanity by mail, which I still have hanging on my wall. This influenced me to choose architecture as my major graduation.

Another factor that influenced my choice was that my father was a builder and developer. This also contributed to my discomfort with the lack of housing because, in a way, I had the tools to "build homes for people." I entered college, and in my first year, I started working with him, but our visions were absolutely opposite. I was always looking for laws and opportunities in social housing but very time we talked about that, he would say, "My daughter, the government should be the one to worry about social issues." Until one day, almost 10 years later, after having some back-and-forths in the company and working with other developers too, I agreed with him, so decided to enter politics.

At that moment, I understood that if I could "close the deal" in the private sector I could build one, ten, or a hundred housing complexes during my lifetime, benefiting tens of thousands of people. But if I could change a law or create a government program, I could impact tens of millions of people.

POLITICS AS A PATH

In a way, I have always had one foot in politics. From being a class representative in school to becoming the president of the Academic Directory in college, wherever there was a chance to influence and improve the environment in which I lived, I got involved. I joined a group called "Virada Política" ("Turn Politics") whose main goal was to connect and shed light on the incredible initiatives of civic entrepreneurs that had emerged in recent years, especially after the June 2013 protests. I met many people who, like me, wanted to "change politics." I also joined a "collective candidacy," a movement where a group of people, not just one individual, has a voice within a mandate. I remember

136

feeling amazed at every meeting. I saw Politics with a capital "P" as a tool to construct better futures, social goals for Brazil, changes that would impact millions.

After attending the United Nations Urban Forum in Malaysia, where the connection between cities, housing, and gender inequality in decision-making positions was glaring, it became clear to me that we need more women - three times as many - in politics. Brazil ranks 129th in the world in gender equality in politics. So, upon returning, after some conversations and meetings, I decided to run for federal deputy in the 2018 elections, which were to be held in October. I made this decision around May. If you understand politics, you know that making a decision like this only five months before the elections is complete madness, but at the time, I didn't know that.

I had no political role models, and I didn't know any politicians within my family or close friends. I grew up in a typical Brazilian household where politics is synonymous with profanity. I heard things like, "Duda, but you were doing such great work! Why get into politics?". When I decided to run, I wanted to make it something even bigger. Along with a group of friends who were also passionate about gender equality, we created the "Vote Nelas" ("Vote For Her") movement, which supported female candidates across the country, a true "Rise and raise others" movement.

Campaigning was stepping entirely out of my comfort zone. I felt a pit in my stomach from May until October. I was waking up and going to sleep meeting new people, talking about politics and housing. I was asking not only for a vote for myself but a vote of confidence for Politics, the one with capital letter that I truly believed in. I cried, laughed, and ended up in the most unexpected places for me - from a Masonic store to local soccer games and dozens of people's living rooms. On Sundays I went to Paulista avenue with a stool and a sign that said "Have you ever talked to a federal deputy candidate?", and I made random friendships that are still a part of my life today.

I didn't get elected, but I gained many other things. 12,538 people pressed in my number on the voting machine, making me the second most voted woman in the party for my position nationwide, all from a campaign budget of less than 40,000 reais (around eight thousand dollars) - if you know politics, you'll find this even more crazy.

The experience was important for all the chapters that would follow. I started the first strategic planning consultancy for the legislative branch with two friends, Mandato Ativo, and worked with deputies from different parties all over the country. I became the president of the political party Rede Sustentabilidade in São Paulo, worked in the Legislative Assembly of the state of São Paulo, and had the opportunity to accompany Marina Silva to the United Nations. This trip to NY was absolutely memorable and special, we had a long lunch with Nobel Peace Prize winner Muhammad Yunus. It was beautiful to see them practically finishing each other's sentences; their thoughts were very similar and represented me completely. There was only one point where their vision wasn't exactly the same: for Marina Silva, the answer lay in Politics, it had always been her calling. For Prof Yunus, what governed the world, including politics, society, and communication, was the Economy, and his calling was to become the "Banker to the Poor."

The following year brought the pandemic and also the municipal elections. I was responsible for coordinating the entire party's electoral process in the city of São Paulo. This role allowed me to meet many leaders, the mayor, former mayors, mayoral candidates, deputies, council members, secretaries, ministers. It was a period where I saw politics from a different angle, from the inside.

After the adrenaline of the election subsided, I still felt restless, almost three years since the moment I decided to "get into politics to generate more impact in housing." But the truth was that no one had a better home because of me.

So, I stopped and started to rethink everything.

BUILDER OF BRIDGES AND HOUSES

Politics still resonate strongly within me, especially as a tool. But I began researching and talking to different experts to find ways to help address Brazil's housing deficit. I came to understand that we didn't yet have an organization that prioritized housing in the country, a space for collaboration among various stakeholders, a place of awareness that could bring birth to new projects and models - an Housin Institute. So that was what I was planning to do.

Over the years, it became even more evident to me how much a home is at the center of a range of social problems and how it can also be a solution. "Home is the place of all causes" was the motto of Vivenda, a B Corp and one of the most recognized social impact businesses in Brazil. I was approached by one of its founders, who told me about the start of the largest housing improvement program in the private sector, the investment from the IDB (Inter-American Development Bank), the plans to work along the public sector, and the need for someone with my profile and background to be the executive director of the recent created Vivenda Institute.

There it was, the institute that I was planning to create. I accepted almost immediately, and here I am, two years later, as the president of the Vivenda Institute, a hub for housing innovation through partnerships and multilateral projects. Vivenda currently delivers over 100 home renovations in favelas per month across the country and aims, with new partners and technologies, to increase that number to over 1,000 families per month by the end of the year, and then double the target.

I will continue to visit municipalities across the country and bring more supporters to the cause of ending the housing deficit. This will only be possible with the impact of government programs. I have finally found a way to use Politics to impact millions of people. My role today is to bring together Marina Silva's Politics and Prof. Yunus's Economics, to build many bridges between the private, social and public sectors, so together we build many homes.

Restlessness still accompanies me, but today, I coexist with it in peace. I see it as a strength, not a weakness. It does not come from a lack but from the certainty that I want - and will! - do more every day. I still get involved in many different projects. I've recognized in myself a talent for building these bridges, mobilizing and connecting people - with each other and more recently with themselves and their purpose.

Restlessness connected with a phrase I deeply believe in, the prayer of the Hopi Native American tribe, "We are the ones we've been waiting for," or in my own words, if there is a light at the end of the tunnel, it comes from our own flashlight. Let 's go together?

EDNA VASSELO GOLDONI

E-mail: edna@institutoivg.com
Instagram: @edna_institutoivg
LinkedIn: www.linkedin.com/in/ednavasselogoldoni

THE TRANSFORMING POWER OF A PEARL

I was raised in a small town alongside my five sisters, learning many valuable lessons from my parents. Yes, our family is comprised of six women.

My mother instilled in me the qualities of being an entrepreneur and the importance of sisterhood. She taught me to love, respect, assist other women, and honor them with flowers. She also encouraged all her daughters to pursue their dreams and work hard, reminding us that no one can hold us back if we put in the effort.

My father instilled in me the courage to confront the obstacles that life presents. He encouraged me to trust in myself, to persevere through difficulties, to be truthful, and to share my accomplishments, lessons, and experiences.

At 18, I decided to study Biomedicine in the bustling city of São Paulo to pursue my dreams. After graduating, I returned to my hometown to start my professional career. However, I soon realized that there were limited opportunities for growth in my field.

So, I made the decision to return to São Paulo, bringing along my belongings. My mother accompanied me to the train station, where we shared a final hug. She offered me words of encouragement: "Go live your dream, but remember to come back and celebrate your victories with us."

Initially, I worked in my training area, but it didn't fulfill my aspirations. Therefore, I opted to pursue a career in sales at a prominent insurance company. Through relentless efforts, I achieved my goals and eventually got promoted to an executive position, thanks to my commendable work.

With my extensive experience in the insurance industry, I took the bold step of opening my own business - the Vasselo Goldoni Institute, in 2018, with a sole focus on promoting and empowering women. I am proud to be a pioneer in hosting successful events tailored for female audiences, including the "Mulheres de Sucesso" meeting, which I have organized for over a decade.

Throughout this career path, I achieved important recognition by being the only woman nominated for the Top Of Mind HR award for ten consecutive years, winning three times. Also, an extraordinary moment was when I represented Brazil at the UN Women's World Congress in 2017.

The Institute strives to empower women in their professional lives and aims to reach as many women as possible in Brazil and in the world. I have a special appreciation for pearls and their natural symbolism, which is why I selected them to represent the Institute. So, at each event, I hand out a pearl necklace to each participant, representing the courage, faith, perseverance, willpower, resilience, forgiveness, and love that exists within each one.

And here, I make an invitation. If you are a woman, take a moment to observe the women around you. Is there someone who could benefit from your attention, encouragement, or a friendly ear? Sometimes, even the smallest gestures can make a significant impact and help someone lift their spirits. When we recognize our own strength and potential, there are no limits to what we can achieve.

How can you do that?

- Don't judge another woman;
- Recognize and praise another woman's skills;
- Make way for another woman whenever possible;
- Believe that another woman's success is not your failure;
- Be empathetic to another woman;
- Mentor a woman;
- Help women entrepreneurs.

Despite my efforts, I believed there was more I could do. Therefore, seeing the difficulty of many women during the pandemic, the Mentoring Program for Women "Nós por Elas" was born. A free program that started with the participation of 75 volunteer mentors who believed in this dream.

Our program is committed to empowering women by liberating them from the cycles that have held them back. By sharing stories, lessons, and mentorships, we aim to showcase the talents of women and increase their visibility. It's time to redefine the concept of female power and magnificence and shatter the stereotypes and stigmas that have hindered our progress.

Our Mentoring Program for Women in Brazil has seen tremendous growth since its launch in June 2020. With 1200 women signing up for the first edition alone, we have now become the largest program of its kind in Brazil, having completed sixteen editions. Our network of over 600 mentors is genuinely diverse, with participants hailing from countries such as Germany, Poland, Costa Rica, Mexico, and England. Furthermore, our program has generated an impressive Social ROI of over 18 million reais.

Our initiative has had a resounding impact on the lives of over 4500 women. We are determined to persist in our efforts and empower women through meaningful conversations, solidarity, and fostering relationships. We hold an unwavering belief that women's progress leads to a more just and prosperous society.

I decide to win, how about you?

Let's go together!

ELENA CRESCIA

Speaker coach and content curator for conferences.
TEDxSãoPaulo curator and organizer (@tedxsaopaulo)
E-mail: ecrescia@gmail.com
Instagram: @instagram.com/ecrescia
Twitter: twitter.com/ecrescia
LinkedIn: www.linkedin.com/in/elenacrescia

ELENA CRESCIA | BIO

Speaker coach and content curator for conferences. TEDxSãoPaulo curator and organizer. Curator of The Wellbeing Summit (2022 and 2025), the Skoll World Forum (Oxford 2023), and SOCAP Social Capital Markets Conference (San Francisco 2023). Director of the educational program TED-Ed Clubs in Brazil. TEDx and TED speaker. Participated in 20+ official TED conferences. Over 11 years of experience as a speaker coach and content curator. Elena has trained over a thousand people to speak in public. Masters degree of International Affairs from Columbia University (New York). Masters degree in Financial Evaluation of Development Projects from Sorbonne (Paris). She has also studied at Singularity University and FIA-USP.

ELENA, EDITOR OF IDEAS

Since my first day as a content curator for conferences, I've made a commitment that at least half of our speakers would always be women. It was precisely my commitment to invite women, many of whom had never spoken in public before, that turned me into a professional speaker coach and conference curator. I wanted to help each one of them shine on stage, deliver their message in the best possible way, and ultimately make their mark on the world. And it was by helping others that I also found my own mission.

SELF-ESTEEM OF THE SOUL

I will never forget volunteering with Vivi Duarte in Grajaú, a vulnerable community southeast of Sao Paulo. We would go on Saturday mornings to meet a group of young women, high school students, who were thirsty for knowledge, connections and much needed conversations.

The students thought I would offer a class on self-esteem. I explained: "I won't talk about how to look in the mirror and like what you see. I want you to respect your ideas and talk about them without fear. Your perspective on the world matters. It's the self-esteem of the soul we'll be talking about."

We talked about their past experiences speaking in front of their classmates. When we're young, we're used to having some people who are more talkative and others who are quieter in the classroom. And usually, they keep these roles thru college, and later in the workplace. We go through life listening more to the ideas of extroverted and charismatic individuals and listening less to those of quiet people.

Do you really believe that only charismatic people have good ideas? Of course not!

Public speaking is not just for charismatic individuals; it's for anyone who has something interesting to say. Speaking clearly, concisely, and knowing the message you want to convey are tools we should learn at school. The good news is we can learn public speaking skills and even enjoy the experience.

Those girls in Grajaú have big dreams and an immense desire to achieve them. They are preparing themselves to occupy spaces that rightfully belong to them!

But it's not just high school students who feel insecure when speaking in public. This happens to many of us. I remember myself, sitting in a classroom, blushing, my heart pounding, and my voice sounding weak; my mouth would go completely dry every time I raised my hand to ask a question or make a comment. We experience physical discomfort at that moment. It's the fear of making mistakes, of feeling embarrassed or being judged.

Those who feel nervous are feeling the weight of the responsibility. The responsibility of knowing that they will be taking up other people's time. They want every minute they ask of their listeners to be worthwhile.

I love speakers with butterflies in their stomachs! They are more open to learning new skills, relating as equals, and listening to others...

EDITOR OF IDEAS

We have already organized more than 60 TEDx events in São Paulo. In each of them, we create new role models. Listening to people aligned with their purpose and passionate about what they do is inspiring. Hearing from people who have sought solutions encourages us to try and solve a problem instead of complaining about it.

We also organize annual events to highlight the ideas of women from various fields of knowledge. The common thread in our events is that we celebrate women's ideas. I feel very proud of each woman who faces her fears and accepts our invitation to share her ideas on stage. Part of my role is to find people with an idea that deserves to be heard and help them craft their talk. And that's how I became an editor of ideas.

WHAT MAKES YOUR HEART BEAT?

On September 29, 2015, Luciana Fornari published this text:

"On World Heart Day, as a cardiologist, I should talk about the benefits of a healthy diet, regular physical exercise, and the importance of staying away from cigarettes. And truthfully, I want to do that. I do it every single day for countless patients, and I firmly believe that prevention is everything (not just in terms of cardiology)."

"But perhaps today I want to say a little more than that. To speak not only of the heart that beats but also of the heart that feels, suffers, loves. And beyond diet and exercise, I would like to prescribe a little more compassion, a little more empathy for others, a little more forgiveness and understanding, a little more love...."

Because, believe me, a heart with perfect coronary arteries is of no value without the capacity to love; a structurally intact heart is of no use without the ability to see others.... Because this fleshy heart inside our chests lives for a time and a day, it is the journey of all. The other, it beats forever within the souls that enchant life....

WORLD HEART DAY. (OF BOTH HEARTS)"

I loved Luciana's message! Coming from a cardiologist, the idea that we need to take care of the fleshy heart, as well as the heart that feels our emotions, it's beautiful. I reached out to her to invite her to be a speaker at TEDxSaoPaulo.

"I loved your text, Luciana! I'd love to talk to you."

"Hi Elena, it's a great compliment that you liked it! Let's do it... whenever you want."

We had a long phone conversation.

"Elena, I don't think I'm the right person for you. I've never spoken in public before. If you want, I can introduce you to the director of the Heart Hospital. He is often invited to speak at conferences and speaks very well."

That was exactly what I needed to hear to be even more certain that she was the one I wanted. That text was hers. The idea was hers. And it was she who wasn't being heard. I pretended not to hear her intention to avoid the invitation and made the invitation simpler.

"Forget about the speech and the event, let's just meet for a coffee"

A few days later, we met for a coffee. She was still unsure about speaking at the event, so I decided to show her that this difficult endeavor was made up of simple little tasks. The first step was to go from a paragraph to a page, expanding on the original idea.

"I think it's really great to see a message of more empathy and compassion coming from a cardiologist. My suggestion at this moment is for you to write this same text a bit longer, using a more conversational, oral language. See if there is any research and scientific data on the benefits of compassion. Some people write directly on the computer, while others record themselves on their phone and then transcribe the audio. See what feels more natural to you."

"I'll do it! I love challenges... and I'll send it to you to review."

Just two days later, she sent the expanded text of that original idea.

"It's a draft... Let me know what you think."

Her text begins like this:

"What makes your heart beat? My job is to ensure that your heart, this fleshy pump that exists within your chest, beats the number of times it was programmed to beat....

I studied for this, to contribute to making sure your heart beats properly until the end, and I continue to study diligently, as cardiology is one of the medical specialties that has accumulated the most technological advancements in recent decades. And rightly so, as the diseases that affect your heart and cause it to stop are the leading cause of death in Brazil and the world. And no one wants to die, especially not before their time...."

"But whenever I look at a heart inside a patient, it intrigues me with a question that goes beyond medical and physiological aspects: ultimately, what does your heart beat for?"

Luciana's talk at Sala São Paulo is published on YouTube. I highly recommend it.

In Luciana's case, my role was to give her a little push; the message was within her, clear and powerful, but she thought that speaking in public was not for her. Once she accepted the invitation, Luciana took this challenge very seriously. She wrote the text and rehearsed a lot. The result was a standing ovation from over 1,200 people.

I love seeing the effect that public speaking has on people. They gain confidence, credibility, and I see personal and professional growth. It works as a turning point.

Over the years, I see the role we have in creating new heroes and heroines, new role models. In a way, I believe we serve as a seal of quality, of credibility.

GOOD IDEAS DESERVE TO BE SHARED

What criteria do we use when curating speakers for TEDxSãoPaulo? What do we look for in the people we invite to speak?

No prior speaking experience is required to speak at TEDxSãoPaulo. We don't seek professional speakers or people who "speak well." We look for ideas that deserve to be heard. If someone has a good idea worth sharing, that's what matters.

We don't seek out great communicators, experienced speakers, professional presenters, charismatic individuals, or exceptional storytellers. We believe in the power of ideas to change attitudes. We work to make great ideas accessible to everyone. We bring together thinkers, inspirers, and curious souls.

We look for great ideas and good messages. Messages that can move and touch the audience. Anyone with a good idea deserves to be on stage.

We seek speakers to teach, inspire, surprise, and captivate our attendees. Scientists, educators, inventors, entrepreneurs, thinkers, professionals from all walks of life are welcome.

For us, the "x" in TEDxSaoPaulo is a multiplier. It multiplies ideas that deserve to be spread, as well as kindness, connections, smiles, and dreams.

A friend sent a suggestion for a speaker saying: "She's really good, but she's not confident. Maybe you can help her get ready, that's what you do, right?" I replied: "I love working with people who need help to get confident, my problem is with big egos who think too highly of themselves. Want to win me over? Cultivate humility."

We want to surprise our public, bringing new ideas and topics to their conversations, offering new people to admire, especially those who haven't been heard before.

"WHAT ARE YOU WILLING TO FEEL EMBARRASSED FOR?"

This is the title of Felipe Simi's talk at TEDxSãoPaulo. This title summarizes his experience. It was the feeling of inconformity and anger that gave him the strength to face embarrassment for a cause that was important to him.

I use this question with the people I help train for public speaking. It's a fundamental question. We need to shift the focus: it's not about you, it's about an idea that deserves to be heard. You're just the messenger so that idea can reach others.

With good preparation and content editing, you will offer a true gift to your audience. We want the speech to be a gift you offer, and people should feel privileged they were there to listen.

Use your nerves to your advantage. It's precisely because you feel insecure that you will devote time to your script and your rehearsals.

Right before speaking in public, you can remind yourself: "I did my best, and I am here to offer what I did to those who may need this message."

What are you willing to feel embarrassed for? If you're willing to feel a little embarrassed, you're halfway there. If you're willing to pay that price for your idea, then what are you waiting for to speak openly about it?

I'm Elena, editor of ideas. And my way of rising and raising others is literally stepping onto the stage and inviting other women to join me on stage. I love offering women's ideas to the world, one talk at a time.

If you have an orange and exchange it with another person who also has an orange,
each of you will have one orange.
But if you exchange an idea with someone who also has an idea,
each of you will have two ideas.

Confucius, Chinese philosopher

ELISÂNGELA PERES

Founder of the Marcas pelo Mundo news portal. Journalist with almost 20 years of experience.
Instagram: @elisangelaperes1
Youtube: www.youtube.com.br/marcaspelomundo
Website: www.marcaspelomundo.com.br
LinkedIn: www.linkedin.com/in/elisangela-peres

I AM ELI: DAUGHTER, JOURNALIST AND MOTHER

Writing about yourself is an act of self-analysis. I stopped to think about what could I say here with my hand on my head: "Imagine, I don't even have much to say!". How silly is our custom of sometimes not recognizing our own success, of thinking that our trajectory is not as interesting as someone else's.

People have stories and I'm driven by that. I live journalism and bring information to the public! I consider myself an agent of change that multiplies opportunities in people's lives, and I do this through a market that has enormous power with and over society. Today I'll share a little of my journey, which is still at its beginning

My Parents are my Beginning

I couldn't start my journey here in any other way. My parents are the most important people in my life; they are the ones who shaped me into who I am. It was with their love, care, and upbringing that I developed my qualities and convictions.

João Peres and Ivone Biani have always been simple people. They are from the countryside of Paraná, Brazil, and they used to work in coffee harvesting. As I write this text, I remember a moment that left a mark on me when a brand invited me to visit a coffee plantation and follow the process from planting the beans until a cup of coffee was served. I had the experience of harvesting and saw how challenging life was for my parents back then. It made me reflect deeply on my origins.

At one point, my parents moved to São Paulo in search of a better quality of life. My father got a job in a metalworking company and thrived, all on his own, with determination and dedication, even though he wasn't formally educated but had significant expertise in numbers. He worked on many important projects, including

149

some in aviation. It was incredible! I watched closely and saw how he did everything with passion, which always inspired me.

My mother also plays a crucial role. She is pure love and does everything for me. She always supports me in the numerous trips I take, encourages me, and takes care of my children when I'm away. My beloved mother is my biggest support system.

Unfortunately, my father passed away three years ago, and this reality is very hard for me because I always looked to him for guidance in everything in life. He was very wise with his words, guiding me and opening doors for me. He supported me in every moment of my life and lived with pride. Creating ‚Marcas Pelo Mundo‚' studying, and achieving my plans is a way to honor his memory because he never allowed me to give up on my dreams, even in the face of adversity.

They taught me so much that I carry with me, and I truly become breathless when I speak about my parents. They supported me greatly in journalism, and to this day, I am the ‚family celebrity. My relatives find it amazing to see me on the screen. I have a truly wonderful family!

Speaking of family, I will take a moment from the chapter dedicated to my parents to also talk about my children, who have felt my absence from a young age and have always supported me because they understood that my work makes me happy. My eldest, Felipe, already accompanies me on some assignments. He loves topics related to the gaming world, and my heart fills with joy to have him by my side in my work. My little one, Gabriela, will also join me in the future, and I want to show them both that working in a job you love is priceless.

My Journey in Journalism

I love sharing how I got into this field because it was, I would say, quite amusing. My dad bought one of those big VHS tape camcorders because he wanted to make some extra money filming weddings, baptisms, and parties. I used to help him, and I enjoyed both the filming process and what came after. I thought it was amazing! Of course, my sister and I, being curious children, would occasionally (secretly) play with the camcorder.

It was incredible! She would film, and I would anchor the news, and the other way around. Sometimes, we'd even be at the „news desk" (which was really just an improvised setup with a bed), and we'd use the music from the „Jornal Nacional" (a Brazilian news program). But that's not where my journalism journey began. The inclination was already there, though I might not have realized it at the time; it was just playtime for now, you know how things go, right?

Still quite young, I had several „first jobs." I worked as a school assistant, a dental clinic secretary, and, believe it or not, the dentist, for some reason, thought I had a talent for getting my hands dirty - or rather, in this case, in people's mouths - and I became a dental assistant. I participated in some major surgeries that, if I were to describe here, might cause someone to feel faint. No, I'm not the best person for that kind of thing either, I get squeamish, but I really needed the money.

These were important phases for me because before becoming a journalist, I did things that I knew didn't suit me, but I learned, especially from the dentist, that I had to be a good professional, regardless of whether I was in my desired profession. I had to give my best always.

Later, I went to journalism school, and at the very beginning, I landed a job as a commercial assistant for panels and media. However, my passion for journalism had already been ignited. I stayed in the media commercial field for many years, which was enriching because I learned a lot of valuable things. Then, a friend from college suggested I take a course in TV news anchoring, something that had never crossed my mind. But she insisted so much that I applied and passed the test. I admit that after that course, several doors began to open, both in my mind and in my life.

I was well-established in advertising and marketing when I received an offer to join a TV station for hard news journalism. But I was deeply fascinated by marketing and communication, so I initially turned down the offer. At that moment, I made the choice to pursue journalism in a more specialized way, and from then on, I saw my career in this field being built and taking shape.

THE BRANDS OF MY WORLD

I gained credibility and space as the years went by. There were so many assignments that I can't even count, honestly. It's been nearly 20 years of talking about communication and marketing. I interviewed thousands of professionals, iconic people who, just thinking about them, gave me butterflies and made me tremble all over. Wonderful brands invited me for the best assignments and always supported me. It all seemed like a dream to me.

I want to share some of the most special moments. The first assignment I recorded, presented, and edited all by myself was for LG, in Rio de Janeiro, when the brand was launching a cell phone. This was very significant because I truly created the content from start to finish without any help. I believe it was the stepping stone for others to start coming my way. And I say this because right after that, I was invited by Samsung to cover a product launch in New York (imagine how I screamed when I got the confirmation). Visiting that city had been a lifelong dream of mine, and going there for work, oh, it felt unreal. It was one of the most wonderful things in my life.

Since then, I've been to many incredible countries and cities. Many assignments, people, stories, lessons, and, of course, fun. I did all of this while working for a media outlet, which I eventually left to fulfill another dream, which wasn't even that clear at the time.

Shortly after my departure, I received an invitation for the Jeep Experience, an expedition to the Pantanal wetlands in Brazil. At the time, I explained that I was planning to launch a new media vehicle. They believed in my project and wanted me to tell that story, so I went. It was amazing to experience that and, even more, to feel valued. Next, I had the opportunity to cover the Festival El Ojo de Iberoamérica in Argentina, and after that, I received an invitation to attend CES, the world's largest technology fair, in Las Vegas, with LG. These were the first assignments of my solo career.

Marcas Pelo Mundo (Brands Around the World) was being born, without knowing that a pandemic would hit us months later. I became an entrepreneur, still finding my footing, but a lot was already happening. Brands were reaching out to me, but I doubted myself, perhaps out of fear. Who hasn't self-sabotaged, right? But with strength and determination, I created my platform, structured myself, and today it's almost 4 years old. We faced a pandemic right at the beginning, where the idea was to travel the world to give voice to people, but I had to start from my own balcony, with video calls due to social distancing.

At a certain point, I also began working as a master of ceremonies, which is something I love to do. For me, the pinnacle, so far, was an event where I commanded a packed audience on the stage of the Municipal Theater. Being there, where historical figures had also been, was emotional.

I believe that many people and brands saw the passion I have for communication and my work, and I would like to take this opportunity to thank so many people who have been a part of this journey. All I know is that I still have a lot to tell, and I'm excited and up for anything.

Communcication in my Life

Speaking of „one thing leads to another," I've always wanted to showcase the stories not only of brands as companies but of brands as people, of those who are behind it all. They also leave legacies not just for the companies they work for but for society as well. I want to highlight the cool aspects in everyone!

What greatly appeals to me in the communication and marketing industry is the fact that it's a market where we can promote change and foster discussions. An advertising campaign does indeed have the power to help change the reality and issues of a society, and a creative mind can be very transformative for the world.

I believe the industry is evolving, especially in terms of diversity and inclusion, but it's still quite elitist. I hope the sector embraces causes with genuine actions. Truth and essence, combined with creativity, have the potential to bear good fruit; we just need to always bring these three together.

To Women

It may sound cliché, but I really need to talk about the importance of believing in oneself. I came from a humble background, full of dreams and courage. Today, I've achieved quite a bit, traveled to many countries, I am known for my work, and have many victories, but I admit that there were many moments when I thought people wouldn't notice me or dedicate their time to an interview with me. It wasn't easy!

But one thing I can say is that we have to fight for what we want. At the beginning of my career, I would call to request invitations to events, begged for assignments, and that's okay. Humility is a part of any journey, and it's something we must never lose. I myself haven't even reached halfway to where I want to be; my journey is still very long.

"Happiness sometimes is a blessing, but generally it is a conquest." (Paulo Coelho)

ELLEN KISS

Director at Nubank, Professor of ESPM
Designer with specialization in digital transformation and "Design your life"
Educator, advisor, mentor and angel investor
E-mail: ek@ellenkiss.com
Instagram: @ellenkiss
Linkedin: www.linkedin.com/in/ellenkiss/

Have you ever been in a situation where your life seemed perfect on the surface, but deep down, your intuition told you otherwise? I'm not bragging about it, but life was close to ideal: married for over fifteen years (impressive, right?), two tweens, a united and healthy family, an active social life with many dear friends, and, especially, a thriving career. Nothing to complain about except that I was *satisfied*, not truly happy. I felt that something was missing, a certain questioning and a deep desire for change.

After 25 years accumulating professional experiences, I was about to reach an eight-year cycle in a corporate career at one of Brazil's leading banks, heading one of the teams responsible for the organization's most focused project, its digital transformation. It was an extremely challenging project, but it did pay off since it brought both the company and my own career development great outcomes. As for my career, it was rapidly advancing with short promotion cycles, good financial and market recognition and great potential for short-term growth — excellent prospects for the future. Despite the exhausting work routine, I still managed to carve out time in my schedule for some side projects. I would speak at events or other companies facing similar challenges, continue teaching postgraduate courses (teaching is one of my passions), and participate in some networking groups where I built solid professional relationships. The logistics were complex, but I could balance work with a healthy personal life, being present in my children's education, and enjoying leisure time. Overall, the balance was positive and my sense of fulfillment came from being able to influence and positively impact the lives of people and companies around me.

However, strangely enough, with such feelings of personal and professional fulfillment came some rather unsettling questions: what is there next in my life? What do I want to do in ten years' time? Should I continue with a consistently prosperous but undesirably predictable career? Was it the time to take on a leading role? How can my present activity positively impact my future? Am I living my purpose? Which legacy do

I want to leave behind?

So, anchored in my learnings and experience, I mustered the courage to disruptively move away from predictability and provoke transformation once again. At the peak of my career, I quit my job and convinced my husband and children to move to the United States for a sabbatical period. The intention was to explore another culture, a new family lifestyle, learn and expand professional and personal opportunities. My husband took this chance to study while I pursued an experience in a native digital company. Attending an event in Stanford, California, where I met people and spotted interesting business opportunities, helped us decide on the location. So, without a fully defined professional path, we calculated the risk and decided to move to Palo Alto, in Silicon Valley. A strong feeling of enthusiasm about our future life filled us. Little did I know at that time that Silicon Valley would actually be a deep valley in my life.

A valley because the reality was very different from what we had idealized, and the transition, this time, was longer and more painful. The market, business partnerships, contacts with people, everything was more competitive and complex than we had imagined. In addition to all that, just over six months after our move, the pandemic began, and the world came to a halt. Like everyone else in the world, we started living in lockdown, without work, far from family, and unable to travel. Considering the devastating consequences of the pandemic on so many families, we were relatively well off and gained for being close and together.

With the world at a standstill, we were all forced to stop as well. My routine once filled with challenges, learning experiences, people, lunches, and events, turned into endless household chores. Cleaning, cooking, doing the laundry (I was spared from ironing because, in the United States, nobody irons. What a relief). The feeling was that, with the loss of work, projects, classes, for me, I had also lost my worth and my identity. The personality, once well-defined, intense, determined, confident, motivated, and full of life, transformed into sadness, anxiety, negativity, and fear. A profound existential crisis took hold of me, destroying my self-esteem and the motivation I had when we decided to move. It was a difficult period, marked by full days spent in bed in pajamas (rare in my existence), frequent crying spells, family conflicts, deep loneliness, and a profound emptiness in my heart. I thought about separating. I thought about going back. I remember looking at myself in the mirror and not recognizing myself. I couldn't dress myself with my own clothes for they seemed to belong to someone else. I stopped responding to messages from my friends, even the dearest ones, out of shame for my own feelings, as if I wasn't allowed to feel that way. I even started avoiding people and social events because at some point, I knew the question "What do you do?" would come up, and for the first time in my adult life, I wouldn't have an answer. Besides, I felt guilty for knowing that people were facing serious difficulties while I couldn't overcome something so small and apparently insignificant. The absence of my work life had taken away my own identity. Changes are painful, especially the internal ones.

The concept of success for me had always been the same one attributed by society: being successful professionally and financially independent. I managed to understand how certain events, like "small traumas" of life, impacted my existence, and, most importantly, I managed to redefine the value of work, relativize the concept of success and recognition, rediscover my purpose, and expand my awareness of self. I realized how much we blindly live to fulfill others' expectations, not our own.

The insights that provoked this change came from my own previous journey. Firstly, the restlessness and need for change had been present at other moments in my professional path, driving me to anticipate stability and make my own moves as a protagonist. Secondly, I understood that the most significant changes were the ones that contributed the most to my growth. Both in personal dimensions, like getting married or becoming a mother, and in professional dimensions, like moving to England for a master's degree or transitioning from entrepreneurship to a corporate position. These profound transitions shaped who I am. Lastly, evaluating my journey of over twenty years in the design and innovation industry brought me pride and gratitude.

Today, years later, stronger, and more centered, professionally fulfilled, I realize that I'm back to being the protagonist of my life. I'm writing it from a different perspective. Of course, I still have doubts, but my decisions now are intentional. I recognize that despite the suffering, that period allowed me to dive deep into myself and promoted some self-discovery. There were many therapy sessions, women's groups, biographical work, readings, transition courses, certification in compassion, spiritual retreats, and the completion of a master's thesis on "design yourself." Only then did I realize how disconnected I was from myself, how I was not in the driving seat of my own life and as such I was being taken to a destination that hadn't even been chosen by me.

By sharing my process of change in this book, I intend to normalize that it's okay to go through this. Feeling lost and alone is part of the transition process. The pain is neither lesser nor greater than the pain of other people. By bringing this subject to the table, it expands knowledge, allows people to position themselves in the process, and helps them navigate transitions with more ease. Knowledge like the messy middle, that phase in which the past has been abandoned, but the next chapter hasn't started yet, helps people understand where they are in the transition process. At this moment, identity is lost, and old values no longer fit. That is exactly how I felt when putting on my pre-transition clothes. Instead of trying to go back to the past, one must be prepared to accept uncertainty and anxiety and use creativity to build new stories and meanings. It's impossible to force the clothes to fit. It was necessary to build a new wardrobe without high heels and tailored pants. Accessing this content helped me not to resist, to understand and accept the chaotic, messy middle of my transition, and make room for new chapters to emerge.

While studying transition, I learned that the concept of a linear life, where a series of events happen in an orderly manner, only exists in an idealized world. The idea of a linear transition from childhood to adolescence, adulthood, and old age; or from dating to marriage, children, and the empty nest syndrome; or from intern to analyst, manager, executive, and retiree; none of these logics fit the current dynamics of life. Real life is composed of a series of unplanned events, some progress, others regress, victories and defeats, some voluntary transitions, others involuntary. Therefore, our ability to navigate transitions will become increasingly crucial. Since we cannot control the events that impact our lives, we need to acquire the skill to control our response to them. Transitions are harder that we think, but more necessary than expected.

On the one hand, these moments cause discomfort, disorientation, and anxiety, but on the other hand, they represent opportunities for reassessing the meaning and purpose in life. For some people, meaning lies in achieving freedom, independence, autonomy, and control over one's own life. For others, a sense of belonging and community building is more important. And there are also those for whom the most valuable meaning is attributed to contributing to a cause and the mission of making the world a better place. For me, it's a bit of all three, and today I intentionally design my future so that my actions are aligned with my purpose, and I live a meaningful life. I hope each one of you have the courage to do the same. And, more importantly, find a group of women who can be part of this journey with you.

Women can rise and raise others but rise inwards in search of self-knowledge, fundamental for true transformation from within.

This text is dedicated to the women who were by my side through the suffering and learning of my transition process. You not only raised me up but also supported me and created the necessary field for my personal growth. Giuliana Tranquilini, Flavia Simon, Anna Maria Carbone, Laura Fragometti, Patricia Madeira, Tonia Casarini, Carolina Bruchilari, Maria Rita Haber, Maria Lucia Teixeira. Especially to Iolanda Steele, who reminds me daily to ask the divine to help me connect my thoughts, my words, and my actions."

ERLANA CASTRO

SXSW Speaker, Creative Strategist, Researcher, Author, Educator, Learning Designer, Content Curator. Founder at #ESGpraJÁ Creative Community. Co-author of the Antifragility Radar and The Business Model (RE)Generation, creative tools for ESG innovation.
Website: www.radardaantifragilidade.com | www.esgpraja.online
LinkedIn: www.linkedin.com/in/Erlana

RISE, RAISE OTHERS, AND ALLOW YOURSELF TO BE RAISED!

This is a powerful mantra that encapsulates the spirit of growth, collaboration, and mutual support happening right now among us women, beautifully manifested in this book. Let's break down the elements:

Rise: This suggests personal elevation, growth, and development. It implies overcoming challenges, improving oneself, and reaching new heights in various aspects of life.

Raise Others: This encourages not only personal growth but also lifting others around you. It involves being a source of support, inspiration, and empowerment for those in your community or network.

Allow Yourself to Be Raised: This part emphasizes the importance of being open to receiving support, learning from others, and accepting assistance when needed. It acknowledges the interdependence and reciprocal nature of growth and support.

Rising yourself relates directly to your appetite and attitude for self-development. This has always made a lot of sense to me. Challenges and changes excited me since early ages, and this always felt like a superpower. Because of that, I had a very special way of managing life, opportunities, and my own creativity.

My grandma Cora always said, "What doesn't kill you makes you stronger." Later, I found the same idea expressed by Nietzsche and identified even more with it. Recently, a Lebanese mathematician based in the US and named Nassim Taleb, specialized in epistemology and dedicated to the uncertain and volatile world of finance, forged a powerful and buzzlike word to contain this idea. He called it "antifragility" and summarized the essence of the term better than anyone else:

"Antifragility is beyond resilience or robustness. The resilient resists shocks and

remains the same, the antifragile gets better."

According to Google Trends, in Brazil, the term antifragile started gaining popularity around 2014, probably with the translation of Taleb's bestseller of the same name. But it was in February 2020 that the search for the term exploded, together with the arrival of the Covid-19 pandemic. The interest in this idea reached a new level.

In his book, the author reflected on the destructive impact of unpredictability and randomness in the business context and how some companies were able to navigate all this chaos and come out much better:

"One day, I suddenly realized that fragility could be expressed as something that doesn't like volatility, and something that doesn't like volatility doesn't like randomness, uncertainty, disorder, errors, stress..."

At that moment during the lockdown, we all needed to be the opposite of fragile. Resilience or resistance wasn't enough anymore. These ideas didn't capture what we were all experiencing. Like Taleb, we wanted to come out from Covid-19 better, stronger, and more evolved.

We needed a name for it, and antifragility arrived at the perfect time: In the face of the challenges posed by new reality, the fragile doesn't resist and breaks. **The antifragile doesn't resist and gets better.**

Since I have been so kindly "raised" by Taleb's antifragility idea, I will also "raise" two more incredible women that are part of this story: Sabina Deweik, cool hunter, and Tipiti Barros, creative facilitator. Both are my partners along this antifragile journey.

It was mid-2020, and the three of us were challenged by the pandemic and its direct impacts on our lives and careers when we realized that together we accumulated decades of experience and complementary knowledge. So, full of purpose and devoid of pretension, we developed the Antifragility Radar: a creative tool to ground the complexity of the current context in a business strategy, project, brand, innovation, or advertising campaign. The Radar is one of those big ideas where we embark with curiosity, joy, commitment, and end up materializing something larger than ourselves.

As Sabina says, "antifragility becomes a kind of antidote to these incomprehensible times." The secret is to embrace the turbulence and randomness unleashed, facing this chaotic context as an opportunity to evolve and thrive. No other idea represents the mindset we need now.

Our journey with the Antifragility Radar is also summed up in the idea of " rise, raise others, and allow yourself to be raised." Everything started when Sabina, Tipiti and I we were invited to give a workshop on debriefing the "Great Reset", proposed by the global business community at the World Economic Forum (WEF), during pandemic.

The request came from the innovation team of a multinational company that had recently achieved the B Corp certification. The team was tuned in to the WEF movement and wanted to delve even deeper into what was being discussed at the heart of the capitalism. A good example of professional teams that raise themselves and stand out!

As usual, before giving classes and workshops in company, there is an alignment meeting among professors, the school, and the client. The challenge gave to us by the executive education director was: what if, instead of one workshop about the Great Reset, we did two: the first to provide the background of context transformations and, the following, to learn how to operationalize all this knowledge into practice applied to the ongoing innovation pipeline?

"Of course!" We answered together with nothing in our hands except the joy of receiving a new and exciting challenge. How to ground the complexity of the highly chaotic context in the day-to-day business, from now on? What direction to take in your brand strategy and innovation strategy? And above all, how to ensure that the projects, ideas, and businesses strategies that are about to be born already pulsate with the spirit of the times (the zeitgeist)?

These questions echoed in our heads, and we felt a kind of calling: what if we could operationalize this contextual complexity into a creative tool? Wouldn't we be able to help not only that company but many others? After all, navigating and evolving in the new context that unfolded from the pandemic was - and still is - the great challenge of our times.

We conducted a cool hunting task force, collecting and categorizing data, observing, compiling, and discussing a lot. Within few months of research, we've separated the noise from the signal: what do brands, leaders, and businesses have in common that makes them thrive here and now? What constitutes antifragility in the current business context?

We mapped out eight creative dimensions and built a simple and yet powerful reframing tool. After all, antifragility requires a super contextual intelligence and recruits our ability to evolve and thrive disruption, therefore what you need is to be informed and conscious about the deep changes going on and embrace them as part of the transformation in course.

We were so excited about the initial results of the tool and its potential for businesses that we felt like the innovation and ESG sections of major national newspapers or magazines might be interested. We hired a press office that seemed suitable, but after some long meetings, we received only recommendations for coverage in smaller media, local radios, etc. We questioned the head of the press office why they didn't think of introducing us to national expert big media, as they covered these topics, and we were three experienced researchers with a great business tool in hands. He replied harshly something like "these media are not really interested in you and your research."

At that moment, we realized a frightening subtext: what did three mature women in their 50s have to say about disruptive innovation? Do we even exist for the innovation ecosystem?

Certainly not... in 2021, a Brazilian startup hub called Distrito counted $9.43 billion in investments in startups in Brazil. An unprecedent figure, two anc a half times larger than that in 2020. However, only 0.04% of the total was invested in startups founded by women. Read it again: 0.04%.

Even today, women in Brazil, in general, have little space in the innovation ecosystem, about 15%, on average. According to other recent survey by the Women Entrepreneur Network Institute, among 3,500 interviewed entrepreneurs, only 2% had businesses in technology. The data are exhaustive in these regards, and if you cross it with the age group, women 50+, then it is a real cold shower.

However, to our great joy, a few days later, we've received an email from the SXSW Festival confirming us for the lineup of their 2022 edition in Austin (TX), to present to the global creative community our Antifragility Radar. We were embarking as speakers for the world's largest innovation and creativity festival, thanks to our project and willing at representing many other mature women from the Global South countries, occupying the space at the business innovation field. As Caetano Veloso says,

"it's incredible the force that things seem to have when they need to happen."

Bringing the Antifragility Radar workshop to the SXSW Festival was a creative challenge an octave higher than what we were expecting. This festival is a reference for the world, and being there is an important achievement.

We decided to submit the Radar to the Festival curators thanks to Tipiti's bold approach; and we only had a few months to refine the tool and launch it internationally. In addition, creating the workshop experience, making a cool video, a website, photos, and rehearse everything in English! Now it was all about rising ourselves more than ever and being able to raise many others through occupying that space of privilege and visibility.

It only happened because the three of us were in the same movement of rising and raising others. This unlocks a kind of energy that runs a bigger gear than us. Synergy is that: when the whole is more than the sum of its parts. On the other hand, this whole also elevates us individually and magnifies us. All in all, to enter this flow, we need to keep three things in mind:

161

The first thing is to abandon the idea of symmetry and embrace the perspective of synergy. In other words, seek a powerful creative synthesis among the three of us and not demarcate or compare effort or territory. Converge on a bigger idea, where $1 + 1 + 1 = 111$.

Tip number 2 is that to arrive to the maximum common denominator, creative friction is necessary. Invest time, energy, and repertoire in this exchange of ideas. Discuss, diverge, converge, reflect... that's what takes an idea from the minimum to the maximum. Don't be afraid of friction!

Finally, to enter this flow of rise, raise others, and allow yourself to be raised, we must reprogram our operational algorithm: from competition to collaboration. To disassemble the competition prompt (habits, routines, neural pathways, assumptions, etc.), we will need consciousness, presence, and intentionality.

The caliber of today's contextual challenges requires us to do things differently, better, and faster, with more constraints and less resources. It requires letting go of our egocentrism and focusing on synergy from our inner power and presence in life.

Rise, raise others, and allow yourself to be raised, all at the same time... The point is to recognize the interconnectedness of personal and collective growth. I call this catching the flow. And flowing is about being able to dilute, amalgamate, and grow together.

That's the journey to antifragility.

FABIANA ANTACLI

Director of Communications, PR, and Culture
E-mail: fabiantacli@gmail.com
LinkedIn: www.linkedin.com/in/fabianaantacli

LIKE MOTHER, LIKE DAUGHTER

I am a lucky woman but also with a lot of determination and perseverance. I am lucky to have extremely loving, generous, and present parents who spared no effort for my education and my happiness. They taught me to believe in myself and to respect myself and others. If I can be half of that for my daughter, I will be the most fulfilled mother in the world. So far, I think so good.

I am fifty years old, and despite passionately believing that my ID is incorrect, my career says otherwise. I have over thirty years of experience in communications, public relations, and international affairs, working at some of Brazil's largest and most important ad agencies.

I started studying Advertising by chance, as I did not get into the Business Administration course I wanted, and because, at that time, it was the most desired within the field of Communications. I have always enjoyed speaking, and although nobody believes it, I was an introverted and shy woman until I started working. Perhaps because in my adolescence, I struggled a bit with being chubby, having curly hair, and not being among the so-called popular kids. However, I have always been incredibly happy and surrounded by many friends who still see me as their advisor and listener. So, since I did not know what I wanted to study and enjoyed communicating, I ended up in this profession where I proudly remain.

When I was in college studying Communications, at a time when "who you know" (connections) was everything in this field, I also decided to learn Languages because I thought I would not be able to get a job at an agency and might become an English teacher. I even took Latin classes! And tried out for a teaching position at a school, but I did not pass. It was through a friend from that college who saw a job internship advertisement in a newspaper for one of the country's biggest and most coveted agencies at that time that my life started to change. I didn't enter that selection process, but I started meeting people, attending lectures, interviewing them for college assignments, and things started happening. I even worked for a political committee, kind of representing the agency where I would spend two decades of my life without actually having set foot there. Everything worked out, and shortly after, I landed my long-awaited and dreamed internship, I quit Languages and started studying at night to dedicate myself to working during the day at the coolest agency of that time, responsible for memorable campaigns that made history in Brazilian advertising.

A bit of luck? Maybe. But undoubtedly, due to a lot of determination and perseverance. For two years, I earned a minimum wage and nothing more. Companies were not obliged to pay interns at that time. Many people told me that I should leave, that I was being exploited because they did not hire me, working days and nights like crazy. But it was not in vain, and I do not regret insisting and staying there.

I started as an intern and went through numerous challenges, facing sabotage from some women (yes, women). However, with honesty, generosity, genuine embracing of the company's values, helping everyone around me, and with a lot of resilience, I climbed the ladder, building up my career. I became a director and even worked for Latin America. It was not easy, but I made it. Through my own merit and effort because giving up is a word that does not exist in my dictionary.

While studying, I started dating my now ex-husband and friend just before I started working. After a few years, we got married, and sometime later, I became pregnant with my daughter Giovanna, who came into the world when she decided, precisely when I was about to complete 41 weeks of pregnancy! She was almost born at the agency since I worked until the last possible day because I wanted to make the most of every second of my maternity leave. And that is what I did. Unfortunately, I could not afford or had the means to take a sabbatical year like many people did that time to dedicate to motherhood, but I always prioritized the quality time we spent together.

I have always traveled a lot for work, and when she was still breastfeeding at ten months old, I had to go to Miami. I remember the many frozen bottles I left with my pumped milk from weeks before and how much I struggled in the hotel room to prevent it from clogging. Phew. But everything turned out fine, I came back, and she continued breastfeeding for a few more months, to my relief.

Since she was little, she had to get used to my travels – of course, she expected presents on my returns – and I always made it clear to her that I was very happy in what I was doing and that I am a fulfilled woman professionally, doing what I truly love. Unlike some people I know who are still not pleased. As I always say, we spend most of our time working, so it must satisfy us, make us happy, and give us great pleasure; otherwise, it's not worth it.

But I imagined that she would never want to get anywhere near this profession, due to maybe some trauma, because I worked so much and perhaps did not give her enough attention – that feeling of guilt that accompanies us even when we know we did the best job possible with our children – but no. To my surprise, she decided to follow my steps. This filled me with pride.

She has always resembled her father. But recently, everyone says she is becoming more and more like me. Even physically, but mainly in attitude, in the way she treats and deals with people, both at work and outside. She is generous, affectionate, dedicated, and a perfectionist in everything she does, and undoubtedly, my much better version, which makes me even prouder.

Giovanna has always been interested in my stories and adventures of traveling the world. And I have always taught her to appreciate diverse cultures and traditions and encouraged her to explore new places and experiences, to discover her passions and talents.

At 18, she went to Costa Rica to do volunteer work, cleaning beaches and taking care of animals. After several tests, she landed her dream job as a cast member at a Disney Park in Orlando, selling pretzels and popcorn for three months. While still in college, she secured her first job, an internship at a multinational beverage company through her own merit, amidst the coronavirus pandemic.

Today, she works at a large advertising agency, a competitor of the one I am at, and she is gaining recognition and admiration from her colleagues and superiors. And just like me, she is always willing to help others and influence the lives of those around her.

Speaking of courage, in 2022, I left DDB group, where I had worked for almost 30 years, and joined BETC HAVAS. I was incredibly happy there, immensely proud of the work I did and the results I helped achieve, and eternally grateful. But it was more than time to start a new adventure as soon as I turned half a century. Because it is never too late to start and redefine your dreams, begin a new chapter in life, take on new challenges, and start writing a beautiful new story.

What I have always sought with those who collaborate with me is to be a friend. I am not anyone's boss because, as I used to say, only Indigenous people have chiefs. And it is by being a friend that I make girls-women feel strong, secure, and confident in dealing with anyone in the company or outside of it, comfortable enough to open up to me about any issue, knowing that they can rely on me for anything and at any time, to advise them in their professional or personal lives, give them a little push to take action or make a decision, knowing that we will never let go of each other's hands.

And I do the same with my daughter. I believe in her and her potential and encourage her to make decisions and do things without fear of making mistakes. To step out of her comfort zone and always be open to new things and the challenges that will come with determination and courage. Like famous adman Nizan Guanaes, whom I had the honor of working with and learning from for over twenty years, used to say, "Make mistakes, but make them quickly," this way, we can change course and move forward because we learn through mistakes. And she knows that I am and will always be here for her and because of her.

I have always encouraged Giovanna not to be afraid of the world, despite obstacles and challenges. To be strong and believe in herself, to make her dreams come true. Respecting herself and others. Nevertheless, the phrase I have always said to her since she was little is, "Don't do to others what you wouldn't want them to do to you."

I am thrilled to see her become such an incredible, strong, and determined woman and - modesty aside - following in her mother's footsteps. She is kind and generous, with a successful career ahead of her and a heart full of love and empathy, also inspiring me to be a better and better person.

I taught her values and always believed in her potential. We shared stories, mistakes, lessons, plans, and dreams - both at work and outside of it. I always let her walk on her own, make her own choices, and, more importantly, take responsibility for them. But she knows that I am and will always be by her side to advise, guide, and support her in all her choices and decisions, even if they are complex or challenging. I throw the lifebuoy away in the pool, but I am always on the edge holding the rope.

I confess that when we are both working from home and inevitably, I sometimes find myself listening to her participate in a call, I restrain myself from interrupting the conversation and giving my input on what she should do. Sometimes, it is stronger than me (hahaha), but I know she must learn on her own. Now and then, I tell stories of things I have been through and what I did to overcome life's adversities. But I cannot and do not interfere in work matters because I think it is important that she experiences setbacks and faces adverse situations to learn and grow from her mistakes, emerging even stronger.

How do I feel? Fulfilled to see that I am leaving a legacy of love and inspiration, of work with dedication, commitment, determination, and passion not only for my daughter but also for many other "daughters" I professionally had and still have spread around.

My wish? That she has good health and is always happy in all areas of her life. That I can genuinely have served as an example and inspiration, that she achieves success and feels fulfilled and pleased in her work, as I do. And we continue together, colleagues in our profession, partners in life, and my great love, looking to make a difference in people's lives and in our country through our work.

Precisely to make that difference, I raised her into the group "Uma Sobe e

Puxa a Outra" (Rise and Raise Others) so that she can be inspired by the success and overcoming stories of so many amazing women there and also that she can raise and encourage other women of her generation.

FABIANA FRAGIÁCOMO

Co-founder @Gloppies, board member OneYoungWorld, content curator/creator ex-marketing executive of financial market (Itaú, BankBoston), ex- head of Communication NGO (Ayrton Senna Institute), designed of First Cause Marketing Forum; ex-ballerina
Website: www.gloppies.com.br
LinkedIn: www.linkedin.com/in/fabianafragiacomo/

LESS HYPE, MORE HIPPIE

The year 2014 presented good prospects. Everything was running smoothly. Family, marriage, no financial trouble, my two loving and healthy children, and managing schedules and tasks like most women in this country. I was working with a committed team and with bonds that extended beyond the bank's cubicles. At that time, I was leading the insurance marketing team at Itaú and had delivered an education content platform that was well-received by the bank and achieved great visibility to the business and the area director. I received an outstanding evaluation and bank shares. As a result, I was rewarded with the chance to attend an international conference. To complete the generous package of life, I embarked on a fifteen-day princess trip with my husband throughout Eastern Europe, -after eight years without any couple's time - with the best hotels and restaurants in the region, sponsored by his work. I started the trip with a sinus infection that wouldn't go away. In the shower, I felt a lump in my left breast, but without much concern, the trip went on its way, and I enjoyed it, despite the everlasting sinus infection. I experienced memorable moments, like an exclusive opera at the palace in Vienna and the best train trip in an imperial wagon: A dream. The good news ends right at this point.

From dream to nightmare

In a regular appointment scheduled by my gynecologist, I began the saga. He asked me to have an ultrasound with his imaging partner, who strangely whispered in my ear she had cured herself of cancer. She tried to reassure me with the phrase "it's better to have cancer than diabetes, after all, the first one still has a chance of cure." I wasn't sure if I understood the comment made with such confidence. But the sequence of events showed the confirmation of breast cancer. The doctor who would perform my surgery gave the bad news regarding the surgery and its possible aftermath. However, he advised me to enjoy the trip to the United States.

Despite the beautiful days I spent in San Diego enjoying the Congress, I was trying to digest the news about my health, trying to accept my new condition. It was October and television showed massive advertisements for breast cancer prevention.

Fifteen days later, I went into surgery and woke up seven hours later with implants and tremendous pain in my frontal muscles. The recovery was slow, and a month later, I started chemotherapy. I felt very strange walking into a wig store with my hair on and leaving with a brown wig with well-groomed locks. My head was shaved with my face turned away from the mirror, so as not to immortalize the sight of a 40-year-old woman who was still quite vain.

I continued to work and face the weekly doses of chemotherapy. I would spend three days at home and three days at work under the uncomfortable looks of my coworkers who probably felt uneasy about perishing. Facing the infernal heat of the wig, changes in taste, body aches, and weakness... nothing was as intolerable as the fear that came in the middle of the night: With children aged between 8 and 3 years old, I saw myself as indispensable in their lives, unable to cope with my possible absence. Even though I recognize that my husband could not have been braver during the period of my extreme vulnerability, deep down he was drowning in his own.

The highlight of this period was that, to "accelerate" my treatment, my oncologist suggested that I take a double dose of chemo reducing the treatment time by one month. So, after the first double dose, two days later, I had a physical collapse, I felt tremendous pain and later I was diagnosed with an infection in my implant. The infection kept me in the hospital for 25 days, with misunderstandings and disagreements among the doctors and the multidisciplinary team treating me. After a while, they decided on a new surgery to replace the implant on the 20th day of hospitalization. The surgery was successful, and I would only stay two more days in the hospital. Before the end of this terror-filled phase, I was still hospitalized when my 3-year-old son, during a visit, asked me, with a bright smile, to go to school on Mother's Day. With this innocent comment that shook my already damaged structure, I held back my tears and made a decision "tipped off" by my doctor. He said: "Patients have morning walks that are encouraged by the medical team. Would the nurses miss you if you leave your room for an hour?" And with this tip, I felt empowered. With this mission in mind, on Mother's Day, I left my room for my morning walk. With the hospital wristband wrapped around my sweatshirt, I headed to the pick-up point. I took the first taxi available to my son's school. I got out of the taxi thinking about the crazy thing I had just done and headed to the classroom, where

I found all the mothers sitting in a circle and my husband, the only father of course, sitting with our son on his lap. Writing about this still causes a lot of emotion as I remember his smiling face looking at me at that moment. Joy overcame the craziness. We returned to the hospital and, believe it or not, I entered as a visitor of myself.

2016 – FROM THE BANK TO THE CLASSROOM

By the beginning of 2016, I had hair again, and was already doing physical activities. Little by little my life was beginning to return to "normal." However, I was already a woman with a tough story, fears, and new dreams.

I was involved in an innovation project with Box1824, where I met Paula Englert at one of the meetings. She mentioned Singularity, and the comment left me intrigued and fascinated by the place I would still discover in the pursuit of myself. I asked a little about the school, and then I organized myself to attend in August.

In May, Itaú went through a restructuring that did not favor me. With fears, but with the certainty that I no longer wanted that life, that business sector, and that culture, my manager, aware that I had other dreams, left me an opening to look for other opportunities in other areas, but the decision to leave was already made. The next day, I received a call from Edson Britto, from the *Ayrton Senna Institute*, telling me that he was leaving the organization and that he saw in me the profile to replace him in Marketing. I started the conversations and interviews without much excitement, but at the same time, I had a blank page I could write on. I accepted the job still a little unsure but negotiated my start at the institute after a trip to San Francisco.

The experience in San Francisco was an explosion of insights. Contact with researchers, scientists, and futurists opened not only a window, but a portal of connections and possibilities. It was only there that I learned about networking. I met people from various fields who sat for coffee and shared a moment with me. They were interested in getting to know what I was doing there. A simple handshake, a smile, and "what brings you here" can already be a passage to another world.

On my return, I was completely transformed. There were more giant waves in the tsunami that hadn't stopped yet. Afterward, I came across the impacts on innovation, those of education, inequality, and the world of the third sector. My arrival at the institute was pure amazement: from the careful and gentle speeches of educators to the educational level of professionals. Unlike the corporate market, there were more masters and doctors per square meter in the institute than in the bank in the entire holding company. From hype to hippie. It was a tsunami because I realized that I had lived in a little bubble and had much less knowledge about social issues than my presumptuous mind imagined. My worldview was that of a white, middle-class woman who studied in private schools and worked in companies without any diversity. This dive into the universe of public schools unfolded a reality that awakened in me a critical look at my past and my own professional experience. I had become another citizen.

I brought my professional background from the second sector in Marketing, my experience in team management and innovation. And in return, I received a research laboratory in education and human development and public policy. Generous people pulled me and trusted my ability, such as Thiago Fernandes, Bianca Senna, Emilio Munaro, and the restless Viviane Senna, not to mention the team and the relationships I built there.

I experienced positioning work, content, and disruptive education events to the creation of the First Cause Marketing Forum, podcasts, research, articles, interviews, and lectures. I was happy with the new knowledge, producing, creating, and managing. However, knowledge also generates anguish. And it revealed the abyss of education, not only of public-school students but also of private school parents.

I attended several meetings at my children's school and tried to bring the knowledge I had acquired. While participating in parent meetings, I realized that the school would not change if the parents didn't change. This understanding led me to create a group of parents that I called *Pais Antenados (Wired Parents)*, in which I started sharing innovative content. At the same time, I met a woman who would become a great friend and my greatest supporter, Veronica Filgueira, a lively and generous Argentine mother of four who helps everyone. With many shared values and purposes, we joined forces. She, as a content producer for Accenture, shared her content on her networks as *Gloppies*. With this name, which for us means creating citizens with a global mindset and a hippie soul, we joined our activities and founded the *Gloppies* movement. Our focus was to impact and transform parents' views, seeking to translate how technology and the context demand new skills for our children. Through workshops, events, and content on WhatsApp groups, we talked about everything from Society *5.0*, socio-emotional competencies, quantum computing, and social causes. Skills to empower parents to empower their children.

ENTREPRENEURSHIP FOR A CAUSE

With the pandemic and my daughter entering adolescence, the challenges became bigger. Beyond the learning loss that she and students around the world suffered, social isolation left its marks. Veronica went back to Spain, and I decided to pursue a program for teenagers. Thus, in 2022, I started a new chapter in my life.

An old dream of a more authorial career. I transformed *Gloppies* into an organization that, in addition to working with parents, directly works with teenagers and the school community. Inspired not only to strengthen the self-esteem of teenagers but also to prepare them for the new Green Revolution that the planet is going through due to the climate crisis. Thus, the *Revoluteen program* develops *GreenSkills*, connecting them with nature and expanding their knowledge of Biomimicry and Regenerative Economics, and also encompasses future literacy so that they can deal with uncertainties and become protagonists of healthier, more inclusive, and sustainable futures.

At this moment when I am embarking on a new journey, I look at my mother and mirror myself on her strength: She is my greatest supporter, the educator, director, and founder of a senior college and a school. She is many things, but her greatest legacy was being a reference of a person who always took her life in her own hands guided by values. Thank you, Vera, your strength, and courage flow through me. With her, I have come this far, and with her, I will continue to rise and raise others, so that this society is diverse, peaceful, and nature centered. Less hype and more hippie.

FÁTIMA PISSARRA

CEO at Mynd, the forefront of Brazil's largest agency specialized in influencer marketing and entertainment is a psychologist, journalist, and marketing professional, an expert in connecting brands and artists.
E-mail: fatima.pissarra@mynd8.com.br
Instagram: @fatimapissarra
Twitter: @fatimapissarra
LinkedIn: www.linkedin.com/in/fatima-pissarra-12560a/

PURPOSE

Fátima, among many names, I came from a promise. My mother already had three children but wanted another one. However, cancer forced her to stop, and in order to conceive again, she would have to stop taking medication for nine months, which posed a great risk. But she didn't give up. Ten years after my youngest brother, my mother went to Fatima in Portugal and made a promise that if I were born healthy, she would name me Fátima.

I was born in Curitiba, Paraná. I never faced hardships in my life or lived in precarious conditions. On the contrary, however, all my memories are of my parents teaching me that the most important thing is self-respect and respect for others, and that in life, everyone is equal. I have no recollection of anything contrary to that. And what they always told me was that I should be my own king, my own queen, the owner of my life, and not depend on anyone. I should always fight for what I believed especially in myself.

Throughout my adolescence, my siblings played a fundamental role in shaping who I am today. They were always motivating me to be fearless and that I was capable of changing the world. Encouraged by my brother, who said, "Go live in the world, go to a different place, learn, live!", I pursued a degree in journalism at the Federal University of Santa Catarina.

I have always been very positive. For me, everything always works out. You know that book "The Secret"? People tell me that's me. But not because I read the book, but because I always believed in myself. I wanted to be happy, to communicate and connect with people, to achieve things, to do new things, to change lives.

At the beginning of my professional life, I went through some situations of anxiety. Bosses demanding, me trying to fit into different places. At that time, "quitting" wasn't an option. I needed to build a career, earn my salary. There were responsibilities that made us accept situations that made us sick. I felt the need to get closer to spirituality. I always believed in life after death and reincarnation, and I took a four-year course at the Spiritist Center, alongside my second degree in Psychology.

All of this foundation was crucial for me to get to where I am today, and I knew it would be the groundwork for my achievements. Everyone I worked with and built a connection, a friendship with, I wanted to exchange, grow, and inspire. I always believed that the more people I could help, the bigger the chain I'm leaving as a legacy and energy, with more people rooting for me and cheering for my success.

For 10 years, I worked in marketing companies. I never dreamed of becoming an entrepreneur. I was happy working in those companies, delivering results, pushing forward. I worked happily and motivated. I went through all departments to learn more. Wherever I didn't know something, that's where I would be, talking, asking questions, building friendships and knowledge. I wanted to have a say in everything because I knew it would shape my understanding and make me more well-rounded to explore the world further at some point.

Then one day, I won a seat at an event through a lucky draw, and once again, luck was on my side. My guardian angel, Ricardo Marques, sat next to me and said, "Let's start a business. I'll be by your side to help you build your empire." He listened to me for 30 minutes, and it was enough for him to tell me that I was capable of anything, that I was the most generous and intelligent person in the world, and that I could believe in myself because I would succeed. Ricardo didn't just pull me; he launched me into flight, something I didn't even know I could do. And it was in that moment that the whole world opened up for me.

When Ricardo and I opened Vevo's operation in Brazil, it could have been just a media sale. But I wanted to revolutionize the music market. Everything people told me was impossible, I went and did it. That's how I met Preta Gil, my second godmother. We worked on some projects together, and Preta has always been one of the most generous people I know. She would talk to me and give me many ideas. It was on one of those days that she said to me, "Why don't you manage artists?" And I replied, "Only if you become my partner." She said, "Of course! Deal." And she pulled me into her generosity of exchanging, sharing, and together, we created Mynd. At that time, still with Vevo, Ricardo Marques went on to help others fly and sold his share to Carlos Scappini, a great gift for me. One thing I can't complain about is having problems with my partners. My partners are the best people I could have by my side! They always believed in all my ideas, fought alongside me, and made everything work out in a positive and inclusive way.

When we established Mynd, I wanted to take a step further. It was the first thing with my name on it, a brand that would be mine, and I couldn't help but infuse all my purpose into it. I knew that everything in the past was for me to learn, and now I needed to put it all into practice and finally change the world. My idea was already disruptive. I wanted to have a company capable of understanding the world and its people from multiple perspectives. Something that could transform and, through my hands, lift many others to soar.

And that's how so many incredible stories were created, turning my life into an ocean of achievements, with wonderful people around me who did everything possible to make it all happen. From the very beginning, I told Preta, let's change the world. And so, we set our goal to work in a way that would transform lives, to do what no one else was doing, to promote respect, diversity, and, most importantly, to create a space where everyone can be equal.

Our first artist at Mynd was Pabllo Vittar, at a time when her career was just beginning and growing rapidly. It was at one of Pabllo's early events that I met Priscila, better known at the time as "Mulher Pepita." When I saw her for the first time from a distance, with her fit body and voluptuous legs, I thought, "If I look at her too much, she'll come and give me a smack." That's when she turned to me, with the sweetest voice I had ever heard, and offered me a drink. She told me she had recently undergone surgery but nothing could stop her. She was so kind, friendly, and attentive that all my prejudices vanished in an instant. I fell in love with her in that moment. Shortly after, I invited her to visit Mynd, and when we sat down, she expressed her intention to quit her career. She shared her dreams with me, and I said, "Let's make them all come true". We launched her program on Instagram together, which became one of the platform's biggest audience successes. Nowadays, this trans woman is one of the "owners" of the letter "T" in the LGBTQIAP+ acronym. She is a mother, a symbol of transformation, respect, and showing everyone that it is possible to change the world.

Together with the team, we set the goal of having 50% Black employees. It was one of the biggest challenges of my life. When you come face to face with veiled, structural prejudice that you didn't even think existed, you confront all the racist issues within yourself, all your mistakes. The only way to make it possible was to require that only Black individuals be hired until the representation reached 50%. There were protests and complaints, but yes, we did it. In 2017, the issue of race was still in its early stages of discussion, without major platforms. Our learning process was gradual, happening in the midst of our everyday lives, but it did happen, and I am extremely proud of it. Today, with 400 employees, 50% of whom are Black, it's not just those within the company who are growing and learning; it's their families, their friends, an entire ecosystem that is changing the world.

With this change in 2017, we felt confident in starting our casting with diverse personalities. Everyone felt welcomed when they entered the company and identified with it. I still remember when Yuri Marçal, a Black comedian and actor, came to Mynd to meet us. He sat in my office and said, "Where do I sign?" I looked at him in astonishment, laughed, and said, "Let me tell you how we work." And he replied, "I've never been in a company and seen so many Black people. This is my home; this is where I'll stay until you tell me otherwise."

I realized it's not about one person; it's about many. It's about people seeing themselves, feeling capable, feeling embraced. It's about believing that it's possible and spreading that belief in every speech, in every word. Every time someone sat in front of me, I thought about how I could transform that person's life, how together we could make the world a better place. It may sound cliché, but it's not. Every thought I had about the more than 400 talents at Mynd was about being a helping hand, pulling each of them up, bringing light, giving visibility to their best characteristics, their most brilliant qualities, and bringing forth everything they can achieve, all while believing in their purposes. Often, I was the first one to believe in them. They would sit in front of me with sad eyes and say, "No one believes in me." And I would respond, "If you believe in yourself, I will believe in you too."

Believing, achieving, changing the world—everyone can do it. Sometimes people just need someone to listen to their voice, to be there for them, someone to believe in them, comfort them, and say, "I'm with you." I didn't do everything to get where I am today, but everything I did brought me here. And every day, my purpose becomes stronger, pulling more and more hands, making more and more people believe that they can make a difference. Together, we will change the world to a place of more respect, more love, where everyone can be equal. Does it seem far away? But if each person does their part, plants their seed, nurtures it, and never stops planting over and over again.

FERNANDA MOSANER

Director of Marketing Communications
E-mail: femosaner@gmail.com
LinkedIn: www.linkedin.com/in/femosaner/

PULL YOURSELF UP!

Have you ever had the feeling of not being good enough? That existence crisis that occurs at certain moments in life, you know? With me, it happened frequently: I often felt insufficient. But I'm here to speak openly that despite it all: yes, you are capable! Competent and talented in your own way, in your own story, in your own context.

The star sleeps in the sky
The rose sleeps in its garden
The moon sleeps in the sea
Love sleeps within me.

(VINICIUS DE MORAIS, Lullaby of the Rose, 1958)

THE RESTLESS CHILD

I was born in São Paulo in the 1980s, into a middle-class family. My father was an entrepreneur, and my mother is a publicist (and piano teacher) who has taught us daily about the struggle for life and to be generous, sensitive, and empathetic towards others. I also have an uncle and an aunt (my godmother) who live in Italy, and they were like my parents, guiding me through numerous moments in life.

Middle child (with an older sister and a younger brother), I was a hyperactive child, and my parents strived to offer as many activities as possible. From a young age, I took piano lessons, played tennis, went swimming, did tap dancing, ballet, computer classes, skating (and some other activities that I have certainly forgotten by now). Of all of them, the only one I stuck with for most of my life was piano (mainly because, when I didn't feel like practicing, my wise mother made me do it, recognizing the sensitivity and talent I had). Today, I can only be grateful for her insight because my life would revolve around music forever. It is also said that even as a child, I had a keen commercial/ negotiating side and sales became part of my life (handbags, jewelry, athletic wear, cosmetics). Along with my computer classes and tutoring gigs, it helped me achieve my first dream: a student exchange program in Germany at the age of 16.

Music

Music was responsible for bringing me closer to the family I stayed with in Germany: a couple and their four children, all of them musicians playing different instruments - French horn, trumpet, trombone, violin, cello, and of course, piano. In fact, there were two pianos, and I had a great time playing duets and chamber music with my German host. Music is a universal language and it united us, creating a strong bond that continues to this day.

I've always studied in renowned schools and colleges with fully-funded scholarships, and my first job was an internship at the São Paulo Symphony Orchestra Foundation (Osesp Foundation) at Sala São Paulo (the hall where the Orchestra plays). I started as an intern, and after three months, my boss accepted a job offer from another institution and recommended me to take his place. I remember feeling insecure when assuming his position, and today I realize that he was the first person to "raise me up" professionally, even making me aware of my capacity: "Fernanda, you are already doing the work required for this position, you will handle it! I wouldn't even consider recommending you if I wasn't confident. It will work out." At the time, I worked as an editor for publications and printed materials, managing the communication content of the projects.

At this job I had the opportunity to conceive the first social responsibility material for the foundation, besides leading internal teams and had the privilege of coordinating the rebranding of the Orchestra's logo. I also interacted with various journalists in the cultural field, other cultural organizations, guest artists, and government bodies. My passion for institutional projects grew, and I had the chance to participate in national and international tours. It was also at the Osesp Foundation that I met my first husband, who is still a musician in the orchestra to this day. We were together for seven years, and during that time, I stopped playing the piano, assuming that he was the "professional musician" in the house, and I would be a mere amateur by his side. I was consumed by my own insecurity. I stayed at São Paulo Symphony Orchestra (Osesp) until 2015 before embarking on my journey at the Baccarelli Institute in Heliopolis.

MARKETING, MUSIC, AND INSTITUTIONAL RELATIONS

Based in Heliopolis (the largest slum in São Paulo), Baccarelli Institute is one of the main nonprofit organizations in Brazil, offering music and art education to more than 1,200 socially vulnerable children and young people. At the Baccarelli Institute I engaged in institutional relations, leading memorable projects which I am very proud of, such as the release of the film "Tudo que aprendemos juntos" (The Violin Teacher), directed by Sérgio Machado and starring Lázaro Ramos (a famous Brazilian actor, television presenter, director, writer). Based on the story of the Heliopolis Symphony Orchestra, the film premiered at the 43rd São Paulo International Film Festival, with a free open-air screening in Heliopolis. I was also involved in the creation of a documentary by TV Cultura in Switzerland, featuring three students, through a partnership I coordinated between the Consulate of Switzerland, Swisstour, TV Cultura, and the Baccarelli Institute. On that occasion, I selected the students who would travel, conducted interviews, coordinated with the press and communication departments, and accompanied the students during the trip, representing the institute in the country.

I can say that at the Baccarelli Institute, I accomplished numerous achievements, including a fundraising campaign with companies and individuals. I served as a spokesperson for the institute in projects and visits from foreigners, using my strong language skills in English, German, Italian, and Spanish. I designed multiple partnerships with consulates, foreign universities, and conservatories, as well as with Brazilians famous magazines, institutions and other prominent foundations and companies.

Another achievement was the connection with the Belgium Consulate, which enabled the Heliopolis Symphony Orchestra to host some prize-winning soloists from the International Queen Elisabeth Competition (one of the most respected music competitions). This partnership continued for years after my departure from the institute, and I was subsequently honored and recognized at the General Consulate of Belgium in Sao Paulo, in the presence of representatives from the Baccarelli Institute, the Belgian delegation and members of the Queen Elisabeth Competition.

In 2018, I was invited to become the Artistic Director of the Percorso Ensemble (a group of musicians dedicated to promoting 20th and contemporary century repertoire), which provided me an excellent opportunity to invest in the artistic side of my career, leveraging all my knowledge and repertoire in this area. I was "raised up" by the conductor of the group, but often, I was my own driving force, pulling in companies, people, and businesses.

DIRECTOR OF MARKETING AND COMMUNICATIONS

Contacted by the president of Dançar Marketing, I moved on to my current position as the Director of Marketing and Communications at the business group, that for over 40 years have been conceiving projects and creative solutions, connecting people, brands, and opportunities for clients such as AstraZeneca, Samsung, Vale, Deloitte, Banco Pan, SulAmérica, among others. I designed communication strategies for various projects, such as the tours of tenor Andrea Bocelli, the exhibition of Rita Lee (a famous Brazilian rock singer, composer, and writer), the Best of Blues and Rock festival, the Arts SP (visual arts and graffiti project), and the eFestival music competition, among others.

In this scenario, what do I enjoy doing the most? Managing projects, workflows, processes, leading people and gaining knowledge. I have always had a very rational and analytical thinking and my strength is definitely mathematics. To be honest, I never dislike any subject: humanities, sciences, or biology. In fact, at the end of high school, when I had no idea what to pursue professionally, I took vocational tests, but the results were inconclusive, justified by this notion of having "multipotentiality" – which, for me, was a general mental confusion. I was afraid of being capable of everything but not good enough at anything. In the end, I attended an exam preparation course to apply for engineering and I changed my mind for a humanities course. So, I chose to go into communication (they say I'm communicative, by the way), but this strategic and analytical side continues to be very present in me and my career. I love calculating, creating templates and standards, even though I have a creative vein that I express more through music, arts, and other moments. I had the opportunity to create a project inventory spreadsheet, both at the Baccarelli Institute and at Dançar Marketing, gathering key data throughout the history of both institutions.

In 2022, I applied for a grant from the São Paulo State Secretary of Culture to join CreativeSP, a government program that assists creative economy companies in São Paulo to internationalize. The grant was for participating in SXSW (South by Southwest), in Austin (Texas, USA) and I was one of the ten selected (out of over three hundred applications). I was ecstatic.

NEITHER SHAKESPEAREAN TRAGEDY NOR OPERA BUFFA

Fear of not being intelligent, not being attractive enough, or not being capable of achieving my dreams were some of the ghosts that haunted me, even though I had a supposedly successful journey. Looking back at my childhood, I see that impostor syndrome was such a prevalent part of my life that it inevitably led to self-sabotage and low self-esteem. I constructed a perception of myself associated with incompetence or inadequacy in my mind. I sought security from others, desperately trying to embrace my vulnerability, and failed. Because we are the only ones responsible for our own confidence, and we can only rely on ourselves.

While I was conquering the world, I was losing the continents of my relationship. I became pregnant, and the person with whom I imagined sharing my life chose not to accompany me on this journey. Our story ended in a delicate moment, and I am experiencing a sort of rebirth, where despite some downward pulls, I have the fulfillment of realizing the greatest dream of my life (to become a mother), which constantly lifts me up. Why did I tell you this? Just to say that we will inevitably have those who pull us, both up and down. And there is nothing exceptional about it: at one moment, we are at the top of the Ferris wheel, and at another, we have a limited view of the horizon below. While on one hand, I encountered hostility, contempt, and abandonment, on the other hand, there was a great deal of support from family, friends, colleagues, and all the women (without exception) who co-authored this book with me. The group "Uma Sobe e Puxa a Outra" (Rise and Raise others) symbolized, for me, an infinite network of support, from which genuine and true relationships derived, which will remain forever in my memory. It is in this context that my story intertwines with the stories of the admirable women here (and of many others in the group who are not in this book). To all of you, my gratitude for so much love and support. I thank Natasha de Caiado Castro for pulling me to participate in this group and Chris Pelajo, my sincere thanks for pulling me to co-author this book.

My advice? Pull whoever is at your reach. Take pride in your own story, be more generous (and less demanding) with yourself, do not be ashamed to ask for help to face the difficulties of life. It is legitimate and reasonable not to be a wonder woman all the time but remember that you are your greatest strength. Do not let anyone pull you down and understand that others may pull you, but you have all the tools to "pull yourself up" and soar in ways that make sense in that particular moment of your life.

In the words of Maddalena Casulana (an Italian composer from the late Renaissance, the first to have her works published), let us "show the vain error of men in thinking that they alone possess the gifts of intelligence and that such gifts are never given to women" (MADDALENA, 2023). Together, we are stronger. Generosity, sisterhood, empathy, support networks, and respect are the foundations of our group. So, when you rise, raise another woman. And keep pulling yourself all the time: it is the best thing you can do for yourself!

REFERENCE

WIKIPEDIA. Maddalena Casulana. Available at: https://it.wikipedia.org/wiki/Maddalena_Casulana. Accessed on March 1, 2023.

FLÁVIA CALDEIRA

Senior Director of Operations and Strategic Communications at LLYC Brazil
Journalist, MBA, corporate communications, reputation and crisis management
Email: flavia.caldeira@llorenteycuenca.com and flaviacald@gmail.com
LinkedIn: www.linkedin.com/in/flavia-caldeira-8156761

THE PURSUIT OF RESPONSIBLE, CARING LEADERSHIP

"Have you arrived?" The WhatsApp message in November 2016 was never answered. It was the continuation of a recurring chat with my husband, Paulo Julio Clement, whom I had been married to for 20 years. He was a commentator for FOX SPORTS and was on the Chapecoense flight. We met at O Globo newspaper, where we worked for a long time. I had been dating him since I was 25, and in a matter of seconds, I stopped hearing his voice and, worse, sharing his life. Yes, I had shared almost all my entire adult life with PJ. I lost the love of my life in an accident. And just like the plane, my world came crashing down.

Theo, my son who was seven years old at the time, has been my priority since the accident. I use everything, from respected therapists specializing in grief, to traveling the world, to ease his pain. I do not want him to grow up with a sense of "nostalgia for what hasn't happened." We are doing very well on this journey. Theo makes me want to be a better person every day. It is to set an example for him that I demonstrate and practice solid values every day. But I get up to work every morning for me.

I like to take care of people, run projects, and share victories. I do it for myself, for the team, and for Theo. And why am I telling you this? Because what has always sustained me is my support network. It is in that 'village' – family, friends, and work – that I seek the strength and support to keep going and grow. This is also the concept of the network that moves the whole "one climbs up and helps the others" movement, which I am very proud to be part of.

I was pulled up by the talented professional and my dear friend, Maria Fernanda Delmas, but I follow the participation of several other friends and women that I do not know but admire from a distance: it's a group that makes me very proud.

I am the Director of Operations at LLYC Brazil, a global communications, digital marketing, and public affairs consultancy that helps clients address strategic challenges with solutions and recommendations based on creativity, technology, and experience, to reduce risks, seize opportunities, and take care of reputational impacts.

Founded in Spain, LLYC celebrates its fifteenth anniversary in Brazil in 2023 and has a diverse advisory board. With it, we periodically share knowledge and actions that make us more empathetic, respectful, and - why not say it? - better. The company has global recruitment policies focused on diversity and structured internal programs that get real results. Among them are Challenger, for young talents, and the Internship Program, for minority groups.

Gender equity is real. In Brazil, 66.7% of our employees are women. More than half the directors (51%) are women. Globally, 62.9% of employees are women. And it is not just talk. It is practical. For example, Naira Feldmann, Director of Engagement & Intelligence, went through her first pregnancy at LLYC and took on the challenge of developing three areas in Brazil just as she announced the arrival of her second daughter. In 2022, she was promoted while pregnant, and Joana was born, beautiful and healthy. During her maternity leave, the business went well and was very profitable. This was a legacy of her management. Sara Paez, a professional in the Talent area, was hired when she was pregnant. Pedro was born, and she continues to shine, with her clinical eye for people. There are several other similar examples.

I lead a team of just over 40 professionals. Throughout my career, I have developed people and encouraged several women to take on leadership and management roles. It is a legacy that I make a point of developing wherever I work. Leadership in these times involves much more than a focus on results. Today, being a leader requires skills such as peripheral vision, reading people, the ability to improvise, continuous change, and, especially, the ability to solve problems without stressing the team.

Leadership is careful listening. The needs are different, the personalities are varied. Each employee makes a different and rich contribution to the collective. So, you must be alert and provide resources that serve individuality. A good manager acts and commits to people. A good leader makes a difference in the lives of those around them. They inspire.

One of the fastest growing areas today is Talent Engagement. Perhaps this is because the corporate world has realized that taking care of people is critical to the success of organizations. I know our talking about transformation, sustainability, and the humanization of business is nothing new. But for this to happen, consciousness has to be expanded. That is where Conscious Capitalism comes in.

Created in 2010 as the result of the merging of the ideologies of Raj Sisodia, a renowned university professor and author of several books on the subject, and John Mackey, a co-founder of Whole Foods Market, the Global Conscious Capitalism Movement presents the only sustainable path to a new era in which collaboration and purpose go hand in hand. The main goal is to leave a more positive legacy for future generations. The idea is to transform the culture and the way business is done. "It's about having a purpose that aligns with what the world and society need. Companies have an important role to play in solving society's problems," Raj explains.

It was from marketing research that Raj identified a correlation between business and negative social impacts, such as advertising, eating disorders, and body dysmorphia. As he was born in India and lived in the West, he decided to unite the Eastern mentality (focused more on the collective) with the business world. For him, profit, although fundamental, should not be the main objective for a company, but a consequence of a positive impact that the business provides. "What really matters is 'how' you make money and 'what' you spend it on," he sums up. So, Conscious Capitalism is based on four pillars:

A Greater Purpose

A company's purpose should be much more than simply generating profits: it is the cause the company exists for.

Conscious Culture

This is the incorporation of underlying values, principles, and practices: it connects stakeholders to each other and to their purpose, people, and processes.

Stakeholder Orientation

A business should generate different values for all the stakeholders.

Conscious Leadership

Leaders are responsible for serving the organization's purpose, creating value for all the stakeholders, and cultivating a Conscious Culture of trust and care.

For these pillars to be assimilated within companies, leaders must develop self-responsibility and socio-emotional skills - which are directly linked to the expansion of consciousness. I got to know the movement through Mariana Clark, a psychologist friend with more than 20 years of experience who specializes in mental health, loss, and grief. Mariana is a Talent Engagement Advisor at LLYC and working with her is a daily learning experience. In presenting Conscious Capitalism, she highlights the nine competencies that a leader must develop so that change can be actively implemented in corporate environments. They are:

Self-awareness: we must be aware of who we are, how we relate to each other, and what impact we have on those around us. It involves understanding essential values and respecting one's own limits and needs for a creative, rather than reactive, experience. Self-aware leaders act in line with their core values, are consistent, and respect themselves and others.

Integrity: Leaders of integrity are deeply attentive to the words they utter, and have a high level of awareness and coherence, because they understand that their behavior is an example. What is the level of coherence between the discourse adopted and the actions taken?

Cognitive Flexibility: also understood as adaptability and resilience. It is the ability to anticipate change, learn quickly, and navigate between dualities and conflicts, flexibly and resiliently.

Empathetic Communication: Conscious leadership can create pathways for information and knowledge to flow to everyone clearly. This skill also involves nonviolent communication and building healthy relationships based on trust, transparency, and humility.

Relational Intelligence: the ability to see multiple realities and perspectives for the same situation, to navigate with respect, openness, and compassion for our personal and other's feelings, and to understand each other's reasoning, context, intention, and needs. Leaders with high Relational Intelligence are empathetic and adjust their behavior for the sake of the quality of relationships – so generating a space of genuine presence.

Creativity: we must use collective intelligence and imagine superior solutions to highly complex situations and problems. Conscious leadership can recognize discomfort, stress, and the demands we make of ourselves only as the early stages of creativity.

Inspirational Influence: Leading by example is key. We have to engage people for the sake of the evolutionary purpose of the organization, to connect with people genuinely and authentically, and to generate influence through honest discourse and coherent behavior.

Shared Value: the ability to deliver that which generates shared value frequently and consistently, engage the team for a greater purpose, and guide with clarity and assertiveness. Leaders with an orientation to generate Shared Value manage, even with limited resources, a constant pace of delivery, in addition to decentralizing power, aware of the impact that the business generates for the scenario they are in, and for the world.

An Orientation to Serve: conscious leadership must also be at the service of people, demonstrate humility, recognize limits, and develop ways for people and teams to develop together. It also involves visualizing the business and people broadly, and clearly understanding how best to serve them. Leaders with an Orientation to Serve are responsible for guiding the organization on its evolutionary journey in searching for something greater than mere financial return. These leaders form their teams with assertiveness – where there is complementarity and diversity, and people are serving their personal purposes and those of the organization in their best versions.

In the study "Conscious Capitalism and Caring Leadership," by Mariana Clark, Naira Feldmann, Talita Monaco, and me - Flavia Caldeira - we explore the theme further. Here I have set out just a few concepts. It is everything I believe in for the management of the future. I hope we have more and more women in leadership positions. And that they truly exercise caring and affectionate management.

FRANCINE ROSSET

Marketing and technology executive, entrepreneur, mentor for leadership programs and volunteer for social causes.
LinkedIn: www.linkedin.com/in/francinerosset

ABOUT SELF-RECOGNITION

Personal or professional life stories are usually built with the adversities that appear along our path. It seems that the pursuit of success is an eternal loop for most people I know, and even those I don't know. Constant challenges that can arise, sometimes in childhood or early in our professional lives, start creating our self-defense mechanisms, which, over time, begin to define us as individuals, often more than they should.

Giving up on plans, procrastinating on projects, declining invitations, among many others, become constant behaviors out of fear of judgment and the apprehension of things not working out. Thoughts like "I don't deserve this.", "Is it meant for me?", "Oh, imagine, I'm not that good", become frequent in various situations, limiting our possibilities for growth and fulfillment. The fear of failure is a strong trigger to activate these mechanisms, and it happens in two ways: consciously and unconsciously. Both problematic, if in the end, the conclusion is always that it's not good or not meant for us. It's not about being pessimistic, not at all; it's something deeper that directs these automatic responses.

A comment about a work you did, a comparison with someone else, a simple joke that didn't resonate with the intended intention, or even a constructive criticism at first. There are those people who are more sensitive and vulnerable to these external influences, affecting their perception of the world and leading them to create less positive reactions, placing more obstacles, not celebrating their achievements, and not fully experiencing something that really is going quite well. It's a negativity that appears in the most subtle way possible, and it generates self-defense, initially necessary but eventually harmful.

Let's clarify. I'm talking about two things here, and one triggers the other: "Sabotage", the act or effect of sabotaging, hindering, or harming an activity. "Self-sabotage", acting against oneself, consciously or unconsciously.

One permeated various situations in my life, the other lingered for a while.

My first professional experience was an emotional roller coaster. I dreamed of being a creative professional and was certain that I had found the perfect place for me – an environment of brilliant minds that would give me the opportunity to learn and grow. However, the reality I encountered was very different from what I expected.

Day after day, my routine consisted of spending hours doing the same task over and over again – the boring routine of cutting out images. I was stuck in a monotonous routine and felt stagnant, without the opportunity to do what I had come there for: to be creative. Even after a year of work, nothing had changed, and there was no prospect of change. No one seemed willing to teach me something different or give me a chance to show my potential. After all, who put this girl here anyway? I felt sabotaged by the lack of opportunities for learning and professional growth. However, the worst sabotage came from myself. During this period, I won an award for a project I had created in college and submitted to the One Show, one of the most renowned and coveted festivals in the advertising industry. It was a great achievement, but I didn't share it with anyone there. After all, it would be pointless to mention it.

I sabotaged myself, believing that winning an award wouldn't bring me the opportunity to receive a briefing and finally get an opportunity to create. I thought I had no chance to grow there.

I was already acting against myself. While I was dedicated and believed in my abilities, I was also aware that I was in an incredible place to learn. However, my vulnerability, being young at the time, spoke louder than my inner confidence, and my subconscious sabotaged the pride I had in my first award, which could have possibly made them see my potential and unlock the opportunity I was seeking.

Sabotage followed by self-sabotage.

I left my job with the absolute feeling that I was just occupying a seat. What remained was the certainty that I would never work in a creative role again. It wasn't meant for me.

Years later, in a different field, at a job I had been in for some time, a new opportunity arose to move to a more interesting place, in a position that would undoubtedly boost my career. It was a huge company, with the opportunity to work for a globally recognized brand. Like everyone else, I had the right to receive a job offer and accept or decline it. At least, it should have been that way. But it didn't happen.

One phone call led to another, and the person who had made me the offer received a call from someone at my then-current job: "You can't proceed with the offer to Fran, she's very valuable here, and I can't lose her." Said and done.

It would have been helpful if the place at which I was working had made a counteroffer, a career plan, or at least a conversation about how well I was doing there and how they wanted me to stay. But none of that happened. The resignation speech that I had been rehearsing under the shower for days and gathering the courage to deliver went down the drain. The offer of a new opportunity was kindly withdrawn, due to a favor for a friend.

Sabotage.

I've been in situations where I've heard, as a form of "compliment," that I earned a certain salary, but I was worth twice that. How productive of me! Or that the promotion was mine, but they would give it to someone else because, after all, I could wait a little longer.

When we are young, it's not always easy to discern right from wrong. We fall into the temptation of believing that patience is indeed necessary, and that simply being part of a big company means we should be grateful. But it's not quite like that.

I could go on here, writing pages and pages with various stories describing my experiences. This succession of sabotaging that we go through along our journey ends up impacting the way we see ourselves, shaping our behavior and the self-defense mechanisms we create when we become aware of our past experiences. It amplifies over time and becomes detrimental to our future.

I've always had a strong (and frustrated) creative side, and it was during the pandemic that, in search of an escape, I found an opportunity to embark on a hobby as a business.

I stumbled upon an idea that began in my free time as a therapy, one that eventually turned into a business, without my expecting it. My hobby was making accessories for my personal use, with the intention of bringing color and joy to those difficult days we were all living through in the pandemic. It was during the lockdown period when support and empathy were needed. I came up with a name inspired by my children, created an Instagram account and pursued this alongside my professional life.

I started posting photos for my friends to see the pieces I had created, so that they could choose which model they wanted as a gift. They were "fun" items, and I would send them out in an attempt to brighten their days.

Then, one day, I received a message from a stranger: "How much?" I immediately thought, "Sell? How so? I don't even know how to do it properly, let alone imagine it!" I sold one, two, ten, a thousand pieces, and it didn't stop there. My therapy had turned into a business. And let me tell you, it seemed quite promising. I did everything myself: buying materials, creating the pieces, producing, taking photos, promoting, shipping orders - everything.

Three months after my first sale, I was approached by several leading fashion and business magazines to promote my brand. I participated in fashion editorials for Vogue, L'Officiel, GQ, and many others. Influential opinion leaders and influencers started wearing my accessories. I sold them in multi-brand stores in Brazil, the United States, and Europe!

I was becoming an entrepreneur, but I never recognized it as a business. To me, it would always be that little thing I did as a hobby, and I had no idea how it had succeeded. Whenever I received a compliment, my automatic reaction was, "Come on, it's just a silly thing, it won't amount to anything." It was almost as if my response made interested people lose interest. Myopia prevailed, and I couldn't see the success that everyone else apparently saw, and if you really want to know, I was ever embarrassed by it.

Self-sabotage in its purest form. No one had sabotaged me, except for one person: myself. I had the ball in my court. Everything depended on me, and I don't think I even need to explain what happened, right? I sabotaged something that had a natural trajectory for success, one that could still be thriving.

THE PAGE OF MY "BUSINESS" STILL EXISTS ON INSTAGRAM, BUT IT MERELY EXISTS.

Today, I can look at this sequence of events and understand everything that happened there.

For years, I focused solely on the negative aspects of my experiences, sabotaging my own potential and ignoring the positive possibilities. But then, driven by the stories of other women, I began to see myself differently. Seeing the vulnerability, insecurity, and imposter syndrome that permeate the stories of successful women was comforting and liberating: So, it's not just me?!

I began to see opportunities instead of limitations. I understood that adversity and external influences don't define me. Over time, I have won awards, took on incredible roles in various renowned companies, expanded my professional horizons, explored different areas of expertise, embraced entrepreneurship, and today, I can look back and see everything I have built. That only drives me to pursue goals that I still intend to achieve. I have an active voice and I am determined to make a difference, in my life and in the lives of so many other women who have experienced or are experiencing something similar, when they question their own abilities.

Today, I lead a team composed of 60% women, and I dedicate hours of my day to listen to them, advise them, and mentor them, providing a safe space for vulnerability, and helping them realize that success depends solely on us.

Adversities will always happen, but it's all about how we deal with them. Sisterhood. The empowering, transformative, constructive, and necessary power of sharing and exchanging experiences.

Self-sabotage was a consequence I did not consciously choose. But it came to me, and if it's coming to you, I hope that in some way, I inspire you to go against the flow. If we're going to engage the fray, let it always be in favor of success. Let's go together, because when one rises, she raises others.

GABRIELA COMAZZETTO

General Manager for Global Business Solutions at TikTok Latam and member of IAB and MMA Boards. Recognized as Woman to Watch in Brazil and Caboré Winner in the Professional Vehicle category for Meio & Mensagem. One of the 10 Successful Women by Forbes Brazil 2023.
Email: gabriela_schwery@hotmail.com
Instagram: @gabicomazzetto

I am Gabriela, daughter of Nane and Rick, and Tita's sister. I was born in São Paulo and I am 43 years old. I grew up in a large family and always dreamed of having a big family of my own. My parents encouraged me to believe that I could be anything I wanted to be and that the limits were within myself. I was always full of energy and loved sports. I played everything, including soccer. Yes, soccer, at a time when it wasn't considered a sport for girls. But that was never a barrier in my home, and my parents always supported me and made me understand that I didn't have to limit myself.

I started working as soon as I entered college (I studied Business Administration at FAAP). My first job was at Itaú Seguros, in customer service. It was a very important time in my life when I began to understand what empathy was. Still in college, I saw a poster announcing an internship program at an entertainment website called "Fulano. com.br". This was in 1999 when the internet was still in its early stages, and I became an intern there, selling banners when no one knew what that was. I spent two and a half amazing years at Fulano, learning everything about the digital world and sales, and that's where I truly discovered what I wanted for my life and career.

When I was almost graduating, I was hired as a sales supervisor at Ambev. A wonderful company that taught me a lot about focus, discipline, and management. After nearly 5 years, I joined Microsoft, returning to the digital world. I spent 9 years there, where I learned a lot about people management and the crucial balance between business and people. After that period, I went to Twitter, for almost 2 years and then joined Facebook as the Commercial Director responsible for retail. I spent 4 years at FB, where I had the opportunity to build an amazing team and create many incredible things. But at the beginning of the pandemic, in April 2020, I received a phone call that would change my life and my career. I was offered the opportunity to launch the TikTok for Business operation in Brazil. It was an invitation filled with fears and insecurities since we were experiencing a pandemic, but it turned out to be the greatest gift of my career in terms of learning and growth. In December of that year, I joined the company to launch the platform in the Brazilian market, and since June 2021, I have been building and solidifying that operation throughout Latin America.

What brought me here? A mix of curiosity and openness to challenge myself, as well as the courage to take risks and a very positive energy. My greatest characteristic is always believing that things will work out and focusing on opportunities rather than problems.

During this journey, I met my husband, Luiz. Then, my daughters started coming. The first one, Rafa, came with Luiz. When we got married, Rafa was one year old. Then, every three years, Luana, Gigi, and Duda arrived. As I mentioned at the beginning of this text, I always knew that my most special role would be as a mother.

Even though work is a fundamental pillar in my life, I never thought that having children would be a barrier, and I never thought of giving up on that dream. Throughout each stage, I planned for it to happen, and of course, I was fortunate to have a wonderful support network that was and still is crucial to me. My mother, the amazing Nane. Zezé, who has been working with me for 15 years, and my husband, Luiz, who always shared everything with me without distinction and is just as much a father as a mother to our girls, besides being a great source of encouragement to me. And mentors, incredible individuals who support, develop, and inspire me.

For me, having children is motivation. It brings me even more energy, a desire to achieve, inspire, and build. Through my daughters, I want to do even more, I want to pave an even more beautiful path for them. I want to show them and all girls that we can have and be anything we want, and our happiness and choices are in our hands.

The question I hear the most is how do I manage everything? And my answer is always to simplify and, of course, to organize. I am very organized, and I have a life mantra that says, "We will always find time for everything that is important in our lives." And I believe that to be true for myself. I exercise every day, I study Spanish, I work a lot, I travel, I take care of the girls, the family, and still find time to enjoy life and friends. And, of course, to give attention to the my babies, our dogs, Tapioca and Sushi.

And if I was afraid throughout this journey? Of course, a lot. But I never let that fear paralyze me. I focused on building alliances and bringing people I trust to join me on my journey, and they are the ones who strengthen me every day and push me forward whenever I falter.

After all, we don't do anything alone, and I have been fortunate to meet people throughout each stage who have been and continue to be essential to my learning, growth, and transformation.

What do I still want to do? A lot. I hope to see my daughters grow up, well and happy, and to continue positively impacting people and businesses. I want to continue being an agent of change in our society. I have the opportunity to be a woman leading a business, and I want to help more women to have the same opportunities. There is still much to do. This "Sobe e Puxa" community is about that, about women inspiring women, women positively lifting up other women, opening up spaces, and fostering paths.

This book is a crucial chapter in that journey. Having thousands of amazing women sharing their journeys and inspiring so many others. These are emotional stories that everyone relived while writing this book, and now, I invite all of you who have made it this far to tell your own story on the following pages. It only depends on you, your strength, courage, and passion. Shall we?

GABRIELA ONOFRE

Publicis Groupe Brazil CEO and Partner at Unico IDtech Brazilian unicorn startup. 100 Women of Innovation (2023), Women to Watch (2020), startups investor. LinkedIn: www.linkedin.com/in/gabriela-onofre

EXAMPLES INSPIRE AND ENCOURAGEMENT AMPLIFIES

I was born in a house of strong women. My maternal grandmother was proud to have attended college at a time when education was not seen as something necessary for women. Unfortunately, she had to follow my grandfather's career and ended up not practicing her profession. My mother pursued two degrees and always worked. She was independent, and that was always very inspiring. On my paternal side, two other strong women marked my childhood, my grandmother, and my great-grandmother. We used to spend vacations with them when they would host the whole family and manage that house where more than fifteen people would eat and sleep. The men came on weekends. From them, I learned to take care of myself, to take care of others, and I understood the power of collective strength and care.

The responsibility to grow came quickly. My father, an architect, went bankrupt during one of Brazil's numerous financial crises. A few years later, my parents separated, and my mother had to change jobs to support us. She worked tirelessly, often on Saturdays and Sundays. It was the three of us, her, my sister, and I deciding every month how we would move forward. We changed schools, sold our car, and closely monitored our expenses. This mutual support strengthened us. I got my first job at the age of 15. I worked as an extra salesperson on Fridays and Saturdays at a highly successful shoe store in São Paulo, managed by two very hardworking sisters. Another example of strong and independent women.

I decided to study engineering. I had a knack for math and was always curious about how things work. I needed to attend a public institution because we couldn't afford a private college. I decided to go to Unicamp because I believed that food engineering was the profession of the future. My mother preferred that I stay at Poli (USP) because she couldn't afford the expenses of housing and food. The fact that I needed to support myself led me to do many things in college, including working at the junior company, where I served as the marketing director, an experience that ultimately shaped my trajectory. Those were incredible years. I met lifelong friends, my husband, and I learned to be independent. But it was also the first time I encountered prejudice. Engineering has always been seen as a male-dominated profession. "An engineer?" many people would question. "Oh yes, in food engineering," as if we didn't study calculus, material resistance, mechanics, unit operations, thermodynamics, and so on in the same way. But I never let any label prevent me from moving forward.

I ended up working in marketing at a company full of engineers, Procter & Gamble. Besides being a great business school, it was a place of great inspiration. Even back then, 25 years ago, there were many women leaders: managers, directors, and presidents. Moreover, there was a culture that encouraged leaders to develop the next generation. However, I didn't realize how valuable the exchanges and examples were at the time. It was common for us to have conversations with senior leaders when they visited the country for business reviews. They would tell us about their career choices, how they managed different roles as professionals, wives, and mothers, how they dealt with their bosses, and how they approached international assignments. These examples always propelled me and encouraged me to believe that I could be whatever I wanted to be. Another common practice was seeking mentors. Creating a support network with more senior individuals who guide, question, and support you in different stages of life. Many of whom I still carry with me today.

But it was only when I became a mother that I realized my responsibility in creating support networks. I went on maternity leave thinking that I no longer wanted to work. That my role was to be a mother and there was nothing beyond that. However, the months I spent away from work made me realize that working fulfilled me. I decided to exercise a company policy and work part-time with half the salary until my child turned one year old. Many said it wouldn't work because even though the policy existed, nobody had put it into practice. But I made it work. It was very empowering for me to return to my career with much more confidence, but it was also a milestone for many other women I worked with.

I started to be sought after as a mentor by younger women who were getting married, planning to have children, and wanted to understand how I managed to balance everything. I looked for data and realized that precisely when women are advancing in their careers, becoming managers, that professional moment often coincides with personal life changes such as marriage and motherhood. And that's why there is a gap in the advancement of women in director and C-level positions within companies. Together with other directors at the time, I created the first women's group at P&G Brazil. In the beginning, the exchanges were less structured, but the fact that we shared our challenges and doubts, and that we were united with the goal of supporting more women made this program enduring. It is immensely gratifying to see how many women from the next generation now hold senior management positions.

This experience awakened in me the responsibility to be an agent of change and to give back the inspiration and encouragement I received. I was privileged to have examples of strong women throughout my journey who made me believe in myself. I also understood the power of support networks and how female networking can be important for career development, emotional support, dealing with "imposter syndrome", balancing multiple responsibilities, realizing that we don't have to be wonder women, and most importantly, opening doors and possibilities for us.

My subsequent career changes were always based on strong networking. I reached Johnson & Johnson through its president in Brazil, whom I met at corporate events where we were among the few women representing our companies. I joined *Unico Idtech* because a close childhood friend supported and encouraged me to make a career change. She made me realize how ready I was for the challenge, opened her connections to me, and provided guidance.

Working in a technology company brought me back to a more male-dominated environment. For a while, I was the only woman in management, but also a voice for bringing others in. At the same time, an innovative environment is more open to the new. We structured affinity groups - women, LGBTQIAP+, Black people, people with disabilities - often minorities within companies, but not in society. As we grew, we were also able to increase the number of women in leadership positions. Today, we make up just over 30%, increasing our capacity for influence and mobilization to bring more equality to our workplace.

Outside of work, I mentor women and entrepreneurs. I believe that connecting them to a strong support network, encouraging them to think big, will make them believe in their potential more quickly.

I have been privileged in this journey, but I only realized it as I added new roles to my narrative. Today, I understand the power of example and support networks, and I believe that we all have the responsibility to lead change, making the world around us a place of greater equity.

After all, examples inspire, and encouragement amplifies.

HELOISA GLAD

Managing Director Brasil at Kenvue
E-mail: hglad3010@gmail.com
LinkedIn: www.linkedin.com/in/heloisaglad

COURAGE

"The course of life wraps everything up, that's how life is: it heats up and cools down, tightens and then loosens, settles down and then becomes restless again". I start with this excerpt from "Grande Sertão Veredas", Guimarães Rosa´s masterpiece because I believe that, still to this date, for a woman to assume her choices and feel at peace with them, it takes a lot of courage. Following a non-linear path can bring anguish at times. But at the same time, there is nothing more liberating than having the courage to live fully and consciously according to your choices.

I was born in São Paulo and, from an early age, I was able to learn this lesson. The women in my family bravely leapt into stories considered unconventional until they achieved a liberating life.

Enedina, my maternal grandmother, got married at the age of 25 in the 1940s to a younger man. She was a complete exception to the rule of the time, when girls married around the age of 18 and usually to older men. Later, to definitively break the taboos, she divorced around the age of 50, when she decided that my grandfather's infidelities were no longer to be tolerated. She was always way ahead of her time. Following her heart and seeking to live in peace with her conscience was not what her contemporaries practiced. Once she became independent, she opened her own clothing store and became an entrepreneur of fashion retail. She would travel frequently to Rio de Janeiro, one of the fashion capitals of Brazil at that time, to buy clothes considered extravagant, with bold colors and necklines, and then bring them back to enchant the women in her city. In some way, she fulfilled daring dreams for those women. I was still a little girl and I loved to travel to Rio with her, where she would spend most of the time looking for new fashionists and trends. I saw her talent and hard work and I was filled with admiration. Across the years Grandma worked non-stop and was always full of energy. She never remarried. She said that her freedom was her most precious possession. She passed away at the age of 99, exactly as she wanted, because she always said she didn't want to be so old as to reach 100 years of age.

Enedina had three children. Among them was Dinalva, my mother, who was a history teacher and classical pianist. At the age of 21 she married my father and moved to São Paulo with him, leaving her hometown Londrina and her family behind. At that time, she also decided to quit working in order to dedicate to motherhood. Far away from her relatives, in that big and intimidating city, she raised her four children with my father, with limited supporting network. But she lived and stood by her choice. Without a doubt, my mother was courageous.

These two women and their life stories have left deep marks on me. They have always influenced me in my relentless pursuit of self-fulfillment and independence.

When I was 6 years old, I started classical ballet classes and soon fell in love with it. I believed that being a dancer was my great destiny. It was a sort of an unconventional profession to pursue, but I was determined to work hard for it. After eleven years of dedication, an injury ended up making that dream impossible to me. I then decided to study business administration and started working in several different internships in parallel. I wanted to learn and explore.

Four years later I graduated from college and started working for a global company. At that time, I realized that the world was much bigger than my own little world, and that there was so much to explore. The prospect of pursuing a global career in business management was exciting and the possibility of meeting new people, exploring new cultures and learning new languages, attracted me deeply.

At the age of 24, I married Fernando, and we moved abroad to experience some of those things that fascinated me so much. After five years of marriage, I finally felt the desire to become a mother. And Fernando also wanted to become a father. It was our time to embark on this new adventure.

Nicole was born in 2004, when I was still living in the United States, freshly graduated from my MBA with a new job. At that time, I experienced a similar challenge my mother faced when mothering in a different environment, without any supporting network, except for my husband, who has always supported me greatly. I spent Nicole's first year of life trying to balance work and motherhood, and I was truly focused on making it all work. I believed it was possible to manage both roles with skill, patience, and dedication, but deep inside I was not sure if I was accomplishing it.

I lived with this anguish for a few months, and when Nicole was almost 1 year old, we decided to go back to Brazil. Despite my insecurities, my daughter seemed to be growing up very healthy and happy. And my career was also progressing rapidly. Gradually, I began to realize that my personal life and my work were not two different "entities", and I needed to integrate them. As she grew, I learned to better balance time spent with her and at work. It was not easy, but I was convinced that I needed to focus on balancing time between my family and my career. It was a continuous search for self-fulfillment and freedom. Despite being convinced of my choice, I faced many moments of anguish, especially when I had to travel and spend days away from my daughter. When those moments hit me hard, I convinced myself that one day I would feel that it had been worthwhile. I knew that one day my daughter would grow up and understand me, just as I now recognize that the journeys of my mother and grandmother had been right for them.

One day, when I went to pick up 9-month-old Nicole from daycare at six in the evening, I vividly experienced the duality that many women understand. I needed to finish something important at work that night, so I didn't hesitate to go back to my office with her in tow. In those days, home-office was not an option. I set up a small table for her to have a snack, gave her crayons and paper, and there we remained until 8:30 p.m., when we finally headed home. In those days, I thought it was normal. Today, I would do it differently. And that's why I find this story so striking. This challenge, this guilt that we fight very often, is what connects so many women around the world. We make choices every day, and we are not sure if they are the right ones. And then, when we face moments of insecurity, those choices, sometimes represented by an event like this, come back again and again to poke at us.

Even when we are fortunate to have a partner that helps us share responsibilities, the role of 'caregiver' is often attributed to us as mothers. It is a role that, until very recently, most women accepted without questioning. It is as if having a helpful partner didn't really matter, because this feeling is intrinsic to being a mother. We are constantly learning to deal with it, which ends up weighing disproportionately on the scales of our life. I am aware that I speak from a place of privilege socially and economically and that so many women out there carry much heavier weight than I do. But I also realize that the burden, the guilt and the doubts are elements that in fact unite all of us.

I was maturing as a mother. I was embracing this learning journey and enjoying it so much that, when Nicole turned 5 years old, I chose to embark on this adventure again. And this time my gift came in a double dose. Our twin daughters Caroline and Sophia were born in Brazil, where, this time, I was blessed with the privilege to have a support network, despite still being away from my relatives. I remember fearing the twin pregnancy, but I was convinced that I wouldn't stop working. The first six months after their birth were difficult, and I think I handled it only because I had wonderful women helping me every day with the routine of the girls. It was during that phase of my life that I began to realize the importance of women building their support network. We have an unmatched ability to help each other, which gives us incredible strength. We understand and empathize with each other's feelings.

With three daughters, the work at home was tripled, and my career also demanded more and more. In this context, the feeling of not fulfilling the roles very well was inevitable, and it bothered me a lot. However, I started realizing that striving for perfection in all roles is nonsense, or worse, an illusion. The only thing I could do was to give my best in both roles, and that should be enough. And when I thought it wasn't sufficient, I would think about the countless women around the world who found it impossible to meet all the demands placed upon them. I would remind myself that we are not alone, and that thought was comforting. Embracing our choices regardless of what they may be requires courage and, obviously, resilience to let go of many things. This conviction was gaining strength within me. I also learned that if I wanted to pursue my career, be a mother, wife, daughter, among many other roles, I needed to find time for myself. I started finding my moments: a trip with friends or a full afternoon reading a book. Those things made me feel good, and I had gone for years without realizing it.

Over the years, my daughters grew up and went through phases when they criticized my absences at school meetings or that I couldn't always give them attention. Today, as I write this, I still hear that from my 13-year-old daughters, Caroline and Sophia and, I confess that it still bothers me. In my mind I go back to that old fear of one day regretting and realizing that they had grown up and I didn't make the most of my time with them. But I have learned to live with it more constructively. At 19 years old, my eldest daughter is entering adulthood, giving me some comfort in my heart. One year ago, she left home to go study abroad and this was symbolic for me, as a divided mother for so long. Seeing her embark on a path of independence was, in a way, a validation of my choices. It was time to see if my "model" of being a mother and a professional would have a positive impact on her development.

Today, I see in my daughter a young entrepreneur, who is very determined in reaching her goals. I clearly see those traces of independence, present in those who inspired me – that desire to fulfill dreams and to learn, but also to keep evolving as a person. My admiration for her is infinite. While she inspires me, I also know that she admires me. When I reflect on her admiration for me, I realize that the mother who also loved her career indeed had a predominantly positive influence on her daughter's life. Could my imperfect mothering model be effective? Caroline and Sophia still teach me every day, but I feel more mature and fulfilled in those roles. Or at least I am at peace with it.

As a mother of three, I have learned that each one has her own personality and way of seeing things. Each one teaches me in their own way, and I feel so privileged to have them in my life. I also feel privileged to have a supportive husband, who has a very positive influence on their lives as well.

The more mature perspective I now enjoy allows me to say that no woman should feel guilty. Every woman can aspire to achieve her dreams. They may want to be just mothers or combine motherhood with other roles, or even choose not to be mothers without feeling guilty. None of them should be afraid to pursue their dreams. It is worth it. That's how we inspire and uplift one another. The positive examples we set in raising our children, showing them that anything is possible if we work hard for it, are incredibly powerful. In my learning journey, I feel that I inspire and "lift" my daughters up every day so that they can become whatever they want to be, just as my mother and grandmother "lifted" me.

HELOÍSA SANTANA

Executive presidente - Ampro – Associação de marketing promocional
LinkedIn: www.linkedin.com/in/heloisasantana/

TO ALL WOMEN, A SHOUT-OUT!

I dedicate this chapter to the marvelous women who encourage me to believe in my potential, to believe in life every day, and to believe that the best is yet to come. Thank you to all the women who have shown me that faith, courage, and resilience are fundamental ingredients for survival. A round of applause for this tireless network of feminine strength and support!

A marketing professional with a specialization in Finance and the Third Sector, I have been working in communication and marketing for over 30 years, with the last 16 years focused on live marketing. I have worked with advertisers, agencies, media outlets, and industry organizations. Currently serving as the Executive President of AMPRO (Promotional Marketing Association). I am a speaker on representation, with a focus on Diversity and Inclusion. I was a judge at the Cannes Lions in 2022 and 2023. Also, I was elected one of the 13 Personalities in Tourism by Skål International, and in 2023, by PROPMARK, as one of the top 10 female leaders in the communication market in Brazil.

WHEN THE CURTAINS RISE

I am moved! Yes, my thoughts are racing as I write and think about the various women in my journey. The feeling is like watching a movie with a disordered script, as many memories outside of chronology pass through my mind, "choosing" to share a piece of my life. There are many female presences: women from my family, those who are no longer with us today but hold a special place; childhood friends, those from school benches, theater, and professional journey; the younger ones who challenge my beliefs and patterns - Bia and Bella, you lead this group, thank you, my dears; and finally, her, one of the most intense women I have ever known, my mother, the first one to pull me along.

When my parents separated, I was less than 1 year old. My biological father always lived far away, so two men ended up taking on the father figure role: first Tom, my beloved and late godfather - who was there in important moments with his fun, affectionate, and wise style. It was to his house that I wanted to escape when things got tough! Then Luiz, my mother's second husband, a friendly stepfather who spared no effort to show that a father-daughter relationship goes beyond a birth certificate.

My mother was a strict woman, but also joyful and spontaneous. She had a light that transformed any gathering, to the point that our house was always filled with people, especially on weekends.

Lurdinha, as she liked to be called, belonged to a generation where affection was not the main ingredient in the mother-child relationship. In her strict educational plan, there was little room for negotiation once she made a decision. Making mistakes was unthinkable for her. Naturally, this had unpleasant consequences for my psychological well-being. One of my sisters used to say, "Mom is great outside the door, but once inside, she transforms." Determined, she distanced herself from her original family to migrate to São Paulo. She arrived as a domestic worker, and her determination made her a nursing technician. She raised her three daughters with dignity and tight finances, but always concerned with providing us with the minimum education and necessary stimuli to survive in the concrete jungle.

Influenced by the home environment, especially by my sisters, I began to take an interest in communication, culture, and the arts. And there were those two wonderful and inspiring women pulling me in. Thank you, Edna, thank you, Edilene!

Continuing with life and heading towards pre-adolescence, I studied performing arts at the Macunaíma Theater School, initially pushed by my mother: she saw me as a shy and withdrawn daughter, when, I was extremely timid. The classes started to pull me out of my shell, to make me think beyond prejudices, and to see life in a different way, free from constraints. I found myself interested in various stimuli, such as: diverse and mixed groups of people, music, cinema, and theater. Today, I understand that all of this contributed to directing me towards a career in advertising.

I come from a poor family, which naturally led my sisters and I to start working at a very young age. My sister Edilene, for example, started at the age of 14.

In my case, I remember it vividly. I was FIFTEEN YEARS OLD, and it was the first day of my school vacation. Promptly at 7 a.m., I woke up to the sound of Lurdinha abruptly opening the curtains of my bedroom window. She "invited" me to get up with the surprising news that I was enrolled in an intensive typewriting course for thirty days, and here's the detail: at that time, that course could last up to two years. My vacation was taken over by something I hadn't chosen. I felt unjustly treated, not knowing what fate and this woman were gifting me: the curtains of opportunities were opening, but I only realized that years later.

Unlike other girls my age, I already had in mind where I wanted to work, something that would connect me with people and brands, something fun and creative, and nothing related to exact sciences. That's how I pursued a technical degree in design and later graduated in advertising and propaganda. Afterwards, I pursued several specializations and never left the field.

My first professional experience was at the Industrial Engineering College (FEI), working as a secretary for over 100 professors and around 2,500 students. How would that 16-year-old girl describe that experience? From the managers and professors, predominantly men, I received requests like: "Heloísa, make three hundred copies of this test on the mimeograph machine," "put these professors' pay slips in their mailboxes," "post the grades on the notice board." And some privileged students tried to financially bribe me to get the answer key for the subjects they were failing the most.

At the age of 21, I worked as a salesperson at a luxury accessories store on Oscar Freire Street, which was frequented by a very outgoing customer. Every time he visited the store and saw me reading, he would ask about what I was reading and started showing interest in my plans for a professional future. Very generous, and he took a liking to me. During one of his visits, he introduced me to a leading tourism company, without revealing that it was one of his own companies. "Seu Walter" (Mr. Walter) simply recommended me to talk to a certain manager. And so, my journey in marketing began at one of the largest tour operators in South America.

Parallel to this early professional path, I joined various groups and strengthened my circle of friends. One of the groups I enjoyed the most was a diverse group - we were in the pre-college phase, and our trademark was organizing surprise weekend trips and activities. It was delightful because we never knew where we would end up, but the experiences and the thrill of discovery were fantastic. The dynamic was to come up with a theme, for example, "park attire," and off we went, a group of 25 people, having a picnic in the park. Oh, how I miss that dear group.

There was also the group of Black people, introduced to me by my mother, who at one point became fixated on the idea that I didn't see myself as a Black girl. From that group, great friendships emerged, like the one with Patti: when I went on my first exchange trip abroad, she helped me with all the details so that I could connect with the destination in the best way possible. A few days before my departure, she handed me a beautiful handwritten letter, meticulously detailing how to make the most of London and stay safe on this long-awaited trip. She asked me to open it on the plane, at the turn of December 24th to 25th, as it was her Christmas gift to me. And so, throughout my life, I became part of many different groups: those from the various jobs I had, Weberland, the Girls from Moema, and so on. I firmly believe that they helped shape my ability to join (and also add value to) different types of groups of people.

THE PATH I FOLLOWED.

Always observant, I would watch the leaders in the places where I worked, even those from other fields. My curious gaze sought opportunities to be pulled in all sorts of ways, often without knowing what the next challenge would be.

When I returned from Europe, I chose to work in advertising agencies. With that decision, a new chapter began learning to "sell communication." As I say it here, it seems like a straightforward journey, but it wasn't. I had in mind that any misstep or unsuccessful performance could have profound impacts and even lead to unemployment, which was not part of my plans; therefore, I couldn't afford to make mistakes.

Among the managers I worked with, most of whom are still friends to this day, there is one in particular with whom I had a mutually beneficial relationship. Oh, Isabela, thank you for all your pulls and for always telling me that I have "the strength of delicacy." And so, I experimented with various sectors and cultures in companies, advertisers, agencies, media outlets, and recently, another curtain opened: the opportunity to work in one of the most representative entities in the national marketing field, AMPRO (Brazilian Association of Promotional Marketing), where I have the honor of representing around 70% of women in the industry. In AMPRO, I also met incredible women who propelled me on this journey of over thirty years in the profession. Thank you to all who have pulled me, starting from the hiring interview!

THE MOMENTS WHEN THE RUG WAS PULLED FROM UNDER ME.

I realized that most of the time when the rug was pulled from under me, it was due to a lack of trust attributed to me on two fronts: my gender and the color of my skin. My abilities always need to be doubly proven. For example, in meetings, my words are often not heard, but when they are repeated by other people, I observe them being applauded and valued. These incidents happen repeatedly.

Once, I participated in a selection process at a multinational agency, and despite having all the necessary qualifications for the position, the company's president expressed reservations about my candidacy. The reason? He feared that my being Black would harm his company's business. Despite this racist discrimination, I had the support of my direct manager, who hired me. The curious thing about this story of prejudice, among many others I have experienced, is that it was revealed to me by that manager 18 years later. Dear, a big kiss to you. Thank you for pulling me as well!

To this day, I face challenges stemming from racism and sexism. However, giving up on my goals, dreams, and aspirations has never been an option. Furthermore, I have always encountered generous individuals with big hearts who have helped me to keep going. Is it luck, or is it that those who pull others will also be pulled?

If I could play the game of creating 3 pulls for younger women, they would be:

1. Let people "pull your curtains" - Those who pull your curtains are taking you out of your comfort zone. Stepping out of it can be uncomfortable and scary, but also incredibly rewarding. We are accustomed to staying within our bubbles, but sometimes it's necessary to burst them in order to evolve. Success and growth often require practicing things that make us uncomfortable.

2. Choose one or more women you admire and get close to them! - That's right, just approach them. This woman may be much closer than you imagine, such as a family member, a friend by your side, or someone you follow on social media. Identify the reasons for your admiration and create connections from there. Sometimes, she may not even be aware of what you admire about her.

3. Pull for representation - Always advocate for representation. Be an agent of opportunity to create space for Black women, people with disabilities, LGBTQ+ individuals, and all the gaps of prejudice that you can help prevent. Pull people with the most generous gaze you can possess.

I conclude this chapter by pulling the next story and expressing gratitude for all the pulls I have received.

JANE DE FREITAS MÜNDEL

Head of Marketing and Market Intelligence at ESPM (espm.br)
Instagram: @janedefreitas
LinkedIn: www.linkedin.com/in/janedefreitas/

THE *FLÂNEUR* AND THE PHOENIX

THE GIRL AND THE *FLÂNEUR*

A girl stands before a blank sheet of paper. She has something to tell. Stories to write. She visits her memory like Walter Benjamin's *flâneur* (the great observer). Or is it Baudelaire's? She lifts her gaze and, facing a mirror, I realize that this girl is me.

It has been a while since I met her. Not like this! Not so deeply. She soars, she glides, she lets herself be carried away by the pathways of memories as if they were shop windows of feelings and emotions. I observe her enjoying this moment, and taking her place before the paper, I begin to portray what she finds on this journey.

I am the firstborn of a couple who had three children. My parents were financially disadvantaged but rich in love and care for the family. Unfortunately, they did not have the opportunity to graduate. In the 1970s, my father was the fourth case of a kidney transplant at Hospital São Paulo in the capital city. In a way, he was a living experiment for science. Fortunately, the procedure proved effective and gave us eleven more years of life with him. That was one of the reasons why my parents postponed their dream of higher education. They only managed to complete high school when my siblings and I were in elementary school. I witnessed every obstacle, every tired eyelid during that period. They succeeded! However, due to my father's physical condition, death lingered in our home.

My parents have always been instrumental in my upbringing and education. They encouraged and valued education greatly, believing that it could help me change my life. They taught me the most important values: honest work, respect for others, love for knowledge, and dedication to my goals.

I wanted to go to school at the age of two. I remember it well. I studied in a public school when, at the age of 8, I discovered encyclopedias. I started researching everything. Seeing my interest, a teacher, Ms. Gemma, began to work on topics that allowed me to deepen my knowledge, discuss things freely in the classroom, and expand my repertoire. It was a time when I researched my father's illness, travel, diverse cultures, and death.

An enthusiast, Ms. Gemma was the second female figure to encourage me, to give me wings, to pull me up in life. The first, and the most special one: my mother, Izabel. A strong, courageous, and determined woman, she did not hesitate in the face of the difficulties brought about by my father's vulnerability. She plunged into the workforce, fighting for a place and assuming the role of provider for the family. At the same time, my father, extremely intelligent and creative, discovered his domestic side and became the "master of the house," cooking wonderfully, singing, composing, and playing music, engaging us with his stories and his worldview. A world that he knew was not his own destiny but glimpsed in my journey and that of my siblings. My father taught us that anything was possible, as long as we wanted it deeply and made it happen with ethics and respect. My mother taught us the "how." Thus, my model of femininity was forged by strength and determination.

After much dedication, academic excellence, and perseverance from my parents, I fulfilled my dream of studying in private schools with scholarships. There, I encountered different consumer realities, cultures, and lifestyles. I believed that I could be part of it and change the life script that was written for me.

THE FLÂNEUR ACCELERATES ITS FLIGHT.

One day, in the spring of 1988, I received the news that had haunted us forever: my father had passed away. The feared visitor, death, had finally settled in. A mixture of pain and relief. Longing. Mourning! The certainty that from then on, everything I achieved would be in his memory. Studying and graduating became a matter of honor, a passport to a new story.

I completed high school in a small town in the hinterlands of São Paulo, where my family had moved after my father's death. I was eager to return to the big city and start my adult life, as I had planned.

I left my mother's house, bid farewell to my siblings. Fear and hope. I went to São Paulo and lived with the family of a great friend, Ana Beatriz. She was essential in many ways. And it was she who introduced me to my great love, who would become my journey companion.

I started working to pay for my studies right from the beginning. I passed all the selection processes and chose a renowned Advertising and Marketing school. My interest in the field arose in the height of my adolescence when I watched a classic

REAL LIFE STORIES FROM INSPIRING WOMEN

TV commercial, followed by an interview with the copywriter of the ad, Camila Franco. What an inspiration! During the four years of the course, I was granted a partial scholarship and worked hard to finance my education. I graduated with honors and applause, standing up, from the institution's president, who surprisingly was on the panel for my thesis.

Dad, Mom, I did it. For myself and for you!

THE YOUNG WOMAN AND THE ACT OF DOING.

The girl takes a breath. She seems exhausted from the intense emotional wandering through her mind. But wait. She is no longer a girl! Before the mirror and the paper stands a young advertising professional. I continue recording her encounter with the past as if it were my own voice.

A challenge had been thrown at my TCC (Final Coursework) group by a professor: to start a communication agency that culminated in an entrepreneurial initiative, my first business experience. It was the mid-1990s.

My friends and I, newly graduated and partners, worked together for four years. I discovered the pleasure of working with advertising discursive strategies and communication logics to positively influence human behavior.

During a client visit, I received an unexpected job offer, financially irresistible. I left our partnership in the venture. That was the gateway to experiencing an evolutionary sequence of corporate changes and endeavors in major multinational advertising agencies. Patricia, my great manager, inspiration, and friend, was the one who propelled me. With that, I developed an obsession for understanding and experiencing intercultural communication, studying English and Spanish and exploring the world. Soon, at the age of 32, I became a Director of Account Management and Planning. This new reality was now mine. I could finally experience the lifestyle I had discovered during my time in private schools, and which my parents helped me believe was possible. And just as I was pulled up, I also offered to pull others up.

It didn't take long for the university where I had graduated to invite me to join their teaching staff. I was returning to my house of knowledge. The contact with students definitively transformed my understanding of the teaching-learning relationship. It gave purpose to my life and increased my sense of responsibility towards the community.

I felt ready for a new challenge: to build my own family. After eight years and seven months of dating, I married Paulo (the one introduced to me by Ana Beatriz).

My pillar, best friend, and great supporter. I postponed the dream of being a mother to consolidate my professional career. When I decided the time had come, pregnancy didn't happen. Without thinking twice, I decided to face IVF (In Vitro Fertilization).

THE WOMAN AND THE REBIRTH

The success of the IVF came on the first attempt. A boy was on his way. Our Felipe: desired, dreamed of, and eagerly awaited. Pregnancy was something incredible. I felt complete, fulfilled, admired, a woman. I cherished every detail, every movement, and every centimeter of my belly. Every gaze, every demonstration of care and attention from my husband. I felt protected!

My son was born through a scheduled cesarean section. He was born beautiful, healthy, and perfect. However, that intrusive visitor that surrounded my childhood decided to make an appearance. This time, it loomed over me in a daunting attempt. After returning from delivery, I suffered a severe hemorrhagic shock caused by a condition called *Couvelaire uterus*.

I became a statistic. I refused to welcome death. In exchange for my life, I gave up my uterus. It was either it or me. That was the deal with the visitor who stayed by my side several days until realizing its defeat. Mourning! I knew that at that moment, I was giving up the chance to experience once again everything that pregnancy had gifted me with. I never felt any less of a woman because of it. Quite the contrary, I clung to faith, medicine, my family, and most importantly, my immense desire to witness the life journey of the being I had just given birth to. I lost a part of myself, but I felt relieved and grateful to be alive! A second chance was given to me, and I received it with great responsibility.

I understood that miracles happen. Everything is possible! After all, wasn't that what I learned?

Building the long-awaited family was a significant step in my life. I decided to take a break from the agency's pace to focus on motherhood and my emotional well-being. I needed to assimilate and transmute everything that had happened. I continued teaching and consulting to stay active and connected to the industry. As a gift, we moved to the United States, where we stayed for two years as expatriates. There, I studied, traveled, took care, received warm hospitality, and made lifelong friends. I found myself in many ways.

The flâneur pauses in the air, fluttering.

The Professional and the New Knowledge

We returned to Brazil with a heavy heart but with many achievements and future expectations. As soon as I landed, I received an offer that was once again impossible to refuse, but this time on an emotional level: to work at the same institution where I was already teaching, with the mission of structuring and leading the Marketing and Communications department. My two professional passions united in a single company: communication and education. It was a fulfilling experience, a gift wrapped in satisfaction.

Breathing the air of an educational institution for over forty hours a week stimulated in me a desire for constant updating and expanding of my repertoire. To embrace the countless challenges that were presented to me, to lead relevant, diverse, and multifaceted teams, and to continue my personal and professional development, I immersed myself in academic extensions, MBA programs, and a master's degree. I pursued various specializations, attended events, engaged in networking, and received invitations to speak and conduct workshops.

In an upward spiral of my career, I experienced both heaven and hell. The latter was served on a platter by those from whom I expected sisterhood: women. I was struck in many ways, feeling sadness and disappointment. In a moment of vulnerability and uncertainty, oxygen came through the hands of my own team (special beings, more than just friends) and a man. Someone who looked at me, looked out for me, regardless of the circumstances.

This revitalizing breath came at a price. Once again, I found myself at the negotiation table, letting go of an area that I loved, that fulfilled me, to answer a distressed call for restructuring a new department. A call that urgently needed my expertise. It was painful to let go! Once again, I clung to my faith and saw expectation transformed into hope. I responded to the call. And I reaped joy.

The flâneur is at peace!

In this overview of my story, I see that I have achieved and continue to achieve, I have risen. I have made and continue to make friends. I have fallen and gotten back up. I have surprised and been surprised. I recognize the moments that have marked the path of this woman who positions herself with maturity to inspire, encourage, and value others as she would like to be valued; to lift others up as she would like to be lifted.

I think of the girl who, amidst the legacy of her parents, believed she could make a difference in the story of her family and took the reins for a new reality. This is my ongoing project to be visited by the *flâneur* of memories and to be recounted at some future moment.

The woman appears reflective. A long blink emerges with a faint smile. Wandering through her memories stirs her soul deeply. I know she is enveloped in a feeling of fulfillment and gratitude. I also know that she will stay there for a while. So be it!

JULIANA FIUZA

Founding Partner at mesttra, founding Member at Rise and Raise Others, headhunter, CPO & business consultant
E-mail: jugasparf@gmail.com
Instagram: @julianafiuza_
LinkedIn: www.linkedin.com/in/julianafiuza

DECIPHERING ONE'S POTENTIAL

At the age of 16, I began working as a secretary in my father's medical clinic. I mainly took care of scheduling appointments, but my curiosity led me to question and understand more about the orthopedic cases that came in. I had the opportunity to observe complex surgeries and was amazed by humanity's intelligence and uniqueness created by God. Although I had accompanied my father on medical calls throughout my entire life and contributed to the care and preservation of human life, over time I realized that medicine was not my destiny. Perhaps in part because I felt that it was incumbent on me to choose a profession that I would follow for the rest of my life. I now understand that it is no longer like that. Very few people have just one job or career for their entire life.

In my restlessness to get to know a new country, a new culture, and of course, to learn English, strongly encouraged by my mother Eliana Fiuza (a strong and courageous woman whom I love very much), I finished high school and set off for Sydney, Australia, with only a one-way ticket. As soon as I felt more confident in English, I began my studies in Marketing at TAFE College in New South Wales. In addition, I worked in the hospitality industry, which allowed me to learn about people, customer service standards, and the importance of teamwork to ensure excellence. It was an enchanting experience. During the six years I lived in Australia, I devoted myself to both my studies and work.

Upon returning to Brazil, I was recommended by dear Mariana Gaspar to translate candidate dossiers for a renowned executive search consultancy. My interface with the headhunter team intensified, and I was eventually invited to work there full-time. It was then that I decided to enroll in a degree in Business Administration at Anhembi Morumbi University. Despite not having much experience as a headhunter, I took on leadership roles in the search processes, identifying potential candidates for specific positions in different companies. In addition, I also conducted end-to-end projects, dealing directly with clients -- a task that I always enjoyed doing.

HUMAN POTENTIAL IN TECHNOLOGY

After a few years of general experience as a headhunter, I started to work exclusively in the technology and innovation dimension. I had previously recruited technology professionals for other companies, but this time was different: a multinational corporation asked us to recruit 30 software engineers in an integrated single search process, which I had never done before. To accomplish this, I gathered the internal team and directed the recruiters' activities in order to optimize the process and achieve the desired result. Interviewing over 100 software professionals was a fundamental requirement of this process. I was deeply moved during the first interviews, as this brought me a greater understanding of human potential in technological developments versus their impact on business and society transformation. Most of the interviewees, usually young people between 20 and 28 years of age, showed similar characteristics: they were keenly interested in technology, were mostly self-taught, and had a certain obsession for problem-solving. How powerful! But there was a lack of purpose and vision beyond the typical perspective. In my interviews, I made a point of asking: Why do you do what you do? Most of the interviewees couldn't answer with certainty. This intrigued me. In the end, we managed to recruit the necessary professionals and proceeded with the next client projects. Until then, I thought innovation was synonymous with technology, but after this experience, I understood that technology was merely a "means" and not an "end," and that innovation should permeate all dimensions.

INNOVATION

While serving various clients and observing the growing demand in the IT market, I began to have increasing difficulty finding qualified professionals. The demand was high. At this stage of my career, I worked for large companies in various areas and 99% of these companies were interested in a profile of professional that we call "Talent." A Talent" is difficult to define or describe. "Grit," is what specialists define as passion and persistence for long-term goals (as studied by the father of positive psychology, Martin Seligman [2019]). When you manage to find a person with this characteristic, the character trait is easy to identify. Then comes the dilemma that all recruiters face: When a candidate is a genuine "Talent," they are often so harassed by recruiters that they do not even answer messages or phone calls. The goal is to find a talent with true grit.

To solve this dilemma, I plunged headlong into the world of technology.

I participated in numerous innovation and business transformation events, truly connected with ecosystems, and met many people who shared my passion: creating value. It was critical for me to elevate my understanding of what companies really need as an organization and seek in candidates, and vice versa. I deepened my knowledge of strategy and employer branding management, of how employer brands could become more attractive, to arouse the desire of qualified professionals who are harassed by companies. I sought courses and certifications in employer branding to better understand how companies can use their marketing and human resources to create experiences that attract the best professionals. With this, I published an article about how this new relationship between marketing and human resources can answer the main questions that a desirable candidate brings to the table: "What will this company add to my professional experience and development?" "What is the culture of this company?" Today, these questions are increasingly easily answered with a search on the internet, on Google or social media. Thus, it is important to reflect on what message you would like to convey at each stage, what form and format is required for the interaction to occur with the desired impact; how does one get a clear focus on the target audience? That was when I understood that I needed to innovate my role within the recruitment process.

This innovation began with the Living Lab. I remember that one of my clients at the time, a large beverage company, was looking to hire a team of analytics specialists to deal with suppliers. It is not common to find professionals with analytical competence in the area, who have skills (and interest) in project management, negotiations, and a concern for the deadlines of third parties. I went looking for new ways, because the traditional hunting process would not be the solution, given the delivery time and the mismatch between the market and the company. We approached some of the main professionals in the area and invited them to a kind of "Petit Comité de Analytics" aimed at the client. At the same time, we instructed the company to receive "the talents" in a way that recognized and affirmed their with the brand.

The interactions were extremely productive, and the people really connected. The employer brand had the chance to demonstrate its value proposition, and the candidates interacted, displaying their competencies, skills, and attitudes. They recognized each other's analytical way of being and performing, as well as identifying with the culture of the organization. As expected, the hiring was successfully completed.

During this project, I saw with a new degree of clarity the potential for innovation in the recruiting process, of connecting people and companies. At the same time, there were still not enough qualified people available. So, I launched a new challenge for myself, in the form of a question: What if I could include more people in these processes,

214

create talent flows and connect them with companies? What if it were possible to empower people so that they were qualified for the positions that I was accustomed to recruiting for? After all, we are going through the "Reskill Revolution" -- in other words, increasingly, professionals will have to adapt to a more dynamic job market that demands new skills that were not previously developed or even known.

That's how, with Mariana Gaspar and Gustavo Albuquerque, we developed a Bootcamp for people with disabilities and ended up training 70 students at the time (a project that is worth sharing, but at another time).

EDUCATION IS THE BRIDGE

This purpose for teaching and development was exactly what I found at Mesttra, a startup that aims to accelerate talent and innovation through new formats of attraction, selection, training, and connection between people and companies. I was introduced to Gustavo Maierá, an innovative and restless "ideator" (one who constantly generates new ideas and fresh perspectives), to meet a specific hiring demand. However, the purpose of transforming people through education spoke louder, and I fully immersed myself in the founding of a company dedicated to this. Since then, more than 400 people have been trained with a 96% employability rate.

More than promoting innovation, my goal and that of the company is to envision the construction of desirable futures for everyone. We believe that techno ogy is a great tool to solve humanity's career and employability problems (which are many nowadays, don't you agree?). We do this in an intelligent way, measuring impact anc serving large companies in their people strategies.

WOMEN IN IT

The technology industry has traditionally been dominated by men. However, women are increasingly migrating to technology careers (albeit slowly) and gradually taking their place. In our training programs, we strive to include at least 50% women.

Diversity plays a key role in forming technology teams. As technology becomes increasingly complex and interconnected, people with different educational backgrounds, knowledge, and perspectives are needed. Through diversity, teams develop more innovative solutions, reach more users, and generate better results.

Technology, in turn, "empowers" people and should be developed based on values, ethics, and purpose.

I attended Tristan Harris's (2023) lecture at the SXSW (South by Southwest) innovation festival, which takes place annually in Austin, Texas. Tristan is a co-founder of the Center for Humane Technology, worked at Google, and now is an advocate for the ethical use of technology. His motivation comes from his deep knowledge of Big Tech mechanisms, which connect people in superficial ways and tend to promote a kind of loss of perspective and self-awareness on social networks. "Technology is undermining wisdom and consciousness," he says.

In contrast to the lack of diversity and the need to rethink the way technology is developed, there is a great opportunity for social renovation, repair, and transformation. After all, everything starts with the foundation, and companies reflect society. My view is that technology is neither good nor bad in itself -- the problem lies in companies' solitary dedication to scaling up quickly for financial gain, at any cost.

Finally, what does the story of the seven-year-old girl at the beginning of this chapter, and her superhero father, have to do with all of this? Like a doctor who saves lives, technology can be used for the benefit of humanity, empowering people, helping to build values in organizations, and contributing to our understanding of our purpose on earth. Just like the superhero, technology is a means of helping people and contributing to a better world. Many people ask me if we will be replaced by robots. The answer is "no" - if we don't work or act like one. We will most likely be replaced by more technologically qualified people than we are. Technology extends our capabilities, and our greatest asset is our humanity. That is why we need to act. If we are not able to program the world, we will be programmed by it. Shall we, together, transform realities?

REFERENCES

BOCCIA, S. Tristan Harris - debate os pecados das big techs e por que ainda nos rendemos a elas. Época Negócios. Available at: <https://epocanegocios.globo.com/Tecnologia/SXSW/noticia/2022/03/tristan-harris-debate-os-pecados-das-big-techs-e-por-que-ainda-nos-rendemos-elas.html>. Accessed on February 20, 2023.

DIAMANDIS, P.; KOTLER, S. Abundance. Rio de Janeiro: Alta Books, 2018.

SELIGMAN, M. Authentic Happiness. 2nd ed. São Paulo: Objetiva, 2019.

LAÍS MACEDO RIBEIRO

President of Future Is Now, CJE council member, mentor for IFTL and Abstartups, networking specialist.
Email: laismacedo@futureisnow.group
https://linktr.ee/_laismacedo
Instagram: @_laismacedo
LinkedIn: www.linkedin.com/in/laismacedoribeiro/

"FROM INTERN TO PRESIDENT"

My small and peaceful hometown, Andradas, had already announced it: the Mantiqueira mountains were not barriers for me. Today, 15 years after leaving home, when I meet someone who was part of the first phase of building my life, a generous reaction of recognition comes with optimistic phrases like "I always knew" or "you were always a dreamer." This stirs something in me. Indeed, I've always been a dreamer. I remember the Laís who wished for so much, and it all comes to my mind in a hazy way because I remember vibrating with the intention of growth, impact, and significance, but without a name, position, or form. It's challenging to name something that you don't know exists.

I am a fortunate daughter. Luck, blessings, and something grand brought me into a powerful family structure of resilient people who didn't represent that dream in terms of titles, attire, or Faria Lima buildings but in a worn T-shirt smelling of sweat and coffee from my father when he returned from the roastery or my mother, always elegantly selling shoes, dresses, and ideas. In those simple and honest attire, I learned to dream, understanding that the dream was my place of access and transformation.

The entrepreneurial DNA of my parents, which led us through a life of ups and downs, instilled in me not only the desire for construction but an absolute lack of fear of the new. I always saw, within our home, that work not only dignifies but also provides the muscular structure that life demands for confrontation. Resistance to obstacles is overcome through work, the reason to work, and the references of those who introduced us to the verb is what changes the course of our lives.

With that strength and courage, I crossed the Mantiqueira mountains to experience enchanting São Paulo, which presents you with the binary condition of understanding its buildings and streets as a concrete jungle or, when within these spaces, veins and lives run, the road diverges, and you can be generously introduced to the city of affection. This was the São Paulo I wanted.

I arrived with the mistaken idea that in São Paulo, nobody knows each other. The vision of a young girl lasted only a few days before I began to understand the city's configuration in my initial steps into the market. São Paulo is the land of networking, who recommended you, who you know, who opened that door, who vouched for you. Life is networking. As a newcomer, I needed to build my network of relationships.

And so, I began my journey of connecting with people. I aimed to connect with influential individuals in all the places I frequented. I sought relationships with prominence. I made myself present with authenticity and responsibility. I needed to build my story.

Life then led me to the opportunity to work at LIDE, the best and most powerful networking reference in my world of intentions to meet and connect with strategic and influential people in the business environment. An internship position welcomed me to a new world, one that was so uncomfortable and showed me that it was in this place of not belonging that I wanted to build my place of being and becoming. Not with this clarity and maturity, of course, because a price was paid before reaching this understanding, and that price was not cheap.

The dreamer in me emerged early on. There I was, an intern, wanting to be everything but the lowest-ranking position in that company. I wanted titles, salaries, status, access, people. I wanted everything that emerged among brands, luxury, superficiality, competence, networking, and influence. It was all there. What a whirlwind. Decision-makers crossed my path, and I followed discussions that changed the course of the country. Presidents of the largest national and multinational companies, governors, ministers, opinion leaders, all at the same table. What luck, what honor, what madness, my God!

Curiously, the more unprecedented it was, the less uncomfortable I felt. I found myself in those spaces and got lost. Everything was so new and strange. Dreams led me to the group's management in four years. At that moment, I was completely lost. I adopted the company's name as my own. I believed that just being there gave me access, a network, and a seat at the decision-making table. No, not at all. That's when my sandcastle crumbled, and I realized I needed to become Laís Macedo and no longer Laís from LIDE. Whenever I questioned myself, "Will they reply to the @gmail email?" my immediate answer was no, clearly announcing the mistake in how I was building my path in that space.

It was also when I adopted my name and surname as a new direction and strategy for my career that I began to act with much more strength and courage. 92%

of my clients were men, white, over 60 years old. I was a little girl in that space. I never accepted that condition. Every day, Laís from LIDE, and now Laís Macedo, fought for her space and against the commonplace and normalized sexism in my life. I collect the disappointed looks of the CEOs who expected to meet the executive manager of LIDE in their luxurious offices or came to me at our imposing office but encountered a 1.57m girl with braces, a rural accent, and a child's face. Disappointment often overshadowed neutral looks, and, of course, there were almost no looks of admiration in that initial contact. It's no wonder that very often, before even introducing myself, they would ask me for coffee and water while they waited for the LIDE manager. "Hi, I'm the LIDE manager (with a knot in my stomach). Nice to meet you, Laís Macedo (my powerful phoenix reminding me of everything that surname carried). My starting point for meetings was not the reason for their existence but rather the place to disarm the disappointed CEO on the other side, trying to prove to me, to show that despite being a woman, young, and entirely outside the standards of their reference for a successful executive manager, I was a capable person, and that meeting was not a waste of time for him or me.

It was in this space and condition that I developed a valuable skill, to thrive on the contempt, insecurity, and disappointment of others. It was in the negative feedback, even if unspoken, about me, that a force dominated me, and with every conversation, meeting, or interaction, I only thought about how impeccable I would be in every move, word, delivery, and strategy. "You're going to have to accept me." "I didn't come this far for nothing." And it worked, but it was physically and emotionally exhausting. I didn't mind, I don't mind. I didn't come this far for nothing, and it's only the beginning. Now I knew how to name and shape dreams. I dreamed of being the general director of LIDE before turning 30. When I stepped in there at the age of 20, as an intern, I told myself and everyone who asked me what I was doing there.

Life has a way of crossing our carefully laid plans to show that not everything happens on our terms or in our time. Thank goodness. In 2017, a branch of LIDE called LIDE FUTURO, which was previously a project within the group, took shape and showed great promise. It was the LIDE's anticipation movement, the environment where we envisioned the group's future. New leaders were entering the decision-making spaces. Leaders equally qualified to the LIDE members but wanting to consume and experience networking in a different way.

In the face of the group's growth potential and deliverables, as well as the need to embark on an entrepreneurial journey, precisely to foster entrepreneurship, the group took flight and became a spin-off from LIDE. The board joined with the freedom for anyone who believed in the model to enter the partnership and take control of the company. Eleven people wanted to become part of the partnership. I was also invited to become one of the partners, leave LIDE, and take on the role of CEO at LIDE FUTURO. So, at the age of 27, my dream of a future in entrepreneurship took shape alongside 11 other partners.

Eleven men and one secret, that was our partnership. Between the years 2017 to 2021, I learned, relearned, took deep breaths, reflected, and questioned. On one hand, I questioned models; on the other, I questioned my competence. My efforts never seemed adequate and sufficient. They were 11 fantastic men from whom I learned and got inspired, but the hidden feeling that I didn't teach them anything or was never enough for their expectations regarding our business drained me. On one side, I saw a generous look in some of them towards the evident exhaustive dedication of my leadership; on the other side, looks of doubt and questioning about my capacity. It's no wonder I couldn't run; I felt that I always had to walk, hand in hand with some partner who would dictate the direction and pace of each step, and that limited me. I never seemed sufficient or ready. And maybe I wasn't. I drew inspiration from my 11 partners, but inspiration didn't seem enough.

I had plans and dreams for our company, but they didn't seem viable or prioritized. I saw our group mirroring society. The members, mostly men, and similar discussions and speeches projected themselves in our spaces and events.

I feel that these were years in a cocoon, a tight but promising cocoon, one that nurtured me to blossom into a colorful and free butterfly. It was the courage to break the limitations of masculinity in all my contexts of control by someone who was born to be an entrepreneur because she was born to be free. It was the ability to break free from an abusive and suffocating relationship to begin to recognize the strength of my freedom. It was in this blossoming that I had the courage to propose to the boys the purchase of the partnership. I needed freedom, to face my fears, and to walk in the direction of my beliefs and at my own pace, even if it meant a mix of sprints and contemplative walks. I needed to find myself, I needed to stop being defined by them. Them. Clients, colleagues, exes, partners, CEOs.

I bought out 10 of the 11 partners. Majority freedom arrived, and with it, the truly new, what makes me question my capacity, decision, and resilience daily. Resistance redefined every day, that feeling in life, "do you really want this? Then prove it." And we prove it. I'll never know if it's stubbornness or courage, but I just know that this entrepreneurial excitement and its butterflies in my stomach inspire me. It's the liberation from my cocoon.

And I took the president's seat. What changed with the title under my name? Very little. After 13 years of relentless pursuit of that coveted title, I understood it's much less about vanity and more about responsibility. Initially, I enjoyed the feeling of accomplishment and freedom, but then I found myself intimidated, questioning if I was truly capable of being there. I convinced myself that I couldn't continue without my male partners in the partnership. It was then that I became aware of the misguided place of dependence they had shown me, and where I had ended up. I severed these imaginary ties and began to search within myself for the new direction for this story. This place arrived in a positive and exciting way, a place of opportunity, but as I looked around, seeing so many groups like LIDE FUTURO, led by men and repeating patterns in connecting like-minded people, at tables with veiled prejudice and the course of the country being determined by the same hands, I renamed my position and understood that this is a seat of responsibility.

In every space I occupy, the places I've come to navigate, in every step on the stage and presence at those tables of like-minded individuals, I am never alone. I never speak for myself. It's about never normalizing the coffee request (with all due respect to the noble waiters, but just because I'm in a boardroom doesn't mean I'm there to serve them). It's about being heard, recognized that I've earned my place in that space, and when I speak, it's not about confrontation but the informed need for construction. It's about speaking to honor my space and all the women who made this possible. My warrior grandmothers, often silenced but who used their strength to build their stories and pave the way, just like so many others. Our powerful ancestors, how much pain and struggle went into us being here today? For all those who have gone before, for those who are here now, and for all the other women and stories that are yet to come, I will make my presence known, occupy positions, spaces, and opportunities with the responsibility of the femininity that pulses within me.

Simone de Beauvoir, the French philosopher, wisely said words I often find myself thinking: "May nothing confine us, may nothing define us, may nothing subject us. May freedom be our very substance since to live is to be free."

And so, my book ended with the paragraph above, but the life of someone who takes risks moves at a rapid pace, and in this case, it was no different. Between telling my story and the days following the book's planning, another turn of events. After nearly 14 years, the opportunity to fulfill a dream knocked on my door: to expand my group in a way that not only represented my intention and ability to connect inspiring leaders who hold positions of influence and decision-making but to do so with more reach, purpose, and impact. It was time for my solo flight, without the LIDE brand with me. It wasn't just about scaling my group and strengthening the quality of the foundation even further but also about redefining why and how we do what we do.

In the first 15 days of making this decision, anxiety overtook me. "Who am I without LIDE FUTURO?" "Is this powerful networking network Laís Macedo's or Laís Macedo at LIDE FUTURO?" Doubt and fear overwhelmed me, and any decision during that period was hard to make with clarity and confidence. However, it was through a courageous and authentic move and interaction with numerous people in my network, sharing my new plans with conviction, that everything truly took shape.

The answers to the countless questions of doubt and anxiety had always been within me. None of this is about a rash and ill-founded decision; it's all about nearly 14 years of a story written with focus, resilience, commitment, and courage. That is the foundation and certainty for everything that follows: a story written by a brave and accomplished woman.

Nice to meet you, Laís Macedo.

LEILA STERENBERG

Journalist, documentarist, tv anchor, international politics expert
E-mail: lsterenberg@hotmail
Twitter and Instagram: @leilasterenberg
LinkedIn: www.linkedin.com/in/leila-sterenberg-65a14b1a

THE AMAZING WOMEN WHO BROUGHT US HERE

It was on a Sunday afternoon that I received the unexpected invitation to write the lines that you are now beginning to read. It was a rather unusual Sunday in my life, as just two weeks prior, at this time, I would have been getting ready to go to work on this day of the week (or, for most people, the "weekend"). It was precisely April 16th. The sun was shining in Rio de Janeiro. I had gone for a run in the morning, stopped by the supermarket, and arrived home slightly short-winded (my grandmother Cleia, whom I will talk about later, loved that expression). I was focused on taking a quick shower and then going with my boyfriend to visit an artist's studio (Zemog, whom I recommend, if you're not familiar with). André (the boyfriend) dreamed of buying one of his artworks for the apartment where he had recentlymoved into. We had an appointment, and it wouldn't be appropriate to be late. After visiting the artist in the neighborhood of Santa Teresa, we returned to my home in Laranjeiras and had lunch, which consisted of a slow-cooked beef rib that had been roasting since mid-morning, under the watchful eye of my daughters – about whom you will also learn more soon.

All this introduction is to say that what would have been a lazy afternoon, marking my recently acquired Sunday freedom, suddenly turned into a challenge with a WhatsApp message: to write 12,000 characters – or six pages – by the following morning. Of course, I accepted. Firstly, because I believe in this project, even though I am just beginning to get to know it. Secondly, because I love a deadline – and I don't know if that's why I became a journalist or if, throughout my life in newsrooms, I grew fond of deadlines (often extremely tight, sometimes mere minutes, especially in television). But what exactly should I write? What is the "topic"? My experience in being raised and raising other women? Would I have something to say about that? After a few seconds of reflection while talking on the phone with the coordinator who had contacted me, I realized that, yes, I did have a story to tell.

This story has two starting points: the maternal and the paternal. My maternal great-grandmother Carmosina, the mother of my mother's father, was an "arretada" (or brave) woman - and I don't even know if this Brazilian slang already existed in the interior of Piauí, where she was born in the second half of the 19th century. Carmosina came from an important family: the Pires Ferreira. But instead of making a "good marriage," as was expected of young ladies back then, she committed a sin: she fell in love, still being a teenager. She fell in love with a poor cousin, a suitor whom her father did not approve of, with the last name Braga de Carvalho. Despite her father's disapproval, she married him and had a son - Murillo. To make things worse, this Braga died prematurely during the pandemic known as the "Spanish flu." He left Carmosina with a young son and limited prospects in life. What did she do? She moved to Rio de Janeiro, the capital of the Republic at the time. She initially lived in her uncle's mansion, Marechal Pires Ferreira (for those familiar with Rio, it's on the corner of the street with the same name, in Cosme Velho). Realizing that she would end up becoming something like a housekeeper or a companion to her wealthy cousins, she decided to do something almost unthinkable for the time: she moved with Murillo into a boarding house and got a job. She became a janitor at the Institute of Education - famous for its students in white shirts and pleated skirts. That's how she raised my grandfather. And she did it very well. He became one of the top students at Colégio Pedro II, went on to study law, and from there, he soared to a brilliant career in public service. He became the director of DASP (the Department of Administration and Public Service, which was significant in the Vargas era state apparatus) and died (still young, in a plane crash) as the second president in the history of INEP (yes, the one that administers the national exams, including the National High School Exam - Enem - that aims to assess the performance of students at the end of their basic education).

Fast forward to 1939, in the village of Lipcani, now Moldova, formerly part of Bessarabia, a region of Romania. My grandmother Tuba, the mother of my father (who had not yet been born), had gone to visit a relative. When she returned, their house had been destroyed. My grandmother was Jewish and, at that time, anti-Semitism was being fueled by the state, with the Romanian dictator Antonescu being an ally of Hitler. My grandfather, Janchel, had been living in Salvador, Bahia, for seven years, where he had gone to "make it big." He played music on the streets of Pelourinho, worked as a salesman, but he never made much money. He never had enough savings to allow my grandmother to leave the confines of Eastern Europe and join him in the adventure in Bahia with my two uncles. However, the signs of the Holocaust accelerated their journey: my grandmother sold what was left and, with the help of the family (who were grain merchants), they crossed the Old Continent (including Nazi Germany) and arrived in the tropics.

Summarizing what happened next: my grandmother became pregnant, and my father, Max, was born. He was less than two years old when my grandfather had an ulcer crisis and died in an ill-fated surgery. My grandmother didn't speak Portuguese yet and didn't even have enough money to bury her husband. She took a loan from the Jewish community, arranged the funeral, and bought a cart of charcoal. The teenage children helped to package the fuel - which was used for cooking at the time - into small cans and they went door-to-door selling it. That's how she started a business, which evolved into a mattress manufacturing company and later, in Rio de Janeiro (my father being already a teenager), into a small furniture factory and store. Needless to say, all three children obtained university degrees from federal universities and took charge of their own lives.

It's also worth mentioning my grandmother Cleia, the widow of Murillo mentioned two paragraphs ago. She became a teacher, in a positivist family where all four daughters had to have a profession. Her mother, my great-grandmother Áurea, studied piano with Ernesto Nazareth, who would come to their house to give lessons, even if my great-grandfather wasn't present - which was not common at that time. It was with Dona Cleia that I spent the most time during my childhood and adolescence, as my mother, Cleia Maria, separated from my father when I was 6 years old, balanced a public job and various architectural works, sometimes designing houses, sometimes working on the revitalization of historical buildings, and sometimes building theaters. Cleia-mother (or Cleia-grandmother to me) was tough.

If my brother and I received perfect grades in school, the comment, accompanied by a gleam in her eyes (revealing her pride in her grandchildren), would be something like, "You're just doing your duty." And she would buy us books, many books, encouraging intellectual audacity from an early age. I was about 16 years old when Grandma Cleia said, "You can read Flaubert now." I tackled "Madame Bovary" from her collection. Of course, I didn't understand much - and years later (this time in the original French), I had to reread the book. Another suggestion from my grandmother: when she deemed my English and French relatively proficient (which, by the way, I learned at the public school I attended, Colégio de Aplicação da Uerj), she suggested that I study German. Grandma Cleia's suggestion was an order.

Last but not least, my mother. Cleia-daughter or Cleia Maria or "Maizinha" (although I think only my grandmother called her that) could have written "The Years" instead of the Nobel laureate Annie Ernaux because many of her experiences were almost like snapshots of an era - and of societal transformations. She was a student teacher and had a fiancé with a fancy car, a friend of the Jovem Guarda (a Brazilian musical movement). She broke off the engagement because she fell in love with my father while studying Architecture (she was not Jewish, he was Jewish, back in the late 1960s - imagine the shock to both families). She lost her virginity before getting married, took birth control pills, and hid friends from the student movement in the backseat of her red Karmann-Ghia to smuggle them out of the Fundão (UFRJ campus), smiling kindly at the Army guards who were watching over the campus during the military dictatorship in Brazil. Despite being white, she frequented Umbanda and Candomblé temples, sometimes taking me along. She got me involved in samba schools long before it became fashionable among the middle class in Rio de Janeiro. She was the first female civil servant in the State of Rio to obtain permission to work in long pants (until the early 1970s, only skirts were allowed). She convinced the then-Secretary of Education (she was part of the architectural advisory at the department) that pants would be more comfortable, as supervising construction sites (and climbing ladders and scaffolding) in a miniskirt wasn't exactly a good idea (at that time, a skirt that wasn't mini was out of the question in her and her friends' wardrobes).

It is in the strength and courage of these women that I hold on to when something goes wrong - and in these times of "polycrisis", there are many things that can go wrong. I thought of them in times of heartbreak, the kind that knocks us off our feet. When they take away our bread as well: it was these powerful women that I focused on a few days ago, when I was informed that my journey in the company where I worked for 25 years had come to an end. "What am I going to do now?" I asked myself, with a question mark in body font 30 at the end of the sentence. The answer, for now, is: "I don't know yet." But the addendum to the answer is: "If my great-grandmothers, grandmothers, and mother found a way, so will I." I know I have to move forward - and this accidental matriarchy that has formed behind me has laid the foundation for the path I will build as I advance.

I don't believe in taking shortcuts: I believe in effort, dedication, and sweating it out. I also don't believe, pardon the vulgarity, in cheating: I believe more in cooperation than competition. I have always been the one to recommend friends for internships and freelance gigs that I couldn't take on. I prefer to share the motherhood of a project with a brilliant colleague rather than have the pretension of shining alone - and lonely. I think it's a feminine logic that reaches us with ancient roots in the kitchens and sewing circles of our ancestors.

I also believe in teaching our daughters to be less princesses (waiting for a supposed prince) and more queens on their own journeys. I speak from experience: I am the mother of two girls, Laura and Elisa, now 20 and 14 years old, each with their own personality and unique interests, each carving out their own space - and receiving a few scoldings here and there from the mama bear who is writing to you. Setting boundaries ceased to be the exclusive role of the paternal figure a long time ago (apologies to the fathers of psychoanalysis for this heresy). I give them the hard truth, just as they do the same with me, which has become even more necessary at this moment as I begin to crawl in professional reinvention.

That being said, I realize the length of my text, which shouldn't exceed 12,000 characters, and I discover that I'm already approaching 11,000. I also realize that I have much to say. I could list my professional accomplishments - live coverage of events about which we had almost no information, impromptu simultaneous translations in five languages, interviews with powerful and talented men and women from different corners of the world, a documentary made with passion but limited resources, numerous work trips to remote places, and so on. I choose to state that if you, the reader, want to know more about that, you can Google it or ask ChatGPT because it should all be there.

Here, I will reserve the remainder of my space to say that this moment, 2023, is of unparalleled richness for us women, at least in countries committed to democracy and the pursuit of gender equity (because we are still in pursuit). Today, we can talk about ageism in companies. We can criticize the red pill movement. We can debate gender prejudice intertwined with racism. We can applaud older actresses who win Oscars. We can openly discuss our orgasms and affections. We can choose whether to dye our hair or let it whiten freely, embracing the passage of time. We can wear shorts after 50 (and I do so frequently). We can choose to marry or not. To have children or not.

Let us live up to the Carmosinas, Áureas, Tubas, and Cleias in our lives - and be worthy of the Lauras and Elisas who will come after us. And let us tread this path together - authors and readers - each with our own tools, perspectives, and voices. This book is exactly about that, and I am honored and pleased to be a part of it. I hope that this brief account, which now comes to an end as the Sunday sunset approaches, will be a small contribution to this beautiful road ahead.

LÍVIA MONTEMOR

Growth, Digital Media & Digital Marketing
Opening ways for brands and users in the digital universe!
E-mail: lipgm@hotmail.com
Tiktok: www.tiktok.com/@midiapower
LinkedIn: www.linkedin.com/in/lívia-montemor/

1984, THE BEGINNING OF MY JOURNEY

This is the space to tell a perfectly imperfect story, a summary of important experiences and lessons learned that helped build solid steps on my ladder of life. This chapter involves some of my greatest loves and is imperfectly amazing because it's simple and like any journey it has ups and downs that I believe make us stronger and more interesting.

I believe that life is an eternal climb where the more paths to the top the more complete we feel in every way, we find peace, serenity, balance, we care less about small things.

I didn't think I was capable of writing a story that would capture your attention, and I realized that in this thought, there's much more of the imposter syndrome than I could imagine. And it was with the support and encouragement of some friends who pulled me up that I could see that I did have something special to share. I set aside that syndrome, and here it is!

So, I decided to release fear and insecurity and write this chapter to tell this part of my story with my heart regarding supporting as much as respecting the women around me.

I'm not going to report here a great professional pull I had or an epic moment when I pulled someone...

It is a true story of small moments and countless daily exchanges, which add up to fabulous results.

It was the title of the book that inspired me to write, and it was writing that I was able to realize the immense value that small, good attitudes have when carried out spontaneously with love, affection and especially sisterhood.

My story around being pulled and pulling women started on the day I was born. It was a home already composed of three people, my father, my mother, and my older sister.

It was in this love-filled home that I arrived as the fourth member!

And five years later, another girl arrived, my younger sister, and that's how we formed this family, the "Montemor's," a home with one man and a quartet of strong-willed women.

My father has always been (and is still) our foundation, the rational side, that presence which brings security and eliminates fears. It's as if wherever he is, nothing bad could ever happen. His involvement in this story is crucial because he has always encouraged us, raised us to be independent, always gave us space, and showed us that the world could be ours! He has never taken away our right to express ourselves as well as our shine and the freedom to come and go, and he has never failed to praise our achievements. He has always been there to help us raise every stone and cover every hole that appeared in our paths.

Having him supporting us was essential for me to grow confidently and freely to conquer the world responsibly.

My mother is the emotional component, bringing balance alongside reason. She celebrates our achievements, cries with us in our pain, propels us forward, embraces our craziness, and is a fantastic companion.

My sisters are a delightful mix of a little bit of everything. There's love, friendship, jealousy, fights, affection, laughter, and tears, longing, and a desire to be apart... But we protect each other, love each other, and are truly friends. I love their company!

And it was with this select feminine nucleus that I learned in my daily life that if we were together, everything would always be easier and lighter. Always having someone to share with is the best of sums. Many times, it was also chaotic. However, even this chaos had its positive and comical side. Can you imagine the four of us getting ready at home for a wedding? Or that day when one decides to borrow something from the other? It's chaos!

We are very similar and very different at the same time though. Each one with their qualities and flaws, complementing each other throughout life. Even after a big fight, we never stop supporting each other.

Although we have had countless disagreements, they don't represent lack of love because disagreement always causes discussions that enhance our relationship. Disagreeing is part of the process. But they can hurt and bring the fear of losing ourselves, of not being together anymore. But they are essential and continue to be important for my growth in order to rethink attitudes, see things differently, and value those who love us even more. After all, no sky is blue all the time!

It is the sum of these moments that make this journey worthwhile!

And it is because of this context that I cannot say that I learned to support women or be supported by them. In my life, it has been something intrinsic, a part of who I am.

Being raised in this family with valuable principles and having the privilege of sharing life with three other women has taught me to always lend a helping hand, to want to see others grow, to support, help, and have empathy.

Highlighting some meaningful passages, when I was only one year old, a household employee planned to kidnap me, and my older sister, who was four years old at the time, but who also used all her strength to stop her. She screamed desperately, pulled me from her arms, and tried to prevent the woman from taking me out of the house. It was the determination of this little girl that made our mother arrive in time and prevent the progress of that abduction. Maybe it was this story that made me grow up safe and also brought me the instinct for protection.

It was with my younger sister that I shared the best nights of laughter in my life... We were both in the same bed for endless nights watching shows on Discovery Home and Health, laughing, fooling around, and imagining ourselves in those episodes of Say Yes to the Dress. She taught me that love is sharing small moments.

I could tell endless stories about my mother, the countless times I cried in her lap, the magic teas that only she makes to cure my rhinitis, the scolding for the times I was going the wrong way, all the encouragement to see me grow and for every time she surprised me.

I can sum up our relationship in 4 words: Love, honesty, welcome and friendship.

However, as I grew up, formed bonds outside the family, became a friend, a leader, and a mother, applying all these learnings became inherent in me.

It took me a long time to understand the value and greatness of growing up in this fantastic nucleus with such solid values, and now I am aware of it, and I think it's wonderful!

It's incredible to be able to constantly be a small step on their life's staircase and on the lives of other people around me, especially women, in different ways. And I say especially women because it is with them that I feel most comfortable and relevant in being able to bring a word, a gesture, advice that makes sense, creating contribution and having exchanges.

I have learned that small acts have great value. Whether it's in that tight hug, that genuine smile, that hello on the street or even that casual conversation on the corner of the house, a piece of work advice, the encouragement to a coworker, the outing with my sisters, listening to my mother's laughter or tears, conversations with a friend about her children, or recommending that new therapy I discovered among many other things.

In each of these small gestures I am contributing to these women and they to me, it is a reciprocal sharing. And that's how I want to continue for my whole life... Being a contribution to other women!

AND HOW CAN I NOT MENTION THE MANY TIMES I WAS PULLED...

Throughout my almost 40 years, there were many women who reached out to me, who gave me professional opportunities, who supported me, who helped me to make dreams come true, listened to me, listened to me many times in silence just because they knew that what I needed was to vent and they gave me that friendly shoulder.

I register here my immense gratitude to all of them for all the exchanges, for all the contribution and for making me see that a life without women around would not be so light and full of joy. I certainly wouldn't be so happy!

I especially want to thank the most important woman I know: My Mother. She is my inspiration and my best friend! She teaches me to be my best. She has taught me since an early age to help others whenever I can and that every time, we collaborate with someone, we are creating a solid step on the stairway of their life and ours once help doesn't have to be material, but it has to come from the heart. A word or a smile could be worth millions!

GOING BACK TO THE BEGINNING...

I didn't believe I would have a strong story to include in this powerful book because I wanted to find a grand story that could change a woman's life one day...

But now, after diving into my experiences and writing this chapter, I can realize that what matters is not a single grand story, but all these little fragments that have undoubtedly changed many stories!

It's about knowing that there is not THE most important step in the climb of our lives, but rather how solid and generous the stairway we form along the way is!

With love, I dedicate this text to my parents and my sisters!

LUCIANA PACHECO

Founding partner of Mirá Sustainability, develops projects in the Amazon rainforest, mentors black women. Former sustainability and communications executive for big companies.
Instagram: @lucianapacheco
LinkedIn: www.linkedin.com/in/lucianapachecos/

IN THE MIDDLE OF THE WAY, THE RAINFOREST

I look forward to the end of the day to repeat the ritual I love doing the most int the Amazon rainforest: boarding a skiff boat towards a smaller river. There, while the boat is anchored, I enjoy the night, without rush, and I try to empty my thoughts to be able to listen and feel the forest that pulses strongly inside me. The greatness of its trees, the smell of the wet forest, the sound of the animals... Everything balances me, transforms and energizes me to continue working for the good of that environment and its people. The first time I set foot in the Amazon rainforest, I said: "Everything I do here will always be small". I know that for a fact everyday.

Working with sustainability and investing in actions in the Amazon rainforest were not in my career plans, they simply happened. I was taken there, after a long journey in Corporate Communications with a lot of learning, most of which came from women.

I chose to be a journalist without knowing exactly which path I would take. Among other experiences, I was a producer for a famous rock band, I worked as a press officer, but I found myself in the corporate world, where I embarked on an executive career. I soon realized that my strong personality and insistence on saying what I think caused some discomfort in leadership. But I never considered doing it any other way. Companies are tough and they taught me to create a protective shell around myself. The problem is that I also became a lot tougher.

I led communications teams for large companies and shortly before turning 40, fortunately, I got closer to the sustainability area. It wasn't love at first sight. At the time, it was up to me to take over the area after a colleague left. Today I realize that I was in the right place, at the right time to discover the true meaning of my professional journey.

As a journalist, I keep a close eye on social issues, which makes me fight against injustices and fight for what I think is right. But I realized that to do well in sustainability it was necessary to go further and dive deeply into this new topic. I took a master's degree in sustainability at FGV (Fundação Getulio Vargas), in São Paulo. There began a profound change in my life and career . I got into a new tune that changed the way I acted and that reflects on who I am to this day.

During my master's degree, along with many years of therapy, I realized who I truly am. I am a white woman, with green eyes, daughter of a white mother and a black father, a man for whom I have huge admiration, a friend for all hours. They gave me a lovely brother and a very special sister. I was born into a middle class family in Rio de Janeiro's with access to the best schools and to cultural and international experiences. I have understood the extent of my privilege In recent years, and learned that I can use it to work towards more equality and diversity wherever I go.

My mother, Maria Helena, was the first woman who supported me, and today I realize her strength in me. She didn't judge me when I decided not to have children, despite her great desire to be a grandmother. She was proud of all my achievements, even telling me to take care of myself when she noticed how overworked I was. She was moved by my stories and talked about going to the Amazon rainforest with me, to see the work I was doing up close. My mother, a workaholic woman, the most loving mother in the world, who worked in education her entire life and taught her three children to do volunteer work from a very early age, unfortunately didn't have time to discover the Amazon rainforest with me. She passed away knowing that she was the backbone of my transformation. We talked a lot about it while hugging each other and understanding that her journey was coming to an end. We agreed that she would continue to follow everything from wherever she is.

The feminine strength in my family also comes from my affectionate aunt Sonia. Since my first job, she has always encouraged all my new professional steps. My sister Isabella, with whom I share every moment, gave a new meaning to the word love in my life by allowing me to become an aunt and also a kind of grandmother to the twins Joaquim and Olivia. My cousin Anna, my faithful sidekick, is always by my side, laughing, crying, helping me with every challenge and thrilled with each victory.

My parents raised me for the world, always telling me that I could be anything I wanted to, that I shouldn't depend on anyone and that I just had to believe in my dreams and go after them. I believed in this and I go through life making my own choices and conquering places. At the same time, I began to understand that not everyone has the same opportunities.

MY DIVE IN THE AMAZON RAINFOREST

While working in the retail sector and heading communication and sustainability areas, I noticed that I could take advantage of meetings and discussions in the company to bring the sustainability subject to the center of the debate. And so I did. I talked to other executives and proposed initiatives. I also perceived the marketing area – communication's rich cousin - to be able to take a fresh look at projects, with gains for the human society, for the environment, bringing more reputation for the company. From talks to talks, I gained allies who, like me, were proud of what we were building.

It was at this moment that the pragmatic and objective executive paved the way for a more flexible professional, willing to use all her connections for the common good. I understood that working with sustainability is like an ant's work, built by many hands.

Bruna Saboia was the first woman who helped me in sustainability. She was the area coordinator when I took over as an executive. There were many lessons that I learned with her and the main one was that we must always fight to do what we believe in. Together we developed great projects and became excellent friends. Up to this day, when people ask me why we have to do this and not that, I answer: "Because it's the right thing to do".

The strong technical base that I achieved at my master's degree and my daily work revealed the extent of our country's inequality. This scenario made me dig deeper into social projects and to work with local communities, primarily in Rio de Janeiro and São Paulo. I also had the opportunity to develop work projects in the Amazon rainforest and that was the beginning of my enchantment working with indigenous peoples and riverside communities.

I understood that this kind of work could help keep the forest standing and create a positive impact. I met fantastic people who took me by the hand and taught me a lot. I started traveling to the Amazon rainforest three times a year. On each trip, always staying at the local communities, diving in the 'Rio Negro', having many conversations and making connections with local population, I've developed projects that brought them income and helped us win their trust.

I continued to develop projects with the Sustainable Amazon Foundation (FAS), that brought connectivity and education to the communities that live in the middle of the forest. Therefore, these experiences have transformed me.

I started to feel moved by those people's stories and by everything that we were doing – something new that I hadn't learned after so many years in the corporate world. This experience began to reflect in my way of leading. That tough person, who demanded results at any cost, gave way to a more human leader, closer to people, who learned to practice active listening and has a more sensitive attitude – even though the necessary demand for results remains to this day. The big difference is the way I started doing it.

Every time I travel to the Amazon rainforest, I come back refreshed. There, I learned the importance of observing nature, of seeking answers within myself. I realized that it is possible to have much more productive days when I reflect on what I am doing and don't just act automatically. On the other hand, with each return there, my uneasiness increases with the experiences and learning.

From this perspective, the desire to focus just in sustainability became increasingly stronger. Designing sustainability strategies and inserting them into the business, with a transversal perspective and thinking together with the teams, has become my routine in recent years. Over time, I enjoyed doing this so much that my days became lighter.

I changed jobs and had another opportunity to be among incredible women, in a new environment, in a new city to lead a team made up mostly of women, already integrated with its own way of working. Not all of them were welcoming, but I met Vanessa Romero who pulled me in, teaching me the true meaning of the words empathy and sisterhood. With her very careful look at people, I learned to discuss projects from the perspective of what each one could deliver best at that moment. We achieved beautiful results together.

I began to go to meetings full of enthusiasm and cheering with the teams every time we managed to implement a project. But I also like to rack my brains when I realize that the paths are wrong. And in sustainability we are still making a lot of mistakes. We have a historical debt to black and indigenous peoples, just as we need to learn to truly respect the rights and desires of LGBTQIAPN+ people. We have an environment that screams through forests, rivers and seas against all the evils that man has caused for hundreds of years. We live in a Brazil whose social inequality is inhumane. But as an optimist, I also believe that we have a great opportunity to reinvent ourselves and start over. It is possible to do this in many ways and I chose to be part of it for good.

A FUTURE CALLED MIRÁ

With more than 20 years of experience in the corporate world, and a little tired of it, came the decision to begin together another journey. Less than a month after leaving my job as an executive at a large corporation, I had breakfast with Milena Herdeiro, a friend that I had worked with seventeen years ago.

Even though we have followed different professional paths, we've always continued connected, exchanging experiences. And it was there, in that cafe, that our paths crossed again and we decided that we wanted to return to an old project of creating something together. Once again I was raising and being raised.

The universe was conspiring in favor of that old project with Milena, who in addition to being my friend, would also become my partner. I soon started doing lectures to companies boards and institutions. As I told people what I was doing, ideas emerged and turned into consulting proposals. Over the next month Milena and I talked a lot. There were meetings, coffee, wine and lots of reflection thinking.

Not by chance, our personal lives were going through very similar moments; we were at a turning point and wanted to do something that really represented us. And, in October 2023, Mirá Sustainability was born, with the aim of helping companies and institutions to include sustainability in their business strategy and create a positive impact on human society and environment.

'Mirá' means humans, people, nation, in 'tupi-guarani' language. It arises from the union of two women that complement each other professionally and believe that it is possible to build a better world, based on justice and the defense of human rights, based on gender equality and the diversity of races and thoughts.

'Mirá's' future is to help to create a legacy, through creativity and innovation, thinking about the planet we want to leave for future generations. This is our cause and it is urgent, so we started quickly. We have no time to lose.

I go on full of energy, living this new moment.

LUCIANA PALMEIRA LANGER

Head of Customer Relationship Management at Banco Bradesco. 20 years of experience in Marketing, Communication, and CRM across various industries. Voluntary mentor.
LinkedIn: www.linkedin.com/in/lucianalanger/

GOOD GIRLS GO TO HEAVEN...

I grew up listening to my dad, always very loving, telling me: *"Daughter, don't question so much! Only good girls go to heaven."* Saying that I became a feminist when I was a teenager was almost a sacrilege for a girl who studied in religious schools in Paraíba*.

For those who don't know yet, the main characteristic of feminism is the fight for gender equity and, consequently, the participation and respect for women in society, aiming for equal rights and opportunities for all genders. And for years I kept quiet. It wasn't easy to express my progressive position in the patriarchal culture of the Northeast where I was inserted. The homes of my friends followed the same dynamics of this social system where men hold primary power and dominate leadership positions, moral authority and social privilege.

Even after completing college and moving to São Paulo, a big and diverse city, I didn't feel sufficiently encouraged. Criticism from friends, family, and coworkers made me feel intimidated. Who hasn't heard phrases like: *"Here you come, again, advocating for women's promotion... This will harm you at work. You better not mention your opinion to your boss!"*.

One day, my aunt said to me: *"Luciana, if you continue with this idea of feminism, you won't be able to get married. Is that what you want?"* Well, I have been married for thirteen years and continue educating my husband. I didn't marry a feminist, but every day I do my "preaching" and one day he will "convert".

In 2016, when Gabriel, my second son, was born, I found myself with an even more outstanding obligation, to ensure that my boy does not become a sexist man. I have a duty to teach him that we should all be feminists – men and women – just as I teach Helena, my eldest, and my husband, as I just mentioned. To reaffirm my belief that change in favor of gender equity needs to be in all environments of society, not just in the family, I want to tell you that on the same day I returned from Gabriel's maternity leave, I was kindly invited to a meeting in HR department.

I was so happy, expecting lots of hugs, after all, I had achieved all the goals before giving birth. My area and I were one of the best evaluated in the organization, we accomplished great things, with a lot of partnership and teamwork with the more than 340 business units of the company at the time! I felt remarkable. I was one of the top-rated executives in the company. Alongside my team, I had made significant contributions that are still being adopted by the company to this day. So, I was sure someone would promptly enter the room with a gift, a cake, and everything! And me, well, I was already preparing a speech to thank them.

Then, the Human Resources manager appeared and said to me: *"Hi, Luciana, it's great to see you again. But, well... I came to tell you that the new director of the department, he decided that for your position... He wants someone who's 100% available. And we know, Lu, that the first years of a child's life require more attention from the mother. So, you're being fired. Take this as a gift."*

I was shocked! I wanted to tell her that I could be both, mother and professional, that the dismissal wasn't a gift. It was a bomb! I was being fired in the midst of my postpartum period, still breastfeeding, in a stupid way, with an even more stupid justification. But I was so astonished that I couldn't say anything, all that came out was: *"Oxente!"*

The "catastrophe" of being fired left me depressed. I went through a painful postpartum period. I lost 15 kilos in a few days, just like magic! People would say: *"Wow, you look great, you don't even look like you've had a baby."* They didn't know that my thinness, considered a desirable attribute, was actually a result of great suffering. We don't always realize what lies behind the stereotypes we value so much!

I also became part of the sad statistic revealed by Getúlio Vargas Foundation, which shows that, depending on education, up to 50% of women lose their jobs after maternity leave in Brazil. I couldn't stop thinking: *"What about everything I gave to this company all these years? And the awards the organization received because of the hard work of a team I developed?"* Meritocracy seemed like the biggest fake news at that moment. But I couldn't stay inert. Between one cry and another, I focused on what I needed to develop and I structured a career plan with clear objectives to be achieved. I went after them, drooling, like a wolf that sees a bunny in the forest and is eager to devour it!

At the same time, I knew that when the judge blew the whistle for the race of life, I had taken many steps ahead. After all, I am white, upper-middle class, have degrees from the best colleges in the country, am married, cisgender, heterosexual... All of this, in Brazil, brings a series of social advantages. So, even as a woman, a northeastern

Brazilian, and a mother of two, I knew that soon enough, I would be well employed again.

The thing is, the certainty that it would be much easier for me was causing me enormous discomfort. I remembered Audre Lorde: *"I am not free while any woman is unfree, even when her shackles are very different from my own."* That's why on the day I was fired, I suffered not only for myself but for all women, especially those belonging to marginalized groups.

And what about them? What about those who were left behind? What about those who saw their promotion to a leadership position postponed or never happen because their boss chose another man to move up, often due to unconscious biases? These questions kept swirling in my head, and it was in the midst of so much suffering that I founded my purpose: helping other women get there!

As I could predict, shortly after, I had already returned to work, very well repositioned, even better than before. I gained experience in other industries; I was the only woman to hold a high leadership position and directly report to the CEO at the second-largest company in the world for automotive aftermarket parts distribution – a predominantly male industry. That never frightened me. Today, I hold an important position in a highly prestigious bank that allows me to do more than my role, as a senior CRM manager, and to put my mission of helping other women into practice as well.

However, even today, when I share what happened to me, I still feel vulnerable. After all, people's imagination is still permeated with unconscious biases, such as: *"If she were truly competent, she wouldn't have been fired."* But I am convinced that women cannot allow themselves to be labeled. Motherhood does not make us worse professionals. On the contrary, it strengthens us.

Nowadays I understand that I have more than a job, I have a mission. As the philosopher and American activist Angela Davis said: *"I am no longer accepting the things I cannot change. I am changing the things I cannot accept."* Therefore, despite being molded to be shy and obedient, I can no longer be silent! Well, when I was little, my dad told me that good girls go to heaven. It's been a while since I've been telling him, with all due respect, that all the other girls can go wherever they want to go! Fortunately, he agrees with me!

* Paraíba is a state located in the Northeast region of Brazil. The Northeast is known as a more macho region, where patriarchy is still quite evident.
** Northeastern Brazilian expression denoting surprise or confusion.

REFERENCE:

MACHADO, C. PINHO NETO, V. The Labor Market Consequences of Maternity Leave Policies: Evidence from Brazil. Available at: <portal.fgv.br/sites/portal.fgv.br/files/the_labor_market_consequences_of_maternity_leave_policies_evidence_from_brazil.pdf>. Accessed on April 10, 2023.

MABEL FERES

Founder of VivaOmYoga.com
E-mail: mabeferes@gmail.com
Instagram: @mabelferes.yoga

TRANSFORMATION AND THE SEARCH FOR SPARKLE IN THE EYES

Sitting in a circle around the fire, we were all immersed and fully present in that unique moment. The harmonium set the tone, the mantras vibrated through the body, spreading throughout the space. Once the music stopped, everyone's expressions were of serenity and calmness. And so, I finished the first day leading the yoga and meditation program I had spent several months developing. I was initially restless about putting into practice what had previously existed only on paper. But at that exact moment, with the group I was guiding, all my worries vanished. Empathy, acceptance, and a unique sparkle in our eyes were present all around the circle. But it wasn't always like that, neither in my career nor in my life.

THICK DUST

That distant morning is still etched in my memories. The smoke was dense, and the air filled with dust. Some people were screaming, others were running, others were trying to seek shelter. I was in Broklyn, New York, Tuesday, September 11, 2001. It was a little past 10am, and the first tower had collapsed. "The other one is going to collapse!" "They closed the bridge!" Desperate voices filled the air as I pushed against the flow of people on the Brooklyn Bridge, determined to get closer to the World Trade Center. I had already sent my first photograph half an hour earlier to the Brazilian weekly magazine, Época. The image showed the North Tower disintegrating into a giant trail of black smoke against the blue sky. Now, with adrenaline pumping through my veins, I was driven by my photojournalist instincts to reach the other side of the bridge and capture the unfolding events. I did not even consider any of the risks involved.

It wasn't an almost visceral need to capture the photo at any cost that led me to photojournalism. Though I had to develop that skill to adapt to the profession. My first assignment at O Estado de S. Paulo, one of the main newspapers in Brazil, was covering the explosion at a large shopping mall in 1996. The editor sent me to the collective

241

funeral of dozens of victims. The mission was to photograph the faces of their suffering relatives. I returned to the newsroom with tearful eyes, a lump in my throat, and no "good enough" photos, much to my editor's disappointment. However, I pressed on and learned to enjoy the adrenaline of chasing scoops and fighting for the best angle in extreme situations. As a young woman competing in a mostly male field, I was eager to prove myself. But deep down, it was all just dust.

During the early days of my career, I worked the night shift at the newspaper while attending classes during the day for my master's degree at the School of Communication and Arts at the University of São Paulo (USP). I also conducted research, wrote my dissertation, and prepared my weekly photojournalism lectures at the University of Mogi das Cruzes. At 25 years old I was not much older than my students, and my energy and curiosity were overflowing. Life was a rush – and I loved it. Eventually, thinking that the madness had become somewhat monotonous, my then-boyfriend (now husband) and I decided to change things up. He accepted a job offer in New York.

THE PATH OUTSIDE

The 14-year chapter of my life in the US started with my arriving in New York for the first time amid freezing January weather. Our apartment in Midtown Manhattan was on the fifth floor and, of course, the apartment complex had no elevator. What a struggle it was to climb those stairs with three extremely heavy suitcases. However, they weren't as heavy as the pile of expectations, which quickly turned into a heap of frustrations. Everything was difficult: the bone-chilling cold, the culture shock, the city's dirtiness, and the feeling that the phone never rang enough. It was chaotic, and I wasn't prepared for it.

The difficulties were enormous, but opportunities began to appear, and I was driven to embark on new ventures. With a group of Brazilian professionals, we launched the startup NY24h.com: a digital guide to New York, in Portuguese, filled with fresh content during the internet boom. Alongside that, I worked as a correspondent for magazines and newspapers. Over time, I participated in exhibits, published books, and paved new paths in that place where, no matter how much you do, it's never enough.

We were in our fifth year in NY when I took on the position of photo editor at AOL Time Warner. Those were productive, creative years, filled with the pregnancy and birth of our first son, Victor. But they were also times of suffering and mourning. We lost five family members in that short period of time. And the distance made the grieving even more profound. The last person to pass away was my mother, diagnosed with leukemia when she came to help us with the baby. The diagnosis preceded months of grueling treatment. We spent our days, my mother, the baby, and I, in endless chemotherapy sessions at a hospital in Manhattan.

After my mother's death, NY became an even darker place for us. We had already been considering seeking a better quality of life when an opportunity arose in San Francisco. The three of us packed up and moved there. It required a lot of adaptation and brought new interests and challenges. One of the biggest challenges was the three miscarriages we went through before the birth of our second child, Bruno. Despite the obstacles, life continued to bring challenges and also great rewards.

I kept my position at Time Warner and, during a work trip to New York in January 2007, I was invited to photograph an up-and-coming English artist who was in the AOL studio to record a podcast for the launch of her first album. Her presence was impressive, and her heavy eye makeup and distinctive hairstyle were striking. In the small studio, there were only the producer, the cameraman, the sound technician, the guitarist, and me. As she began to sing "Back to Black" a cappella, I felt every hair on my body stand on end. By the time she sang "Rehab," my eyes were teary. Her voice sounded like a whole orchestra. The camera clicks came out trembling. After that day, Amy Winehouse became the only voice heard on all the radios in New York. Despite her eventual tragic end, that day in the Studio remains a memorable moment for me.

At that time, I already understood - and sought - what I loved photographing the most:

> *portraits. Portraits offer the possibility to see the truest essence of people, the subtle sparkle in their eyes that manifests itself between clicks. Throughout my career, I took hundreds of portraits of all kinds of people, famous and not-so-famous.*

THE PATH INWARD

I knew very little about self-discovery when I started my first yoga teacher training course. I had already practiced enough to understand that those few hours on the mat each week guided me to a state of tranquility that resonated in all aspects of my life. I felt a visceral urge to surrender more and more to that experience.

São Paulo was once again our home. I established Studio X+X with a colleague, specializing in photography and audiovisuals to cater to the editorial and advertising market. It was just the two of us, both former photojournalists, offering a feminine perspective in this male-dominated field. The studio went far, but we encountered several obstacles along the way, facing them with great determination. However, it came at a great cost and required a lot of struggles.

After my initial yoga teacher training, which I undertook without the real intention of teaching or changing careers, I couldn't stop. In a short period, I pursued two more immersions in India, guaranteeing my international certification. I spent over 500 hours studying in Rishikesh, one of the yoga education hubs and a place of pilgrimage on the banks of the Ganges River.

The continued practice of yoga not only balanced and strengthened me but also shed light on my own habits, attitudes, encounters, and ways of acting, allowing me to discern what served me and what did not. I quit smoking, acknowledged that I didn't enjoy eating meat, and alcohol lost its importance. These and other small habits gradually dissolved and, what's better, it happened with gentleness and without holding onto resentments. In this process, the frantic struggle to position our studio lost its meaning. While still at X+X, I started teaching yoga almost as a hobby. Suddenly, teaching became everything I wanted to do.

The dissolution of the studio was a natural step. For a while, I taught at various schools while still identifying myself as a photographer. It took therapy and a lot of meditation for me to embrace my new profession on the yoga path and let go of my identity as a photographer. The decision was influenced by my periodic trips to India, a place as intense as it is magnificent, constantly reminding us of the power and importance of spiritual development. It inspired me to follow the path of self-discovery, which had no turning back.

In the first year of the pandemic, I built a digital platform from scratch to meet the need for remote teaching for my classes. Viva OM Yoga became one of my most cherished projects. From the initial sketch to the completion of the platform and the growing participation of students from various corners, from California to China, everything flowed with an unprecedented naturalness in my life. The feeling of being on the right path and in perfect balance had never been so clear. Special projects took shape, such as "Integral Professional," aimed at managing anxiety through yoga and meditation, which I put into practice at the Women's Hospital in Rio, collaborating in the comprehensive health recovery of nurses dedicating themselves to women in fragile situations.

THE SEARCH FOR THE SPARKLE IN THE EYES

When I started this retrospective, I imagined I would be telling a story of career transformation. After all, I had spent over 20 years working in photography, constantly reinventing myself: from being a photojournalist and professor in the 1990s to working as a correspondent, an entrepreneur, a documentary filmmaker, a photo editor, a businesswoman and a commercial photographer. With each change, there was a complete reinvention that culminated in the biggest one. Eight years ago, at the age of 45, I left photography behind and embraced yoga as both a professional practice and a way of life.

An important lesson I learned is that even seemingly extreme changes do not mean starting from scratch. The new career began with more confidence and many more emotional and professional resources. I brought together the creative, academic, and corporate experiences I had previously lived to Viva OM.

Today, my work is a blend of many life experiences and lessons. It incorporates the methods and professional dynamics I learned in New York and California, the overflowing spirituality I encountered in India, and the warm connections I experienced in Brazil. All this goes along with my own vision, clarified through yoga, that helps me extract the best of each culture and transform it into something unique. It reveals that I am doing what I truly love and believe in.

I have arrived at this point with the clear objective of cultivating, reaping, and teaching paths to a healthy and balanced life, both physically and emotionally, one breath at a time. And, above all, I am certain that I share this path of growth with my students. The progress of one is shared by all, in a constant collaborative, empathetic, and loving circle.

As I come to the end of this account, I understand that today I am doing what I have been doing for several years: seeking paths that are not always obvious, moving towards what makes my eyes sparkle. I am incredibly happy to realize that I am now doing it with a purpose rooted in self-discovery and the belief that well-being and happiness can be taught, nurtured and, above all, shared.

MARCELA MIRANDA

E-mail: marcela.miranda@seastorm.ventures
Website: https://seastorm.com.br/
LinkedIn: www.linkedin.com/in/marcelacmiranda/

GESTATING STORIES

Motherhood can arrive in a woman's life in many different ways. Some are caught off guard. Others plan the conception for years. And there are those who pick an already born child to love. That's my case.

I've built some companies over my professional trajectory, I've ventured and even founded a startup factory, however, my greatest challenge was - and is – being a mother. The journey with my kids didn't start with the gestation, nor with coming out of the maternity ward with a "little package" of a person wrapped in a warm blanket. It was not Instagrammable. It started on a stressful day, upon the return from an international trip, with an empty fridge and a pantry that lacked even a little bit of sugar.

The day was November the 9th of 2017, end of the afternoon, when two children, an 8-year-old boy and a 6-year-old girl, arrived at my apartment, and in my life, brought by a social worker. My kids came through the door of my home after a two-year long adoption process. I've often asked myself, if I wanted to have kids or to give birth, for, over time, I've discovered that these are two distinct concepts of motherhood.

I was born in Alumínio, a city in the countryside of São Paulo, into a simple and large family, which never seemed to stop growing. My Christmases brought together dozens of cousins (50 maybe), aunts, uncles, grandparents, presents, a lot of food, and mattresses spread throughout the floor for everybody to sleep together and to continue enjoying all that confusion. That was the concept of family that I knew and that, one day, I hoped to have for me. Carrying on the childhood dream of motherhood, at 10, I moved to Campinas, a bigger city. Working at 15, I lived in the US at 20. Back in Brazil, I interned at Compaq, a major multinational. Leaving with a new job, I moved to São Paulo's capital.

I was 32 when I decided to leave the corporate world to become an entrepreneur. At the time, I opened the first site of imported beers in Brazil and the bar, Bierboxx. Next came the creation of a few more startups, Grumft, Mediatech; CBYK, a technology company, and, finally, Seastorm Ventures Builder, a startup factory. I started in Marketing and TI, uncommon for "girls". GEM's (Global Entrepreneurship Monitor) research shows 55% of female entrepreneurs focus on cosmetics, fashion, and food. Female participation in science, technology, and engineering in Brazil is around 20%, per IBGE.

Having gone through the early stages of entrepreneurship and already managing more structured companies, side by side my business partner, who became my boyfriend and current husband, Guilherme, I recalled 10-year-old Marcela and her childhood dream of becoming a mom.

Guilherme's mind was set on changing the world, not on being a dad. But he agreed to take on the adventure of paternity, after a lot of conversation, which, by the way, put us on a new path: adoption. I was already 36 years old, we're at the height of Seastorm VB, and we had just started the fintech Trigg. Since I wanted to have 2 children, I didn't know if I would be able to get pregnant quickly if I had the age or the stamina for it. Besides, how would I fit the routine of a baby into my life?

More and more, adoption was becoming a real possibility and the best decision for this moment in our lives. For Guilherme, there was also the social issue, of so many children wanting and needing a family. It was a choice to be made – and I felt that the choice was mine.

I started studying this new world: the process of adoption. It became clear that it was not a simple and easy path. By September 2021, The National Registry of Adoptions (SNA) had over 46 thousand habilitated candidates and approximately 6 thousand children and teenagers available for adoption. In some cases, the process could take months, even years to be concluded. And what is the reason for the disparity between the number of habilitated candidates and the quantity of children and teenagers available?

Because most are after an idealized profile: they want babies up to 2 years old, white, healthy and without brothers. And these children are not available! Those who don't fit this profile stay in shelters waiting for a family. And, the more time passes, the bigger the child gets, and lower are the odds of adoption. What we most find in the registry are children above the age of 7, groups of siblings and children with special needs, many of them who've had contact with HIV, who possess hydrocephaly, or some kind of disorder.

And here I started a journey: I entered support groups for adoption, I started to read reports and stories – some of them very happy, others incredibly sad. When a child arrives with a family, notwithstanding what has befallen her up to then, it is imponderable: anything can happen, even if she receives all the love possible. That's because, with the child, comes a whole lot of pain, rebellion, doubts, trauma, and the fear of being abandoned again. By the way, a fear that stays forever with adopted people, with triggers that bring back that same anguish, even when they are inserted in structured and loving families.

I decided to follow that path. I was sure I wanted to be a mother, and giving birth was not a priority. For Guilherme, it was always the choice. For me, it was a path slowly built. And, since we'd opted for adoption, we decided to take on a large family. We'd accept up to 3 siblings, with the oldest, at the most, being 7 years old.

The process started in 2015. We're evaluated in all ways possible. Documents, aptitudes, emotional, social, and financial conditions. We received many visits from psychologists and social workers, as well as individual and couples' interviews.

In January 2017, over a year after having begun the process, we finally made it into the SNA. It's then that we got to a difficult part. Choosing the profile of the child you want to have; what's the color of the skin, of the eyes, the acceptable level of infirmities, gender, race, region of origin, ethnicities, number of siblings. It's not the best part of the process, but it's an analysis of everything we'd be capable of living with and for them.

In August of the same year, we received a call from the social worker. They'd found a couple of siblings, and she was sure of one thing, they were our kids, even though the oldest was about to turn 8 and the youngest was 6. She suggested we meet the children, no strings attached, at an event that would take place at the shelter they were staying at. It need not be said that, though they hadn't been born from me, they'd been born for me. It was my childhood dream finally coming true.

The time estimate for the judge to clear the children to be sent home with us was January 2018, with the possibility of them arriving for Christmas. During the adaptation phase, we stayed with them every weekend, with them returning to the shelter for the rest of the week. We had even found a new apartment to be remodeled in time for the definite arrival.

At the same time, we're scaling Trigg, which was going full steam ahead, with daily work hours of 18 hours. A business trip to Israel came up, and we let the judge know that we'd stay away for 2 weeks in October. Everything proper and in perfect order. Right? Of course not! On a Thursday in Tel Aviv, my phone rang. The social worker informed me that the judge had approved the children to come live with us, and we could pick them up. That same day.

Panic and joy, all mixed together. I informed them that we're only scheduled to return to Brazil in 10 days. The social worker gave us an ultimatum: if we didn't pick up the kids by November the 9th, we'd have to wait until January because the judge would go on vacation and then be on recess. We got off the plane in Brazil on the 9th, at 7 a.m., and by 4 p.m., I had two kids. They had no clothes in their bags, and I had no food in the fridge. "Mom, we're kind of poor, aren't we? We don't even have sugar", said my daughter, on her first day home.

As many say, every positive has its negative, Yin-Yang, black and white, night and day, the sun, and the rain. With my dream also came... my nightmare.

REAL MOTHERHOOD

About the kids: they are amazing! Of all the problems we could have had, we had only the simplest, the easiest. They arrived and embraced the whole family: parents, cousins, uncles, aunts, and grandparents. They wanted endless love, and that's what they got. Polite, studious, adaptable, fun, eager to explore the world and discover life. On the first trip to the mall, they rode the escalator for 15 minutes straight. They loved the first day at the new school.

They were fascinated by the buildings and traffic in São Paulo. They also arrived filled with fear, uncertainties, and doubts. They questioned, tested, doubted, argued, cried, pouted, got angry and screamed. Even today. But They never doubted that they are absolutely loved and that they were seriously wanted.

About Gui: He, who didn't want to be a father, became a great dad. He taught them about stars, the sea, and respect. He taught them how to ride a bicycle and how to deal with technology. He drew a family tree to explain our family and introduced our values. And today, he is certain that he would do it all over again.

About me: I simply freaked out! When I saw myself responsible for 2 kids, I thought I was never going to relax again, never take my eyes off them or divert my attention.

In my mind, I needed to accelerate their lives, to make up for all the lost time, to live 7 years in 1. They had to ride a bike, to dance, to learn to swim, to be good students, to speak properly, to eat with the proper silverware, to read daily, to eat healthy, to play soccer, to have friends, to spend time with the cousins and grandparents, to visit Disney. All at the same time. I forgot to breathe!

I stopped being a daughter, a wife, a woman. I could only be a mother. My marriage survived because Guilherme held things together. I would cry in the shower, questioning what I had done with my life. Then I would wipe away the tears and help them with their homework.

Everything became heavy. I set my motherhood bar way too high. I think I didn't have a bout of depression nor burnt-out because I wouldn't allow myself to get sick, tired, or dispirited. I was always smiling, however, deep down, I wanted to disappear. Leave my 650 square feet apartment and go back to my first 105 square feet apartment.

I couldn't understand how my friends enjoyed being mothers, even had fun with it and I found it "a drag." Everything I did was to ensure that they reached a standard of excellence. However, where would I draw the line? I had no idea. I dove deep into work, directing all my energies to build an incredible company. And, if I could, I would stay at the office and not return home.

Until the pandemic came, and I had to lock myself at home with them. What for many was a torment, staying locked at home with their own families, for us was a chance at redemption and to get closer again. We (re)discovered and (re)connected with each other. We left São Paulo and moved to a house in the countryside. I may have reconnected myself with the 10-year-old Marcela. I learned to observe and understand the signs in my children, which had been invisible until then. I started to see and understand the differences between them. I finally relaxed.

I lowered my expectations and demands, started to enjoy family moments and small pleasures, like having lunch together and playing ball in the backyard. I started smiling more with them and for them.

It took a lot of therapy, a pandemic, and many hugs from my children for me to finally give birth to the mother who had always lived within me. And sugar has never been lacking again...

References:

GEM - https://ibqp.org.br/gem/
IBGE - https://www.ibge.gov.br
SNA - https://www.cnj.jus.br/sna/

MARGARIDA YASSUDA

President BPW Brazil (2020-2022) Vice President Women for Water Partnership (2017-2022)
Representative of Brazil – G20 EMPOWER (2020-2023)
Instagram: @margaridayassuda
LinkedIn: www.linkedin.com/in/margaridayassuda

LEADING IN A TIME OF GLOBAL CRISIS

"We can't achieve changes just by wishing for it. Change requires deliberate control of force. It can occur through revolution, but it can also happen through thoughtful planning, carried out with purpose and determination."

I begin this chapter with the vision of change from a visionary woman who inspires me greatly: Lena Madesin Phillips, founder of BPW Business & Professional Women in 1930, who always fought for women's rights in all spheres. Lena used to talk about change, which on a very essential level is at the heart of the story I have chosen to tell you.

I have been a member of BPW (Business & Professional Women) an international organization for more than 20 years. It brings together women from all working sectors across 100 countries, offers networking and business opportunities, and has consultative status at the United Nations. On International Women's Day (March 2023), I met Natasha de Caiado Castro in a queue at the UN in New York. She brought me into a great group of women called "Rise and Raise Others". I'm always up for a challenge, whether it is big or small. That is why I accepted to write a condensed version of my history. I'm grateful to Natasha for motivating and inspiring me!

In late 2019, without any prior ambition I was elected the national President of BPW Brazil. My term began in January 2020 with a three-year strategic plan already in place. However, on March 19, we were hit with a shock: Covid 19, "lock down", a worldwide pandemic declared by the World Health Organization.

Days before the pandemic was declared, some BPW members and I enjoyed an almost empty Manhattan. The city lacked tourists, and numerous restaurants, bars and museums were empty or closed.   The memories of those moments with our friends will stay with us forever, considering that we had not travelled abroad for more than two years.

Returning to Brazil, I had to face as President this terrible reality. I felt the atmosphere that had settled in the minds of many members. A lot of fear, insecurity, restlessness in the face of this invisible enemy. Since the virus was severe in certain regions of Brazil, we could not be inert, waiting for it to end. We needed to inspire dynamism, optimism, hope, and most importantly, "unity" among all members, regardless of distance.

Thanks to the generosity of some high-savvy associates, we connected via WhatsApp and provided training for new users on how to use Zoom, YouTube, Instagram, and other online tools. In case someone faced connecting trouble, many others were there to assist them technically and emotionally. Our motto: "No one left behind neither disconnected" We taught many members to deal with digital tools, run virtual events, and play as moderators and panelists. In short, it was a period of learning and exchanging knowledge and sisterhood.

Health, education, violence and abuse against women, the environment, women in politics, the 17 Sustainable Development Goals (SDGs), gender equity, diversity, and other current issues were among the many online events organized by the hardworking women.

Since February, before Covid, we were already planning the yearly national congress with the venue and date chosen. My God, what should we do, cancel it, or wait for the pandemic to end? The executive board and I decided not to cancel like other institutions did but to explore options. We moved forward, only adjusting how we would do it. We chose a national virtual event instead of an in-person conference! Decided, let's get to work, research the alternatives on the market!

That was our best decision. We planned to repeat the same operation in 2021, a year when everyone would still have to wear masks, limit gatherings, and follow other health rules. Brazil recorded the shocking figure of almost 700,000 victims of Covid, fortunately only a few members were included in this statistic.

Parallel to the day to day living with Covid, a small team organized the national conference virtually. We were dealing with newly learned technology and innovation, something challenging and unprecedented for all of us. Strategic planning played a key role in making both small and big decisions. This planning process, I must say, was especially enjoyable, pleasant, and enriching, even during stressful times. After hiring a technology company, we outlined our requirements: online sessions, in the evenings, scheduled for four consecutive days, each one lasting two and a half hours. The program emphasized multiple expert discussions, breakout rooms, foreign guests, simultaneous translation, and participants from all over the country. The trust and involvement of the nearly 400 members played a crucial role in our achievement. One day, they will surely share their virtual experience and proudly claim their role in the history.

I was very often in touch with presidents, national committees coordinators and associates. Many of the concerns and anxieties were related to maintaining their businesses that generated jobs, or how to keep their local BPW association active, very impacted by the lack of face-to-face meetings.

Once, a therapist told me that she had started offering virtual appointments after realizing that in-person appointments were no longer possible. This big change transformed her practice, and many other professionals began to rethink their business models. The introduction of this virtual services generated also psychological help and support to many women, whether they were BPW members or not, preventing bouts of depression and anxiety. Psychologists and therapists provided all services voluntarily. The pandemic made us rethink our lifestyle, and technology now is definitely part of our lives.

We experienced many virtual moments of sharing, learning, teaching, good laughs, music, happy hours, conversation circles and so weeks and months flew by. Who would have thought that we would host the traditional BPW Candle Ceremony, online, with hundreds of emotional faces lighting candles in front on their small screen accompanied by John Lennon's song "Imagine". It was truly unimaginable.

Leading a team can be a source of conflict even when you know the members but imagine organizing everything without ever meeting them in person and living in different states with different cultures. It seemed like a major obstacle! We had to overcome feelings of fear, unfamiliarity, and prejudice and stick with what we had decided previously. Clear goals, specific objectives, and set deadlines were essential to uniting them all. I am really proud of our great BPW team, which is made up of twenty-four clubs from all over country, and without whom our success would not have been possible.

Once being volunteers, all required attention and affection in their own time and space to feel valued, welcomed, and proud of being at the forefront of pandemic-induced changes. We had to understand the skills, needs, strengths, and weaknesses of each one, motivating them to do their best and building their confidence and safety. In essence, I was confronted with a lot of emotions that I learnt to overcome.

In many moments, I felt insecure and alone in the decisions I made but I always considered that we cannot please all the Greeks and Trojans, but the most important is to be supported by the majority. I have a strong personality and committed to achieving my goals. I think my strength comes from my grandma, the first great woman in my life, who came from Japan to Brazil at the age of 14 to start a new life and had a very difficult time, losing her husband when her oldest child was only 10, but never gave up and eventually became successful.

In reference to BPW's roots, the business committee dared to organize international business rounds with associates from other countries. Each participant would be given a one-minute elevator pitch to showcase their product. Initially, everyone found it impossible to present themselves in only one minute. However, with training, they all realized that it's about learning how to summarize and present objectively, clearly, and friendly. Those who were brave, at the end felt proud of their achievements. From then on, we began to better promote the business and skills of our professionals more effectively, showing that distance would no longer be an obstacle to doing business.

On November 2021, in the general assembly some changes of BPW Brasil constitution and financial records were approved online under Brazilian law. Additionally, the President and Executive Board   of BPW International were elected by voters from different countries and continents, demonstrating the success and permanence of using technology for group decisions.

During my presidency, two governmental elections took place in Brazil at national and local level. We claim that BPW is a non-partisan organization. However, that does not mean we should not support members who demonstrate bravery by stepping into this male-dominated field. Political awareness is necessary and urgent since women make up 51% of the population. In these three years, we witnessed women entrepreneurs striving to keep their businesses operational and, as a result of their resilience, several jobs were retained. In fact, we must have more voices in the spheres where important political and economic decisions are made and always affect us.

Time flew by, and in my last year as President we were finally able to organize the dreamed in-person event, postponed for 2 years. It took place in Campo Grande with the presence of 300 members, a record, plus the international President's delegation. We rock!!! All wanting to hug and meet their virtual friends in person.

For me, it was an unique adventure to head an NGO during a worldwide crisis, confronting the most diverse feelings and obstacles such as fear, insecurity, courage, pride, and hope. An incredible and outstanding journey. I hope that by sharing my experience, I have conveyed important values and beliefs to inspire more women to remain conscious and receptive to new opportunities, no matter how chaotic their surroundings may seem. No matter how fast you are going, look around, be aware of changes, and see opportunities in seemingly chaotic situations. Opportunities are always created by chance. Serendipity.

Throughout my journey leading volunteers, I have been fortunate enough to have had the support of many wonderful women. I don't mention them so as not to forget or be unfair, I would like to express my deepest gratitude to each one of them. Their simple yet powerful words of encouragement has allowed me to view from a different perspective and use creativity to find innovative solutions. It was an immersion within myself, in search of strength and serenity to overcome the various moments in which many other women sought comfort and security in the Organization of which they were part of. Thus, new answers and new challenges came, relying on some essential elements: courage, confidence and determination.

I would like to end this chapter with one more thought from Lena Madesin Phillips, the same one I quoted at the beginning of this history. "Women today ought to realize two essential things for their future: they must see themselves as capable, independent, and free individuals, and they must understand that opportunities are attainable. Nevertheless, they need to have faith in themselves, a distinct comprehension of their potential, and the bravery to accomplish it in order to take advantage of these opportunities."

MARIA GAL

Presenter, actress, and owner of the audiovisual production company "Move Maria."
Website: www.movemaria.black
E-mail: contato@movemaria.black
Instagram: @mariagalreal
LinkedIn: www.linkedin.com/in/mariagal/

I AM MARIA, I AM BLACK, NORTHEASTERN, AND A WOMAN

Since my childhood, I dreamed of being an actress. As a child, I would mimic the lines of soap opera characters, took ballet classes, and enjoyed going to the theater with my mother. It was during ballet class that I started learning about theater and became enchanted with improvisation lessons. To please my parents, I went to college, but my goal was to dedicate myself to an artistic career. In 2001, I began moving towards my dream and haven't stopped since then.

THE JOURNEY IN THE THEATER IN SÃO PAULO

Right after graduating, I started a professional theater course at Teatro Vila Velha, a renowned institution in Salvador. When the theater season ended and I returned to Salvador, I felt my heart beating stronger for São Paulo, and that's when I decided to go back to study. During this process, having already gained experience with the Bando de teatro Olodum, an important group composed solely of black actors in Salvador, I noticed the absence of black actors in the São Paulo theater scene. This led me to desire to start my own venture in this field. So, within USP, I created a group comprised of black actors, along with other colleagues.

Everything was developed in an artisanal and cooperative manner, but it was a starting point to unleash my entrepreneurial side. I remember that when I left for São Paulo, I had only a thousand reais with me. It was just me, my determination, and my goals. There were many challenges to overcome. I even rented a room at the time where the landlady wouldn't let me cook because she didn't want the house to smell like food, and I didn't have enough money to eat at restaurants. To get out of that situation, I worked as a waitress, even though I didn't know how to properly hold a tray.

Audiovisual in the Marvelous City

My interest in the audiovisual field began during a trip I took with my aunt when we stopped at the gates of Globo, in Jardim Botânico. I still have a photo of me with the great Ruth de Souza at that location. Since childhood, I have had the desire to live in Rio and work in television. That's why I moved to Rio de Janeiro.

When I arrived in the Marvelous City, I knew very few people. Looking back now, I can't even imagine where I found so much determination to start from scratch, carrying only a project in my arms. Oh, how much I needed a good network! I know the value it holds.

I followed my intuition. I arrived without any job prospects, always facing "no" as the certainty but seeking the "yes." The project was to stage a children's show that addressed respect for differences, based on Lázaro Ramos' first text. Little by little, I started learning how to raise funds and navigate incentive laws.

Beginning as an actress on TV

In 2012, I started with some small roles and then I was called to be part of a soap opera. The initial contract was for 7 months, which turned into 5 years, composing a very important chapter in my journey as an actress, not only because of the responsibility but also because of the size of the role and the economic stability it provided.

On the other hand, as the popular saying goes: "Good fortune in business, bad luck in love." During this period in Rio, I also experienced an extremely abusive relationship. And in those moments, if there is no financial stability, the situation becomes even more complicated.

"Your skin tone is not marketable"

In 2017, I was called to audition for a film. I kept progressing through the selection phases, spending the little money I had to travel to São Paulo. I remember how much I needed that role, especially for financial reasons. The decision came down to me and a white actress. The director chose the white actress because, according to him, "her skin tone was more marketable" than mine, simply because she was white.

What year were we in? 2017, full swing!

How can a director simply think that an actress cannot portray a certain character because of the color or tone of her skin? Well, this was not only his thought, but also the mindset of a large part of the audiovisual industry.

Although I was prepared for this racist attitude, I experienced firsthand how deeply rooted this cancer is in the communication and audiovisual sector, both in front of and behind the cameras.

People usually think that acting is all about glamor, but an actor is a laborer, chosen from the perspective of a director, a screenwriter, or a producer who often carries a RACIST BIAS. Of course, we are making progress. Nowadays, we see more black actresses and black leads, but it still does not reflect the Brazilian population, which is made up of 56% black individuals. How many black female talk show hosts have you seen in Brazil? How many movie posters featuring dark-skinned black women do you remember? Have you ever questioned this?

I realized that I couldn't just wait for the phone to ring and for them to call me because it never did, and I had bills to pay. And when it did ring, it was for situations like: "You're not approved because of your skin tone, or they're small, stereotypical characters." Like any other professional, as a black actress, a dark-skinned black woman from the Northeast, I seek protagonism, challenges, professional and economic growth.

THE ENTREPRENEURIAL SIDE IN THE AUDIOVISUAL INDUSTRY: MOVE MARIA

This weekend was a turning point in my life. After much crying and pain, whenever I remembered that I wasn't selected because I was a dark-skinned black woman, and the director believed that my skin wasn't marketable, a rage ignited within me that transformed into the driving force to unleash my entrepreneurial side in a grand way.

I had opened a sole proprietorship and this audacity led me to expand the company so that it would be able to produce audiovisual content. At that moment, my mindset was focused on creating projects and taking courses in screenwriting and production.

The name of the company? "Move Maria" - Narratives that shape the world. It's an audiovisual production company focused on creating and producing films, series, digital media content, and literacy programs centered around racial and feminine themes that are commercially viable while adding value to society and commercial partners.

This talk show was created, hosted, produced, directed, and written by diverse black women. Have you ever watched a nationally broadcast talk show with these characteristics? I express my gratitude to Gerdau, who believed in the project, in me, and invested in the program. Without them, it wouldn't have been possible.

THE GREATEST VALUES AND TIPS

I need to mention the importance of networking because, as a black woman, a woman from the Northeast, an artist, without resources, migrating to the Rio-São Paulo axis, it is crucial to have resilience, focus, and faith, especially to meet the right people who are open to offering the opportunities we deserve.

Yes, entrepreneurship saved me! This entrepreneurial spirit I developed started as a form of survival. "The phone wasn't ringing for me." But I turned the problem into a solution, a form of empowerment, of fulfillment, which brings light to many other Marias, black women from the Northeast, and women. Through audiovisual content, we foster new narratives with representation, both in front of and behind the cameras, and that are commercially viable.

Move Maria has synergy with a concept called impact entertainment, coined by Jeffree School, which aims to create the change we want to see in the world, moving society, our partners, and investors to take action. We aim to raise awareness and promote racial literacy through the new narratives we are building for the audiovisual industry, showcasing the real Brazil. Who benefits from this? Everyone! Our children and grandchildren. Our Brazil.

THE IMPORTANCE OF FAMILY

The first person who pulled me up was my mother. I remember her calculating how to pay the bills. This woman, without much education or significant job opportunities, has immense wisdom and intelligence.

She had to not only be a woman but also the head of the household since my father wasn't very present. She always motivated me! She enrolled me in the best schools, educated me, and inspired me to be the master of my own destiny, independent, to appreciate numbers, and to be the protagonist of my own story.

THE GREATEST DIFFICULTIES

In Brazil and around the world, unfortunately, it was only after the cruel murder of George Floyd during the pandemic that people started talking more about diversity, representation, and racial injustice. It seems like there was a boom of awareness, at least within certain circles, right? Because until then, for many people, racism didn't exist in Brazil, although for many it still doesn't. All my difficulties were within this context, related to various prejudices, combined with cultural challenges, adaptation, and self-esteem (yes, black invisibility takes a toll, making you believe that you're undeserving and that big goals are impossible).

One issue was my accent: I worked on my pronunciation to neutralize it, so that I wouldn't only be called for Northeastern characters. There were also many challenges when starting my entrepreneurial journey: dealing with bureaucracy, organizing finances, finding role models who shared my goals, and partners who empathized with my purpose and were willing to invest in my business, although this challenge still exists.

Regarding self-esteem, as the great Abdias do Nascimento once said: "Black invisibility also robs us of the possibility to dream," to believe that we can reach certain levels and be whatever we want to be. To break free from this daily invisibility, therapy is essential!

Another issue is the "emotional difficulty" because when you migrate alone from one state to another, you not only leave your comfort zone completely but also become orphaned. Orphaned of affection, friends, family.

I still remember, to this day, walking on Avenida Paulista in tears, with no prospects for the future. At that time, I couldn't even share the pain of hopelessness with my mother because she would have forced me to go back to Salvador. I had no one to turn to, no contacts, no support. That's why, today, as far as I'm concerned, I will make it easier for other women. I want to be a facilitator of networking, lifting up Marias and black women.

It is possible to achieve success despite the difficulties, as long as you maintain courage, focus, and faith. And to privileged allies, I have a challenge for you: let's build new narratives together.

Take the first step with faith, even if you can't see the whole staircase.

MARIA PAULA

Actress and Peace Ambassador of Brazil
E-mail: mp.paz@icloud.com
Instagram: @mariapaula_brasil
LinkedIn: www.linkedin.com/in/mariapaula-brasil/

PEACE AND THE ARTS

Confession: I am blessed to have an incredible career in entertainment as a television and movie star, theater performer, and a public speaker, but I have discovered that my most precious talent lies in making contributions as a communicator and addressing deep issues to people through humor and empathy. In my current role as the Peace Ambassador of Brazil, I have found my bigger purpose beyond entertainment: helping to cultivate a peaceful mindset in a country that uses violence as a way to deal with its horrible and shameful social inequality.

THIS PATH AND PURPOSE ACTUALLY BEGAN WITH MY ANCESTORS.

My grandmother, Augusta, got married at the age of 14 and had 11 children. Her strength and intelligence sustained the soul of our family. Even in the submissive role typical of that time, she laid the groundwork for me to become a role model of freedom for my generation. My grandfather, Manoel Soares, dedicated his life to his community. Our family's saga began in a remote region of Brazil where the religion of Kardecist Spiritism culminated, and my grandpa played a special role in its development. According to this religion, when someone navigates between the material and spiritual worlds, they are called a medium. My grandfather was one.

While my grandfather was trained and working as a dentist, he also helped all kinds of patients who came to his house in search of healing. He would enter into a trance and channel the prescriptions. In fact, he not only provided care to the entire underprivileged population of the region but also paid for the medications they needed. As a token of gratitude, people would send him gifts such as chickens, eggs, bags of rice, beans. Whenever my grandmother became pregnant, my grandfather would accurately predict who was joining our family within the first few days of gestation. Certainly, there was no way to know whether the baby would be a girl or a boy when no such

260

medical exams were available. Yet, he could tell! In fact, he claimed to know the spiritual name of each little soul that was entering this world through my grandmother's womb. My uncle's names are Labieno, Camilo Flamarion, Ayres Soares, Demóstenes, Rolando, Edwiges, and so on. These are not typical Brazilian names at all, but since the first ten children my grandmother had confirmed my grandfather's predictions, she didn't complain or claim the chance to choose her own children's names, knowing in previous lives they had that very same names. In this way, they lived in harmony.

However, during my grandmother's 11th pregnancy, my grandfather went out fishing, contracted an unknown disease, and passed away. My grandmother feared what would become of her since she could no longer rely on the generosity of strangers. In fact, a couple of weeks later, the provisions indeed stopped arriving. The relentlessness grew along with her belly, and a few weeks before her due date, she heard a knock at the door. It was Chico Xavier, who would later be recognized as a great medium, but at that time was just a teenager. "Dona Augusta, I am here on behalf of Mr. Manoel Soares, with a message he's sending from beyond." Interrupting him hysterically, she exclaimed, "You cannot be here to tell me that the son-of-a-bitch wants to name the poor child I am carrying inside, the very child he left in my care to raise alone along with the other 10."

"So sorry, that's precisely what I came here for. Mr. Manoel sends his respect and informs you that the girl is supposed to be called Gilka, and she will bear a dark oval birthmark on her left shin."

My mother, Gilka, was born with that exact birthmark, and the limited financial resources available didn't prevent her from being raised with love and care. She never had dolls or bicycles, but the entire town took good care of her. My mother displayed artistic talents from an early age. In school plays, she always took on the lead role, even if it required her to paint on a mustache and portray a boy to captivate the audience with her incredible performances. However, when she married my father at the age of 23, my mother gave up her artistic career. Societal norms at the time did not allow a woman to pursue both an artistic path and be seen as a respectable mother. And so, she chose us. Ultimately, my parents had three children in three consecutive years: my brother Cyro, my sister Cinira, and my other sister Guta (named Augusta after our grandmother). Seven years later, I was born. And then during a family trip when I was just a toddler, my mother was holding me in a hotel when she spotted Chico Xavier. She felt too shy to approach him but to her astonishment, as soon as he laid eyes on her, he walked straight in her direction. "Gilka! Have you moved to Brasília?" he asked. They had never met, but he knew her and her name. "Maria Paula will become very famous," he said. "She is a beacon of light, destined to bring lots of joy to this country."

Because I had heard them my entire life, I grew up considering it very natural to hear such stories, in which people would send messages from beyond and predict the futures of the little ones. Unlike my mother, I had the opportunity to pursue a career as an artist. Every time I step on stage or look at the camera, I breathe with trepidation and feel the energy of all the women before me: my mother, my grandmother, and so many women who were denied their chance to shine. I took my chances and influenced Brazilian girls of the 90's and 2000's generations, encouraging them to pursue their dreams.

I have always been aware of how fortunate I have been for my opportunities. I was admitted to the University of Brasilia at the age of 16 in the field of psychology. I had an early start as a public figure. At 18 years old, I was selected to be part of the first team of VJs on MTV Brazil. And then just as Chico had told my mother, I became famous as a TV star as the only female of the cast on the hit television show Casseta e Planeta (a Brazilian TV show similar to Saturday Night Live), and making people laugh brought me great joy. And then I became a mother. When my first daughter Maria Luiza was born, Brazil's Minister of Health invited me to be the face of their Breastfeeding Campaign. The purpose of this campaign was to emphasize the significance of exclusively human milk diet for the first six months of a baby's life. They selected me to be featured in national broadcasts, promoting this important message. On the other hand, the Minister of Labor surprisingly did not guarantee a six-month maternity leave for mothers. So, I engaged in a campaign to rectify this injustice. When the new law was approved, effectively increasing maternity leave from four to six months nationwide, I realized that my credibility as a public figure could be used to improve the lives of people in my country.

When my second child, Felipe, was born, I had an outstanding opportunity to be even more impactful as a prominent female voice for my country. The highly respected Fundação Oswaldo Cruz research center had successfully pasteurized human milk and invited me and my son Felipe to be the faces of the milk campaign, which aimed to encourage mothers to donate their milk. Felipe gained a "milk sister" named Juju, who was born prematurely and was struggling in the intensive care unit. Desperately in need of help, she received my milk which ultimately saved her life. It was surprising how quickly our campaign achieved the outcome of the rapid reduction in the childhood mortality rate, an achievement that was expected to take years to be accomplished.

While I was thrilled to realize that my work was bringing hope to so many women and children in my country, I soon understood that there were invisible portions of Brazilian population that required urgent attention as well. I developed a program to create breastfeeding rooms inside the penitentiary system and gave speeches around the country to incarcerated women who were giving birth in jails. It was overwhelming to get to know those women and learn about the outrageous amount of suffering they were being subjected to. And yet, it was so reassuring to witness the transformation of their relationship with their babies happening right before my eyes. I would say simple things such as: no matter where you are, the bond between a mother and her children can be established in a healthy and strong way. If you're willing to give your love and attention, it doesn't matter if you're in a palace or a cell; it is perfectly possible and essential to nurture that bond. In addition, I had the opportunity to work with countless NGOs from all over the world, such as the Smile Train to provide palatal lip surgery to indigenous children from the Amazon Forest.

The diplomatic roles I engaged in allowed me to experience unique situations including hosting Princess Mary of Denmark during her visit to the Fernandes Figueira's Hospital and escorting Queen Sylvia from Sweden on her visit to a center for abused children, where we highlighted the wonderful work that had been done there.

But the reality is that despite all of this good work and progress, Brazil has a lot of progress to make. We were indeed the last country on earth to officially abolish slavery, and our prisons are packed with black men and women. The nation still struggles to integrate our indigenous heritage, and we need solutions to these basic problems in order to set the transformation of our society in motion.

I'm surely not going to step into the big picture that includes colonialism and old forms of exploitation, but it's impossible to ignore that Brazilian rates of starvation are outrageous. As a Peace Ambassador, this means that I am committed to helping my fellow Brazilians to understand that we need to break the ongoing cycles of violence, and the way to do that is through cultivating virtues of forgiveness, acceptance, humility, honesty, and peace towards one another with actions that reflect those virtues.

I believe that being in a position of privilege comes with the opportunity to lead in order to create true change. I feel honored to combine my artistic talents and academic career to be a conduit of peace and to work on real solutions. I put in the time to keep learning and expanding my education and have also developed Danssage, a technique of art therapy that facilitates human interactions through dance and massage. I am the author of the nonfiction book "Ultimate Freedom", published in 2011, and I received my master's degree in mental health in 2018 at the University of Brasilia. I am a contributor to the ongoing project, The Power of the Character, published in 2022, where I am part of a team responsible of training teachers in public schools in Peace Education.

Confession: I call myself a "psychonaut". If an astronaut explores the outskirts of the vast universe, my object of exploration is our world within ourselves. Whether on stage, on screen, or in life. I dedicate myself to observing, performing, and collaborating in the construction of an increasingly peaceful experience in this journey known as life.

MARIANA FERRAZ

Sales Director for Key Account, C&C and Dufry at Diageo
Instagram: @maferraztoledo
LinkedIn: www.linkedin.com/in/maferraztoledo

MY CREW

Mariana Ferraz de Toledo is the daughter of Edna and Mauro, sister to Juliana, a proud mother to Betina, wife to Fernando, and the niece, cousin, and friend of a vast list of people that wouldn't fit in this book.

"Her crew is large, and there's always room for one more on her boat. She connects people, no matter how different they may seem from each other." This statement, spoken by a friend, accurately defines who Mariana is.

Living surrounded by people is a life choice for Mariana. She has a genuine fondness for people, a lot of people. She strives to maintain emotional connections with everyone, navigating through a busy schedule.

But this intention is not in vain. Mariana enjoys knowing how people are, offering advice, listening, building bridges, and bringing everyone together with the goal of creating a large family where everyone helps each other live better lives. Whether in her personal or professional life, she doesn't believe in a real division between these two frames.

Does it always work out? Of course not! But her crew never stops growing.

My Paths

Mariana is part of a generation of professionals who have contributed to the consolidation of the Brazilian digital market. Currently serving as the Growth Superintendent at BV bank, she leads the team and the digital customer acquisition strategy, an area in which she has specialized. In the financial sector, she was part of the team that launched Banco Original and later led the digital acquisition area at Santander.

Before that, Mariana worked in agencies that played a key role in the growth of digital communication in Brazil, such as AgênciaClick Isobar and AG2. In these roles, she assisted and supported major brands like Sadia, Gerdau, Petrobras, Natura, Toyota, and Bradesco in taking their initial steps on the internet. In the retail sector, she managed the digital marketing for C&A and the acquisition of individual clients for Webmotors.

MY HARBOR

I was what my parents affectionately called a "child with a lot of energy." I imagine it must not have been easy to deal with a little one who sang, jumped, and made a mess all day long, and, to make matters worse, didn't want to sleep at night. To be able to work in peace and with the best of intentions, they enrolled me in every available activity in the small town of Socorro, in the suburbs of São Paulo, where I was born and lived until I was 18.

Let's say it worked. I directed my energy to learn the flute, karate, chess, piano, and more things that I barely remember. But among them, one thing marked me forever: being part of the Adventist Church's girl scout group my paternal grandmother attended. The Pathfinder. Yes, even my grandmother Olímpia got involved! But in this case, I think she took care of me while I took care of her. I was trying to expend energy, and she was escaping from the mandatory company of her macho and alcoholic husband. My grandmother taught me to look for solutions for difficult situations. She showed me that we don't only live with those we want, and that people can be both good and bad at the same time. There, I learned respect, affection, and solidarity. I learned not to leave anyone behind—a lesson I carry for life.

As I grew older, questions took up more space in my life. Religion no longer suited me, but it was challenging to leave a place that meant so much to Mrs. Olímpia. I didn't want to hurt her. Even today, I can remember the feelings generated by my first dilemma. But it was time to explore other paths.

At the same time, in my mother's family, composed of various strong women but with my grandfather as the backbone, I learned that staying together—despite friction—is better than going alone. I learned from him that any reason is valid to gather around a table to laugh, talk, and why not, cry. I learned that memories have the power of recollection when experienced in rituals.

This gregarious heritage is so strong that I became the successor of the communion traditions of the Ferraz family. Even 20 years after moving from the city, I regularly return to Socorro to organize Christmas, family lunches, birthdays, baptisms, and even casual meetings to gather everyone. From this family, I inherited a sense of belonging.

I AM THE ONE WHO SAILS ME

The spirited and clever girl ended up in the first private school in the city. My parents probably thought there would be more support for someone who never stopped for anything. However, a few years later, an unexpected financial crisis seemed to put an end to this privilege. My father told my sister and I that we would have to leave school. But I couldn't accept it. I recognized the influence I had at school and had no doubts: I went to talk to the principal about what we were going through and left with a scholarship for myself and another for my sister. I don't remember exactly what I said, but it was a fact that I was convincing. I believe this was my first memory of taking responsibility and solving problems.

Socorro is a tourist town and therefore receives many people from all parts of Brazil. During my high school years, I made great friends from São Paulo, who were very important to start flirting with the possibility of going to college there. Every time I went to São Paulo, I felt that the crazy city completed me. Strangely, it calmed me. But what's the best way to move to the capital?

The answer came at a vocational fair at Colégio São Luiz - where my daughter studies today. I received a brochure about the course: Social Communication with a focus on Multimedia, an exclusive course at PUC SP. I had no idea what that meant, but it was communication; it must have something to do with me. Besides, it was exactly where I wanted to be.

I took the entrance exam and passed. The most challenging step came next: convincing my parents. In addition to the natural concern about their daughter leaving home, there was also the cost. My father even asked for a year to save some money to support me. I remember our conversation on the stairs of my house and my harsh sentence: "Dad, if you haven't planned it until today, it won't happen in a year." "I'm going, and we'll figure it out." And we did!

They fought hard to help me, and I also did my part: I got a scholarship, found an internship in the first semester, did freelance work, and luckily, I could also count on the support network of friends I had in SP. Thus began my life in the metropolis that I discovered was as crazy as I am.

In the second year of college, I started dating Fernando, who is now my husband. We wanted to spend New Year's Eve in Garopaba, Santa Catarina, a beach in the southern part of the country, but again, there was no money! Since I was studying multimedia, learning to create websites, something almost nonexistent at the time. We started calling dozens of inns and hotels offering to create their websites.

We managed to make the site for 6 inns. We stayed at one of them as barter, and with the money received from the others, we spent New Year's Eve. It was our first achievement together. But, there's always a catch, we didn't think that the pages would need updates. The new year begins, and a huge number of calls from the inns demanding many changes and many hours of work. After a few months without success in containing the volume of requests, I understood that there was only one way out: I threw away my phone's chip and changed my number. Thus ended our first venture with the indispensable lesson learned: the importance of project scope and its management. This was widely used in the following years in my career.

I started my career doing everything. If there was an opportunity, I accepted and embraced it. I did press clippings, karaoke subtitles, reporter for a samba school website, layout for an independent film cover, 3D modeling. On the outside, I was working hard to pay the bills, but inside, I knew that there was a ladder, and I was learning everything necessary to climb its steps. And that's what happened. I knew someone at work who then changed jobs and, after a while, called me to work with her. From friendship to friendship, from job to job, I got to know myself better and learned more about the job market. I didn't know exactly what I wanted to be. But I knew I wanted a leadership position.

In these more than 20 years in the job market, more than 10 were spent working in the business area in advertising agencies, and the rest in the retail services market, I have always been at the forefront of digital marketing and acquisition. I am a proud 40-year-old woman who feels honored to be part of the old guard of the internet and the possibilities it has created.

I am convinced that what brought me here was a great network of people, women, and also some men, who recognized in me the desire to achieve and gave me an opportunity. My determination, good humor, humility to learn and recognize mistakes also support me on this journey. It doesn't matter if the glass is half full or half empty; I will always try to find a way to complete what is missing.

I am from the world of action. I am always in motion. Tell me a problem, and I'll start running to find a solution. Show me people in conflict, and I'll set out to make them rebuild their bonds. This requires almost omnipresence and, of course, extensive and tiring control.

Not by chance, the first time I was in therapy, the label of "controlling" quickly came strong. The one who keeps everything within reach so as not to deal with something that doesn't go as expected. The one who seems to do things for others but does them for herself. To be necessary to be loved. Who never? It wasn't easy to recognize myself in this place. To recognize that light and shadow go hand in hand and that while I would like everything to go well for me and for those I love, I was also controlling everything all the time. But life is what happens while we make plans. And she had more to teach me.

Who Sails Me Is The Sea

What is the ultimate lesson for a controlling person? I would venture to say that it is motherhood. I am no longer the priority, much less my career. In fact, not even my body is just mine anymore.

I planned for a normal delivery, had to have a cesarean section at 39 weeks. I took a breastfeeding course, but my milk dried up, and I had to give supplements; I became the crazy woman with the breast pump. I hired a nanny before my daughter was born to ensure that when I returned to work, she would already be familiar, and I would be confident for this return. The nanny resigned in the first week I went back to work.

Babies cry, and we have no idea why!? I spent the night awake watching her sleep. And an hour before dawn, she already wanted to play, and I wanted to give her all my love. But I needed to get ready, work, organize her day. How is it possible to manage all this!? Where did my memory, my energy, and my hair go? Everything disappeared! I really thought I was going to go crazy. No matter what I did, I couldn't navigate myself; it was the sea that sailed me, and it had a delightful smell and a beautiful name: Betina!

How lucky I was to have bosses and colleagues at work who, for the most part, were mothers at that time. The mantra "it will pass" made me more confident, and the fear stopped when I realized that pregnancy would not harm my career when I was promoted during my maternity leave.

Having these women around me was essential and inspiring. Breathe and don't freak out! I understood that it won't be possible to juggle everything all the time: there will be moments when I will be a better mother than a professional, in others, I will be a better professional than a mother, and that's okay; it will be in the way it can be. But it will be with a lot of intensity and love!

The controlling Mariana, who had a 12-month agenda planned, ended up giving way to a more flexible, more spontaneous, and perhaps even a little lighter Mariana. Today, my daughter is 6 years old and challenges me every day to question what is care and what is control, and I love this challenge and the way we are discovering this together.

Ahead, An Iceberg And A Captain

Covid-19 pandemic. I, like all inhabitants of planet Earth, collided with a massive iceberg. Everything seemed so certain—my career, friends, and family. How do you suspend so many desires and ambitions? Who guides us when everything seems like fear, losses, and uncertainties?

At that time of the lockdown, I was leading a team of more than 50 people. All goals and projections were not only being achieved but surpassed. I was very fulfilled. Everything was so valuable to me until life is at risk, then the numbers become secondary. The company, for reasons beyond my understanding, decided not to adopt remote work, not to flexibilize shifts, even during the critical, pre-vaccine, phase of the disease.

As a people person and someone who seeks solutions to difficult situations, I fought my private battle. I did not accept the company's decision. I met with the team and created a work plan that would not jeopardize either the operation or their lives. The following months were filled with endless meetings with HR under a lot of pressure, and a team that responded excellently, driven by the affection of having a captain on this ship.

For me, the calculation was simple: what is success when an executive delivers the numbers but puts people's lives at risk for them? Not only theirs, but mine as well. Being in person kept me away from my daughter, my husband, and my family, who were sheltered at home. It's not just Covid itself that makes us sick, but the fear and loneliness it imposed.

I won this battle, but I also lost. After the storm passed, I preferred to change ships. I left the bank and decided to explore the exciting world of startups.

The position was higher, although the company was smaller. To gain the trust needed to climb this ladder, once again, I relied on my network. People who see me with generous eyes and reinforced the certainty of my competence. I climbed and brought many people with me. People who liked to swim and faced challenges with joy and commitment. All good, nothing guaranteed.

I found myself adrift. The way I take responsibility for people was not part of the company's culture. There is a thin but concrete line between being innovative and making the necessary changes for the business to thrive and being inconsistent and inconsequential. People are the heart of the business. They are the bureaucrats of the street. They are the ones who turn into reality what was once just words on a bunch of slides. Just as the famous yo-yo effect is not healthy for our bodies, gaining and losing weight at the frequency dictated by our feelings, it is not healthy for a business to exercise this same dynamic at the mercy of numbers.

This storm drained me. Without strength, I decided to return to my port. For the first time since I entered the job market, I was without work. But I say this only in the formal sense of work. Deep down, I was working on everything in me. I met myself and met many people, including this group here. It was intense work to discover how I could reconcile the dream of being a respected executive without giving up my values, my humanity. Although during my journey, I was fortunate to be led by women but also by many men who supported me. Here at Sobe e Puxa, it was empowering to understand that I am not alone. Women together, moving the indices that measure success.

But Is She Really A Captain?

I am a woman. How do I know that? I feel it every day. Sometimes in the skeptical gaze, sometimes in the requests or "compliments" that only a woman hears. But above all, I know that I am a woman because I do not fit the parameters of an executive as it was traditionally defined.

This position, until recently, was occupied only by men, characterized by a suit and tie and the necessary aggressiveness to override whoever was necessary. Of course, such an executive had to be stern, very serious, to be respected.

Not out of rebellion but out of essence, I couldn't be more different. My weapon has always been good humor. Even in the worst moments, I will laugh and make others laugh because I consider laughter a weapon of resistance. Whoever laughs stays alive because they can feel!

Putting this out into the world is not easy, but I was fortunate to work with people, both women and men, who did not conform to the standard and inspired me to create my way of being, and this way has humor as its seasoning.

I remember one of these situations now. My colleague, who is now a lifelong friend, and I were at a huge event promoted by a client for the inauguration of the system for which we were responsible. Champagne in hand, smiles on our faces, and the system simply did not work; it crashed! I noticed my colleague's legs trembling, pulled her aside, and said: don't fall apart! I'm going to open this champagne, and you're going to drink it in the bathroom. Don't ruin this makeup because I need your innocent face because no one will argue with you. We laughed while our eyes twitched nervously. We laughed to survive the embarrassment, and we survived!

Humor, which I have often criticized myself for exercising, I now see as a strategy for creating bonds. Humor has the power to melt hierarchies; those who laugh join the group because they understood, because they shared the moment. That is connection. I agree with Schopenhauer when he says, "good humor is the only divine quality of man."

In the company I currently work for, I feel free to be the captain I want to be, thus writing my daily logbook, collecting people and lessons. Accepting myself as I am, and therefore having more flexibility to accept the people around me with less projection and more affection. This is a significant challenge that I believe accompanies many women: being less rigid with oneself. Only a person who knows how to embrace and forgive oneself will know how to forgive and embrace others. That is the management

I believe in and seek because technology is the real input; people are the raw material.

No matter what ship I am on, I will always be navigating in this sea of people, striving to build results that make sense for everyone involved.

MARIANA MANIERI

Sales Director for Key Account, C&C and Dufry at Diageo
Instagram: @marimanieri
LinkedIn: www.linkedin.com/in/marimanieri

I AM MANY MARIANAS

I always wanted to be an executive, but also to build a family and have my close friends near me. And just like many others, I wondered if it would be possible to balance all these pillars. This Mariana here wanted it all, and giving up was never an option. That's what I want to talk about, believing in your purpose and pursuing it, because nothing in life appears or happens by chance.

THERE'S THE EXECUTIVE MARIANA.

My father was the inspiration for my entry into my commercial career. He was a salesperson, and I have beautiful memories of when I was little and on vacation, visiting customers with him. I had fun with the order forms and watched the relationship he had with the customers. I also loved going to the office, where I not only played with taking orders but also typed on typewriters and helped the secretaries with the photocopy machine.

My first job was in a multinational company when I was 15, as an intern, juggling administrative assistant and secretary assistant tasks. There, I did a little bit of everything. On Sundays, I also worked as a receptionist at a steakhouse owned by my neighbor. Even at a young age, I always wanted to work, which is why I started so early. Being able to earn my own money, gain independence, and help with the household bills made all the difference to me.

When it comes to being an intern, I understand. I spent six years interning at different companies before actually having a signed contract. I joked that I was the queen of interns. I learned a lot and even left one job for another with lower pay because I knew that this move was important to achieve my ultimate goal, which was to become a trainee at a large company. I was young and had the chance to meet more people and gain new experiences. That was a golden opportunity for me, and I always embraced the opportunities that came my way.

My father passed away from cancer when I was 17. He was the financial provider of the household, and his illness and passing made my family reinvent themselves. My mother, who hadn't worked since getting married, took on the role of a sales representative with my sisters, and I started to contribute even more financially at home. I'm proud of how my mother, my sisters, and I reinvented ourselves after my father's death.

My first sales position came at the age of 21 at Unilever. After much planning, my dream of becoming a trainee was realized in 2004. After six months of training and a quick stint in logistics and marketing, I moved into a sales supervisor role, still as a trainee. Twenty years ago, this field was much more male-dominated. In the commercial region where I worked, there were only two women: myself and another trainee.

I thought a lot about it when I started writing about my professional life, whether I had experienced any sexist situations, discomfort, or anything of the sort. But, in a very natural way, I didn't think about it. Some things happened, but I preferred to ignore them.

Upon self-analysis, I discovered that I unconsciously shielded myself in various ways. I wouldn't dare mention my age, thinking that besides not being seen as a more mature professional, it could trigger jokes. I also refused to wear skirts, and my red lipstick stayed in the closet from Monday to Friday. I was afraid, and these were alternatives I created for myself to try to gain more respect. It's the kind of thing you only really think about when you're very young. Today, where do you think my red lipstick is? It never leaves my lips!

I believe that this shield wasn't the best way to deal with the situation, but at that moment, it was what I thought was right. If I could go back in time, I would do things differently. I would fully embrace who I am without hiding behind sexist stereotypes to be accepted.

Male-dominated rooms no longer intimidate me, and I feel empowered by the experiences I've gained over the years.

I was in a good place, a large company with many opportunities for growth, but I wanted more autonomy, and I was in a hurry. So, my first managerial role also came quickly and at a young age, in a new company, Danone. I was hired by a director to implement the trade marketing department, and we did great work there, where they gave me the autonomy I needed to showcase myself and grow.

After two years at Danone, I achieved another thing I always wanted: international experience. I went to England in 2008 to pursue a postgraduate degree in Marketing. I came back to Brazil in 2009 and soon secured a position at Nokia, an industry different from what I already knew. Learning the dynamics of another sector was very exciting and transformative.

After that, I joined Mondelez, where I had incredible experiences working with excellent professionals. Those were pivotal years in my career and personal life, nurturing true friendships that still endure today. Almost five years later, I returned to Danone, now in my first role as a director. Along with this change in position, another significant milestone came, something that was still missing for me to feel complete.

AND THERE'S THE FAMILY, FRIENDS, AND MOTHER MARIANA.

I have long-lasting friendships. Friends who know my essence, stand by my side, and accompany my journey. We laugh and cry together. They are a fundamental part of my story.

My husband is an amazing man. The man I truly wanted to marry. Besides love and chemistry, we share values, a vision for the future, respect, and mutual admiration. I know I can count on him at any moment. I wouldn't be where I am today if it weren't for him. And I also gained a stepson whom I consider my own.

I have an indescribable love for my sisters and mother. I can't imagine my life without them. They are the foundation of my upbringing.

Speaking of parenthood, I became pregnant while at Danone, two years into my role as trade marketing director. That's when reality hit me. I knew I was capable of continuing to work, but I was afraid of no longer being seen as a talent. There weren't many women in leadership, let alone mothers, so I was certain that it could change everything for me. But even though I was afraid, I wanted to inspire other women, and I did it with great fulfillment.

Overall, I had a very smooth pregnancy, feeling extremely powerful by exercising my position while nurturing a baby at the same time. I used to say that my child would be born as a salesperson. I have several photos of meetings I conducted where other women took pictures and sent them to me, saying I looked beautiful. I worked until the last day of my pregnancy – I had a meeting in the morning and gave birth to my child in the evening.

It was a very special pregnancy. That made me feel powerful and energized, and I wanted to convey a message of empowerment to all my colleagues, which is what I want to share here. We should not think of not accepting another position because we want to get pregnant. A healthy pregnancy is not a barrier to your career. Don't let fear overcome you. It is possible.

I started at Coty upon my return from maternity leave. It was a new challenge, in a different company, and at a special moment, which was the mother's return to work. My debut was at the sales convention, where I needed to travel for almost a week. I told the company that I would only go if I could bring my young child and the nanny (paying for their expenses personally). The company was very humane and empathetic and immediately accepted my proposal.

I know the stories of friends who were not as fortunate as I was, and even people close to my personal circle who were dismissed shortly after returning from maternity leave. I also experienced a situation in a job interview at a large multinational company where the first question the male manager asked me was if I had or planned to have children. Who starts an interview like that? Obviously, I did not work for that company.

A few years ago, a few companies in Brazil began to institutionalize extended paternity leave. It's very interesting to hear the fears of men who decide to take advantage of this benefit. The fear of stepping away, of being deprioritized, of how they will return to work. It is wonderful to give fathers the opportunity to connect with the newborn, in addition to being a great support for new mothers. At the same time, when we talk about equity, this is a great example of action that companies can take by offering the same benefit to men and women. I am happy that at Diageo, the company where I currently work, we have implemented this practice. The men return very happy and grateful for the experience.

Balancing the various aspects of life is not easy, I'm not romanticizing it. But it is possible to have children and continue working as long as you have a good support network, whatever it may be.

Guilt? Did I miss out on spending time with my child because I had to travel? Did I not give enough attention to my family or friends as I would have liked? Yes, there will be guilt. But I learned to work with that feeling because I know that I give the best of my time to each part that is important to me. There will be moments when it is necessary to focus on a specific area. That's okay. Accept it and don't neglect others.

How did I become all these versions of Mariana?

I knew from a young age that I wanted to have a family, get married, have children, and have a career where I could progress. Everything I achieved professionally and personally was the result of merit, planning, reflection, trial, and error. I learned from past relationships to have more clarity about what the ideal partner would be for me. Age reinforced the point that we don't go anywhere alone. The journey accompanied by your family and friends is what makes the difference. I love celebrations, and I make sure that the people closest to me are by my side during important moments.

On the professional side, I always wanted to grow and be significant. At the same time, not having certain privileges at the beginning of my career, like not studying at the most famous college or not doing an exchange program, sometimes made me feel insecure when the interview process became more challenging. But I never let that stop me from pursuing my desires. I can be better than others in many other ways.

To make it happen, I pursued things. I learned to speak English by listening to cassette tapes, singing, and translating Madonna's songs, and taking every opportunity to speak English with foreigners in the multinational companies I've worked for.

However, individual merit alone is not enough if you want to grow. In entry-level positions, connections may not matter as much, but as you start to advance and your level of influence increases, relationships and politics become crucial. I ask you: how do men connect? Through post-work football games, happy hours, lunches, and events that we often can't attend due to personal reasons. That's why you should build your network, invest in moments of connection that make sense to you. I realized this more explicitly later in my career.

And I say this because ambition is important, but building relationships is essential, including having good role models – after all, we don't have to be alone. It's a game of influence, and you can and should play it. As a team, help each other, be genuine. The more women rise, the more we can inspire and help others get there.

I believe that it is only possible to be happy if we have balance, achievements, and joys in the different spheres of our lives. I am very proud of my journey, and I hope that my story can serve as inspiration for women who also believe in this mindset. Despite all my efforts, I know that I am an exception, and I want there to be thousands more exceptions like me. That is my purpose: to inspire and help other women reach wherever they want to go.

MAYTE CARVALHO

Chief Growth Officer Cubo NY
E-mail: maytecarvalho1@gmail.com
Instagram: @maytecarvalhos
Website: www.maytecarvalho.com.br
LinkedIn: www.linkedin.com/in/maytecarvalho

SAY NO TO OTHERS AND YES TO YOURSELF – THE ART OF SETTING BOUNDARIES

We were raised to be quiet, kind, and submissive. But besides that, we were also taught from an early age that we need to deserve love. In other words, that love is tied to performance. You are good when you get good grades in school, when you win a trophy, when you are praised by the teacher, when you win the essay contest or get into college.

And we believe it because we are afraid that at any moment, the person taking care of us will abandon us. And then we learn to justify ourselves, to apologize, to explain ourselves, even as adults: "I have to go, or else I'll lose my job!", "She'll be upset if I say no."

If you've ever thought or said something like that, know that you're not alone. I catch myself self-justifying or thinking that I should justify myself too! A little neurotic. Especially when I set a boundary. When I say no: "I don't want to go to that event", "I don't want to take that trip", "I don't have availability for this project." Here comes that little voice saying, "Oh no, they're going to hate you for that!"

I imagine terrible things that the other person will think about me. Deep down, it's as if I become that scared child again, who doesn't feel good enough. But the truth is, we don't need to prove our worth. We don't need to apologize for setting limits and drawing boundaries. Nor for our ambitions, needs, dreams, and desires. Even if they bring up the insecurities of the people around us.

We just need to be.
Being is enough.
Being is sufficient.

For a long time, I established a dynamic in my life called performance-based love. I always wanted to be top of the class, to win prizes and be recognized. All of that to be loved by my parents, the teacher, my friends - to belong.

The problem is that because of that, I would apologize before even speaking, I would justify myself all the time. If I turned down a job opportunity, I felt like a cruel person and would apologize. If I declined a friend's invitation, I felt like a witch and would apologize. I even ended up providing services for my boyfriends: making websites, writing reviews, becoming their career manager just so they would value me.

Say no to others and yes to yourself.

But over time, and with a lot of therapy, I learned to let go of that pattern, that unnecessary scheme. I learned to separate self-sacrifice from love. And that's what we'll do now: we'll learn to say no to others and yes to ourselves.

First step - Be aware of freeloaders and manipulators.
Some people will take advantage of your difficulty in saying no. Identify and list who these people are. Sometimes it's a coworker who takes advantage of you and overwhelms you, sometimes it's a lazy sibling who doesn't help at home, or a friend who doesn't know when to leave. Start setting boundaries. It's no use complaining and doing nothing about it, communicate and ask. What is your responsibility in the disorder you complain about?

Second step - Always be transparent.
Don't make up excuses to say no, as they will easily be contradicted by Instagram, mutual friends, etc. Be honest. Use nonviolent communication if necessary (fact + observation + feeling + request). Nonviolent communication involves taking responsibility for your own needs instead of accusing the other person. Instead of saying, "You were late picking me up, and now we'll arrive late to the event," say, "When we agreed on eight o'clock and you arrived at nine, I felt sad. Can you pick me up on time next time?"

Third step - Start with a positive statement.
Before saying no, acknowledge the other person's request and make a positive observation. Begin by saying, "I understand that...", "I'm glad you thought of me," and then explain why you can't fulfill the request. This way, it's clear that you have good intentions, and it becomes easier for the other person to respect your decision.

<u>Fourth step - Putting yourself first.</u>

Ask yourself: What do you lose with this? Or gain? Weigh the pros and cons of saying no. As writer Stephen Covey says in the book "The 7 Habits of Highly Effective People," "Every time you say yes to a situation where you should have said no, you say yes to the other person and no to yourself."

MEL MAGNUS

Strategy and Finance senior executive, investor, board member, mentor/mentee, life-long learner
E-mail: melissa.magnus@me.com
LinkedIn: www.linkedin.com/in/melissa-magnus

FINDING MY FREEDOM

I wasn't born free. I was born restrained by my context and the mental models of the generations that came before me. I dared to be different: I chose not to marry, not to become a mother. I simply refused to conform to my "female condition." Instead, I pursued a career in one of the most male-dominated environments I knew: the financial markets. And I succeeded. At age 44, I have never been closer to achieving unconditional freedom. If nothing else, I hope this account may serve as an inspiration to many other women who have not yet had the chance to tell their stories. And may it serve as a reminder that freedom lies, above all, in allowing oneself to be free.

I am the eldest of three sisters. My parents were born in German and Italian immigrant villages in the South of Brazil. My father worked for a bank, and my mother was a schoolteacher. Armed with their dreams, they decided to try life in São Paulo, the country's business capital. I was one year old. The move was not easy for anyone, especially after the birth of my two sisters. My parents worked tirelessly; and as the firstborn, I inherited the responsibility of taking care of the household and my younger siblings. At 8 years of age, I found myself in a strange place: not an adult, not a child, not a sister, not a mother – but yet a care-giver to my siblings. It was a role I somehow fulfilled until college. I often wonder whether this responsibility caused me to not want children of my own, since I had already practically raised two.

Over the years, my family and I moved back and forth between the south and São Paulo, so that by the age of 12, I had already lived in seven different houses and attended four different schools. With each fresh start, I made new friends, only to lose them again. Money was tight, carefully allocated to pay the bills. We grew up watching our expenses. There was not enough money for restaurants or family trips, but that didn't stop us from attending private schools, taking English lessons, ballet, and swimming. During the school holidays, we spent time in the South with our aunts and cousins while our parents continued working. Despite their constant absence, the one thing they instilled in us was the importance of education as the foundation for a better life and the path to financial security. With that mindset, my sisters and I immersed ourselves in our studies, finished high school, and got into top-tier universities.

Like any normal kid, I grew up drawing, assembling small theatrical performances, browsing fashion magazines, and watching music videos. I dreamt of traveling and freeing myself from the mundane routine of sacrifice and resilience that came with limited finances. I wanted to become a fashion designer, an architect, an artist, a writer. I wanted to explore the world! But when I got accepted into both architecture school and GV Business School, my father said: "Aren't you going to choose GV?" So, I did. I chose to specialize in Finance. After all, since the focus was on making money, it seemed like the right choice. I started working during my first semester in college, teaching English to beginners in my spare time. Soon, I landed my first internship at a bank, then another, and finally at Credit Suisse, where I was hired after graduation.

The world of investment banking can be fascinating to any newcomer. There was talk of the stock market, interest rate curves, trading, local and foreign investors, confidential negotiations, and obscene amounts of money. As a junior equity analyst, I wrote reports on companies listed on the stock exchange. I had access to CEOs and finance directors, as well as portfolio managers from major funds worldwide investing in Brazil. I worked hard, traveled extensively, spoke more English than Portuguese, and felt like I was part of something important. But all that glamour hid a pernicious dark side: rampant moral and sexual harassment, frequent pornography on computer screens as if it were wallpaper. Some men in the office would show explicit images to the younger girls aiming to shock, assess their reaction, judge, and oppress. It was common for older men to leave long-term marriages to marry young girls they had met and harassed in the workplace, as a rite of passage into the hundred-million-dollar club. I kept focused on my reports and spreadsheets, trying to distance myself from the environment. It was then that I decided I wouldn't marry someone from the banking industry. More than that, I didn't believe in the legal concept of marriage. I wouldn't let my freedom be restricted by a marriage certificate, and most importantly, I wouldn't depend on anyone financially.

After four years at Credit Suisse, I decided to pursue an MBA. So, I applied to nine American schools. I got accepted to a few, including Harvard Business School. I spent two years in Boston and completed my degree in 2004. The MBA years were tough: I was challenged by the course; it was a competitive environment and I often felt lonely.

But those years also afforded me the chance to grow into myself and form friendship bonds that would last me a lifetime. During my MBA, I seized every holiday and break between semesters to fulfill a long-standing dream: traveling the world. I visited India, Japan, Lebanon, Egypt, Indonesia, Malaysia, China, Vietnam, Cambodia, Thailand, South Africa, and Hawaii, among several other North American and European cities. These are cherished memories I keep close to my heart. Upon graduation, I secretly took as much pride in my travels as I did my diploma.

After my MBA, I wanted a different and better work environment, so I decided to venture into healthcare. I interned at GE Medical and accepted a job offer at J&J Medical Devices and Diagnostics. However, back in Brazil, my father's teachings spoke louder: I needed to make money. After all, I had the debt from my MBA and my travels to pay off. So, I headed back to the financial market. I wanted to work in private equity, where I could directly contribute to the development of companies. I reached out to the leading Private Equity shops in the country. The responses I received fell into two categories. The first and overwhelming majority were direct or veiled statements, "We don't hire women." The second category, job offers that didn't match my experience and qualifications. By invitation, I returned to Credit Suisse.

It was the beginning of 2007, and the Brazilian stock market was experiencing its best year ever. Foreign money was pouring into the financial system, and entrepreneurs, bankers, lawyers, auditors, and advisors jostled for a piece of the pie. And although concepts like governance and compliance seemed finally integrated into the work environment due to advancements in financial system regulations, the truth was that things had gotten worse. Ethics and "doing the right thing" looked great written in the "Mission and Values" statements, but were concepts far removed from reality. Anything goes when it comes to making money.

Soon, I was assigned to work on IPOs (Initial Public Offering). At the time, Credit Suisse had come up with a new type of bridge loan whereby the client company would take on debt before the IPO and repay the Bank in cash and shares at the IPO. The higher the Bank would price such stock in the IPO process, the more it would profit. Detail: banks are supposedly neutral agents servicing both investors and companies alike. This created a conflict of interest that compromised that neutrality. After two of these IPOs, the CVM (Brazilian Securities and Exchange Commission) finally banned them. One of the companies went bankrupt a few months after going public. An investigation was launched to uncover the facts, resulting in the arrest of company executives. Years later, the mentor of this type of bridge loan would have his name linked to the *Car Wash* corruption scandal.

In another episode, I was tasked with raising money for a company whose main asset was a farm that had been fined three times by the Ministry of Labor for practicing working conditions akin to slavery. And I could go on and on with the stories. At this point, I questioned myself: was all this right? Even if it was legal, was it ethical? Was this the only way to make money? In the case of the farm, I couldn't disguise the facts and escalated the issue. It hit compliance in New York like a rocket and after circling the upper management of the Bank, exploded on me. I was labeled incompetent and abruptly "fired," as if I were responsible for the facts. The whirlwind caught me by surprise, and it took me some time to recover. When I tried to return to the job market, I found doors closed in other banks, influenced by some of the same people who had fired me. I spent months at home in depression. I thought to myself, how could this be happening? I had done everything right: graduated from GV, with honors in one of the semesters, got an MBA from Harvard, won awards as an equity analyst, and was one of the first women in Brazil to be certified Chartered Financial Analyst (CFA).

I eventually found a job at an institution named Safra that posed a significant challenge: a commercial bank that aimed at becoming an investment bank. It was a joke to those in renowned banks like Credit Suisse. Even without a name, without a track record that qualified it to do what it was proposing, I accepted the challenge. And I made history. We conducted major M&A transactions, including the largest one at the time in the Brazilian pharmaceutical market, and participated in various stock offerings, achievements that put us on the map as an investment bank. After three years at Safra, I received an invitation to join BNP Paribas, a French bank with limited operations in Brazil. I had just been promoted to director, but to join BNP, I had to step backwards one level. They said it would only be for a year, but in practice, it became three. Even with a lesser title and limited resources – the team was small, and the bank focused on a few, mainly European clients – I began to carve out my space. Within a few months, I connected with my international counterparts and other product areas where there could be cross-selling opportunities. I understood where the bank's strengths were and how I could leverage them. That was how M&A franchises in Consumer, Agribusiness, Pharma, and Cement were born – franchises recognized in the market that expanded throughout Brazil to Latin America and beyond, putting BNP on the map of investment banks active in Brazil, much like Safra. During the nearly ten years I spent there, I made money, saved, and invested wisely in new asset classes such as CRAs and FIDCs, private equity, tax-incentivized debentures, bonds, startups, equity funds, and fixed income. At the age of 44, I found myself with enough financial stability to live comfortably for the rest of my life. I had finally achieved what I set out to do.

But that wasn't enough anymore; I lacked a new purpose. I thought to myself: What else does life have to offer me? So, after two years of reflection and negotiations, I decided to leave BNP. Shortly after, I ended a 16-year relationship -- a relationship that suited well the banker version of me but was no longer aligned with who I had become. I was eager to reinvent myself, my way of living, working, and relating to others. Eager to seek out new life experiences, explore new roles, industries, technologies. I desired a journey with room for my curiosity and creativity, a lighter and more humane way of being. And so, now I find myself in this next phase in life, much like being suspended in water: I look around, choose what to hold onto and what to let go of, but I can't clearly see beyond the horizon just yet. It is a place of unrest but also of excitement, discovery and growth. I always believed that life was too long for just one career. And I always believed in radical change. One thing I'm certain of: this new chapter, however it unfolds, will be on my own terms. And that is priceless.

MONIQUE LIMA

Co-founder and CEO Mimo Live Sales
Instagram: @moniqlima
LinkedIn: www.linkedin.com/in/moniquelopeslima

GET THE CHILLS AND HAVE FUN!

Welcome to my life in ten thousand characters. I'm Monique Lima, CEO and Co-founder of a retail technology startup called Mimo Live Sales. A B2B SAAS pioneer of Live Shopping in the Latin American market. I started working when I was 15 years old. I wanted to buy a pair of jeans and my mother told me that I needed to work to get it. She could pay, but she wanted me to understand the value of things and especially of work. I am a working mother; I understand that seeing my mother work ng all my life was an inspiration for me. Every time I travel for work to give a lecture, I tell my children everything. I don't say I'm leaving for work. I explain to them that I'm going because I'm building something exciting, and everyone wants to hear about it. I show them photos and make my children feel part of this new world I'm building. So, back to jeans... I bought my first pair of jeans after working at my mother's photography studio. Between the ages of 16 and 17, I worked in a shopping center in fashion stores. I understood that working was great, I got my money and, to be honest, I spent everything on clothes... Time to go to university. I studied cinema and applied for an internship at MTV. Everyone's dream was to work there at the time. Marcos Mion had "Piores Clipes", a famous show, Tata Werneck was joining the team along with Marcelo Adnet and other great VJs - which to this day are references of a golden age on Brazilian TV. I thought that if everyone wants to work there, it will be difficult to get in... I needed to do something different. I couldn't just send my resume and wait. So I edited a movie at the university, it was an MTV ad. I chose Billy Elliot's movie and made a 30-second movie about how the music made the protagonist feel free. It started with him feeling grounded and silent. When the song arrived, he started dancing and ended with a scene of him happy and kicking a door with the phrase "MTV sets you free". I think I did a good job. He gave me an award at the university. So I entered my resume along with the movie and got the job! The first cliché message here is: you never achieve greatness by doing the same things as everyone else. I worked as an intern for a year and then I was promoted to assistant producer. I did everything, edited the programs, directed VJs, went after new

TV shows and ideas... As long as my bosses didn't stop me, I was learning something new and improving every day. Second necessary cliché: Everyone is born with the "NO", so let's live our lives chasing "YES". After two incredible years on MTV, I went on a university program to study cinema in Madrid. So I left MTV crying... but I went to this new chapter. Well, Madrid... Have you ever been? It's my favorite place in Europe. Maybe it's because it's beautiful, maybe it's because it's clean, maybe it's because the food is amazing, maybe it's because of all this! Cinema, Friends, Gaudí, Good Food, Party Time and Fluent Spanish = Check! Time to go back to Brazil. I applied for a job at Schurmann Company. I still remember my first interview and my first impressions of all the places I worked. I remember that I thought David should be a good leader, a person I could learn from and I was excited about the possibility. I think you can capture if a person is good at what they do in a 5-minute chat. You can see if they have what I call a "punch". Punch is sparkle in the eyes, it's wanting to do things so much that you get excited just explaining and telling other people. That's why at Mimo I always have to do the "punch filter" before people enter the company. After producing 4 films and the pre-production of "Little Secret", I decided to try something new at an advertising production company called Sentimental Filmes. I love Cinema, but it takes a long time to get the money, be on set to film it and take it to the cinema. When I found out that in advertising people made a new movie every week, I thought this was my kind of place. Yes, I like speed! So, at Sentimental, I was on the set at least twice a month. Great productions for major agencies and brands such as Visa, P&G, Itau... Digital was starting to grow and the costs of the movies were the same. But since everything that went digital needed to cost less, we needed to build a plan on how to create amazing movies, with the same people, the same equipment and less money. Go figure...? As a doer, I am passionate about making it happen and working with challenges. I LOVE it when someone says something can't be done. It's all about telling stories. Every negotiation is about telling stories. You need to understand the gaps and fill them. In the end, we found a way to make a simple and great production. The concept "a camera in his hand and an idea in his head" of Glauber Rocha, worked. We also did some crazy live actions. Nothing will beat the day we made this huge live activation in a real football game for an Insurance Company, and while my assistant was being arrested for filming on the field, I gave permission for the action to happen. We had all the licenses to film in the field, we had 16 cameras scattered around the stadium. But the guy just didn't listen to me and didn't want to look at the contracts we had in our hands. So he asked who was in charge (it was me) and I didn't answer. At that moment I thought: "I'm a 26-year-old woman... he won't think of me coordinating an activation of 300 people". So I kept quiet and looked at my assistant - by the way, he had the punch - so he understood my signal and said "I"! And I felt the adrenaline of someone who was bold enough not to throw away a million plus activation and complete the mission I signed up for. I began to understand that I had an incredible ability to deliver difficult tasks and work under pressure. I received the proposal to go to this strange job description "we need someone to make things happen, regardless of the format" at the DM9Rio agency. I thought "this is me". At the time, the agencies produced TV films, OOH, digital films and digital campaigns, but not technology services and products. So, in less than a week, I left my parents' house (for good) and moved to Rio. The best part is that, in the interview, my future bosses gave me a challenge for a project that I had no idea how to deliver. And I told them I could deliver! As Amy Cuddy says, "Fake it Till Wil Make it". I had never entered an agency. I didn't know what to expect and I got chills in my stomach... Third important cliché: If it doesn't give you the chill, you're not building anything new. I was loving Rio so much that I didn't want to throw it away. So I had to get around it. I started to get to know people, ask what they did and why, and I began to understand the business of an agency. And one day that challenge that seemed impossible came true. It wasn't easy at all and it's an amazing story. But I don't have enough characters to write, so if you find me, ask me. After this project, I won my first Cannes Lion. I started doing several other projects connecting major brands with ESG, innovation and technology. I also worked with Coby Bryant, Serena Williams, Luciano Huck, Billie Jean King and other celebrities. We didn't just make movies, we did real actions. Services, technological products that brands still use. We went from talking to doing it. From DM9Rio, I went to W+K (Nike's global agency) and then to Africa DDB, where I stayed longer. Together with the incredible teams, we brought the first Glass Lion in Cannes for Vivo and UN Women, for MyGameMyName, the first Grand Prix for AbInbev with Tag Words, we did the first Beer Sommelier Course for the visually impaired, we made many debuts. In total, I won 48 Cannes Lions. Basically, I trained my brain to see gaps and think of ways to solve them with technology. So, when I look back now, I understand that I used to build startups for big brands. And the day came when I felt like I wanted to build my own business. It was at the beginning of the pandemic that no one knew what would happen to the world. Some layoffs started to appear and there I was resigning. At that time, I was Director of Special Projects of Africa DDB, I had an incredible team, a good salary and bonuses. The cherry on top? I was 6 months pregnant with my second child. Everyone said I was crazy. But I just had to do that. It was the perfect timing for the business. Live Shopping was already huge in China since 2016 and I didn't understand how it hasn't arrived in Brazil yet. We are the first to adopt social media. From Orkut to TikTok, Brazil is always at the top when it comes to social networks. So, I thought that if there is nothing here so far, this is a great opportunity to start. Pandemic hit, retail doors closed, brands and people will need it. I looked for a product and technology expert and typed a message in a WhatsApp group "C-Level Power Women" and a friend, Laura Florence, connected me to Etienne Du Jardin. We co-founded Mimo in June 2020. We did two tests at my sister's shoe store, Blue Bird Shoes. It was a very bad experience with friction and redirection to the purchase. But it was good. A lot of engagement and sales, even without a technological solution. That was it, POC proved it! If people liked that horrible experience, I had to build a Live Shopping in one screen solution just like in China. An important note: the frictionless live shopping tech that we've build at Mimo converts 30 times more than E-Commerce. It is indeed the next revolution of digital sales. So I asked to leave Africa and my former boss Sergio Gordilho invested at Mimo in the same conversation. After him I talked to Nizan Guanaes, Sabrina Sato and Luciano Huck who also invested. So with these names I went to the market and chose people I admire with complementary skills and offered Mimo's investment. We have a rockstar team of angels: João Pedro (from Play9), Natasha Caiado (Wish), Ricardo Dias (Adventures), Camila Salek (Vimer), Ricardo Natale (Experience Club), Andrea Bisker(Spark Off) and Daniela Graicar (Pros) are also our investors. Mimo is the main Live Shopping player in Latin. We have the biggest number of Lives done for clients like: Bauducco, Samsung, Wella, Carrefour, Bayer, and other 150 brands in more than 20 different segments. Our startup is a 3-year-old baby. We have 45 amazing talented Mimers. 58% are women, 37% and indigenous people and 51% lgbt+. We believe building with different backgrounds builds stronger products, we build for everyone. We did 3 rounds of investment, and we are only getting started. Mimo is my first company and I have learned more in these 3 years than in the last 10 I can assure. We have struggles of course, we face them every day. Last (not so) cliché lesson is: "Above all be the heroin of your life not the victim" Norah Ephron. So how did I do it? I read about startups, ecosystem, SaaS, innovation, people and culture. I talk to people I want to learn from. I am very effective when I am working. I surround myself with people that have complementary skills, that lift me up, that teach me. I am optimistic, always! I never say no. And best of all: I have fun and try to stir everyone around me. After all, work is not just what you do, and the value you generate, but, above all, the inspiring legacy for generations to come.

NEIVIA JUSTA

Corporate Activist Leader, Communications and Inclusion Senior Executive, Influencer and Consultant.
Instagram: @neivia
YouTube: Líder Com Neivia
LinkedIn: www.linkedin.com/in/neiviajusta/

LEARNING TO JUST CAUSE.

I was born in the state of Ceará, Brazil, three days before Neil Armstrong set foot on the moon. On that same day, Angela Merkel was celebrating her 15th birthday in Germany, and Camilla Parker Bowles was turning the age of twenty-two in England.

I come from a large male family: my father has eight brothers and two sisters; my mother has eight brothers and three sisters. I grew up surrounded by men. Being the first and only lady in the room was constant in my life since I was a girl: I am the firstborn daughter and had been the only granddaughter on my mother's side until I turned eight years old. I was the first tennis champion, the only one to score a perfect ten in the college entrance exam essay, and the first to move to England at the age of seventeen, in a world still 100% analog and non-globalized.

I have always been curious, brave, and ambitious. I wanted to conquer the world, the galaxy. I loved people, stories, numbers, and music. When I had to choose a career, there were no women astronauts, nuclear physicists, genetic engineers nor STEM students. I assumed those places were not for me. "You cannot be what you do not see," says my friend Duília de Mello, a Brazilian extragalactic astrophysicist. At that moment, I put my analytical side to sleep and invested in my social communication talent.

When I started my journalist career in 1992, I became the first and youngest anchor of "Citizenship Day by day", a live 2-hour TV program where I shared the stage exclusively with men. I was also the first and only columnist among seven in a new section of O Povo newspaper. "Saia Justa" became the most widely read weekly column in Ceará during the time I published it.

If I had followed the script written for a young, white, heterosexual, cisgender, and without disabilities privileged woman from Ceará, by that time I should have been making plans to get married and start a family. But that was not the life I wanted for myself. Not at the age of 23! I wanted to carve out a different path from the women around me. For that, I needed to leave Ceará, and I was sure it was impossible to balance career and motherhood.

And so, I moved to São Paulo, without knowing anyone, to pursue a postgraduate degree in Marketing at ESPM, in early 1993. A young and single northeastern woman, with no connection to the city, its culture, or its people. Free, light, and ready to author a real story, with ups and downs, achievements and frustrations, struggle and glory.

Soon, I realized that studying alone would not be enough. I needed quickly to gain a corporate repertoire because, apart from being the youngest, the only one outside the Rio-São Paulo axis, and one of the only five women in the class, I was the only one who had never worked at a large company. At the first opportunity, I landed an internship at a petrochemical company. Experiencing sexual harassment at the age of 24 became part of the learning package. At that time, all I could do was pretend not to understand, suffer in silence, and manage the emotional damage.

As I was about to complete my postgraduate studies, I was invited to participate in a recruitment process for a product management position at Timex, that was entering Brazil. I knew nothing about product management, but as I was fluent in English the CEO chose me and took on the role of my first mentor. And so, at the age of 25, I became a manager at the company behind Ironman watches, a sensation in Brazil in the mid-1990s.

The following years were absolutely focused on my career. I started a second postgraduate degree in administration at FGV and took advantage of a vacation period to do an exchange program in Barcelona and accelerate my fluency in Spanish. By that time, my first boss at the petrochemical company was working for Natura and recommended me for a position there.

It was October 1998, Natura had just been named the company of the year by Exame magazine, and there I was, taking on the role of product communication manager, leading the company's advertising area, in the process of building its new brand.

I spent a little over 5 intense years there, leading innovative communication work: we questioned beauty stereotypes, encouraged the bond between mothers, fathers and children, saw makeup and fashion as identity expressions, and advocated for the sustainable use of Brazilian biodiversity. At Natura, I learned that life is a chain of relationships, and a phrase from one of its campaigns has echoed in me ever since: "What world will we leave for our children, and what children will we leave for the world?"

I was working at Natura when I turned 30, and finally, I started to believe it was possible to balance career and family. I reconnected with Eduardo, whom I had known since 1989. We started dating, got married, and I became pregnant with Luiza, who was born in July 2003, 5 days after I celebrated my 34th birthday.

I went on maternity leave, and, during that time, I experienced the joys and challenges of being a full-time mother, sharing this experience with a husband who worked in Rio and commuted back and forth. At the end of the 5 months period, I decided not to return to the company: I had not brought a child into the world for her to live in Natura's daycare. And certainly not for her to live in an apartment in São Paulo with a live-in babysitter while her parents worked in different towns. There was no remote work, no hybrid model, and no flexible hours at that time.

I left Natura in early 2004 and became an entrepreneur. Alongside my role as a mother, I took on the management of a luxury accessories brand in which I had become a partner in 2002. I had the privilege of being present in every stage of Luiza's early years and, as Julia was born in September 2005. I continued with my parenting-entrepreneur project, learning new management skills: people and time management, conflict resolution and prioritization, among many others.

In 2008, Eduardo returned to work in São Paulo, and I decided to pursue an MBA. The girls were already in preschool with an organized routine, and managing the brand did not demand as much of my time as I would have liked. I started to nurture the idea of returning to the corporate world. When I left Natura, the prophets of doom told me that it would be impossible. As an optimist I never listened to negative voices.

One day, at 7:30 in the morning, I received a call from an HR consultant at Schincariol, saying she had a corporate communication manager position open for 11 months and she had found my resume on a job site. She asked if I was interested in discussing this opportunity, and off I went. A month later, I was interviewed by my future leader, who saw in me the talent he was looking for and defied all possible biases by hiring a woman who was nearly 39 years old, mother of 2 daughters, aged 4 and 2, and who had been out of the workplace for four years.

And so, I returned to the executive life. Happy and guiltless. Before my first day of work, I sat down with my girls and told them our routine would change; I would drop them off at school and then head to work, where I would spend the entire day. We would only see each other again at dinnertime. I wanted them to know that work had always been an important part of my life and that I would be a better mother by living in these two parts. We learned to cherish and value every minute we spent together in this new routine. We grew and strengthened our family bond. And, of course, I always had the unconditional partnership of Eduardo, raising our girls and managing the household at all phases of our careers.

In 2009, due to a restructuring at Schincariol, we would all have to move to a small city. I chose to leave the company and spent a year in career transition. It was a great reflection and self-knowledge moment. At that time, looking at the revolution that had happened while I was building my parenting career, I understood that I needed to reinvent myself, undergo my own digital transformation, or else I would become obsolete and professionally irrelevant. At the end of that period, I was invited for a selection process at GE, from November 30th to December 27th, when I received the offer to manage the company's corporate communication in Brazil.

At GE, I learned all I know about technology, built a brilliant team, and together, we led the most innovative 360-degree communication project for a century-old industrial-based company in Brazil at that time. We became a reference for the company worldwide. Also at GE, I worked for the first time with Black women, managers like me; I was part of the global women's group; I co-created the local LGBT+ group as an ally; and I was the communication leader for the company's first female CEO in Brazil.

Despite all that experience, I was still unaware of gender inequality in the workplace: I belong to the second generation of women who entered a corporate world made by men, for men, having to believe in and survive the prevailing male meritocracy with no place to report jokes, violence, and harassment, or question pay gaps, unfair evaluations, lack of opportunities and promotions.

In 2014, I assumed the position of Communication and Public Relations Director at Goodyear in Latin America and discovered that I was the first woman on that board in the company's 99-year history in the region. I experienced mixed feelings: the pride of being the first and the loneliness of being the only one.

It took me almost a year to understand the power position I now held. I was invited to a Women's Leadership Forum, and I began to study the topic. I was shocked by my own unawareness and, from that moment on, I was sure I should do everything in my power, with the responsibility and resources I had, to transform reality and make the world a better, fairer, and more inclusive place for all people, starting with women. All women.

What tools did I have? My communication skills, a cell phone, LinkedIn, and the courage to question what nobody seemed to see: where are the women? I started asking this question daily, posting on LinkedIn an image of events, boards, governments where only men were in leadership and power positions, often looking like clones of themselves, with the hashtag #wherearethewomen.

I soon discovered that the discomfort was not just mine: I began to receive images with the request, "Please post this for me but don't reveal the source. I'm afraid of retaliation, of being fired." #Wherearethewomen started to bother men, and they reacted with a brutality I had not known. I became personally insulted and attacked on LinkedIn: "Who did I think I was to dare question male sovereignty?" I persisted. The violence became unbearable, and I almost gave up. But I remembered a quote: "When you get tired, learn to rest, not to quit."

I started studying nonviolent communication and learned to shield myself from attacks. I understood it was possible to focus on the glass half full; if we are the majority of the population and in universities, have more education than men, and are present in all places, why do we seem invisible? That is how I created #herethewomenare, a sisterhood movement that highlights leadership and success stories of women in any field of society.

In 2016, sisterhood was a distant concept in our lives: I started receiving messages from women I did not know, asking why I was promoting them and what I wanted in return. Today, almost seven years later, #herethewomenare has become a kind of recognition seal for our success and activity as a protagonist.

Finally, in 2020, at the beginning of the pandemic, I created #LeaderWithNeivia, a live videocast program featuring C-level leaders, board members, and entrepreneurs representing all forms of human diversity, in total gender equality. Every week, I have 2 conversations on LinkedIn, YouTube, and Facebook. By the end of 2023, I will have spoken with over 150 inspiring women who show us that the success of each woman is the success of all of us. And that is how we continue to make an impact together, just causing!

PAULA BRAGA

CEO of Automotive Business
Instagram: @paulabragaprado
LinkedIn: www.linkedin.com/in/paula-braga-prado

WHO'S AFRAID OF BEING CEO?

IWhat makes a leader? What is a CEO made of? Many elements contribute to shaping a professional with the noble responsibility of guiding a company. However, for most of my life, it appeared that one characteristic stood as the primary prerequisite: gender. I could only observe men at the helm of companies.

Compounding my imposter syndrome is the fact that I operate in a predominantly male and traditional sector, namely the automotive industry. Need more reasons for self-doubt? My career unfolded within a small company, one with fewer than 20 employees, founded by my father—Automotive Business, a content platform, or a means of communication, designed for those engaged in the mobility ecosystem.

Unlike many conventional career paths, I lacked external validation. Over the course of more than two decades in the workforce, I began as an intern, gradually advanced through my studies in Administration, and assumed leadership within the commercial and financial sectors. In recent years, I've undergone a significant transition, taking on a substantial role in conceptualizing and executing the strategies required by my company.

For some time, I was the CEO behind the curtains, hesitant to acknowledge this role openly. I struggled to assert to others that I held this position within the organization. Gradually, I began to step into the spotlight as I crafted and nurtured projects that bore a significant part of my identity and passion. Additionally, this transformation coincided with my father's undeniable withdrawal from the company's day-to-day operations.

Every incremental advancement during these two-plus decades of work was solidified through immense effort, marked by the audacity to break free from the expected mold within my industry's context. Restlessness played its part as well. As a typical Aquarius, I have a penchant for looking to the future, initiating discussions, and striving to make an impact wherever I find myself. It aligns with that old maxim: if it won't lead to change, I might as well stay home.

I have poured my heart and mind into my work, in collaboration with my team, our audience, and our numerous partners. Beyond what may be perceived through my

CEO title, there are many facets to Paula. I am the mother of an inquisitive boy, the wife of my childhood best friend, an enthusiast who revels in physical activity and the sight of daybreak during a morning run in the park. I am the lighthearted friend, a sister to two remarkable women, and the daughter of a mother and father who inspire me every day. With time, I have come to realize that this journey only holds meaning when infused with my truth.

The journey also needs to be collective. It's truly remarkable to witness how my path converged with the perspectives and aspirations of other exceptional individuals who have worked and continue to work alongside me. Together, we've succeeded in shaping the company's purpose, one that I am genuinely proud to refer to as "ours": empowering individuals in the automotive and mobility sector with knowledge, enabling them to make the most informed decisions for the benefit of both their businesses and society.

Today I see that we only managed to reach this strategic approach because I got rid of what I thought I needed to be and became who I am. I admit, however, that I didn't always have such an authentic view of leadership.

More often than I'd like to admit, I found myself adopting the typical postures associated with the old-fashioned command-and-control style of leadership: fearing that I might know less than my peers, avoiding any display of vulnerability, and undervaluing my team's ideas more than I should have. It took me some time to recognize the importance of intellectual humility and use it as a catalyst for change.

Intellectual humility is the quality that enhances our ability to acknowledge mistakes, actively listen, learn, and relinquish our presumptuous and defensive stances. In essence, it should serve as a fundamental prerequisite in any profession.

This perspective isn't solely my own but also aligns with that of some of the world's largest corporations. A few years ago, Laszlo Bock, who was the global head of talent at Google at the time, stated that demonstrating intellectual humility was among his top recommendations for excelling in a job interview.

And, interestingly, for much of my life I believed that one needed to do exactly the opposite to be successful professionally. Even when in first grade, the teacher had to ask me to get something from the staff room or do some favor outside the room to clear my mind. I was a little girl who didn't blink, didn't take her eyes off the class.

It was at the beginning of my school life and the dreaded tests that I discovered my high level of competitiveness. I always wanted to be best in class. And so I was. I felt that winning first place was only up to me and I felt proud every time I got there. This fight with myself was very easy to win.

I pursued this pursuit of excellence all the way through graduate school, earning numerous accolades and distinctions along the way. However, as time progressed, that familiar cocoon of academia began to yield to a broader, more competitive world teeming with exceptionally talented individuals—individuals who surpassed me in various ways. I was no longer the top performer.

Discovering this was somewhat painful and frustrating, but inevitable.

In 2016, that young girl, now a woman adorned with certificates, found herself facing a formidable challenge. Brazil was grappling with the throes of a global economic crisis, and Automotive Business needed fresh horizons. In search of solutions, I delved into my knowledge reservoir, only to realize that none of my prior experiences held the answers I required. The future of the business seemed hazy at best.

In response, I made the decision to enroll in a program called "10 Thousand Women," offered by FGV and Goldman Sachs. The program garnered thousands of entrepreneurial applicants, with only 50 spots available. Remarkably, I was among the select few chosen. A major score to my innate self-importance.

When classes started, I immediately started talking about my extensive resume experience when introducing myself to the group. I thought that stance conveyed self-confidence, courage, intelligence, but, deep down, I sought validation from people.

And none of the other 49 entrepreneurs in the room thought much of my extensive resume. In fact, they didn't care at all. They were all humbly seeking answers and paths for their businesses, openly showing their weaknesses, mistakes, and fears.

Ironically, my initial motivation for seeking out the course was rooted in my own arrogance. At that time, I was more preoccupied with showcasing my strengths than addressing my weaknesses. Little did I know, their stories would serve as the catalyst for a profound turning point in my life.

Their experiences resonated with me deeply because they embodied something I had concealed within myself: immense vulnerability coupled with an insatiable thirst for knowledge. My relentless pursuit of always being at the forefront of everything had earned me countless "congratulations," but it came at a cost. I had spent years ensconced in that narrow bubble, diligently concealing my vulnerabilities. It was a comfortable and controlled existence.

However, as I began to grasp how much I had constrained my own growth, I made the courageous choice to seek therapy. I embarked on a journey of profound self-discovery—a process that was often painful but ultimately transformative. These two years were emotionally intense but undeniably worthwhile.

And only now do I see that all of this made me bring out my best side, which I didn't even know. I felt very ashamed of that arrogance that accompanied me, but, at the same time, proud of that emotional and intellectual humility that I embraced with so much willingness.

The more it grew, the more I saw value in myself, I felt good, I was able to admire people, I experienced self-confidence without needing to rely on dozens of certificates. I empowered myself with that woman who was being born. And if I learned one lesson, it's that no one puts the brakes on a woman who is sure of herself.

Of course, I didn't find the answer I expected for my company in the course. I found a much more powerful one. The experience was much greater than any theory. I recognized myself there, I understood a little more who I am, and I felt enormous strength alongside those women. I started thinking about how I could give back that feeling to society, how to make women access some of that strength that I had found.

That's when the Feminine Presence in the Automotive Sector Project emerged, something that was born from the desire to do more for those who often feel alone, lost and without opportunities in their professional lives.

The initiative was a success, becoming a biannual study on diversity and inclusion in the auto industry and, more recently, a movement for diversity. On the one hand, we map inequalities and challenges to make the industry more representative of society. On the other hand, we highlight great results and initiatives and engage the entire sector in the search for solutions.

In parallel, we built a large project to debate leadership in this industry: we mapped the profile of those who occupy these positions, their objectives, and challenges. After all, as Peter Drucker, one of the great management experts of our time, said, "a company is only as good as its administrator allows it to be".

These steps have consolidated into a huge personal and professional achievement: an annual event promoted by my company that is today the largest business meeting of leaders in the automotive and mobility ecosystem. ABX - Automotive Business Experience was born from the need to bring together in a single day and venue all the people who have in their hands the power to define the solutions we will bring to society.

Consider this: Mobility transcends mere technology, vehicles, and business. It encompasses the fundamental right of individuals to move freely, to access opportunities, and to do so democratically, with minimal environmental impact. Furthermore, it presents an opportunity to utilize vehicles that create quality employment opportunities and contribute to strengthening education in our nation.

Over the past several years, as I've achieved numerous milestones, it has become evident that I can only truly fulfill my purpose of making a positive impact on people's lives, as well as Automotive Business's mission, after I overcame emotional barriers and confidently embraced the role of CEO. Despite the absence of female role models in this position throughout my journey and the many obstacles I faced in reaching this point, it is now abundantly clear that this role amplifies my ability to effect change.

As I conquer the imposter syndrome, I gain not just personal empowerment but also contribute to the collective advancement of all women. Our victories are not limited to ourselves; they extend to the growth and progress of both businesses and society as a whole.

Therefore, I invite you: let's put our fears aside and show the worlc who we are?

RENATA BINDO

Strategy Director at Haleon, a world-leading consumer health company. Responsible for its organic and inorganic growth strategy and running corporate strategic initiatives.

LinkedIn: www.linkedin.com/in/renata-bindo

WHEN YOU REALLY WANT SOMETHING, IT'S ALWAYS WORTH A TRY.

"Dreams don't work unless you do." - John C. Maxwell

If you really want something, you must go after it and do your best to get it. That's been my life motto from a very early age. I learned that I had to **TRY**, really try my best, by preparing and pushing myself. I also learned to **ASK** for what I want and **TAKE A CHANCE** even if the odds were against me. At the very least, a 'no' or a 'failure' would keep me where I was. However, a 'YES' would lead me towards my dreams.

It took me two years to get into the best university in Latin America - the University of Sao Paulo, USP. My sights were set on USP and wasn't going to stop until I got in! First, I explored medicine and studied biology, chemistry, and physics. I didn't make it. The following year I visited hospitals, observed surgeries and dissection rooms......Guess what? I decided to apply for Business Administration!

The focus shifted to math, history, and geography, which left me with a rounder education. Time is never lost when learning! I knew that with a degree in Business Administration I would be able to work with whatever I wanted in the future, from Tourism to the Health sector among others, which proved to be true in my life.

Trying

With my story, I want to show that self-confidence develops by trying. The more you try, the more learnings you have from your failures, the more you end up understanding what you want and the more achievements happen. This generates a positive cycle of empowerment, showing that it is worth keep TRYING to keep conquering. If you haven't seen it yet, watch Steve Jobs: "What separates dreamers from doers," which reinforces the importance of developing a 'ask', 'act', 'make it happen' mindset.

The year I joined USP, my brother went through a selection process at AIESEC, an international organization that helps students to work abroad. AIESEC's vision was to use exchange as a way to promote world peace. After all, if you knew someone from another country, you would be less inclined to go to war with them. I thought it was very real, it touched me. It was also a way to have international experience when you don't have the money to pay for your cost of living abroad or an education. I thought, "If I want to travel abroad, I need to participate in an exchange program." By coincidence there was a small group composed only of boys who founded an AIESEC office at USP. I decided to break the "boy's only" trend and joined them in 2000.

My English wasn't good. I couldn't really read, write and understand English without difficulty. Speaking was almost impossible. I knew I would need English if I wanted to have international experience, so I did odd jobs and raised money for a two-month vacation course in Canada during my first year at the university. I was determined to make this course count, even if it was very short to get to the level I needed to venture out into the world. And it was really short, but it laid the groundwork to get to the language proficiency I needed.

In my third year of college a vacancy appeared - only one! - to do an all expenses paid exchange at Harvard University. The student had to have an interest in social impact and submit a proposal for a long essay on the topic. Luckily, this was the world I was navigating at the time. I worked with the third sector studying partnerships between the public, private and social sectors and was already planning to do my final year essay in the area. I had to fast forward my plan by a year and spent sleepless nights developing the proposal for this vacancy. I studied hard to pass the TOEFL (certificate of proficiency in English). Only on the second test I received the minimum grade needed to apply to the exchange program at Harvard.

Most of the people I talked to about the opportunity thought Harvard was impossible, and not worth trying. However, I always thought "if I don't even try, how am I ever going to get in?" Although those days were really tough and many times I felt demotivated, I decided that I was going to give everything I had in me to achieve my dream. I had to believe in myself and lean on the few who believed in me too. One friend stands out to whom I am very grateful to this day. I told him about the scholarship and he helped me a lot. He could see my potential and drive. He knew this was possible for me and I trusted him. We would review the application and practice the English test together.

I stayed laser focused, took bold steps, **TRIED** and it worked! Harvard's offer came with a condition that I had to arrive at least a month before the start of classes to improve my English. I remember the happiness of the conquest. The achievement was mine and no one else's. Now, **imagine if I hadn't even tried.**

ASKING

My mother always said that she had raised her children for the world. So, I always thought the 'world' was there to be conquered. Harvard opened the doors for me out of Brazil and gave me the taste of wanting more.

After my stint at Harvard, I came back to Sao Paulo to complete my undergraduate degree in Business Administration. My professional experience had only been in NGOs during college. However, I wanted to travel for work (or leisure) and strategic consulting had everything I wanted at that stage: experience in different industries, with different projects, intellectual challenge, a lot of learning, and the opportunity to travel and earn better. In addition to all these, consulting has also given me incredible colleagues and mentors for life.

Getting into consulting was difficult and super crowded. It was also an environment dominated by men and engineers. Again, I had no external motivation, but I still **tried**. At Monitor Group, I was the first non-engineer woman to be hired. And it was there, too, that, once again, I had to get used to being somehow the minority.

In general, they sent consultants to projects outside Brazil only after TWO years of consulting, because they would already be better trained and accustomed to the life of projects. At the end of my FIRST year an opportunity for a project in Colombia appeared, and I **asked** for it! I ended up spending 7 months there, followed by another 7 months in Chile. And so, I started my international career. **Imagine if you hadn't asked.**

TAKE A CHANCE

The taste for travel became a virus that was always circulating in my veins.

After 3 years of professional experience, I decided to return to the University. I wanted to explore the possibility of pursuing an academic life. So, I had to do a master's degree and potentially a doctorate. This time I had Europe as my focus. I always looked for excellence, after USP and Harvard, the University of Cambridge in England had the master's degree I wanted in economic development.

Again, I jumped headfirst to explore the possibility of a master's degree abroad without knowing anyone who had already done so. But as always, I was sure that if I didn't try, I wouldn't succeed (100%), and if I **tried**, I increased my chances of succeeding by at least 50% (since it would be either a 'yes' or a 'no').

In this case, being 'in the minority' helped. By being a woman and from a developing country, I was able to apply for full scholarships for my masters. In 2008 I embarked for England with my studies paid knowing that I might not return. Opening doors and walking through unpaved roads, served as an inspiration for other women to follow this path, including my sister, who two years later got a full scholarship for her master's degree at UCL in London.

After the master's degree I received a "return offer" to return to the São Paulo office of Monitor Group. At the end of my master's degree the world was still in an economic crisis, but I wanted to pursue an international career. Even understanding the difficulty of offices hiring foreigners due to the situation, I **TOOK A CHANCE!** I reached out and showed my interest in staying abroad. To my surprise I was offered a position to be based in the London office. **Imagine if I hadn't taken a chance.**

"Fear kills more dreams than failure ever will" – Suzi Kassem

I spent 10 years living in London, 3 years in Dubai and traveled to more than 55 countries. I have worked for the public sector with economic development, but my primary experience has been in the private sector. I worked in several industries including tourism, telecommunications, media, broadcasting and consumer goods. Healthcare consumer goods became my most recent area of interest.

I've always looked for role models in female figures and strived to be one. I found it difficult to find married women with children in a leadership position. This is a scenario that has been changing but is still far away from being frequent. Reconciling career, family, and motherhood abroad without support from relatives was the greatest challenge.

I have always been asked what is needed to pursue an international career. The first jump is always the most complicated. But the more structured paths are: to go abroad to study, or even better, to get an internal transfer within a multinational company. But nothing will happen if you don't go after it. In this process you need to know that the path will not be easy. Adapting to another culture and settling in a foreign country is already difficult alone, with a partner or dependents will be ever more - but nothing is impossible. **TRY, ASK, TAKE A CHANCE.**

Women are great at building support networks and communities. Be part of the groups that exist around you – in your neighborhood, or at your children's school. If it doesn't exist, create one. In these networks you will get help, support, guidance, and opportunities for collaboration and growth.

What has changed from my first challenges to the ones I continue to face today is knowing that I am not alone. As much as the dreams remain ambitious, and many people continue to disbelieve me or try to demotivate me, there are many more people

willing to support and pull me up. Knowing how to find these people and to leverage my network of contacts selectively, became one of my main strengths. And remember...
DON'T BE YOUR OWN 'NO'

ROBERTA SUPLICY

Founder of Urban Remedy Brasil, Speaker at SXSW, Entrepreneur and Fitfood Wizard, Agritech Specialist, Agribusiness Consultant, President of the Sectorial Chamber of Juices in Brazil, Founding member #riseandraiseothers, EY Winning Women
Instagram: @robertasuplicy
LinkedIn: www.linkedin.com/in/robertasuplicy

I was born in São Paulo and come from a huge and traditional family. On one side, my grandmother had 11 children, 40 grandchildren, and 67 great-grandchildren. She lived to be 104 years old, was married twice, widowed from her first husband with whom she had two children, and then married again, having nine more children, one of whom was my father. My grandmother Filomena was a very strong woman; she was one of the first women to get a driver's license in Brazil. She said she never wore pants but knew how to play soccer. Despite having 11 children, she never raised her voice to any of them. Any mother knows how difficult that is, but in her own way, she always managed to get everyone to do what she wanted. I remember that every Wednesday there was a family dinner at grandma's house, with at least 20 to 30 people. Very religious, every Christmas she held a mass for more than 200 people. At the end of each year, she sent the entire family a printed list with phone numbers, addresses, and professions of each family member so that if anyone needed a lawyer, an astrologer, or a veterinarian, we could find one within the family.

And believe me, my family has everything: a senator, astrologer, lawyers, musicians, veterinarians, entrepreneurs, housewives, influencers, photographers, brokers, researchers... Maybe that is why I love being surrounded by people and have this ease in talking, connecting, and meeting people. And curiosity about so many different subjects. On the other side of the family, I had a movie-like grandma, chubby, cute, and loving. She taught me how to crochet, sew, and cook. She also taught me patience, consideration for others, and how to take care of everyone around with great affection.

My house was always full; my parents had many friends, and they were always bohemian. The movement started and ended late. There was always good music and lots of hapiness. And as you can imagine, I loved all that. I remember when I was four years old, my father woke me up because Pepino de Capri was at home and wanted to sing the song "Roberta" to me.

My father, always very aware and ahead of his time, created some landmarks in São Paulo. He founded a relaxed Rio-style bar in São Paulo called Supremo, changing the city's profile. Every corner turned into a bar. There, he brought together all tribes: journalists, intellectuals, bohemians, high society... Years later, the Supremo basement became a music venue, where many famous artists played the piano that now, luckily for me, "lives" in my house. Maria Rita, Simoninha, Max de Castro, Nana Caymmi, Banda Mantiqueira, among others, passed through there. He also founded the famous Gueri-Gueri band, the first street carnival in São Paulo. If there is this excitement during carnival today, you can blame my father.

I remember that in school and college, there were groups of athletes who woke up early and the group of party. I was part of both.

I have done all kinds of sports: soccer, motocross, surfing, tennis, squash, swimming, water polo. I even became a Brazilian snowboarding champion. In the past few years, I learned how to kite surf and fell in love with it.

It was difficult for me to decide which college to attend. So, I enrolled in two simultaneously: advertising in the morning and architecture at night. After a few months I decided drop out of advertising. I continued with architecture studies while simultaneously working at DPZ, the largest advertising agency in the country at that time, my experience at DPZ provided me with valuable insights into the world of Advertising and Marketing, which continue to benefit me in my current venture, Urban Remedy.

In 1994, I was 19 years old, I left DPZ to start my first entrepreneurial venture. I opened a restaurant called Filomena, named after my grandmother, where we served Mediterranean cuisine. I hired two professionals: chef Alex Atala (recommended by my neighbor and king of São Paulo nightlife at the time, Angelo Leuzzi) and architect Patrícia Anastassiadis (it was her first job, recommended by her friend Daniela de Luca). Although they were relatively unknown at the time, they became very successful in their respective fields. Filomena had six years of success, with a loyal clientele and several awards for best chef and restaurant.

In 2000, we sold Filomena. While contemplating my next move, a friend named Fernanda Camargo indicated me to work on the Arremate, the first auction site in Brazil. Fernanda is a pioneer in impact funds in Brazil, Wright Capital Wealth Management, she is a (sister kind of) friend and great advisor; I talk to her about almost everything.

During this time, my boyfriend (now husband) invited me for a trip through Southeast Asia, with no predetermined return date. I remember talking with my mother about it: "Mom, I'm going to quit my job and travel with Phil," to which she responded, "Are you sure? You just started a new job. When do you plan to come back?"

I replied, "Mom, I live in your house, I don't have children. If I don't go now, when will I?" My mother's response "Go, daughter, and enjoy it!" I left my job and embarked on a six-month journey of learning and exploration. We visited Laos, Cambodia, Thailand, Vietnam and China. The experiences I had during that time could fill several chapters on their own.

Upon my return, while considering my next career move, another friend named Ana Cristina Nogueira, who owned a clothing store, approached me to provide press and marketing consulting services. I hesitated initially, questioning whether I was the right fit for the job. However, Ana Cristina assured me that I had previously demonstrated success in similar roles for Supremo, Gueri-Gueri and Filomena. With her vote of confidence, I accepted the offer. The collaboration proved successful, attracting other clients and leading to the birth of RSUPLICY Assessoria e Marketing. Over time, RSUPLICY evolved into RFSUPLICY, with my sister Fernanda Suplicy joining me. Our client portfolio expanded to include notable names such as Sabuji restaurant (where chef Bel Coelho earned her first award), Emporio Santa Maria, Dr Perignon, Vodka Belvedere, Rossignol, Quinua Real, General Prime Burger, Suunto, Dr. Orgânico, Rocco architecture, Q!Bazar, and many others.

In 2003, I married Phil. In 2006 I got pregnant, my concern for food grew, becoming a passion. In 2007, my daughter Chloe was born, followed by my son Gabriel in 2009. Throughout their early years, I continued to breastfeed and reduced my client workload, but never ceased working. I carried my children with me in a kangaroo carrier wherever I went. The passion for motherhood was instantaneous, I enjoy every minute. I find it impressive how much we want to do everything better and better for them, and in this role, we learn as much as we teach.

I began attending yoga classes taught by Juliana Loureiro, the most exceptional yoga teacher I have ever encountered. Juliana is married to a childhood friend of mine named Jairo and our friendship blossomed. We engaged in numerous discussions about healthy eating and the profound impact it has on a fulfilling life. Inspired by our conversations, we decided to research and establish a company that could bring exceptional products. As we were contemplating the product selection and import process, Jairo's cousin, who resided in California, introduced us to Urban Remedy, a company specializing in cold-pressed juices and healthy foods. We were instantly captivated by Urban Remedy and its founder, Neka Pasquale. Our aspiration to bring their products to Brazil aligned perfectly with their plans for expansion and search for investors to bolster their production facility. Consequently, we became angel investors in Urban Remedy, securing the rights to the brand in Brazil.

We interned at Urban Remedy in California, mastered their production techniques, imported the necessary machinery and thus brought Urban Remedy to Brazil. This endeavor opened up a new world of passion for me, as I became increasingly committed to helping people understand the significance of food in their lives. At our company, Urban Remedy Brazil, we not only offer delicious, ultra-nutritious, preservative-free, dye-free and fresh food, but we also strive to educate our customers about the transformative power of food. Over the span of eight years in business, we have witnessed the remarkable impact on people's health when they make the choice to change their lifestyle or are motivated by health concerns. Did you know that obesity, diabetes, and heart disease are among the leading causes of death worldwide? Many of these conditions can be prevented or even reversed through dietary and lifestyle modifications.

In 2017, on the recommendation of Bel Carvalho Pinto, we applied for and were selected to participate in Winning Women, a program offered by EY that provides mentoring, management guidance, branding support and leadership development for women entrepreneurs. Great experience, enabling me to expand my knowledge, forge new friendships, and significantly broaden my network. If you are a female business owner, I wholeheartedly encourage you to explore the program's criteria and consider participating.

Motivated by my insatiable thirst for new experiences, knowledge and personal growth, I was invited by a friend Maria Raduan to attend SXSW in Austin, Texas, the world's largest event for trends and technology, and I believe everyone should seize the opportunity to attend at least once in their lifetime. It is a whirlwind of exhilarating ideas, inspiring individuals, and captivating experiences.

In 2019, I received an invitation from Gustavo Junqueira, a longtime friend who was then serving as the Secretary of Agriculture for the São Paulo government. He asked me to actively participate in the Juice Sector Chamber within the Agriculture Secretariat, subsequently, I was elected as the president of the Chamber.

I consider myself incredibly fortunate to have a network of competent and supportive close friends who have always stood by my side. Carolina Maluhy, not only the best architect in the country but now expanding her projects to London, Greece, Portugal and beyond, provides me with invaluable advice and poses thought-provoking questions. Heloisa Guarita, a nutritionist and owner of RGNutri, is my faithful companion in travel and concert experiences. She pursued her dream and is now also involved with the "PREMIO DA MUSICA BRASILEIRA," the most prestigious award in Brazilian music, alongside our mutual friend Zé Mauricio. Cris Barros, my sister in life, teaches me how to accomplish everything with determination and delicacy. As a designer, she has infused her lifestyle into her incredible clothing brand,

Cris Barros. Thanks to her, I have also learned the art of dressing. Without her, I believe I would solely wear jeans and workout attire.

Why have I shared all these stories of connections and invitations? It is because I firmly believe that together we are stronger and in the importance of being open to new experiences, attentive listening and keen observation are vital for personal growth. Cultivating and maintaining relationships profoundly impacts our life path, while our family greatly influences our personality formation. Life experiences help us understand what truly matters and find joy in our work. Some people have positively influenced my life through their skills, relationships and recommendations, both for me and by me.

By being open to new experiences and extending help to others, remarkable opportunities arise.

Through a friendship cultivated at SXSW in 2017, I became one of the founders of this incredible group, "Rise and Raise Others," whose name is anonymous in this book. It has positively impacted the lives of many women, including mine! While I write this chapter for this book, I am also preparing to be a speaker at SXSW 2023 alongside Carmela Borst and Natasha Caiado, discussing how agrotechnology in Brazil can improve health and reduce social inequality.

A connection that arose within the group after I identified a workforce gap in agrotechnology and recommended Carmela from Soulcode (an incredible company that empowers young people in social vulnerability by teaching them, integrating them into the workforce offering them employment opportunities in the tech world) Together, we will showcase the impact this can have on future generations.

ROSSANA SADIR

CEO & Board Member
Instagram: @rossanasadir
LinkedIn: www.linkedin.com/in/rossanasadir/

IN LIFE, I AM NEITHER A SPECTATOR NOR A VICTIM, I AM THE PROTAGONIST

I have developed my career in three cycles, each built upon the competencies and learnings of the previous one. Right after the MBA, my first positions were as a strategist, working at McKinsey, Monsanto, Abril and Avon. In this role, I developed the ability to diagnose the company and its ecosystem, outlining alternative strategic paths, and coordinating teams and projects for successful implementation. In my second professional cycle as CEO, I lead operations for Avon in Ecuador and Chile, and for Amway as President in Latin America, overseeing twelve countries. My mandate was always to transform the business in the long term, while delivering targeted top and bottom-line results. Currently, in my third cycle as a board member, I work across various sectors and market complexities, aiming to be a pollination agent: seeding new strategies, disseminating best practices and ideas, and supporting company boards and management in the implementation.

It is not an easy task to be the protagonist of an international career, with three expatriations and five international moves, or traveling more than 30% of the time throughout the region. I have been asked how to balance work and family, and the answer is simple: it is not about having to choose or split yourself, but rather multiplying and embracing both. I took on my first Director position while eight months pregnant with my first child, and I accepted the first CEO role just one week after the birth of my third child -- conceived in Colombia, born in Brazil, and breastfed in Ecuador.

I had four promotions during three pregnancies, proving the Hispanic saying: "Children come with bread under their arms," meaning they bring fertility and prosperity. Balancing professional and family lives is not a mission for Wonder Women but for a Justice League, as it depends on a solid family network and support team. I am grateful to my parents Raul and Isabel, and my ex and current husbands Alexandre and Marcelo for their unconditional presence and support, which has given me the freedom to make my own decisions.

Agent and catalyst for transformation

Having coordinated strategic planning processes throughout my professional life, I developed my life's mission and purpose twenty years ago: *"Live intensely and happily into new experiences, seeking a constant transformation of myself, and the people and organizations I work with."*

This purpose key concepts are:

- Intense and happy - live with passion.
- New experiences – dare to think and act outside the box.
- Transform and develop – be a lifelong learner.
- People and organizations - change happens from the inside out: we transform ourselves to influence others and the environment.

As an agent of transformation, I have learned that effective and lasting results are not the goal; they are a consequence. Business transformation starts and can only be permanent by developing the team. Devoting myself to listening to and mentoring professionals has become a passion and a source of continuous learning. In supporting various causes, I do not consider myself an activist but an activator. Instead of polarizing discussions (victims vs. oppressors), I seek the root causes of obstacles and support people in developing their own solutions. In the case of women, we face four obstacles in our careers: guilt, comfort zone, insecurity, and prejudice, with only the latter being an external factor.

Seven tips to overcome the obstacles for a successful women's career:

1. **Stretch and expand your comfort zone** – Develop your own strategic planning
process by defining your vision and life goals from an individual, family, and professional standpoint. Allow yourself to visualize where you want to be in each dimension, as by evaluating future scenarios, free from present obstacles and insecurities, you will feel more comfortable exploring new adventures. Aligned with my mission, as my youngest son says, "Mom, your comfort zone is being out of the comfort zone!"

2. **Minimize guilt and increase your satisfaction.**
By having clarity about your goals, define your scorecard and share it widely: as we know, well-understood and clearly communicated objectives become shared goals.

Female guilt has biblical origins dating back to Eve, and it currently manifests itself as a constant sense of falling short and failing in all dimensions. Hence, the importance of defining simple and clear indicators of your desired performance:

- Arrive home from work before 7:30 PM.
- Exercise three times a week.
- Dedicate two hours per day to family time, away from computer and mobile.

After all, as the equation states: *Satisfaction = Results - Expectations.*
If expectations are not clear, guilt will always be present.

3. Minimize guilt through management.

At the beginning of each year, it is customary for executives to include recurring corporate meetings in the agenda, as well as scheduled events and trips for conventions, budget discussions, and market visits. In parallel, we receive the annual calendar of activities from our children's school and the list of upcoming events from other organizations. To balance and keep all my plates in motion, the agenda has become a great ally, by proactively including and coordinating all activities in advance. Being the master of my agenda makes me feel that I am fulfilling all my roles well.

4. Master your insecurity by defining your personal branding.

The Imposter Syndrome is common among all women, regardless of how successful we are in our careers and personal lives. It is present when we don't feel prepared for a new position or challenge, or when women downplay their achievements and presence. To overcome it, it is crucial to define your personal brand based on your competencies, principles, and experiences that set you apart from others. Your personal brand will guide your storytelling and should be reinforced in your presentations, conversations, interviews, elevator pitch, and social media posts.

Avoid the common mistake of most professionals, who organize their resumes in chronological order of birth, education, and positions. Focus on your personal identity and "brand" by describing your competencies and how they have helped you achieve results. In the first paragraph of this chapter, for example, I develop my "pitch," by positioning myself as a transformation agent, reinforced by my experience as a strategist, CEO, and board member.

5. Master your insecurity through a support network.

A support network is a broad concept that encompasses family and friends, contacts we build and cultivate for opportunities and knowledge exchange, plus a third category that we rarely delve into: our community for sharing experiences. In this third network, we move away from the traditional "cocktails and business card exchange" events to forums of discussion or mentoring on concrete issues that affect our personal or professional lives. Throughout our careers, we all face very similar situations, being able to share our strategies and results contribute to our well-being and progress, as we feel less alone and better prepared with an arsenal of tools for action.

6. Deal with prejudice with a feminine approach

I had the privilege of building a fast and upward career with reasonable companies' support. Nevertheless, as women, we have altogether become accustomed to the daily microaggressions that are now widely recognized and condemned, such as mansplaining, manterrupting or bropropriating. Our first instinct is to speak up assertively, emulating male behavior. However, in recent conversations with over two hundred top female executives, I discovered that at some point in their careers, all of them received feedback about being aggressive or tough. When a man is assertive, he conveys confidence and power, but in women, it is seen as aggressive or lacking emotional intelligence. It is not about criticizing or judging, but rather reflecting on how we can act differently – with efficiency and effectiveness. I finally found my feminine voice -- remaining objective and firm in my statements, but with a soft and positive tone of voice, which generally stands out in board meetings where loud male voices clash.

7. Deal with prejudice using your influence

Engineers often say that the shortest distance between two points is not always a straight line; sometimes it requires "successive approximations." At a turning point in my 40s, I decided to transition from being too directive to being a point of reference, with a high ability to influence. Since then, when dealing with complex issues, I usually create an influence matrix, listing key stakeholders, their motivations, and what styles, arguments, and actions may resonate to them. As women, we have several tools for persuasion, and we must learn to use them effectively, as most of the time direct confrontation works against us.

On leadership and motherhood

I was recently asked, "What have you learned at home that you bring to work, and at work that you bring home?" Reflecting on the first question, a sentence came to mind, "Once you become a mother, you will never stop being it." Same as leaders; our responsibility transcends family ties, hierarchical or formal lines, we are eternal mentors. In the words of Saint-Exupéry, "You become forever responsible for what you have tamed."

In a training meeting with managers, I was asked a question related to the second issue: "Are you as good a leader at home as you are at work?" Indeed, it was not the case: at work, we are trained to delegate and empower, give constructive feedback, and build high-performance teams. At home, often we still emulate a command-and-control style, especially when kids are small. Since then, I have applied some management tools in raising my children, trying to be less of a mother who sets limits and more of a mother who opens opportunities.

Regarding my leadership style, I draw upon two reflections that left a mark on me. First, in an academic research, professors presented an image of a school of fish with one fish separated from the group to two sets of students from the US and Asia. The US group interpretation was: "a school of fish with one fish leading it." The Asian students answer was: "A school of fish with one fish that we should include back into the group." I witnessed Chinese leaders being called on stage for recognition, bringing their entire team and giving them the opportunity to shine. Being a leader means being integrated into the team, coordinating it from within, not isolated in a glass bubble.

The second reflection came during my experience as President of Latin America, working with senior Directors for whom the traditional leadership style derived from military hierarchy was not acceptable, with generals in charge and soldiers following orders. I focused on empowering the team, being the last to speak and establishing the direction without detailing strategies. I named this style "Shepherd Leadership," because it exercises leadership by delivering a vision or direction, but positions the leader to walk behind the flock, ensuring that everyone reaches their destination, supporting stray sheep, and allowing them to chart their own paths.

During the pandemic, I left my executive career, reinvented myself and multiplied my influence in new roles such as consultant and Board member, while taking on leadership positions in corporate NGOs. By being plural, I developed myself like never before, and abandoned two concepts that I used to cherish as an executive: resilience and assertiveness -- the ability to return to the original form after an impact, and the certainty of the path to follow. In their place, I embraced adaptability (acquiring new forms) and flexibility (generation of various strategic paths).

For the future, this is what I aspire to: continue in my transformation path, by learning and adapting from new and diverse experiences.

SANDRA CHEMIN

FutureYou founder and CEO
Website: www.futureyou.be
E-mail: sandra@futureyou.be
Instagram: @sandrachemin
LinkedIn: www.linkedin.com/in/sandrachemin

WHAT AM I DOING HERE?

The sound of crashing waves reverberates through our sailboat as we skid sideways. Green water seeps into the cabin. It was worse yesterday evening when the wind howled, blowing at more than 110 kilometres per hour.

At that point, we face the daunting prospect of enduring hours, if not days, on this terrifying roller coaster. In the middle of the Pacific Ocean, facing a tropical storm with our daughters aboard, the question becomes inevitable - What am I doing here?

This question has been guiding me ever since. This story is about how I went from an entrepreneur and CEO to living on a boat and helping organizations navigate change. It's also about what I learned about leadership and finding myself along the way.

I come from a family of Italian immigrants. My great-grandfather left Italy for Brazil with the promise of land and a vision of a better future for his family. They were met with the reality of poverty, the early loss of loved ones, and the indispensable lesson of being together as a family for survival.

When my father was 12, my grandfather passed away, leaving behind a loom in the basement as his sole legacy to his six children. The siblings learned the art of weaving, and worked tirelessly in shifts, weaving barber towels throughout the night. At each month's end, the earnings were entrusted to my grandma, who judiciously decided who was in the most need. From them, I learned never to wait for someone to bring me opportunities, that I had to create my own work. I became an entrepreneur at the age of 21.

Innovation has always been the cornerstone of my work. My first company was a design studio that introduced Apple Macs to Brazil, pioneering desktop publishing in the country. My business partner was a professor at the University of Sao Paulo, and together, we witnessed the nascent days of the internet.

313

We shared a conviction: "This will revolutionize everything." With this vision, we launched Hipermidia, the first digital agency in Brazil, at a time when the internet was only accessible inside the university. A few years down the line, we sold the agency to Ogilvy, a global advertising agency, and I was appointed head of their internet operations in Latin America.

It all happened very fast. Becoming a leader of 250 people with teams in 5 countries, traveling a lot, working with global brands. I was creating the future, and that vision moved me forward. I remember when I met Shelly Lazarus, the CEO. The simple idea of having a woman CEO, leading a company of ten thousand people and being a mother of four blew me away. Shelly wrote me two letters by hand in the years that I worked at Ogilvy. In a time of instant messages, she modelled a level of care that was hard to find. I started to understand the difference between a leader and a boss.

But one day my husband and I received news that would change our lives forever. I was pregnant with our first daughter, and Lucas was diagnosed with an aggressive form of cancer. The doctors said he would have two years to live.

Following months of consultations, we found out the diagnosis was wrong - Lucas never had cancer. Nevertheless, this ordeal had already initiated a profound transformation within us. Reflecting on it, I believe that life gave us the gift of asking ourselves, at 30, what we would do if we only had two years left.

Lucas had nurtured a childhood dream of living on a sailboat. The mere thought of it initially took my breath away, as my only sailing experience was windsurfing as a teenager. However, I also held cherished childhood memories of time spent at sea with my father, an avid spearfisherman. The idea of offering our daughter Clara similar experiences was deeply appealing.

Lucas and I began contemplating the possibility of living his dream. It was a daunting decision. I was living the best moment of my professional life, with a great salary, awards, and recognition.

What was initially conceived as a year-long sabbatical radically transformed my life. We visited more than 30 countries. I crossed the Atlantic while pregnant with our second daughter, Julia. We lived in Paraty, a historic village on the coast of Rio de Janeiro, where we co-founded a Waldorf school designed for social inclusion. We crossed the Pacific and, for the past decade, have been living in New Zealand. I spent over two thousand days at sea, learning to navigate change, and, most importantly, learning who I am.

I have lived many lives ever since. I joined a global network of impact entrepreneurs that is a pioneer in the future of work, participated in the project that created the Global Impact Visa in New Zealand and, with that, the purpose of a Nation.

FutureYou

"You will be the first," said Elena Crescia, the curator of TEDx Sao Paulo. My heart quickened as my eyes swept over the vast Municipal Theatre, filled with an audience of 1,500 people. The year was 2016, and I was invited to deliver two TEDx talks a few months apart. Life was asking me to embrace my journey and acknowledge the different experiences I had lived.

The reaction that followed was overwhelming. Hundreds of people messaged me saying they wanted to change but didn't know how. I remember one afternoon, wind against my face, as I said out loud, "I want to help people find more meaning in what they do, how they live and act in the world." In retrospect, I realized I was utilizing the same innovation methodologies I had employed in creating products, services, and companies, in my own life. The FutureYou program was born that day. Since then, 17,000 people have gone through the program, designing the next phase of their careers.

Elena Crescia, another contributor to this book, states, "My way of rising and raising others is literally stepping onto the stage and inviting other women to join me". Thank you for inviting me to join you on stage, dear friend. That was a pivotal moment in my life.

Leading change

"Are you currently in Brazil? Could you extend your stay? We're charting the course for the next 20 years of Natura Amazonia, and I would like you to join us," said futurist Lala Dehenzelin over the phone.

Natura, one of the world's leading cosmetic companies and a former client, is Latin America's largest B Corp. Committed to environmental preservation, the company safeguards 2 million hectares of the Amazon Forest, collaborating closely with 34 communities over two decades.

What began as a 3-day sprint soon morphed into a much larger challenge. "We're on the brink of acquiring Avon, expanding to hundreds of countries, and changing our business model. The way we used to lead is not working anymore, we need a new leadership DNA. Could you help us?"

The year was 2019. My father, nearing his 96th birthday, was in and out of hospital, and I yearned to remain close by. The opportunity to undertake a new project in Brazil provided a chance to do so.

Crafting a new leadership DNA required a different approach. Transformation doesn't happen overnight. I reached out to our friend Shima in Cape Town with whom I had been creating learning journeys. We shared the belief that navigating complexity and uncertainty required a new suite of human skills. For many years, we looked North, seeking solutions in processes, technologies, and efficiency. Yet the skills needed nowadays are rooted in the Global South, in countries like Brazil, South Africa, and New Zealand. These nations have social skills, creativity, and collaboration. They have deep connections to the land and ancient wisdom of indigenous cultures and traditional communities.

This was the genesis of RE.CONECTA: a four-day immersion in the Amazon designed to reconnect with oneself, others, and our impact in the world. One hundred thirty-three leaders participated in these journeys, co-creating the new leadership DNA of the company.

A few months later, my dad passed away. Shortly after, I found a notebook I had kept upon arriving in New Zealand. In there, I had written that I wanted to remain close to my parents in their last years. That was non-negotiable for me. In hindsight, I had indeed been to Brazil every three months ever since. I couldn't help but smile, realizing that despite residing half a world away, I had been the closest to my parents for the past seven years. This was the moment I realized I was first designing my life to then creating the work to match it. This became a core concept in FutureYou.

Acknowledging my own Bias

Recently, I was asked to speak on Leadership to an audience of 1,200 women. While preparing, I found a folder with interviews from my past. Among them was a cover story from December 1999, featuring 15 pioneering women in the internet industry. *Veja*, the leading magazine in Brazil at the time, rarely highlighted women leaders on its cover. I was among them, and I recall our pride in being part of that moment.

As I snapped a photo of the magazine to share with our daughters, I reread the headline: "They shine in the profession created by the internet pioneers." The English translation of this title fails to convey its whole meaning. In Portuguese, every noun is gendered; each word is assigned either a masculine or feminine form. In the cover story, the gender distinction was explicit. The inference was clear - men had established the companies where women now flourish. The realization stunned me. How many times had I read that article without fully grasping its implications?

This prompted another recollection, a painful memory that I had long since tucked away. Another cover story featured one of my business partners, crediting him with founding the very company I had established. I held a 99% stake in the business at the time, with his share being a mere 1%. This same pattern was repeated with the company that eventually acquired us, and with journalists. No one ever questioned who had founded the company or who was truly at the helm. They simply assumed that the man was responsible. How many times has this happened to you? As I write this chapter, I am becoming aware of my own biases and the extent to which patriarchal culture has been ingrained in me.

YOU ARE NOT ALONE.

This chapter began with an account of the most formidable storm our family ever confronted at sea en route from Tonga to New Zealand. For three days, we faced winds reaching up to 100 kilometres per hour, towering waves of seven meters, and relentless rain that forced us to remain within our boat's cabin for 24 hours. Yet, we were not alone. Sixty-two yachts were out at sea, weathering the same storm. Twice daily, we communicated with each other via radio. One sailor would report, "I am a day ahead of you, and here's what it looks like."

In the early hours of one morning, we heard "Mayday, Mayday, this is the yacht Windigo, and we need help." I had just started my shift when Lucas jumped from the bed to understand what was going on.

The waves had rolled the sailboat a full 360 degrees, knocking the two sailors unconscious. On regaining consciousness, they found themselves bloodied, their boat severely damaged, and water seeping through broken hatches. We assessed their coordinates and realized we were too distant to be of immediate help. However, our friends on the yacht Adventure Bound were within range and promptly steered toward the distressed vessel. For 24 hours, they maintained close proximity and contact until the pair was rescued by a cargo ship.

The magnitude of their decision to reverse course and plunge headfirst into the eye of the storm is difficult to encapsulate in words. Adventure Bound took a week to reach New Zealand, their boat bearing the scars of the rescue mission. But the sixty-two boats were there to provide them with much-needed care upon arrival.

This, I believe, is the power of the 'Rise and Raise Others' movement. We are navigating challenging times, and it is impossible to manage it single-handedly. How fortunate we are to have a strong network of women with whom we can traverse life's tumultuous waters together.

SANDRA MONTES

CMO of Olist, board member, angel investor and mentor.
Instagram: @sandramontesaymore
LinkedIn: www.linkedin.com/in/samontes

THE TWISTS AND TURNS LIFE TAKES

The year 2017 was the worst and the best of my life, and talking about it is liberating.

I am Brazilian, an Aquarius, and I am 51 years old. I come from a large family, with two sisters and a brother: Silmara, Silvana, and Sérgio - yes, we all have names that start with "S." My parents have always been my inspiration: Antonio Romão, a successful economist, and Lourdinha, my mother, a strong woman who was only one and a half meters tall, a pedagogue who became an entrepreneur in her retirement by opening a clothing recycling atelier to honor my grandmother, who was a seamstress with enviable manual skills and always present even though she is no longer in this world.

I am a woman, wife, stepmother, and mother, in that order. The first company I worked for had a great impact on my life, not only because of the experience itself but also because it was where I met my husband - yes, I married my boss. César Aymoré and I have been married for 16 years. We have two children, Bernardo and Guilherme, and I have three stepdaughters: Gabriela, Victoria, and Eduarda. César supported me at an important moment when my career took off in São Paulo; he was a great partner in choosing and believing that this city was our path.

What I want from my life is to give my best to the world, make an impact, and leave a legacy. I am extremely grateful for experiencing the impact of 2017 when I was fired - spoiler - because now I can see that it was the best thing that happened, although it was difficult to understand the mourning that came with it. This experience made me a much stronger and more confident woman and leader, true to my values and principles. I don't enter and leave a meeting quietly; if I'm there, my voice needs to be heard. My life is lived intentionally with a sense of purpose, and I talk about it every day and now, here.

My career: How did I get there and leave "that"?

My father's career was my inspiration. I decided to study Economics in college and started an internship at Citibank. It was my first job, and the finance field intrigued me. I thought that was where I would have a solid career. Embracing the opportunities that arise in the early years of our professional life is very important. It may not always be what you want, but sometimes it opens up new horizons.

After completing my Economics degree, I decided to go to the United States to study English. I lived in Boulder, Colorado, for a year, and besides learning English, I discovered where I truly felt happy. I studied at the university and took advantage of additional learning modules, courses in marketing. It was there that I realized I enjoyed working with people, understanding what they think, how they live, and how they want to live. I returned to Brazil and started a postgraduate course in marketing. Excited about this first transition, I applied for a Trainee program at Electrolux in Brazil.

At Electrolux, I was transferred to São Paulo, where I built the brand with all my strength and learned everything I could about strategy, marketing, and corporate governance, being the only woman in my area. I started as a trainee, until I reached the position of CMO (Chief Marketing Officer) for Latin America, a long way. I dedicated 19 years of my life to the company. I was trained to participate in the leadership board as the only woman in that position. I would wear high heels and dress up every day - as if that supported my opinion and recognition. I remember that something within me still made me feel small, causing me at times to shrink in my speech, voice, and behavior. I believed that a certain behavior was necessary for that management style, but the truth is I was capable of more, and it was up to me to bring that out.

For ten years, I reported to the CEO of Electrolux, Ruy Hirschheimer. He had and still has a significant impact on my career and remains my mentor. We had good moments and some difficult ones, but all of them were important in shaping who I am and how I operate. I also had a dual reporting line, reporting also to Mary Kay Kopt, the global CMO, who was and will always be a great inspiration to me - my first female mentor-leader. She made me understand the true value of listening, generosity, and that leadership means knowing the person beyond their role in the company, above all else regarding them as human.

In 2016, Ruy and Mary Kay left Electrolux. My world crumbled. It was the first time I went through a major change in my leadership team. When you are fortunate to work with such great people, the fear of dealing with something totally new is enormous. We are rarely ready for change; we cling to our comfort zones.

In 2017, after some conversations with the new CEO, we realized it was the end of a cycle and I left Electrolux. I had no idea what it meant to live without my work. I vividly remember that when I got home, I looked into the heart and mind of the person I had been and said, "I need to find myself, I need to take care of the house, acknowledge my children, and focus on my husband." The next day, we traveled to Disney with the kids, and I cried for hours. In my imagination I wanted to disconnect from everything and embrace Mickey with all my privilege. I wanted a break to enter the universe where everything is beautiful but illusory. I returned to Brazil, unemployed, not knowing what to do with my hours and days.

And now, Sandra?

I was scared, afraid, and very hesitant about not knowing how to do anything other than work with home appliances. I doubted myself, couldn't look into other areas; it felt like my end. I was afraid of never being recognized or considered a competent professional and executive - the imposter syndrome. Moreover, financial insecurity haunted me. The situation was comfortable for a year due to the non-compete clause in my severance package, but the fact that I didn't have a salary at the end of the month haunted me. To comfort me, my husband gave me a credit card, but I didn't know how to deal with it. I had always had my own money and been independent, but at that moment, I had to accept that I needed him. It was a great lesson to admit that receiving help, whatever it may be, is part of the process, and it was okay to exercise partnership as a couple during this time. It was the behavior of someone who felt guilty for not contributing, even though I had contributed my whole life.

I started the year with a self-awareness course with Alana Trauczynski that affected me profoundly. She pushed me, made me look inward, and truly see who I was. It took me three months to understand myself and discover my life purpose, both personally and professionally, which I now defend and proudly say is "making a difference in people's lives, generating a positive impact." In addition to that, I started studying the digital world, inspired by my children who are gamers. I wanted to connect with them and have a more common language with them. Technology was the way. I understood that to make an impact on the world, I would have to enter into this new context, speak this language. But how could I do that? How would the world see me?

How did a career transition make me reborn?

My kick-start – or rather, my courage – to leave the offline world for the online world rebirthed me into a better version of myself and I discovered my true personal and professional purpose. It was a tough, intense, and extremely necessary process within a volatile, uncertain, complex, and ambiguous world – a world that I love!

I began studying digital platforms, got closer to Singularity University, and Peter Diamandis' statement about impacting a billion people in the world through technology resonated deeply with me. I took online courses both in and outside Brazil, revised my LinkedIn profile, scheduled countless coffee meetings to hear people's life stories, how they made changes, what they did, and how they felt. I sent emails to headhunters, to people I knew and didn't know, seeking guidance, and most importantly, I asked for help.

I was uplifted by many women: Fatima Zorzato, who clearly told me what my resume should reflect, who I am, and not to be fake; Morena Leite, who invited me to join the Board of the Capim Santo Institute at a time when I didn't believe I knew how to do anything else; Claudia Lebie, a long-time friend who re-entered my life like a whirlwind, shook me up, and never left my side; Denise Paludetto, my neighbor and executive at heart, who knew how to see me, listen to me, and understand me. So many women extended their hand and pulled me back to life! In this context, my friends Paula, Priscila, and Angela, my sisters, and my mother were with me, repeating the lifelong phrase: "Daughter, you've always moved forward and believed that things would fall into place, so why would it be different now?"

I continued on my path, attending interviews, applying for processes and positions, but nothing seemed to align with my desire to bring impact to the world and people. Everything felt cold and distant. I can't recall a day when I allowed myself to sleep until eleven in the morning. It's remarkable how difficult it is for us to give ourselves permission to do nothing.

Then one day, I applied on LinkedIn for a Director of Marketing position at OLX, which clearly required experience in digital platforms that I didn't have. In the interview with Phillip Klein, the CMO, we made a pact. It gave me the opportunity to learn from him about technology and performance in digital platforms, while I brought all my knowledge of marketing. It was one of the most important moments in my life, and I am immensely grateful that he believed in my potential.

Naturally, my arrival was met with apprehension from the team. But once again, it was solely up to me to bring people to my side, to show them that I was there to add value, and above all, to learn. I needed them. I stayed at OLX for three years, the last two as CMO, and it was spectacular. I had people who helped me tremendously in this career transition from the offline world to the online world. José Fay, with his wisdom and his ongoing support of my career, and André Caldeira, who knows the true value of a purpose.

I never wore my high heels again!, and I don't want them back. I started wearing sneakers every day, embracing my height, my tone of voice, and feeling content in my own skin. I stopped using an armored car and started using Uber and the subway. I wanted to be closer to the people I wanted to make an impact. If I wanted change, I needed to start with myself. It was there that I learned to be a simpler, more human person, to expose my vulnerabilities, and to say, "I don't know, but I want to learn."

After that period, an opportunity arose to become the CMO of Rappi, where the purpose was to give people a chance to redeem their time. After a year of wanting to challenge myself even further, I was invited to work at Olist, also as CMO. It is a platform that empowers small and medium-sized entrepreneurs within e-commerce. Once again, my life purpose continued to guide me, impact me, and be "lived into" every day of my life.

During this period, I started mentoring women's groups with the aim of empowering women, using my own example and experiences to prove that it is possible to make changes whenever and however we want. I became an "angel investor," evaluating promising startups. Subsequently, I was invited to be a board advisor at Camil Alimentos, embarking on a new phase of learning and growth, where my career trajectory and transition were essential to that position.

That is why, at the beginning of this chapter, I mentioned that my best version was born out of a career transition and a dismissal. Sharing my story is an honor, and I am grateful for experiencing every part of my life. I don't romanticize it. Of course, it is very challenging to go through such experiences, but what I want to convey here is that it is possible to become whatever we want to be. I didn't change careers at 45 minutes in the second half of the game; I changed at the age of 45 and now I can understand and accept that difficult moment in my life. We are what we share, the sum of everything we experience. I am grateful beyond words. It is just the beginning.

We continue, guided by the light on our journey.

SILVANA ABRAMOVAY

CEO & Co-Founder Amor Aos Pedaços
E-mail: silvana@amoraospedacos.com
Instagram: @silvanabramovay
LinkedIn: www.linkedin.com/silvana-abramovay-marmonti

MY LOVE IN FULL

An entrepreneur, Silvana began her career as a partner at Amor aos Pedaços, a Brazilian pastry chain, where she helped build the pioneering franchise model in Brazil, being responsible for managing both franchisees and the team of collaborators that make up the administrative part of the factory and office. She was part of the Ethics Council of the Brazilian Franchising Association (ABF); her knowledge in retail is shared in lectures throughout the country, such as Alshop partners, Itaú Women Entrepreneurs, and other groups. Her dynamism and knowledge over the years have paved the way for private and corporate mentoring focused on retail, franchising, entrepreneurship, and female leadership on the Mentorela, IVG, and Alumna platforms. She also acts as a guardian on the Angel Us platform, exclusively for women, being part of the management committee of the Leader of the Future and the Women in Retail Institute, and volunteering in various social projects, such as SO+MAR and Cruz de Malta. She studied Social Communication at FAAP/SP and is a mother of three children. She is a foodie at heart, that loves to travel and discover new flavors.

By way of personal introduction, Silvana shares that she is of Jewish origin on both sides of the family, the youngest daughter after four sons: That is why I joke that I learned from a young age to have the necessary grit to conquer my space. Being the youngest of five children, at family dinners I even had to fight for a decent slice of watermelon for dessert. Otherwise, I would always be left with the small, ugly, whitish pieces. Since a young age I have strived to be as independent as my older brothers, something that was encouraged by the women in my life, from which I like to think I inherited their unwavering strength. I have always worked with food, and I now realize how my career choice was a beautiful tribute to the three women that raised me: my grandmother Sima, a caterer who made wonderful Jewish delicacies; her daughter Esther, my dear mother - who is saddened by the fact that she was never taught to cook; and my grandmother Estela, the original foodie, who traveled the world and brought us back gastronomic novelties.

It was following in the footsteps of one of my brothers that at the age of 19 I became a partner at Amor aos Pedaços, a Brazilian pastry brand, just before the opening of their second store. Initially our partnership, whose name can be translated as "Love in Pieces," as we sold slices of cakes, was made up of my youngest brother, Reinaldo, Ivani Calarezi and me. Ivani has now been my partner for almost 40 years, but my brother ended up pursuing other dreams after a decade in the company. Not by chance, he, following the family legacy, he still works in the food industry. Alongside Ivani - a musician, trained as a concert pianist and artist who is responsible for creating all our sweet treats - our company has innovated in the Brazilian food market.

Our company was disruptive in this market, as we created a new way of serving pastries: one where we satisfied our own desires to taste everything when we went to a pastry shop. We allowed our customers to choose the size of the cake slices they wanted to eat, instead of being forced to buy a whole cake, as was the custom elsewhere. Thus, they could choose to eat several small pieces, as many flavors as they wanted. At the time, *brigadeiro*, a Brazilian delicacy, was only available at children's parties, but in our store you could buy it to eat at home. My partner also created a pink sweet for her son on Rafael's first birthday party, called bicho-de-pé, which translates to the name of a flea species in Brazil. At first, people found the name strange, but today it is a national success. I have heard many false versions of the story on why the sweet is named after a flea. The true story is that the name was given by Ivani, who, since childhood, went to her farmhouse and sometimes was bitten by this flea and scratched herself non-stop. Similar to our bicho-de-pé, which we eat non-stop!

The history of my company is intertwined with the story of my life. In fact, it was because of it - specifically a store we opened in a city in the countryside - that I met the father of my three children. In these four decades of entrepreneurship, I have gone through cycles of abundance and economic hardship. We went through four national economic strategic plans and endured changes to our country's currency; we opened stores outside of Brazil and then decided to separate from the partners who were handling our international operations. We moved forward by trusting our intuition, but still had a disappointing experience when we received investment from a fund that is no longer our partner today. Furthermore, we were pioneers in the development of the franchise system in Brazil, being the first bakery in this segment.

It has been a long journey, with many achievements and new beginnings. To survive for decades, it was necessary to evolve alongside the people who made up our journey: our customers, franchisees, employees, and suppliers. I always tried to maintain the premise of being a pioneer, innovative, and even disruptive. With love we created sweets that are part of the emotional memory of generations of customers and a brand with timeless emotional appeal.

Just as there were many phases of Amor aos Pedaços, there were also many Silvanas leading these phases. As Lya Luft said: "living should be - until the last thought and final look - transforming oneself." In the beginning, I was the independent pioneering girl who wanted to be great like her brothers. Soon after, the entrepreneur, wife, and mother stage emerged. How does one balance everything with three children? With stress and difficulty, there were days when I was Silvana, the anxious and worried mother. Every working woman knows what it is like to have to stop a meeting because their child called in sick from school. Yes, I worked a lot, so much so that my children would celebrate on the rare occasions I picked them up from school. But I always tried to attend all parent-teacher meetings and most of their presentations. Luckily, my children always had an incredible father; and when he also had to work, I could count on my mother and my mother-in-law to be "present." Georgia, Adolfo, and Pietro grew up and I consider them my three schools (labs of learning), as they inspire me to innovate and rethink old concepts. I continue to learn from them every day in this world of constant transformation.

Nowadays, when I talk to new mothers who feel guilty for not being able to be in all places at once, I speak of the word "presence." I feel that being mentally present when I am physically with my children has made all the difference in raising them. Mental presence is harder today, as at the time I raised my kids we didn't have cell phones with emails or social media to distract us. Regardless, when problems arose, there was always a risk that these things would engulf me and disconnect me from everything else. So, mental presence requires discipline and practice, but it alleviated my guilt and allowed me to get to know my children, and for them to know that they could count on me, even amid my absences.

There was a time, however, when Silvana "disappeared" for a while: the businesswoman, who had connections beyond her company and her family and friends -- Silvana, the one who networked and had an active social life. Around 2001, an event momentarily broke the rhythm of my life: I experienced an attempted kidnapping in which my factory security guard died in front of me. My life turned 180 degrees. I withdrew and stayed indoors for some time. I had the privilege of being able to take my family out of the country for a few months, until I felt ready to reintroduce them to their normal routine in Brazil.

Many times, I felt paralyzed by fear: I became more reclusive, detached from initiatives in which I previously participated, and faced more "on my own" the challenge of entrepreneurship. I lost the enthusiasm to connect outside of the work-home-leisure environment with other entrepreneurs and women. I slowly healed, and with the complications we had with the investment I mentioned from the outside funding source, I was forced to reinvent myself and reconnect with the pre-incident Silvana. I already knew it was important to update myself, research, and study. I discovered in this new phase that it is also necessary to open up to meet new people, give oneself to others, and receive with gratitude what others can also offer as help. I always knew I didn't know everything, but now I'm living into a new phase of learning with the support of a community, which is allowing me to evolve in all my processes. In this moment of reinvention, I had to learn to abandon my old convictions, attachments, and especially my traumas. I am learning to be more open and more receptive.

I write today as a more light-hearted Silvana, who doesn't succumb as much to the pressure of routine and who understands that processes also need to be enjoyable. I read a quote from Kinsella that marked this new phase of my life: "Success is getting what you want, happiness is wanting what you've achieved." It brings me peace to look at my journey, recognize my achievements, and know that success at any cost, which harms, for example, my health, is no longer worth it.

It was also at this new moment of my life - and because of many lectures from my adult daughter - that I discovered feminism. Whenever feminism came up, I found myself saying, "but I'm not a feminist." Me, a partner in a company led by two women, who started a business venture at 19, a pioneer in a male-dominated business world, didn't see myself as such. I realized that while feminism is something to be proud of for my children's generation, it was still a shameful concept for women my own age. I leaned into a new learning curve for myself and reevaluated my life from another perspective. I changed the lens of the challenges I faced and reconnected with the experience of being a woman in those freshly discovered environments.

Already very comfortable with this new persona of mine, a little before the pandemic, I met Dani Graicar, who created Somos Aladas, translated "We are Allies." She invited me to be a mentor for her project called Mentorela. I accepted the challenge. My generation was taught to have one profession for the entirety of one's life. One job, one company, and then only retirement. I remember how I took a vocational test at 15 and it said I should be a teacher. At the time, I laughed. But now with the mentorships I have been executing, somehow, I finally got there, and became a teacher of some-kind. I, who ended up becoming more reclusive, decided to start going out and meeting women pioneers in this male-dominated world. In the various mentorships I offer, I help women step out of their comfort zone and encourage them.

I feel like I've come out of my cocoon, and I really want to help other women do the same and see the importance of pulling each other up. Much of the female experience is shared: from biological things - like cramps, PMS, and motherhood - to sociological things - like abuse, microaggressions, and the pain of being erased because of gender issues. That's why we have so much to learn from each other. Helping other women has also been healing for me, since when I started my business there were no support groups, which would have helped me make fewer mistakes and feel more welcomed and supported. Thank God the world is changing, and we need to transform people so that they also support each other. I thank Helô Santana, a dear friend who pulled me into this group.

The last and most important message I would give is that entrepreneurship will lead you to deal with others, and you cannot deal with anyone without knowing yourself deeply first, because we reflect our shadows and fears onto others; and confused people hurt and lose incredible people. A company is made up of people, and not knowing about yourself is not knowing about others. This is the the ever-present possibility of failure for everyone.

SILVIA TOCCI MASINI

Instagram: @silviatoccimasini
LinkedIn: www.linkedin.com/in/silviatoccimasini

HOW MANY LIVES HAVE YOU LIVED IN THIS LIFE?

We live many lives within a single life. Sometimes, there are situations that completely escape our control. But it is not these facts that define us. It is the choices we make that completely change the course of our story. Life is vibrant, full of sounds, colors, tones, and emotions... and it takes courage to live these lives. But we are not alone. And that is the beauty of all.

A psychoanalyst, she began her career in 1981 in the field of Education. She worked as a monitor, teacher, counselor, and director in two large private schools in São Paulo. In 2007, she decided to make a career shift, entering the publishing market and specializing in curating national and foreign books. Years ago, she made another turn by pursuing Psychoanalysis and is currently pursuing a postgraduate degree in Psychosomatics at Santa Casa. Having attended to young people and adults for over 40 years, listening and support are the most important tools in her journey.

"Silvia... you have the ability to listen and support... you need to study Psychoanalysis." And that's how my psychoanalyst planted the seed for the next turn in my life.

But let's start from the beginning...

I am the fourth in a family of five children: Luiz Guilherme, Cristina, Cecília, Silvia, and Elvira. All the women had Maria in front of their names.

As I am the daughter of a military man, we lived in several places, and shortly after I was born, when I was ten days old, my father was transferred to Rio de Janeiro. My mother, who was a woman who faced everything, boarded a train with four children (ages seven, five, and two, and me at ten days old).

The four of us were always together, and my brother was the one who led all the games. I have wonderful memories of my childhood. And just when we thought no one else would come, Maria Elvira was born, completing the team.

Imagine a lively family, where every birthday was celebrated with parties. Not to mention Christmas, Easter, Mother's Day, Father's Day... and all the dates we could add to the calendar to celebrate.

We celebrated. I spent my childhood and adolescence between São Paulo and a countryside farmhouse that belonged to my great-grandparents. We played everything, fished in the lake, fed the chickens, rode horses, ate fruits straight from the trees, walked along the train tracks to the town, cycled through the dirt roads. It was delightful!

In addition to the regular stove, there was a wood-burning stove, and that aroma and flavor still accompany me today. It was wonderful! A childhood lived with freedom and lots of joy.

During adolescence, it was in that place where we started going to carnival parties, small gatherings, meeting in the town square, our first romances... in short, a very happy phase surrounded by friends.

My sister Cecilia and I made a great team. We would ride our motorcycles right after lunch, visit friends' houses and farms, and have a great time! We made friendships there that we still cherish today. We were able to witness the teenage years, career choices, marriages, the arrival of children...

Unfortunately, when I turned 19, a tragedy struck our family. Maria Elvira, the youngest at 13 years old, died in a terrible accident on a dirt road in that place where we had the farmhouse.

At that moment, I realized how fragile life was, hanging by a thin and delicate thread that could break with the slightest movement. And then, everything turned upside down.

I left college because what I wanted was to stay at home, a safe place where nothing bad could happen. Those were difficult times, dark times filled with doubts, insecurities, sadness, and lots of tears.

Our family became even closer to support each other, and a network of support formed around us. I remember that, despite having a housekeeper who took care of everything, neighbors and friends helped us a lot in facing everything we were going through. It was incredible because suddenly the doorbell would ring, and things would arrive at our house for us... There would be a cake for an afternoon snack, a pie for dinner. Small gestures that comforted and supported us.

Since adolescence, I had the dream of working and living on my own. It was something I saw in movies and thought was amazing. My father, a very present man in my life, told me that I could work, but that college had to be a priority.

We lived almost in front of a big school in São Paulo, and I managed to get an internship. Three months after the accident, I received an invitation to substitute a teacher. And that's how I started my career in education.

I went back to studying, pursued a teaching degree, specialization, and graduated in Pedagogy.

My career in the school evolved as my love for the profession grew. Being among those children was refreshing, and I had the feeling of being close to my sister again.

Time passed quickly, and from being a monitor, I became a teacher, counselor, and director. I was fully immersed in my profession, with a lot of work and intense dedication to everything related to the education of young people and children. The school grew a lot, and I grew alongside it, absorbing everything with great enthusiasm.

But my professional activities didn't stop there... As I was always very curious and had many friends, other opportunities kept arising, and I would dive into them all.

In my mind, life was meant to be lived intensely, so I didn't let anything pass me by. I did TV commercials, helped a close friend boost his store—I even created an entire summer collection!—worked in casting at a significant production company, did photography... I didn't stop, and all of this brought more life into my life.

After more than 15 years in the school, I decided to take a break, rethink my life and career, and ended up co-founding a luxury boutique in a privileged location in São Paulo with two sisters-in-law. It was a very different time... We organized fashion shows, parties, events. And the most interesting part is that customers always approached me for deeper conversations, advice, a place to vent, and while I was getting involved in something completely different from anything I had done before, I remained closely connected to the area I loved the most: relating to people.

Some time later, I was invited to provide consultancy to two schools, and once again, I found myself being drawn to something I had never truly abandoned.

In these two institutions, I was able to analyze the situation, restructure the entire team, and start a support work. Once again, I began a new life. I felt renewed, with an inexplicable desire to immerse myself in the field once again. And during that phase, several years passed... during this period, I pursued a postgraduate degree in Psychopedagogy and a specialization in People Management.

In 2007, I started feeling that something was wrong, and that I needed to make a change.

I left education and fully immersed myself in the publishing market. A dear friend of mine who owned a publishing house had just closed a contract with a toy industry giant and wanted to create activity magazines. And once again, there I was, diving into a new life. It was an incredible time! We got along amazingly well, and we were able to spend time together while doing a very fulfilling job, witnessing the sales numbers rise, participating in summits and fairs here and abroad.

And then, an excellent opportunity arose with another international giant, but the project had to be developed in a different type of publishing house. I contacted a friend who owned an editorial group specifically in that area, and there I went, along with the contract. A year later, we restructured the entire group, and I entered the trade market.

As I always sought to specialize in what I did, I went to Yale in the United States to take the only Book Publishing course in the world. What an incredible experience! I learned from the industry's greatest minds and had the chance to meet people from different countries with diverse perspectives.

I spent 15 years in the publishing market, and that period opened a huge door to a new life. I specialized in curating works, and my focus was always on personal development. It didn't matter which segment the book belonged to; it had to have a message that would help people reflect on their lives. I felt that was my role: to assist people, even through a book.

I participated in the largest book fairs every year—London, Bologna, Paris, Frankfurt, New York—and the Biennials in São Paulo and Rio de Janeiro. What I enjoyed the most about these fairs was the interaction with people. We exchanged so many experiences, talked about so many subjects... And at international fairs, I conversed with people from all over the world, made friends in various countries, and some of them I still keep in touch with today.

One day, during one of those trips, I paused to think about my future, and something awakened within me again... At that moment, I decided that when I turned 60, I would change my life once more; I would return to helping people.

And that's exactly what happened...

At the beginning of the pandemic, I was in London, and when I returned to São Paulo, everything was starting to shut down. Working from home, curating works, translating, and editing texts, I decided to have a conversation with a former college professor, a psychologist and psychoanalyst—my mentor—and it was at that moment that he said to me, "Silvia, you have the ability to listen and support... you need to study Psychoanalysis."

On the same day, I started researching various courses. I wanted something with academic excellence that would fully prepare me. And that's how this new life began...

Today, I have my own practice, and I provide counseling services to some schools and companies. I love what I do because the exchange with patients is what I value the most.

Psychoanalysis is a deep dive, often into murky waters we never wanted to reach. But having the opportunity to embark on this journey with someone is extremely rewarding.

I am married to the best partner for 20 years, who supports me in all my lives.

I have seven nieces and stepchildren who fill my life. They are fun, supportive, and they joined the family embracing the festive spirit. And to make everything even better, I have three great-nieces who are now my greatest passion; they bring a renewal that fills me with joy. And in some moments with them, I feel like I'm going back in time, feeling close to what I experienced before...

Unfortunately, my father passed away at a very young age. Life's setbacks were stronger. My mother is 88 years old, approaching her 90s with wonderful energy. She works for an NGO, sings in a choir, attends concerts at Sala São Paulo, and steals the spotlight on every occasion. She is an example to all of us.

For me, living is all about having many lives within a single life. How many more lives within this life will I have? I don't know, but I wake up every morning with the conviction that there is still so much to live for, and I will always strive to pursue it.

SIMONE CAGGIANO

Co-founder Zenbox
Instagram: @simonehcaggiano
LinkedIn: www.linkedin.com/in/simone-caggiano

DO WITH PLEASURE, SMASH BORDERS, CHOOSE HAPPINESS

The present moment is the only place with the potential to learn from the past and create the future. All things in our lives have a purpose. I believe that, beyond what happens, the way we react to situations is crucial for what will come next, to build our future. Dream, imprint your dreams in your mind, and nurture them day by day. By doing so, you tune in to that frequency and surround yourself with people who are on the same frequency you wish to occupy.

I have a Bachelor's degree in Agriculture Engineering, a Master's degree in Animal Science from ESALQ, USP, and Texas A&M University. Studied Marketing at ESPM, Executive Education at Singularity, Exponential MBA at Nova School of Business in Portugal. I am certified in Well-Being by Yale and in Neuroscience. Collaborate with the Capital Institute for the development of Regenerative Economics. Was Chairwomen for Live University board. Serve as board member on the Business Council of PUC-Rio and Innovation Committee of IBGC. I act as director at FIESP. Worked in the fields of Agriculture, Telecom, and Automotive. Led Innovation at Audi and served as brand ambassador in Brazil. I was the first woman to be a member of the executive board of the company. Founded the Executive Women's Committee of the Brazil-Germany Chamber. Created the Women Leadership Program at Live University. I am a mentor and investor in startups and a certified coach by ICC. I lived in the United States for seven years.

BOLDNESS, CONFIDENCE, AND PLEASURE: MY FORMULA TO MAKE THINGS HAPPEN

Opening a new chapter of my life. This is exactly where I find myself now. In the past 25 years, I lived trapped in a universe that forced me to shrink to fit in. I can say that I did it skillfully because I reached the top of a professional career that brought me the freedom to live my choices freely. It is incumbent on me to say that it is not necessary to go through what I went through to achieve one's dreams. I had to constantly prove that I was capable in the male-dominated environments. But in the end, everything led me to be the person I am today. And now, with a great deal of emotion, enthusiasm, and reflection, I invite you to get to know me a little better. In the following lines, I share my professional journey, the three lessons I have learned in my career and also the formula that was fundamental to succeed in my endeavors: Taking risks and kill conformity.

I have always been the type of person who can be called a risk-taker. Since childhood, I took the risk of learning by doing rather than being a mere spectator. My roots come from Italian and Lebanese immigrants who managed to build wealth in this promised land, Brazil. Like every third generation of wealthy parents, noble children, and poor grandchildren, I found myself challenged by the question of how I could give back to my ancestors, especially the strong women who came before me, and honor them by conquering territories that previously were rarely explored by women.

After graduated in Agronomy, I spent months making applications in COSAN, a sugarcane mill located in Piracicaba, São Paulo. Until one day, after countless rejections of the type, "We don't hire women here.", I went to visit them and got a job! Working as a livestock manager my routine was being fully active when the first rays of sunlight came over the horizon. With all challenges of the rugged world of a sugarcane mill, I was happy and fulfilled with every surpassed obstacle. Harassment was also part of my daily life, but I developed skills like wit and perceptiveness that allowed me to navigate these rather dangerous waters, with the necessary mastery and skill to keep my job.

My desire to achieve the impossible, was always very potent. Despite recognizing myself as fragile and small, not tall at all, I realized that I was leaving a legacy of opening doors for many women. Even at that time, I understood that a woman's place is wherever she wants to be. It was then that, at the age of 26, I suffered a serious accident that made me rethink my entire life.

It was around four-thirty in the afternoon, and everyone was already tired from a hard day of work, especially an old tractor driver who was ending his career that day to retire. He was a very tall man, and I wanted to help him throw grass into the baler so that the tractor wouldn't have to make another round in the field. And that's when, as I repeated his movements, I fell between the baler and the tractor, being pulled in and twisted by the equipment. It was terrible! When they managed to turn the tractor off, I found myself naked, covered in grease and blood from head to toe. I didn't know what was happening, but I saw my thumb hanging on the baler and blood everywhere. With all my strength, I managed to get out of there, and the truck driver threw his shirt over me to cover me. All the other men who were in the field ran and hid. I left the farm in the late afternoon, and after receiving first aid in the city, I arrived in São Paulo at about ten o'clock at night. My family was waiting for me at the door of the Hospital. During those five hours, doubts and anxieties were mixed with the physical pain of the accident.

To understand the reason for these situations in our lives, we must go beyond the surface, dive in, and pass them through our scale of values. And for me, it meant freedom to expand my potential and do it with happiness, without looking at the damage of losing a thumb in a terrible accident or the limitations imposed by social biases.

FREEDOM IS THE VALUE THAT MOVES ME

Driven by intuition and a passion for horses, I wrote a letter to the top four Quarter Horse trainers in the United States, telling them who I was. I made the following proposal: "I will work for you, and you won't pay me; you will teach me. At the end of the agreement, I will not owe you anything. That is my offer." I received responses from all of them (wow!) and chose the top one. And so, off I went to Texas! I don't need to say how much I regretted giving up my comfortable and structured life. I barely understood what Texans were saying, and I had no idea how tough it was to saddle and train horses. But after four months, I decided I would never leave. I became a horse trainer! It was my paradise!

It didn't take long for me to connect with friends and influential people. Through these connections, I ended up completing my Master's degree in Animal Science at Texas A&M University, and four years later, I started my Ph.D. at A&M. Seven years passed and an event changed my life forever: the birth of my daughter Isabella, a real Texan!

Among the titles I received, the most challenging one was that of mother, because we never get a diploma for that; it's a continuous learning experience for life, isn't it?! In these moments of reflection, taking into account all the stability I had left behind to fulfill my dream, and be determined to take on motherhood independently, I once again encountered the pleasure that the courage to make choices brought to my daily life, along with all the consequences of those choices.

SURRENDER AND LEARN WITH VULNERABILITY.

My mother had always seen in me a great ability to communicate and deal with people. And so, she arranged a job interview for me as soon as I arrived in Brazil for a "vacation." Reluctantly, I went for that interview at Portugal Telecom. I never imagined that from then on, my mother intuitively was laying the first bricks of a corporate career that I had never dreamed of.

Well, the day of the interview arrived, and a Portuguese man sitting behind a desk simply raised his round glasses and asked me, in his best accent, "What can you do, girl?" I replied, "Take care of horses." To my great surprise, he had no doubts and replied, "You're hired!" It was a temporary, part-time job. However, within two weeks, there I was, moving to Brasília, Capital of Brazil with a baby, a nanny, and all the paraphernalia of a household with a child. My daughter was 1 year old at that time. After the acquisition of a Telecom Service provider, it didn't take long for the same man to come up with my new role: Investor Relations. "You speak English well. We're going public, and you will meet the investors." I was shocked! "Investor Relations?" I had never heard of it! But I embraced the cause! A year later, another Portuguese man came and said to me, "You have flair for marketing. Do you want to work with me?" I replied, "I know nothing about marketing!" Unlike me, he calmly said, "That's okay, you have a natural talent."

After four years again, knowing nothing about customer services, I accepted yet another challenge and was promoted!

After five years, a German client invited me for breakfast. He turned out to be the president of Audi in Brazil. During breakfast, he invited me to work for Audi. And once again I was going to write a new chapter, now as the Audi Ambassador in Brazil.

In my 15-year journey with this incredible brand, I felt the pleasure of imprinting my soul's signature on every delivery. Through a total of eight different roles and seven presidents, I also started mentoring young professional women and brought together female owners of Audi dealerships, the Audi Ladies.

Throughout these years, I sought to find spaces for my personal fulfillment in everything I did. Today, it is clear to me that work and life blend together when you do what you love and grow at the same time. What matters to me is who you become every time you achieve a goal and, above all, the refinement of oneself.

NETWORKING IS ABOUT LOOKING WITH COMPASSION AND SERVING PEOPLE.

I value relationships as a way to deepen self-knowledge, and through my skills and networking, I am constantly expanding my knowledge and building a supportive network. Creating those relationships allows me to thrive in any space and not be intimidated by any topic. My restlessness is always the expansion of the soul, seeking more knowledge, more abundance, more pleasure. Thus, I recognize lifelong learning as a lifestyle that always prepares me for the next steps.

With no intention of being an example or to tell a great story, I want to open my toolbox and share with you three lessons and tools that can help you face the challenges in your career. However, I must give credit to two great forces that have been by my side throughout these years, helping me face every bump on the road. The first is

Nasira Caggiano, my mother. She is a sweet and gentle woman with deep blue eyes like the ocean, but also a fortress who, at 85 years, is still working with great determination, running her Lebanese food boutique. The second great force comes from my daughter, Isabella, who with her luminous soul has nourished me with courage and passion for life.

So, let's move on to the lessons and tools:

1. **Lesson: Embrace challenges**. We are never really ready for the next challenge. When you set out to do something, you will encounter people that help you. Therefore, do not be afraid to face the new and accept challenges. Steve Jobs used to say that things only make sense when you look back. I clearly see it in my life. Do not wait to find meaning beforehand; it comes after you face the challenges. **Tool: Confidence.**

2. **Lesson: Do what you love**. One thing I have learned in life is that we **are** our choices, and the only way to be extraordinary at work is by doing what we love. And here comes a very important factor, resilience. If you face the challenges and remain resilient, you will undoubtedly succeed. **Tool: Pleasure**.

3. **Lesson:** According to Einstein, the smart people in the world are the ones who leverage the experience of others to take faster steps and progress in life. Therefore, I say to you: **seek mentors, choose role models**, and follow them. I am confident that success will come to you! **Tool: Boldness**.

TALITA ZAMPIERI

CSO & CMO
LinkedIn: www.linkedin.com/in/talita-zampieri/

BE A SUBMARINE, NOT A SHIP

I asked my husband-to-be: "What my superpower is?"

And he replied, "You are deep; you challenge my arguments, so in some ways, it was never easy to talk to you. I always had to think a lot because I knew that a small amount of thought wouldn't be enough. In this way , you teach our children, and me every day to be a better man."

Then, I thought to myself: I won, I made it, I overcame the prejudices of my nature, and even though I am still under construction, what I see so far is something I am proud of.

Paternal abandonment affects development, self-esteem, relationships; observed from childhood to adulthood. National Fatherhood Initiative - USA.

I am part of the alarming statistic in Brazil of children born without their father's legal registration and personal participation in their lives. I was born into a humble family in the countryside of São Paulo. My mother, at the age of 17, became pregnant by my father, the cool guy in town. She didn't take very kindly the lack of support she received from the man she loved. I was registered under the name of my mother without any reference to the birth father's name.

We moved to the capital of São Paulo when I was a baby. My grandparents had been separated since I was born. So, I lived with a large family of strong women who ran the household.

My great-grandmother was a widow, illiterate, and the wisest woman I have ever met. She taught me a lot about values. Amazingly, she was the most modern among them, with such a visionary outlook on the world and the role of women. Not until I was an adult did I really comprehend how subversive she actually was.

My grandmother only attended elementary school, but she was very clever. Despite the hardships of life, she always showed me the good side of things. She fought bravely for the family's rights, in spite of all limitations.

My aunt studied Science and Math, not because she wanted to, but because it was the only option available to her, just like my mother. To me, she was always my *private power bank* of positive energy.

My mother was always firm and courageous, saying: "Don't give up on your dreams; don't depend on anyone; don't trust that the world will support you; your achievements will be through your own effort."

It was this strength and wisdom that always *raised me* and pulled me forward. I think she really tried to play the dual role of mother and father to me, and I confess that when I was little, I found it extremely hard; however, when I became a woman and understood the challenges of her role, I developed deep respect, admiration, and everlasting gratitude for my mother's effort and dedication.

Ms. Márcia is a powerful woman. Even without the opportunity to have other biological children, she *"adopted"* my cousin/sister when her brother's wife died after Thamires' birth. So, another woman came into to this female family.

There were also three more people under that roof - my uncle Tita and my uncle Júnior, whom I adopted as my father, and me. But with all due respect to the men in the house, I only remember the strength and guidance of the women. They were the first women who *raised* me, they always fought to make the story of my life distinctive.

From an early age, I was enrolled in every course available: many languages, singing, volleyball, arts, theater, piano. There was a deep and compelling desire to make me someone with depth, balance, and truth.

I am deeply grateful for their having the sensitivity to expose me to a world of performance, but also a world of tenderness. I grew up without luxury, brand-name sneakers, incredible trips, but I studied in great schools because my grandmother worked in them to make it possible for me.

"As a guest" in that world I met and learned a lot, and this strengthened my decision that when I grew up, I would be *"a hostess"*. I started working at 16, and my first achievements were helping my family build their first home, and paying for my Ad and Marketing degree at Mackenzie University after winning a scholarship at two other prestigious universities.

After a year of studying, I decided to switch from my stable job that gave me some financial independence to an underpaid internship in my field, full of hope for the future. I started in the marketing department of a pharma industry. Working inside a hospital, I witnessed suffering and I saw the World Trade Center collapse in New York. This profound moment led me to dedicate myself to spreading happiness, fighting for causes, supporting others, *raise women*, and maintaining integrity. Guided by this purpose, I crafted a steadfast plan.

I left that internship and went to work in the beer industry. My learning curve increased. I traveled, dealt with big names in the market, and I participated in two company mergers. Everything was of ultimate importance, but nothing was easy. I also started to learn about sexism, all kinds of harassment, and difficult choices. I began to understand that women in the job market face some fundamental challenges and difficulties, that any small evolutionary steps of progress would be a revolution.

In my career I made a move to the agency side of the business as a strategic planner because I felt that I needed to know different markets, products, at the same time. It worked out very well! I could work on several brands, face different market problems, translate strategies in different ways, and it super charged my professional development. Learning many lessons along the way, I was *raised* by some wonderful people, such as Laura Chiavone who was the first woman to truly empathize with me in the profession. But I also went through things that are still difficult to imagine. I recall that at one event a top agency executive asked me into the room just for the purpose of taking an award off the shelf to show to a powerful client, for the sole purpose of "showing off" the women in the company. This kind of sexist harassment was constant; it happened to many women.

Indeed, throughout my career, I dealt with recognized harassers, and I confess that I always recognized it for what it was, but I was afraid of being harmed for speaking up and revealing myself. However, I developed the ability to push back against it, even though the memories still haunt me to this day.

I have always been passionate about my work. I used to stay in the office for more than 12 hours a day. I am not proud of that. Therefore, my relationships all came from the workplace. At the young age of 23, I ended up marrying one of my clients. I leaned into learning the responsibilities of marriage, discerning my other superpower - being a stepmother to a wonderful girl.

My marriage did not last, but alongside my ex-husband, I built a lot. We came from similar difficult family histories, but we were opposites in terms of beliefs and values. Together, we undertook and created the first Brazilian advertising agency with a focus on retail. We had ups and downs, but we built a team of more than 150 people, serving powerful clients inside the country and across South America. At 25 years old, I was the strategist at our agency, and I felt the weight of this job. On the one hand, I had to work on the front lines with clients, and on the other I had charge of the back office. At this juncture we decided it was time to sell to a large advertising group and get the benefits of shared services.

I continued to grow. Rather quickly, at a young age, because I successfully carried a large portfolio of tasks and responsibilities, I became a director. Everything in my life seemed to come early. In the midst of all the professional challenges, after losing my daughter Nina in the sixth month of pregnancy, at age 29 I became a mother to Tom. My marriage was already on edge, but I was *raised* by Isabelle Perelmuter, an elegant woman who reminded me how good I was, regardless of the difficult moments life brought.

When Tom was 3 years old, in the name of professional, personal, and marital freedom, I decided to *"abandon the ship of entrepreneurship"*. I had worked with my ex-husband for a few years, so I felt the need to go back to flying solo in my career.

I took on an important position at Ogilvy, *raised* by Murilo Lico. I came on board alongside a great team, designed specifically to craft the ideal work model for the agency's main client. In these years I negotiated a steep learning curve and acquired great knowledge. It was there that I learned truly to trust other women and rely on a deep support network. Amazing women *raised* me, as peers, bosses, and clients.

Leaving the agency, my priority was to study abroad with my son, seeking a fresh perspective on the world. This sabbatical was driven by personal growth rather than professional aspirations. Opting for Miami, hoping for regular contact between Tom and his father - it did not happen! I found myself trapped in repetitive cycles, fulfilling the role of both parents. Joined by my grandmother, we embarked on this adventure together, supporting one another along the way.

During our time in Miami, I separated from my ex-husband. It was an important moment, when I rediscovered myself as a woman. I was 35 when we separated, and I felt lost. I no longer knew how to flirt or show myself off as a woman. I only knew how to sell myself as a professional. And that's when my sister Thamires, my cousin Vitoria, and my stepdaughter Bianca - who were living with me in Miami, *raised* me back to live life fully and *"being a woman"*. Thank you the girls for not abandoning me!

When I returned to Brazil, determined to break into the digital & tech market, I was *raised* by Renata D'Avilla and returned to another WPP agency to take on the strategy group, soaring with success. Amidst the pandemic, I joined Africa DDB, where I took the entire food line at the agency. During this time I realized the isolating nature of top executive roles for women. Despite our professional evolution, we were burdened with additional responsibilities while juggling our existing ones, particularly in the *"care economy"*, which was further exacerbated by COVID.

At that same moment, in spite all my achievements, I received some feedback from important people in my life, that I had never truly loved, given myself completely for someone, and opened up my intimacy. In my self-analysis, I discerned that this *"pure reality"* was missing in my life.

I was programmed to conquer and had lived *a life like a ship and not like a submarine.* I was happy and fulfilled, but I had not yet entered the *depths of the ocean of my being.* In my career, everything kept going well. I became the CSO of a top experience agency, *raised* by Ligia Vulcano and Bazinho Ferraz.

I returned to the marketing chair as CMO of a fintech company, *raised* by Marcelo Villela, which allowed me to *fight the fight for women in tech* - where there is plenty of sexism, and lack of generosity. But my *ship only turned into a submarine* in my encounter with my life partner, in 2020: yes, as a grown woman I discovered real love.

Marco Antonio carried me into the depths of my emotional ocean, pulling me miles down in a careful way, so I could rise to the surface again breathing peacefully. He respects my story, my way, my flaws. He allowed me the possibility of being a stepmother again, but now with a present and supportive father. He takes care of my son with the same care and dedication he has for his own children. He was born into a sexist world but has developed himself with great sensitivity, a path he intentionally follows every single day.

Everything I have learned and achieved in life makes more sense when shared with those who want to learn - always.

Although Marco comes from a *"different world"* than I, we share the same beliefs and values. So, here is my advice: professionally and personally, connect with people that share the same beliefs as you. And if you have limiting beliefs that create personal barriers, remove them from your life as quickly as possible. I needed a lot of yoga, meditation, and a circle of naked women at a sacred-feminine-retreat for this to happen - thank you Dany Gonçalves for *raising* me into that moment - to make me believe that I could be a loved woman in the lineage of my predecessors. An achiever and a woman who runs with wolves, yes, but loved and secure in her own desires always.

Nothing is achieved by a mind that doubts.
B.K.S. Iyengar

THAIS CHEDE

Senior Executive I Mentor
E-mail: thaischede@gmail.com
LinkedIn: www.linkedin.com/in/thaischede

THE BEGINNING

In 1962, the Married Women's Statute, Law No. 4.212/1962, was approved, which allowed, among other things, "married women to no longer require their husband's authorization to work." I am Thais Chede, and it was in this year that I was born in the city of Sao Paulo, Brazil.

IT'S ALL ABOUT PEOPLE

In college, studying Architecture and Urbanism, I learned that aesthetics, in a simplified way, consist of perceiving the forms of the world through the senses, observing nature, colors, movements, the sky, and people, among many other things. Writing this text made me realize that this exercise of observation proposed by aesthetics was a valuable lesson in the relationships I built throughout my life. Herein lies a strong connection between the architect, the advertiser, and the executive that I became. In fact, I am an architect who transitioned into advertising and executive roles during my journey.

My first job was as a salesperson in a fabric store, but I, being restless, always kept an eye out for other opportunities that would allow me to build a career in a large company. It was Nórea de Vitto, a friend from college, who first opened a door for me, recommending me for a position at Editora Abril, the largest publishing company in Brazil.. I went to work as an advertising agent at the age of 19, selling ads in Casa Claudia, a decoration magazine.

I enjoyed selling, meeting people, and quickly understood that when you earn someone's trust, everything becomes easier – including in business. I learned early on that building relationships based on trust was my greatest superpower, and the key to that was respect – listening to people, showing genuine interest in what they have to say, and always taking seriously what was agreed upon.

There were several years of great results and of learning accompanied by a lot of effort to integrate myself into a predominantly male environment – as is the case in most companies – where opportunities appeared more for men than for women, the minority to which I belonged.

I had many accomplishments, some disappointments, and some unrecognized merits. There were several times I cried in the bathroom, but I didn't give up. Until the opportunity came to manage one magazine, then another, and one day I was invited by Nicolino Spina, business unit general manager, to take on my first leadership position as the director of advertising for men's magazines.

At that moment, my reaction was similar to that of many women: I hesitated to accept because I didn't feel capable. Surely, there were other professionals more prepared than I. The well-known imposter syndrome was manifesting itself, but that's when my husband stepped in to pull me, or rather, push me. He told that I shouldn't have any fear in accepting and that I should embrace this chance with all my might. Whatever I didn't know, I would learn. And so, filled with fear and without having slept the night before I began, I accepted and dived in headfirst. The work was intense; we assembled an incredible team, with half of them being women, and that first year we nearly doubled the advertising revenue over the previous year.

Soon after, I received an invitation to be the first female director of advertising at Veja, the largest magazine in the country. Veja was a powerhouse characterized by the passion of Roberto Civita, a shareholder, editor, and inspiring leader. There, I expanded my horizons and got to meet many people who taught me, supported me, and became my career co-partners.

Maurizio Mauro, then president of Abril Group, was one of those people, and he advised me to pursue an MBA because it would be essential to my understanding the theory of business management. This would be fundamental in order to continue advancing in my career. I followed his advice and quickly realized that I needed to continuously develop my skills and knowledge.

With hard work, resilience, and a robust support network, I gained confidence. I became a female leader in the advertising market, and later, as general director of advertising for Grupo Abril, I was privileged to sit at tables where, most of the time, I was the only woman. I knew that at those tables, I was representing the company, but also paving the way for other women.

Inspiring Women

The 29 years at Abril were spent in a growing company, in a growing market, alongside talented individuals and some empowered women who, without asking for permission, all left their mark. I became accustomed to observing these women and learned from them to not fear the environment dominated mostly by male leadership.

I want to mention the women who had the most impact on me, who paved the way for myself and many others, and who inspired me to be fearless and never give up: Fatima Ali, Olga Krell, Elda Muller, Deborah Wright, Sandra Sampaio, and Ana Maria Braga. Ana Maria was my boss during my first pregnancy, and she told me something that I will never forget: "Thais, the day your child is born, you will never do anything the same way again. Not even driving a car."

That's when I understood how important it is for us, women, to have women in our professional journeys, to teach us and, above all, to understand us. She was clearly right. It would be a profound transformation in my life, and, from that moment, it became necessary to balance the role of being a mother with everything else. Once again, I wouldn't have been able to find that balance without my active support network.

Learning to prioritize and say "no" was also incredibly valuable in this process, and I wish I had discovered that much earlier.

A New Chapter

I left Abril in 2014, and 15 days later, I began a new professional chapter at Globo, the largest media conglomerate and TV network in Brazil. It was Willy Haas, the general director of business, who extended the invitation to me.

I started as the director of special projects, an area that didn't exist before, and a year later, I became the director of Affiliate Relations Central, a move that represented a significant transformation in my career. It basically consisted in taking on the responsibility for the relationship and partnership between Globo and its 115 independent affiliated television stations throughout the whole country - a complex and completely different activity from my previous roles, that put me outside my comfort zone.

It was a major challenge taking on the responsibility for the partnership between Globo and its affiliates across the country.

In this position, I got to know Brazil, its regionalisms, accents, companies, entrepreneurs, and people who, in a way, continuously contribute to develop our country. I built a new network of relationships, and once again, earning the trust of new partners was the foundation for carrying out my new role. There were many conversations, trips, and discoveries, and I recommend that everyone pay close attention to Brazil because, in addition to its beauty, there are countless opportunities.

Working at Globo was quite a challenge. It was a company that captivated me, and I had to learn and re-relearn lessons, as well as integrate myself into a different business culture, in an environment where I didn't know the processes or the people. I observed, learned, and heavily relied on the valuable knowledge and support of my team. It was a very enriching 8-year experience.

An Interruption

My other superpower is not giving up, being resilient, and that was extremely valuable on numerous occasions, especially in what I'm about to share.

During a self-examination at the age of 44, I discovered I had breast cancer. The work I had done trained me to make decisions, be pragmatic, and developed in me an ability to solve problems. All of that was very useful when I saw my life at risk. I needed everything I had learned to act quickly, and I would do anything to remove that cancer from my body as soon as possible. A surgical procedure that would normally take at least three weeks to happen due to exams and other bureaucratic procedures took place in just four days. At that time, a privileged support network allowed me to expedite the process, and I especially relied on the help of my friend and plastic surgeon, Ricardo Marujo.

I chose to face the illness in my own way because it was my body that was sick. I am a woman who has fears, but also a lot of courage. I fear heights, flying on planes, speeding on the road. I was even afraid of writing this chapter. But I'm not afraid of stepping onto a stage, giving a lecture, facing anyone, and I wasn't afraid of cancer.

I underwent surgery, chemotherapy, and radiation therapy, experiencing all the side effects. I didn't stop working because I was certain that continuing to do what I loved would help me. I shared with everyone what was happening to me, explaining the treatment, the changes in my appearance, and that I would have to wear a wig. I asked them to help me navigate this journey as naturally as possible.

But, of course, it didn't happen exactly as I expected. People who were always there for me distanced themselves because they didn't know how to deal with the situation. People I barely knew came out of nowhere to support me. And that made me realize that everyone reacts differently, and that's okay. Each person will give you what they can at that moment, and it has nothing to do with affection, liking, or disliking you.

It was an interruption to what I called normalcy, a period to reflect on and discover what is truly important in life, specifically for me. I strengthened my bonds with my family, with the friends who are an important part of my life, and I learned to be present in the moment. It's a reflection that we should all engage in without having to become ill, don't you think?

THE TRANSFORMATION

Gender inequality has been a topic and a struggle since I started working forty years ago. There has certainly been some progress, but not at the necessary speed. The Uma Sobe e Puxa a Outra group is a powerful way to accelerate this process by forming an unparalleled support network based on generosity, sisterhood, and respect.

Pulling someone up is to take action towards transformation. It is contributing to creating a society where women can live without prejudice and find a job market with equal opportunities, regardless of gender.

Structural sexism presented itself at various moments in my journey, both through men and women. However, I must admit that sometimes I only understood it after the fact, and in some cases, many years later.

The fight for equality must go on; it belongs to everyone and is for everyone. Taking part in it is a small contribution that I, as a woman aware of my privileges, would like to leave as a legacy for society.

Finally, I leave you with a quote from an admirable woman who represents me:

"I have silly fears and absurd courage."
CLARICE LISPECTOR

I dedicate this chapter to my main support network: to Adriana, my daughter who made me realize that I have always been an active feminist; to Felipe, my son who from a young age defined that my job was always to have conversations; and to Eduardo, my husband, who provided support so that I could invest in my career.

I also thank my family, my friends, the professionals I have met, and so many people I have encountered along the way. Without each and every one of you, this chapter would have been written very differently.

TONIA CASARIN

Innovative human development, well-being, mental health and holistic therapies. Speaker. Global Impact Challenge Award Winner from Singularity University
Lemann Fellow, Salzburg Global Fellow and Eisenhower Fellow
Email: toniacasarin@gmail.com
Instagram: @toniacasarin
Linkedin: www.linkedin.com/in/toniacasarin

I'VE LEARNED HOW TO LIVE WHEN I ALMOST DIED

"f you die before you die, you won't die when you die."
An inscription on St. Paul's Monastery (10th-11th century) in Attica,
Greece.

After my near-death experience, I experienced "ego dissolution" during my first psychedelic journey. It brought about a deep sense of peace and happiness. This experience unveiled the profound mystery of life: we truly learn to live when we come close to death. My journey through life started with the gift of possibilities that the finite nature of existence presented. How many different lives can we live?

Santorini presented us with a breathtaking day, or rather, a flawless one. My husband, Carlos, and I had been enjoying a few days of vacation, during which we delved into the historical richness of Athens, immersed ourselves in its captivating mythology, and sailed through the idyllic Greek waters and islands.

On one particular day, we had dinner by the sea, with the orange shades of the sunset casting a warm glow on our hungry bodies, at a traditional Greek family restaurant. In that moment, Carlos said it was the most exquisite and perfect day of his life. The overwhelming feeling of fulfillness led him to say that he could happily die at that moment.

Yet, as is the nature of life, perfection began to yield to impermanence, a concept I had been continually learning through my meditations as a novice Buddhist practitioner.

On this incredible trip, I almost died. After the sunset dinner, I began experiencing bleeding, a consequence of another miscarriage. It was the second time I was going through that heartbreaking situation. I had to cope with immense sadness while also dealing with the cruel task of breaking the news to my husband. With a trembling voice, I called him into the bathroom. As I looked into his eyes, I shook my head, unable to articulate the words. It was a mix of sadness, shame, disappointment, and guilt that overwhelmed me. I had never imagined I would endure such intense pain again.

I called my mother, who was unaware of my pregnancy, to tell her what happened. Only a mother knows how to comfort us. We cried together: me, my mother, and my husband. After the inconsolable crying and infinite trips to the restroom, I thought I had a grasp on what to anticipate during a second miscarriage. However, life has a way of reminding you that you don't know much.

The morning came. The sun was shining on the enchanted island, but I had no strength to look at it. The brightness of sun light in the room was the most I could enjoy. I was very weak, but I could have breakfast and drink a lot of fluids. I felt better. There was no pain or contractions. The sun marched on the horizon while I was still lying on the bed. That's when I managed to speak with my doctor in Brazil, who recommended checking my vital signs – temperature, heart rate, and blood pressure. Temperature checked. Heart rate checked. Carlos went to the closest pharmacy to buy a blood pressure monitor. When he returned with the device, he asked me to sit down. I couldn't. I had a very strong dizziness every time I tried to sit. The lying position was the only one possible at that moment. Then I had some convulsions and fainted. At that moment, he called an ambulance.

The paramedics arrived asking various questions. I understood what they were asking me, wanted to respond, but the words wouldn't come out of my mouth. I had a mental confusion and was paralyzed. At that moment, I felt fear. A greater sense of urgency filled the air, and no one asked me anything else; they just rushed to get me out of there. Tied to the stretcher, in the labyrinthine stairs of Santorini, I finally arrived in the ambulance that would take me to the nearest public hospital. I thought I was going to die.

At hospital, four nurses quickly approached me and started poking my arms, unable to find a vein. Another nurse rushed and put the oxygen tube in my nose. As soon as the first needle penetrated a vein, they started a bunch of fluids, medications, and saline. At the same time, two nurses did an ultrasound on me, and shortly after, began a curettage. Without anesthesia.

The medical team communicated in Greek, talking over each other; it was impossible to understand anything. Almost no one spoke English. I was in a bed bay protected by a curtain that separated me from the main corridor. The medical team were not wearing uniforms making it impossible to identify who was on the medical staff and who wasn't. Some people open the curtain to 'take a look' on what what that urgency. I felt extremely vulnerable. Amidst the chaos among the doctors, who were clearly desperate about my situation, there was a compassionate nurse. She looked at me and, with a strong accent, reassured me by saying, "Don't worry." I confess I was in a daze and not functioning fully, but definitely, I didn't feel worried. Not at that moment.

I glanced at the wall clock across the corridor and I realized that I still didn't feel any better even after four hours. Carlos was giving me with updates, trying to understand the situation and the medications they were administering to share the information to doctors in Brazil. Additionally, he was trying to change our flight back to California, where we live. He informed me that I needed a blood transfusion, but none of the blood matched with mine. Due to this critical situation, the hospital director decided to call the Greek Air Force plane to transfer me, as he couldn't take the risk of a potential fatality occurring within the hospital. It was a situation where I couldn't afford to die there.

A midwife unexpectedly arrived. She was not on call, but checked her phone in the middle of the night and saw that there was an emergency. The emergency was me. Upon her arrival, she took charge of the situation. The blood compatibility test finally came back positive. Nevertheless, the doctors were apprehensive about initiating a blood transfusion due to my fever. The midwife firmly instructed nurses to administer the blood through my arm. It was at that moment that I finally breathed a sigh of relief. I am immensely grateful to her.

She then engaged in an argument with the Greek Air Force rescue team, who had arrived. Their directive was to expedite my transfer to a better-equipped hospital in Crete. However, she maintained that I was not in condition to board the plane. She insisted that they would need to wait until she had cleared me for transport.

I couldn't pinpoint the exact moment when the midwife gave the green light for my plane transfer. I was covered in wires, with two doctors in the aircraft, essentially functioned as an ambulance with wings. The most distressing part of the flight was hearing my husband's asking me how I was feeling, yet I was unable to respond.

In Crete, they conducted two additional curettages without anesthesia. After that, my memory becomes hazy, and I can't recall what happened. I must have drifted off to sleep on the hospital. At some point later on, I was awaken by the sound of inconsolable crying. It was my husband, seated in a chair beside the bed. For the first time, his rush of adrenaline and anxiety transformed into tears of relief. I was alive.

Returning home was both an accomplishment and a profound shock. When you've encountered death so intimately, it compels you to reevaluate every aspect of your life. Absolutely everything. I found myself in a state of imbalance, realizing that

I needed help. Having been in therapy for years, I understood that the path to healing from this trauma required a different approach.

Since immersing myself in the study of mental health, I was aware of the potential healing of psychedelics. I am privileged to have family members deeply involved in research who guided me through the scientific results. The findings were remarkably promising and demonstrated safety with interdisciplinary scientific research conducted at prestigious institutions. I delved deeper into the potential of these compounds in tackling one of the most significant challenges of our era: mental health. Furthermore, the legal landscape is changing, with countries like Australia decriminalizing and allowing doctors to prescribe MDMA and psilocybin treatments.

In clinical trials, various groups, including veterans, terminally ill cancer patients, and those with mental health challenges, experienced significant benefits from psychedelic-assisted therapies. I embarked on a four-month therapeutic journey, despite no prior recreational drug use experience.

I'm saying goodbye to the old Tonia as I'm becoming a new person. There's been a profound transformation within me, and I no longer require her presence. This farewell instills in me a sense of confidence, security, strength, and empowerment. It's as if I'm rediscovering my true self. I can vividly recall a time when the old Tonia and I struggled together to shape a new version of myself. It was undeniably challenging, but I came to realize that the key was letting go of my old self. In this process, I uncovered another layer of myself, a fusion of the new and old, resulting in a more whole and complete Tonia.

I thank the old me, who taught me the power of resilience. The power of struggle. The power of survival. The power to achieve. The power of persistence. And the power to learn that going through tough times builds character. She taught me that I can do anything I want. I want her to know that she is the most important person in my life. Without her, I wouldn't be where I am today. I value her so much that it's hard to say goodbye. I will always remember her. She is a part of me. Thank you very much for your courage in making me a different person.

The new Tonia explores well-being, healing, and consciousness expansion, guiding those with traumas to transform and find profound gratitude for life as I did. This journey stretches my limits of perception and cognition, offering new perspectives and deeper self-understanding. This process helps me address past traumas, work through unresolved issues, find solutions, and embrace gratitude. It leads to emotional liberation, profound well-being, and increased self-awareness. Challenging limiting beliefs and thought patterns transforms me into a more optimistic, less worried, less guarded and more confident Tonia. More confident in herself and in life. I'm proud of who I'm becoming.

I feel more empathy and connection with others, whether they are known or unknown. Less judgment, more compassion, and a certainty that we are all connected. There is no other, there is only us. The separation of self and other is the result of an illusion trapped in bodies. A deep sense of interconnectedness, reverence, and transcendence that opens space for my PhD in Transpersonal Psychology in 2024.

I am starting my second life. The story of strength and struggle is turning into a story of love and courage. And I am ready to live it. How many lives can you live?

*As I write this story, I am pregnant, with a healthy boy due to 2024.

VANESSA BRANDÃO

A marketeer, TEDx speaker, with more than 20 years of experience, Vanessa is now marketing director at HEINEKEN group in Brazil. During her journey at the company, she has led brands like Amstel, Devassa, Tiger, Desperados and Heineken – which under her leadership has become leader of the premium beer segment, the preferred brand in the Brazil, and the country has reached the mark of the biggest Heineken volume in the world. Before that she worked for 8 years at Unilever with brands such as Dove, Sunsilk, and Persil.

Vanessa is also a mom, a professional voice-over technician, and loves to sing during her free time.

Instagram: @vanessa.brandaoo
Linkedin: www.linkedin.com/in/vanessabrandao

IN PEACE WITH MY FEARS

I have always believed in what people say. No matter if it is a good or a bad message, I always believe. Some people take advantage of this to prank me for the sake of the group entertainment, and, not rarely, I end up falling into the same joke more than one time (and it is indeed funny, I laugh at myself all the time). Others call me naive, and I actually have been when I was younger, being teased by mean "friends" who wanted to tear me down. But nowadays I prefer to think that the truth was always that my brain is wired to be a believer.

The bright side of it is that I believe in all possibilities, that nothing is impossible until we try. And even if things don't happen as we planned originally, they can still be awesome. I am an optimist.

But it hasn't always been like that. In fact, I think I was the most frightened kid I've ever known. I was afraid of the dark, the shadows, the urban egends kids spread around at school, and even afraid of the kitchen microwave that one day in my dreams started to talk, spit fire, and drag people inside it. There was a time that I even had to sleep with my neck covered because I didn't want any vampire from the local soap opera to bite me during my sleep. As if the blanket would save me from becoming immortal. Funny, huh? By now I think you got it that fear was a constant presence during my childhood. But not any fear, it was fear o⁻ things that only existed in my head.

I can say I had a hell of an imagination to create things that would scare me. But as strong as it was this creative imagination, was the ability to ask for help and not try to deal with it by myself. Believe it or not, during my childhood, the way out I found was to put my sister – 4 years younger than I – in front of me while walking around the house at night; otherwise, I would never stand up to go to the bathroom. Sorry, sis, not very protective of me, but I always knew you were better at fighting against the microwave, in case it was needed.

As I grew older, the fear of things that didn't exist was replaced by something very real: the fear of rejection. Let's say I wasn't very popular, nor the most beautiful, not the smartest one in class, not even that good at sports. And being average at all these things, not standing out at anything, made me feel inferior to other kids at school. I was never the first to be chosen for anything by anybody. And I remember that hurt a lot. Thank God I have a psychologist mom that did "in home therapy" with me every day to gradually make me a bit more confident, to the point where I decided to move to a different classroom, and in that switch, I found my place and enjoyed my last school years.

College went smoothly, but feeling inferior to others around was apparently a pattern of behavior that followed me. In a competition with 9 thousand candidates, I was chosen at Unilever for a marketing position at one of the most desired internship programs of my generation. But then, after a couple months, when I compared myself to other interns, I realized that I still felt inferior. I had a very good evaluation and was nominated to the trainee program. Unfortunately, I did not pass, which made me feel less capable than the others. But then I was hired anyway by the company, with a very nice salary for a person of my age. Even then, among the other brand coordinators, I still felt "less than."

Today there is a technical name for this - Impostor Syndrome – but back then, it was just me hearing and believing what people say, including this nasty voice in my head that always tries to doubt me. Because of that, we can say I was dependent on external encouragement to validate myself and make me feel better. While that may be true to some extent, I prefer to think that I am a person who asks for and accepts the help of others. And when you allow yourself to be vulnerable and let people help you, magic happens, because you remove a 50kg weight from your shoulders, and the object of your worry becomes smaller and less frightening.

Letting others help me is my way to deal with fear. And I have a weird relationship with fear, because at the same time it worries me, it also attracts me. I am moved by challenges. And do you remember that fertile imagination that created monsters inside a microwave? Well, it still operates nonstop nowadays, in a problem-solving mode, trying to come up with crazy, daring, different ideas to solve problems of the business and impress consumers with relevant, unforgettable, and never-seen-before experiences. All of this comes with a price: assuming risks. And assuming risks is scary.

It seems to be the cycle of my life: when I feel scared about something is probably because on the other side of the bridge something incredible awaits. This is what makes me face whatever fear I might feel. And I am not talking about sky diving or jumping with a parachute kind of fear. I am talking about the fear of something that might be great.

There was a time during my career that I was demotivated with my job and without a growth perspective. I was even considering looking for another job in the market, because the company I worked for was looking outside for a person to occupy the most desirable marketing position of the company. Again, I was not the first choice for that one also. This was my dream job since day one, but I wasn't even considering asking for it, because in my head, if they weren't considering me, I must not be qualified for it. That was when my husband encouraged me to for it and ask for the position: "What do you have to lose? You are thinking about leaving anyway; you are going to leave without trying?" That was the trigger I needed: I never leave without trying. In fact, my life mantra is, "You never know until you try."

I got the job, but it wasn't like I asked and they gave it to me. I had to go through a tough assessment to be validated, which helped to change the thought in my mind that I was not good enough for the position. "You passed in the selection process, lady! You can do it!". From that day on, I enjoyed the most exciting and adventurous years of my career. That is, until the most recent challenge came my way, an opportunity that swept me off my feet: an invitation to talk at TEDx.

Although I have felt nervous previously when having to talk in public, the kind of nervousness I felt during the months of preparation to talk at TEDx was definitely the worst so far. At first, I entertained flattering thoughts in my head for receiving the invitation, but then I experienced doubts about why they selected me. Then I panicked at the thought of not delivering a great speech, considering it would be recorded forever in TED social platforms. During the process, I had a lot of encouragement from my friends, from my family, and from the TEDx organizers, who helped me with the presentation, with fine tuning my text, with tips for the stage, and with support and validation whenever I felt I was not TEDx material.

What I learnt during my life is that we never do anything alone, even when the task is something only you can do - like breastfeeding your son or daughter, for example. When my son was born, I needed people to take care of me so I could take care of him. If you are a mom you know: it's impossible to take care of ourselves when we have a newborn. We always need people to encourage us and to take care of us, because it is inevitable to be tempted to give up and surrender when things get too hard to handle.

When in 2019 I had an out-of-the-blue-chance to sing at Sunset Stage at Rock in Rio, the fear of facing 40 thousand people for the first time in my life, was battling with the excitement of this once in a lifetime opportunity. Having the encouragement of the stage director, who was by my side until I gained more confidence, and friends on stage to back me up in case I confused the lyrics, was fundamental for me to face this challenge.

In the end, we are humans, and humans need humans to thrive in life, to accomplish things, to have healthy relationships, and to feel happy. Being able to show yourself vulnerable, asking for and accepting the help of others, is the type of freedom that I hope you can have in your life. This is how we rise in life, and by rising we can do the same with other people, helping them to rise too. And, since I am naturally a "believer" and always believed in what people said, I ask you to believe me now. I invite you to let yourself be helped, be taken care of, and do the same for others that are in need. I can guarantee that you will experience a very powerful feeling when you let yourself rise and raise others.

Who I am

A marketeer with more than 20 years of experience, Vanessa is now marketing director at HEINEKEN group in Brazil. During her journey at the company, she has led brands like Amstel, Devassa, Tiger, Desperados and Heineken – which under her leadership has become leader of the premium beer segment, the preferred brand in the Brazil, and the country has reached the mark of the biggest Heineken volume in the world. Before that she worked for 8 years at Unilever with brands such as Dove, Sunsilk, and Persil.

Vanessa is also a mom, a professional voice-over technician, and loves to sing during her free time.

VANESSA BRASOLIN ARICÓ

Hotelier by Diploma and People raiser by heart
LinkedIn: www.linkedin.com/in/vanessaarico

FRESH STARTS BUILDING A LIFE

> *"Our lives will only be understood by looking at the past, but they should only be lived by looking at the future."*
>
> *Oscar Arnaldo Arico*

I am very far from conformity or comfort, in fact I never really understood the meaning of these words. When I started to understand something about the world, I always knew I wanted to explore it but never face it. It was more than clear to me that I had the right to seek my happiness and fulfillment to get where I wanted.

But where did I want to get to?

My dear father always said "Sonia, let her go, if today at 14 years old she doesn't know where but she knows how and everyone follows her... when she grows up she will know where and learn how!!!"

Sonia is a character who is present at all stages – after all, she is a master of what we call "Learning on the job ".

I explain my composition. Daughter of salaried parents, Sonia lost her mother at the age of 10 and had to learn everything on her own – either she suffered, or she won. Each season he lived in a relative's house. She managed to study at the Antartica school, did a teaching degree and walked 10 km every day to teach people who had less money than her. She had to win. Oscar was the son of a player...of the 4 children he was the only one who studied (he worked during the day and studied at night) and graduated. Both with the similarity of working for more than 40 years in the same place. 50 years together, they have lived the routine and know the meaning of the word conquest. They won, each in their own way and both together.

I am the oldest of 2. Gustavo is the perfect description of the best student at school, he entered college at the age of 17, and the list is long.

I... oh, I wasn't that constant girl. I attended a few schools, a lot of kite flying, class leader, owner of the volleyball net on the beach, and there was no bad weather.

If I didn't know something, it was temporary, I had a desire to learn and share that intoxicated me most of the time.

I have always been a collectivist and when something displeased me, I left with lightness and joy... without much fuss.

It was very clear that I needed people and loved screens to be around. I did everything I could to serve those around me. Serving was the key word and involving was the genuine strategy for achievement.

I did half of Public Relations in Brazil and then I went to Switzerland Administration & Hospitality. Daughter of two employees, Gustavo's sister, I'm a surfer living in the snow.

As soon as I arrived it was a shambles and unfortunately – Xenophobia. Yes, it hurt, but there I was – becoming class representative, leader of thematic events, Embassy contact and Leader of the Graduation Committee. My training gave me the opportunity to go wherever I wanted around the world, and my determination for development and cultural diversity and the collective made me an agent of change.

The hotel industry gave me what I wanted most - working with people, SERVING everyone no matter who.

The journey became a purpose – where the essence was to disseminate the concept that service and high collective performance go together. This convergence allowed me to fully emphasize that the best Asset of any company is its PEOPLE.

I always took after everyone. I have always had in me the DNA of being the executor, the one who always gets the job done – through people.

But I have always been restless when it comes to the search for fulfillment and happiness.

The combination of these two characteristics guided me to a career of achievements and succession – where results were delivered ahead of schedule, and proposals for greater challenges appeared easily... and I, seduced by the fact that I could deliver more and create new leaders, accepted -you.

I always thought that in the next challenge I would find myself and stay longer.

But no, I soon became what I feared most - an expert in REcomecos , a professional in the world, but who loved the short time spent in places and the hurricane and earthquake effect.

This profile – caused strangeness among my fans – after all the question was "What is she looking for, because she doesn't stay:

Time passed, achievements arrived, challenges and frustrations. Tears, these are great partners after all they wash my soul. Some regrets and a lot of pride. All the social projects that I led, designed, experienced - I carry them with me, because I still believe in the verse that says "what the right hand does, the left hand does not need to know".

I built my career based on deliveries, commitment to my values and the credibility that my knowledge conveyed.

However, I understand that REcomecos need to be clearly exposed ard explained.

I had the opportunity to live and work abroad for many years – always in positions of leadership and trust. All times involved with operations and people development. I had the same opportunities in Brazil, but always with the belief that I was an excellent "startup" professional – as soon as I structured the team, processes and got the operation online – I moved on to another challenge. And everything was always fine. The truth is that I loved this modus operandis and I loved living like this, with unforgettable and short moments.

But everything had a RE around me, and when more than SUDDENLY I met my husband again (who at the time was just my EX's brother) and once again another decision – either I would leave for Dubai after the new year or I would literally pay to see what my heart was telling me.

My husband was the first constancy I learned to live with. It was not viable to start loving and suddenly , after you conquered, polished, smoothed the edges on both sides, you turn your back and call another leader to experience the "success of the project."

But that was a very timid thought and apparently only valid for my personal life.

When I had the opportunity to take on an extremely strategic role with sensational leadership – I started to become interested in the routine and changing some performance routes – where speed was important, but time was the best ingredient for an effective turnaround.

I didn't stop, I was involved in an NGO, designing large events and one of my favorite hobbies was getting involved in social projects as an executor. I started studying everything from the Constellation to the Enneagram of Healing to understand my search for fulfillment and help others find their path. (I'm not a coach or mentor, I didn't study for that, but I'm glad they exist).

I was about to be promoted, when I fell ill... and found support in the leaders around me. Something was stirring. If I wanted to be cured, I had to have surgery. In the pre-operation consultation we discovered Thiago.

MEEEEEEEOO GOD. It was the first moment of silence in my life. But I thought everything was normal – I would have Thiago and after 4 months I wou d go back to work and take on a new position.

Then comes change and another new beginning. I died a few times in these 6 years of motherhood, and my old job no longer made sense.

I understood that all the experience I had in turnaround, and REcomecos made me get to where I am today, but without a doubt I cannot erase that it was a decision made based on the way I liked to live.

This decision brought me to where I was but it won't take me to where I want to go.

Today I continue to enjoy living in a dynamic, intense, but constant way. Working on several projects at the same time, learning from great women, supporting and serving everyone I can with all the knowledge I have acquired over the years, and donating everything positive that life gave me. I can't change my past, but I can undoubtedly rewrite the future, adding ALL the experiences of victories, right and wrong decisions and how to face the unknown with courage. I have always carried this poem with me, and in the last 6 years, every day that passes makes more sense.

What is your biggest fear?

Our greatest fear is not that we are inadequate. Our greatest fears are that we are powerful beyond measure.

It is our light, not our darkness that terrifies us most. Being small does not serve the world, there is nothing wise in shrinking so that other people don't feel insecure around you.

We were all made to shine like children. It's not just in some of us, it's in everyone, and as we let our light shine, we unconsciously give other people permission to do the same as we let go of our fears. Our presence automatically liberates others.

What I leave for the girls who will read this simple narrative and for the great women who will give me the honor of their time for such reading if they allow me

Don't conform

Seek your fullness

Don't get tired and don't give in

Be true to yourself and your values

Be afraid, it strengthens us

Be respectful – always because you never know the other person's story

Forgive yourself

Start over as many times as necessary to get where you want

Take the risks of your decisions

Have a coach... the best thing in life

Find out who your detractors are... they often cause us provocations that strengthen us

LIVE- the way that suits you

Be proud of yourself, your choices, your values and promote lightness in your deliveries.

Be firm and transparent, don't let yourself be carried away
One act of kindness at a time

Nice to meet you, I'm Vanessa, 48 years old at your service.

VANESSA GORDILHO

Business, Products and Marketing VP at Vibra Energia
Board Member, C-Level, Mentor.
Instagram: @vangordilho
LinkedIn: www.linkedin.com/in/vanessa-gordilho-859270

FROM ABARÁ (typical Brazilian food from Bahia State) TO CAVIAR. ALWAYS.

I have always loved writing. And I have always dreamed of leaving something behind through which my children and grandchildren could get to know me better. I thought of taking this opportunity to share my journey here and, by doing so, inspire other women. But I want to do more than that. I want to share the lessons I have learned while narrating my own growth process. That is how I see my life. I enjoy telling my story, but I enjoy exchanging knowledge even more. It is this exchange that inspires me. And I know that is how I can inspire others too. So, allow me to take you by the hand...

Every day I miss Bahia.

"A 'baiana' (native of Bahia State) is not born, they make their debut." I love that phrase by Zózimo Barrozo. Not because it suggests that "baianos" are better or superior, but because anyone born in Bahia already enters the world covered in palm oil. They come full of rhythm, loaded with joy. People from Bahia have as one of their main goals in life the constant pursuit of happiness.

I was born in Bahia, and a lot of people ask me why I am not there now. So, here is my first contribution to the exchange I mentioned earlier: allow yourself to be grateful for your roots every day. I am very grateful for mine. The energy of Bahia is always very present within me. I have Iansã (the goddess of Tempests, of the Afro-Brazilian religion of Candomble) by my side, and to this day, I have not lost my accent. My origins shaped me, made me who I am. But since I was little, I always had big ambitions. One ambition inhabited my dreams: to bring about change. I did not know the extent of the transformation, I did not know how, I just knew I wanted to be the change. And soon enough, my Bahia became too small for me. Yes, we need to recognize the limitations of our path and seek beyond.

Women of great strength saw in me this desire to grow and gave me the tools to achieve my goals. The first of them all was my mother, a woman who was pure magic. She owned the ballet school where I started dancing. And I still had my grandmothers. One was very loving and was in the religion of spiritism, the other had a more facilitator profile and was a fervent Catholic. A combination that was a true driving force in my life. I not only had clarity about where I wanted to go, but also had the necessary strength, and it came from the women in my life.

We must pay close attention to the people around us. They are part of us, undoubtedly. Often, the push we need comes from our own family, and for several reasons, it takes us a while to realize it. My connection with my mother and my grandmothers, combined with the steadfastness of my father and the love of my siblings, were crucial in shaping the woman I am and focusing on my goals.

Have you ever taken the time to listen to what the people in your family have to say? Have you ever stopped to understand where your energy comes from and how it should be used in your journey?

I BELIEVE IN ANGELS

My mother was an extraordinary woman. She was my guide, my biggest supporter, my hero. But heroes also suffer; every hero has their kryptonite. My mother's kryptonite was depression. It was a tough battle, and she fought bravely. However, at a certain point, the illness prevailed. And in the most abrupt and painful way, it took my mother away from me. Physically away, of course. Because she remains with me, she is always very present in my life. In fact, which is how my mother would end letters and notes, with the word "always." Today, I also use that word, and I carry it with me, tattooed on my arm.

When I lost my mother, I knew I had everything to fall to pieces. She was a reference, and her departure from my life created a void inside of me. The pain of loss eventually transforms into memories, but we still feel those stabs from time to time. It was in that moment of pain that I discovered the existence of angels. Not those winged angels descending from the sky, playing harps. Incarnated angels. Angels capable of illuminating our paths, breaking down walls to open windows when doors close, carrying us in their arms if necessary. They are angels who may even shout at us or utter a few curse words. Because they are people who appear in our lives when we need them the most.

Angels have been on my path throughout my life, but I only realized it when my mother passed away. As I said, I could have gone to pieces. I could have surrendered to pain. But instead, I stayed strong. I began to see people extending their hands to help me overcome this moment. I started collaborating with my coach, who is now one of my best friends. I sought my spiritual guides, appeased my mind, calmed my heart. And the angels did not stop coming. I had friends who offered to take care of my daughters.

Several people who could have gone unnoticed in my life played fundamental roles in my growth as a human being. These individuals pointed me towards paths to follow.

Among the many angels in my life, one was already in my family. We share the same blood. It is my sister, my soulmate. Our connection is beautiful, intense, and genuine. She is very important to me. And this makes me reflect that sometimes people do not see or recognize help or understand where it comes from. But believe me, we are surrounded by people who assist us on this incredible journey called life. And sometimes, we are someone else's angel too. So yes, I believe in angels. And here is an important lesson: the more we radiate goodness, the more we attract these angels.

LIFE IS MY STAGE

I left Brazil at the age of fifteen in pursuit of my dreams, and my first stage was in Germany. There was no internet back then, and I would communicate with my parents through letters or phone calls every 15 days. I felt lonely. But the explanation goes beyond being a teenager alone in a different country. Here is a side of me that can be seen as both positive and negative: I had to be the best, I had to be brilliant, exemplary, and surpass expectations. And in Hamburg, I found myself surrounded by dancers much better than me. What now? How could I cope with not being the best, not being perfect?

Living in Germany may not have been the easiest or most obvious choice. I left the lightness of Bahia for the rigidity of a German boarding school. It was a developed country, but with equal dangers. Today, when I hear stories of girls struggling with bulimia, anorexia, and other disorders, I can only remember how unaware I was of the risks. There were also drugs in the public school I attended for a year. Yes, I had numerous possibilities of getting lost, but I chose the path of discipline. I had an inner struggle, daily. Focus. Discipline. That is how I would become one of the best. That is how I wouldn't lose myself. It was as simple as that.

I found fulfillment. But every time I stepped on stage, I would think: is it worth it? In fact, if you allow me to contribute, just ask yourself… how many times have you been following a path (even a successful one!) but stopped to reflect if it was truly making you happy? My mind was filled with thoughts like these. And it got worse. Am I good enough? Am I all that? The pressure of being there, also contributed to this self-sabotage. Out of fear of not being the best, the exemplary one, of not meeting others' expectations, I quit ballet. If I had the maturity I have today, perhaps I would understand that being consistent – which I already was! – is worth more than being the best. I did not have that maturity yet. I stepped off the stage and embarked on an executive career.

If you reach this point in life, regardless of your occupation, understand one thing: it is okay to change. It is okay to take a step back. It is okay to choose different stages. Just continue being the protagonist of your life.

WHO SAID TECHNOLOGY IS NOT FOR WOMEN?

Back in Brazil, I pursued a degree in Communication. Then, I went on to do an MBA in the United States. I also took several IT courses. I ended up in the financial market. Everything was always done with dedication, enthusiasm, and... questioning. What to do next? I was no longer a dancer, I was not working in my field of study, it didn't match the size of my ambition. And I had not found myself yet either.

I needed to explore other paths to find myself. And believe me, that is normal! Whoever you are, whatever your age, it is normal to feel lost, to not yet feel like you belong to a world, even if the choice to be there was yours. It is normal to dedicate yourself to an area and discover that it is not quite for you. Never doubt that it is normal to have doubts. So, what should you do? Keep searching. Remember the motto of a famous blue fish from a well-known Disney movie: just keep swimming.

It was during this search that I fell in love with the field of technology and technology companies. At the time, this area was not even popular yet. It was the early 21st century, imagine! There was talk about it, but we were still at the beginning of this technological revolution. I joined a company without any idea of what to do. I worked with credit card processing systems. And it was something different. Because in this niche, male executives prevailed. Yes, it was an area like many others, with a "male profile." Many times, I was one of the few women accelerating this process. It is truly frustrating when there are labels, dictating what is for women and what is for men. Fortunately, we have evolved. Not much, but we have.

Working in any field – without labels – is about passion, interest, and dedication. It is about blazing new trails, exploring uncharted territories, facing fears, challenging oneself. And I have a personality trait that drives me even further. If someone tells me that I cannot do something, that is when I dedicate myself even more, fall in love with it, dive headfirst to achieve my goal. Often, I give more than necessary. Because I have that annoying little thing of thinking I am not good enough. And this is not just as a professional but as a mother, as a woman. In that sense, the technology field has been a great achievement. I found myself.

I know that even today, there are fewer women than men in this market. Added to the fact that women are not encouraged to like technology. There is also a societal imposition that makes many not see it as a fun or even sexy field. It is true, we still have that kind of thinking! But there are so many opportunities, in so many roles in this field, that I would simply like to inspire more women to enter this world. If it is my passion, then it can be the passion of many others.

Each one of us has something unique to offer. And just like everything else in my life, I have always placed focus, discipline, and consistency in my work. I would say that is my superpower. I hold myself to a high standard. I hold myself accountable every day. And I had to learn to balance roles and emotions. But I am certain that in the technology field, I found my place. I found the path to the transformation I always dreamed of achieving. Even better: I found myself.

Oh! I also found my best friends in the executive world. It has been the icing on the cake. They are incredible women who entered my life on various occasions, in unexpected ways. They are women I can rely on unconditionally. Got it?

Hold on, now I am a mother!

Let us be straightforward: if you want to be a mother, be one. There are many women who do not feel ready for motherhood, especially while being in the workforce. It is harder, we face stigma. There are studies that show women, after becoming mothers, stop getting promoted, for example. It is an unfair world, we know that. But if you want to be a mother, just go for it. Take some time and make this dream come true.

When we become mothers, our priorities change, but they do not disappear. Opportunities continue to arise. It is all related to the type of mother a woman becomes. In my case, motherhood brought me more maturity than difficulty. Our energy shifts. My daughters have brought me reason, balance, and love. Better yet: MORE reason, MORE balance, MORE love. One is outgoing, funny, always telling jokes, and loves music; she has a beautiful voice. The other is super fashionable, organized, very, very studious, disciplined, and has a touch of British culture: she loves punctuality. It is as if they represent the logical and creative sides of my brain.

Children bring us a unique sense of fulfillment. And after I remarried, this experience doubled. My second husband gave me a stepson and a stepdaughter, Leonardo and Olívia. And now we form a beautiful family of four children. Yes, it is four children – or rather, four pre-teens, as they like to remind us. And they are all great supporters of mine and my career.

Whether or not to have children while being an executive is a matter of how you organize yourself, manage your time, and focus and discipline yourself at work to avoid losing track. Because it is possible to be a productive professional and still be present in your children's lives, even when you are not physically present every single moment. Create special moments and make ordinary situations special. Take them out for dinner, play games, and attend a concert together. Leave notes on their pillows, the mirror, send messages or a song with meaningful lyrics. For example, I organize bingo nights where we try on clothes and organize jewelry and accessories in drawers. It is our thing. Create your surprises. Find creative solutions to be close to your children daily, even from afar.

Is there a lack of spice in that "acarajé" (traditional Bahiana dish made from fried mashed black-eyed beans)

Here's my final contribution. I think many women struggle to see themselves solely as women. Let me explain. We see ourselves as daughters, as mothers, as wives, as professionals. But what about the woman? What are you doing daily to admire yourself as a woman? I believe that even for this, focus and discipline are necessary.

I have a wonderful husband who supports me in everything, who is a partner and joins in all my craziness. We always discuss our relationship. Not as something negative. We sit down to talk even when everything is going well. Improvement is a continuous process. To keep my relationship alive, I even found ways to spice things up. It is an exercise we do, it's about complicity.

But the idea of having spice in life is not solely associated with keeping the flame of a relationship alive. The spice is for us. I need to be that amazing and spicy woman for myself. It is about being the fierce and feisty "baiana" that I am. I need to look in the mirror and see, or rather, RECOGNIZE the incredible woman that I am. It is part of my essence, and I cannot let it fade away.

In conversations with my friends, this topic always comes up. Yes, we need to "spice up" our friendships too, the conversations, not letting certain topics get lost amidst other discussions. This exchange is essential to understand who we are and that we are not alone in our fears, thoughts, and experiences. We need to break paradigms, overcome obstacles, shift perceptions, and understand that being a woman is the greatest privilege.

One day, John Lennon said, "When I was 5 years old, my mother told me that happiness was the key to life. When I went to school, they asked me what I wanted to be when I grew up. I wrote 'happy.' They told me I did not understand the assignment. I told them they didn't understand life." That is me.

VANESSA MARTIN

CEO VM Event Consulting
LinkedIn: www.linkedin.com/in/vanessa-martin-649952a/

PASSION FOR EVENTS & SOLIDARITY

I guarantee that you will receive more than you can give!

My passion and pride for working in events have grown stronger and stronger over the years. It is a great privilege to be part of an industry that does so much for people of all ages and social classes, as well as for companies, government, and the Third Sector.

Events have an immeasurable transformative power in our daily activities. In fact, it is so significant and engaging that few realize its true importance. Have you ever organized lunches and dinners? A 15th birthday party? A wedding anniversary celebration? A special date gathering with friends and relatives? I'm sure you have. Even if it's not your profession, you have felt the strength and importance that I mentioned.

Working in events also includes hosting a convention for 50,000 people, the World Cup, the Olympic and Paralympic Games, or a corporate meeting for 10 participants.

All of these are events. Designed and organized by and for people to achieve their goals or meet specific participants' needs. Over the course of more than four decades working in this industry, I have witnessed unparalleled professional growth among my colleagues. Some of the events produced in Brazil have the excellence to enter the Guinness World Records, like Rock in Rio.

And the multiplier effect of income generation and market impact of the events industry is truly impressive. To give you an idea, just the UBRAFE - the entity active in the Brazilian trade fairs and exhibitions market - estimates that in 2023, the business visitor movement in São Paulo will reach 12 million people, generating around R$ 18 billion. Considering that São Paulo represents about 40% to 45% of the national GDP, it is estimated that the impact for the country in that year will be R$ 35 billion. And these numbers still do not represent the full strength of the industry, as there are numerous other types of events that have yet to be accounted for.

Every city, every state, and every country in the world has the same economic and social importance in the events market as this example.

THE CHALLENGE

But what would you do if you were one of these event professionals and had to stay isolated at home for months on end without being able to work and earn a living?

In March 2020, that's exactly what happened in the in-person events market, where business came to a complete halt, brutally affecting thousands of families across dozens of economic sectors and income brackets in Brazil and around the world.

This was the devastating scenario we were facing. It was a time when the pandemic was devastating and relentless towards the events industry. Overnight, the industry came to a complete stop. And the vast majority of professionals in the field had no knowledge of or familiarity with alternatives to continue working during the lockdown. With travel restrictions in place, virtual events were the only modality that could be carried out.

However, at that time, few event organizers knew how to create and organize online events. Some didn't even know how to use streaming platforms like Zoom and Meet, let alone how to execute an online event for dozens, hundreds, or thousands of participants. Faced with all this, I became deeply concerned and decided to help my peers.

MY INSPIRATION

Together with Gerson Christensen from *SSK Analises*, I had launched the 1st National Survey on Hybrid Events in October 2019, when no one else was talking about it. Suddenly, the pandemic made this knowledge essential for the survival of event organizers.

I decided to leverage this reputation and market recognition to drive some actions that could be taken. As I believe it's much better to teach someone to fish than to give them a fish, I saw content production and high-quality free training as the most precious and valuable multiplying tools I could provide at that moment.

HOW IT STARTED

I quickly began mobilizing to share the knowledge of online tools and essential content for professionals to learn about virtual and hybrid events, all for free.

To expand the reach of these resources, two friends and colleagues joined the effort to organize the delivery of this content online. Robson Lisboa from *Midiacode* took on the challenge of producing special content with me, and Vanessa Chiarelli from *BOP*

Comunicação was an indispensable partner in organizing all the events we produced.

Together, we developed content and various events that could offer possibilities and work opportunities to our colleagues through:

- Explaining what virtual events are.
- Introducing the FAST event design methodology, a practical, fast, and easy-to-use approach created by myself and Robson specifically for virtual and hybrid events.
- Providing information on the necessary digital platforms for virtual events and how to hire them.
- Hosting meetings and conversations with Brazilian and international experts to exchange experiences and best practices.
- Facilitating networking among professionals in the industry.

That's how ED2020 was created, which later became known as *DEE - Digital Event Expert*, a brand name that encompassed all the actions we carried out.

At the time, I didn't fully grasp the extent and impact that this movement could have, nor did we limit the geographical scope or areas of knowledge to Brazil. The needs arose, and we made efforts to deliver the best available in the market.

We did all of this with the genuine intention of helping those who had lost their jobs and income, providing support and guidance to offer tools and know-how that could open new doors of work opportunities.

WHAT WE DELIVERED

As early as April 2020, we started a series of over 50 free webinars and podcasts covering topics in 7 knowledge verticals related to digital events. We had thousands of participants and dozens of national and international guests, such as Will Curran from *Endless Events*, who shared insights on pivoting from in-person to virtual events.

In addition to being the first speaker in the series, Maarten Vanneste, a Belgian expert in multi-hub meetings, conducted a unique 6-week course on Online Meeting Design in the country. Although it was a paid course, the final cost, including simultaneous translation, was significantly lower than what he offered in Europe and in Euros.

Later on, one of our speakers, Leila Bueno, an architect, scenographer, and partner at *Bueno Arquitetura Cenográfica*, sent me the following post:

"When I was invited to speak about scenography for digital events with Mariana Thomé, I had no idea of the potential in this field. In one of the case studies presented during the panel, I learned about Nathalia Arcuri, a digital influencer who was already using scenography in her finance channel. I ended up taking her course, which transformed my financial life. I also realized the reach of the virtual world and launched *Bueno Ensina*, our digital channel for education in scenography. Today, I am aware of the impact that this invitation had on my life and how much value it added to our business. My deepest gratitude."

In the early stages of 2020, we released a free e-book on virtual and digital events, with over 60 pages, which has already received nearly 5,000 downloads to date.

Throughout 2020 and 2021, we created and conducted a 20-hour online course on digital events, with live streaming. We had dozens of classes and hundreds of students. Each of the 5 modules cost less than a regular meal per person.

Adriana Girão, from Fortaleza, Ceará, is the Director of *Result Consultoria e Inovação*. She provided the following testimonial about that period:

"I had the opportunity to participate in the ED2020 and Digital Event Expert events, where I was impacted by so much content and tools that made all the difference in my approach, actions, and digital events that we organized. Moreover, it inspired and encouraged us to hold the 1st Digital Transformation Event in the Tourism Sector, which took place during the pandemic! We are very grateful for this fantastic network of knowledge and extremely relevant content."

In March 2021, we held the ED2020 Experience, a 5-day virtual event with 20 hours of content. Each day focused on a different content track, covering topics such as the future, design, technology, monetization, and corporate events. In total, there were 66 sessions, including keynote speeches, presentations, panel discussions, and demo rooms. Curran and Vanneste generously made time to join us once again, along with other top national and international experts in corporate and entertainment events.

And the best part was that **it was completely free**! This was made possible thanks to incredible partners who embraced the idea of helping the industry, such as Cross Host, the studio that captured and managed the audiovisual aspects, Lets Events, the Brazilian event platform that hosted the online event, and even *Braindate*, a Canadian networking platform, who agreed to participate in the project. All of these companies provided their teams and infrastructure pro bono to make the event a reality.

We had thousands of participants from all over Brazil, and to our surprise, also from 7 other countries in Europe, North and South America and Africa. When we decided to focus our efforts on event organizers, we counted on the exponential impact their work could have, through hiring other suppliers and restarting the financial wheel of the industry.

But the greatest thing is that when you practice the good without expecting anything in return, that feeling comes back to you multiplied. It continuously recharges your batteries to keep practicing good and kindness around you. And the return can come in the most unexpected, spontaneous, and beautiful way you can imagine! And when you least expect it!

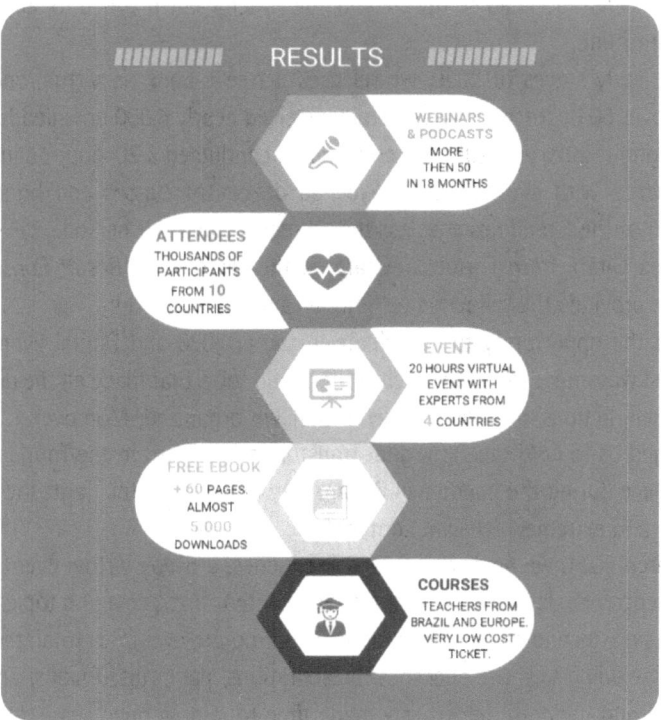

It happened to me a few days ago, almost two years after we started this project. During the *Forum Eventos 2023*, I was approached by a participant after my talk. Her words deeply moved me in that moment and inspired me to write this chapter.

It was Juliana Avila from Vitória, ES, whom I met in person for the first time there. She came up to me, saying she wanted to thank me. Not understanding what it was about, I thanked her and asked the reason.

She said that if it wasn't for our work, her company would have closed down. And she gave me the following testimonial:

"I want to express my gratitude for the wonderful work you all did during the pandemic. You took us by the hand and guided us through a very difficult and chaotic time in the events industry. We accomplished marvelous projects during that period, led and directed by all of you. I want to extend my thanks for the generosity in sharing your knowledge. Feelin' is celebrating its 18th anniversary, and you are part of this story. Thank you so much for the support, the exceptional guidance, the generosity, and everything you did during that period."

This filled my heart with joy and a sense of accomplishment. I don't know other stories of the thousands of people who were with us in one or several initiatives. However, knowing that our effort improved the life of even just one of them is enough for me.

FOR THOSE OF YOU WHO WANT TO TAKE INTO ACTION

If you want to inspire or help someone, first, you just need to have the desire. And it works. You will find a way to do it. But to amplify, to gain momertum and to exponentially increase the results, you will need to gather more people with the same feeling and open hearts and co-create together.

That's what happened with this exceptional group, led by Natasha de Caiado Castro, whose essence is reflected in its name: *Uma Sobe e Puxa a Outra (One Rises and Pulls Up the Other One)*.

Listen to your heart as well to choose whom you will help, organize your ideas, gather people who can contribute, define what you will do, and act.

VANESSA MATHIAS

Co-founder of White Rabbit. Researcher of emerging narratives and innovation. With over 20 years of research experience and vocation, passionate about taking people out of their comfort zone and helping them reimagine their futures in concrete utopias. Columnist, teacher, and speaker at national and international events. Facilitates visions in companies where brands positively impact the systems in which they operate and society.

E-mail:whiterabbittrends.com.br
Instagram: @whiterabbittrends
LinkedIn: www.linkedin.com/in/vamathias

"Who are you?" asked the caterpillar in Alice in Wonderland. This question caught me off guard. At the end of the rabbit hole, who I was at the beginning no longer existed, and there, I no longer knew who I was. My eccentricities were many: strange parties, trips to non-touristic communities, ayahuasca, living with strangers in the early days of the internet. And what did they have in common? They were portals to ontological uncertainty! It was the beginning of the story of opening rabbit holes to allow my own radical reimagination.

OPENING SPACES FOR RADICAL REIMAGINATION

"In this crazy tea party, Alice felt terribly disturbed. The Mad Hatter's remark seemed to the girl like nonsensical words, and yet, it was English. 'I'm not understanding anything,' she said as politely as she could."

"Please, take a look at this soda. Can you tell me, on a scale from 0 to 10, where 0 means you totally disagree and 10 means you totally agree, how refreshing you believe it is? And, on the same scale, how much do you believe its ingredients are reminiscent of the Amazon?" It was the third time we were administering the same concept test for a soda commercial. I couldn't stand seeing that PET bottle and can photo in front of me anymore. The brand attributes always scored low in credibility.

"Why don't people believe that this food is natural and fresh from the Amazon, huh?" Some of the brightest minds I knew were pondering over that concept card. Should we change the location photo? Make the bottle greener? Place a bigger logo?

And ultimately, the main question – but could it be... just maybe... that consumers understand that carbonated water, sugar, acidifier, sodium benzoate, dye, potassium acesulfame might not really be, you know, natural and fresh food? Straight from Mother Nature to your drinking glass?"

I'm sure that looking from the outside, as we are doing now, it's easy to realize that it's not.

Sometimes, the most unfathomable mysteries reside in the obviousness.

There's a legend that little fish were swimming in the ocean; they passed by the big fish, who asked: 'Hey, little fish, how's the water today?' The little fish thought and asked: 'What is water?'"

Water, at that moment, symbolized speaking out loud what everyone knows but doesn't allow themselves to say or even think about. However, in most cases, the obvious is exactly what needs to be said, especially in the corporate context. This time, I had the courage to speak up in the meeting.

But I wasn't a revolutionary within the system – I was part of it. How many meetings had I remained silent in? I also needed to confront the choices I had made myself... More than a decade, month after month, trying to sell a product full of sodium benzoate. It had nothing from the Amazon but the photo. Actually, not even the photo, which was probably from a stock image library; and possibly not even from the Amazon indeed.

For over two decades, I had been doing this – and once you face the water – you think: "What am I doing with my life? What am I doing to others' lives?" And how could I spend another hour in that job, once you allow yourself to think about it?

The Caterpillar and Alice looked at each other in silence for some time; finally, the Caterpillar took the hookah out of its mouth and addressed the girl with a languid, sleepy voice. "Who are you?" asked the Caterpillar. 'I'm not sure who I am right now, Madam – at least I knew who I was when I got up this morning, but I think I've changed many times since then.

Once you see the water, it's hard to "unsee" it. With every project I looked at, that's all I could see. "Am I working to sell more ultra-processed cat food?" Am I working 8 hours to convince someone that shampoo gets rid of split ends? How can I work to sell more stuff to people who don't need it, when rampant consumption is the evil of our decade? How can I contribute to interrupting people's favorite program with commercials that – on top of everything – were a sham?

It's so much budget, concept, branding, insight, big idea, narrative, influence, key purchase decision, ROI, call to action... It's so much analysis of this, analysis of that... My brain was spinning in circles trying to justify a sense of self-importance and relevance in

RISE AND RAISE OTHERS

REAL LIFE STORIES FROM INSPIRING WOMEN

my life, with such sophisticated mechanisms that distanced me from seeing the basics. Selling chips. Selling sugar with a bit of chocolate milk. I looked deep into that rabbit hole and I jumped.

- "Could you please tell me which way I ought to go from here?" asked Alice to the Cheshire Cat.

- "That depends a good deal on where you want to get to," said the cat.

- "I don't much care where," said Alice.

I questioned myself: "Should I sell coconut water on the beach? Make vegan brownies in an alternative community?" Following the cat's advice, I decided that the easiest way to start wasn't to go north or south, but inward.

One thing I was certain of was that I wouldn't make a difference by leaving the system. And yes, I wanted to work within the system. Selling coconut water on the beach wouldn't change the amount of sodium benzoate being sold. I wanted to be an agent of contribution from within. From the company's side, from the system's side, from the side of the agent with the greatest potential for transforming the world. I wanted to be the little fish saying to people: "Guys, are we seeing the water?"

Therefore, I began researching my interests, my desires, where I excelled. And I remembered the original motivation for choosing market research: to learn, to know, to understand, and to discover.

"Curiouser and curiouser!" - Alice cried. "Now I'm opening up like the largest telescope that ever was!"

Curiosity is the essence of doing science. Questioning people's choices daily, what they do and why they do what they do. And what they stop doing to do what they do. The art of "curiosaring" (after all, if Alice can invent words, maybe I can too) is to venture through rabbit holes without knowing where it will lead – or if you'll end up being the same person who entered.

Perhaps we hesitate to jump into the rabbit hole because there's no way to know if, at the end of the experience, we'll still be the same person. Everyone knows the feeling of going through events that make us question our own notion of "self." Did you know there's a name for it? I discovered it not long ago: ontological uncertainty. Many people say this happens after having a child, a spiritual experience, a psychedelic session, or even the first time experiencing an orgasm.

It was in this inner pilgrimage that I realized I am a hunter of ontological uncertainty. It was good to discover that there was a concept for the mental state I sought so many times in life. On my first international trip, at age 15, when I rode a train in Bolivia, next to a lady frying fish in a seat without a backrest, crossing the Andes. In the little doll an indigenous woman gave me during an ayahuasca session.

376

At my first Afrika Burn, in Cape Town, a city that rises from the ashes and returns to them in a week, where the rules of current society no longer exist. And of course, having a child.

There have been many moments of ontological uncertainty in my life. Today, the quest to know the other person I will emerge as on the other side of the rabbit hole is what moves me towards the future. It's no coincidence that this is the profession I not only chose but also built for myself. This desire to dive into the kaleidoscope of futures is what attracted another person with the same desire, whom I now have the honor of calling my partner and who pulled me into this hole. On the other side of it, two people and a completely different company – and, as it couldn't be otherwise, we named our company White Rabbit.

Why? The rabbit is what awakens Alice's curiosity, besides marking the beginning of her journey into a "completely new reality."

In Alice's Wonderland, things are not as they seem, and normal rules do not apply. Alice encounters strange and unexpected creatures, absurd situations, and unpredictable events. She is constantly challenged to question her understanding of reality and to adapt to a world that is constantly changing. Similarly, in corporate life, we often find ourselves in situations where things are not clear or predictable. We meet people who have different viewpoints from ours, face unpredictable situations, or have to make decisions without complete information. Like Alice, we are forced to question our assumptions and to adapt to a world in constant flux.

And, in our company, we invite clients to face the barest realities, to question themselves, and, above all, to imagine. Before the economic crisis, the political crisis, we lived in an imagination crisis. That's where we operate – in the capacity to dream together.

To be able to change in companies, we must first face reality and allow ourselves to question. By doing so, we can expand our understanding of the world and become more resilient in the face of uncertainty. So, it was like this, within the system, within companies, that we began to work with research, lectures, events, curation, content, courses, workshops, and immersive experiences that promote literacy and awareness of spaces for reimagining the future, starting from questioning the obviousness of today.

All our projects are designed to be learning experiences that expand participants' repertoire of the future and challenge them to exercise their own understanding of the future, aiming to lead people to an "Aha state" that expands their minds to the point where they no longer return to the previous normalcy.

And that's why jumping into the hole is the only way to transform. Just as I did with my career, I wanted to be the little ant who somehow celebrated processes of change that open up spaces for radical reimagining.

"Wow, what a strange dream I had!" – said Alice. She then told her sister, as well as she could remember, the strange adventures. After she finished, her sister gave her a kiss and said – "It was a curious dream, dear, certainly. But now hurry – it's teatime."

Do you remember how Alice's book ends? She wakes up and realizes that everything she experienced in Wonderland was just a dream. But maybe you don't remember that she tells her sister all about the dream with the rabbit, the hatters, the strange creatures, and incredible adventures she had there. And then, Alice's sister herself falls asleep and starts to dream... While listening, or thinking she was listening, the whole environment around her was filled with the strange creatures from her little sister's dream.

The long blades of grass rustled beneath her feet as the White Rabbit hurried past. The frightened Mouse stirred the water as it passed by the nearby pond. She could hear the clinking of teacups as the March Hare and his friends shared their endless afternoon tea, and the Queen's shrill voice condemning the "unhappy guests."

Alice's sister remained sitting there, eyes closed, almost believing she was in Wonderland, but knowing that she only had to open her eyes again and everything would return to prosaic reality. Although she knew she was dreaming, she preferred to remain in the Wonderland dream.

If Wonderland didn't exist before Alice told her sister, it came into being when it was shared. All creatures began to have a role outside the dream, all emotions became tangible, that world that opened up when she left the burrow was never closed again, even when she returned to reality.

It was from that moment, when she told the dream, that Wonderland was never forgotten, and that's why it exists in our collective imagination. It's the same with images of futures, possible worlds, that we provoke people to imagine and that, once shared, come into existence.

I became a professional reimagination provocateur, and as such, I invite you: manifest your lucid dreams. Just as the dream doesn't exist before the dreamer, Wonderland also doesn't exist without Alice.

VANESSA SIMÕES

Founder and Partner at VSX Pessoas (Executive Search and Leadership Consulting Firm) and Board Member
LinkedIn: www.linkedin.com/in/vanessasimoesm

THE FLIGHT OF THE BUTTERFLY

In a world of icons, we may find ourselves small and insignificant. But what I've learned throughout life is that it is in the apparently small things that we find the true essence of humanity. The world is made up of ordinary people who become heroes by overcoming their own challenges in their daily lives, and not just in public recognition, social media posts and large institutions.

We are all heroes, but we need to acknowledge it within ourselves first. And I believe that we begin to recognize ourselves when we understand and share our stories with each other. So, let's do it!

My story is simple, probably similar to many other Vanessas, but it is unique at the same time. And it is this jewel that I want to share with all of you.

I am the daughter of my father's second marriage, in a time when divorces were still not well seen by people in Brazil. For a fresh start, my parents have moved from the capital to the countryside; but growing up far from the family and being treated like the ugly duckling has had significant consequences for my self-esteem. This has impacted me for many years and was another challenge on the way to carving out the space I wanted.

My paternal grandparents were Portuguese immigrants who, through hard work, had built a good life. Even with little formal education, my grandfather has taught me the importance of never stop learning. He read the encyclopedia yearbook every year and showed us the changes that were going on in the world.

My maternal grandparents have immigrated from Italy. They have formed a large family, and when my grandfather passed away at an early age, my young mother had to work. But she stopped working when I was born, like many other women did.

My parents did not go to university and have worked hard so that their daughters could have the best possible education. That's what they would leave for us. Thus, I grew up hearing my mother saying how important it was to have a career and be independent. At the same time, I was sure that I wanted to have kids, which was totally possible to reconcile in a high school girl's mind.

I had many doubts about which career path to follow, but since I preferred to work with people, Business Administration ended up being the natural choice. I chose to study in the university that would help me become the best possible professional. My uncle, at that time, told me that if I wanted to find a wealthy husband, I should have chosen another college! Anyway...I wasn't the best student, but I have always been very dedicated and knew that I needed to make an effort to stand out.

My identification with Human Resources area has occurred from the beginning, despite the jokes I heard from friends and colleagues, since this field was the least valued in most companies in the late 1990s – low salaries, distant from the strategy, and where the next CEO would certainly not come from. But none of this made me change my mind!

I moved to São Paulo at the age of 17 to go to college, but the most important moment of this cycle was when I travelled abroad. I was granted a scholarship from the university to study in Germany for a year. This happened at a particularly challenging time for my family because we were going through a period of significant financial constraint due to my father's leave from work.

I went to Germany with the money I had (I had saved a large portion of my internship salary since I was studying at a public college) and willing to work there to support myself. I studied during the day and worked in a restaurant at night, until I was raised for the first time in my career. I was a trainee at ABB in Brazil and my boss put me in touch with the HR Director in Germany. It was a wonderful opportunity to work there and lead global projects for the department. That experience has made me consider new possibilities: in Germany, the HR field was already seen as emerging, aggregating and essential for companies, while in Brazil we were far behind that. I decided to try out different fields and environments.

Back in Brazil, I went through several selection processes. One of them - to work at a large Brazilian multinational company – was deeply disturbing. I went through the 10 stages of the process and in the last one, the Director asked me (this was year 2000 and I was 24): "Imagine you already have kids, there is an important meeting, and the school calls you saying your child has had an accident. What would you do: attend the meeting or pick up your child?" With no hesitation, I answered that I would get my child. He stood up, thanked me for being there, and said that we didn't share the same values. Today, I tell this story with a smile on my face and the joy of seeing that we have come a long way, and these kinds of situation "almost" don't happen anymore.

Few women have raised me throughout my career, but the first one did that at that moment of change, when I understood that I wanted to explore new horizons and prove myself as a professional outside of HR. I became part of a team that was building a startup funded by Citibank, in a time when this word wasn't even popular yet...

I experienced incredible things during those years outside of HR. I have tried different businesses, such as the corporate area of the Bank, learned a lot about the business world, collaborated with clients in several sectors, learned about diverse topics and built relationships with professionals all over the world. I have also experienced the challenges of being a woman in a still very male-dominated environment, where the senior female leaders proudly said that they have prioritized career over family.

I was at a company that was admired by all and where many people would like to work, but I asked myself if I liked that job. I was recognized for my work there and received a job offer to move to USA. And then, a major turning point happened in my life: I said no. I decided to decline the expatriation and follow my heart: return to working in HR and invest in building my family with my boyfriend, who became my husband and has been a great supporter throughout my journey.

Return to working with people was a milestone in my career. The maxim that when we do what we love everything flows more easily is real, but challenges were not lacking.

I have migrated to the HR department of a renowned multinational strategy consulting firm, where I have experienced heaven and hell together. On one hand, I worked with the smartest and most well-educated people in my entire career, had the opportunity to develop myself rapidly in a noticeably brief period. On the other hand, it was hard to be in a male-dominated industry, without the international MBA that they all held, working at a frenetic pace. I had developed some skills I hadn't needed up to that point, but I have demanded a lot from my body, and it didn't handle it. It was 2007, I was newly married and was going to host my family for Christmas dinner. I woke up with half of my face paralyzed, and the doctors thought I had had a stroke. Thank God it wasn't a stroke! I had facial paralysis caused by a virus due to stress and low immunity. I used to (still am sometimes) one of those people who tend to be workaholic, but at that moment my body collapsed. We didn't know if my face would return to normal, and I needed rest, physical and speech therapy.

Fortunately, we live in a different reality today. But being away from work for a month back then was considered shameful, a sign of weakness and lack of dedication. It was an ultimate sign to change priorities, which were 100% focused on work until that moment. To prioritize my health and find quality time to take care of myself and the family I was building.

All this learning has made me choose to change once again. I have been in therapy, coaching and studied hard. I knew I wanted to continue working with people, but I no longer saw myself in HR. So, I decided to join an Executive Search and Leadership Consulting firm.

People usually think that the Executive Search industry is more diverse for dealing with people, but there was another male-dominated industry where women still needed to fight for their space. Despite all of this, I was able to seize the opportunities and developed rapidly.

My dream of becoming a mother came true, but upon returning from maternity leave with my first child, I was informed that my biggest client had been transferred to a peer. I lost the client that would make me become a partner for being out for four months to take care of my baby! "These things happen all the time", said my friends and colleagues. I swallowed my disappointment. And it hurt. In the following years, I tried to juggle the responsibilities, but I must confess that I suffered when my son asked me why the mothers of his friends had stayed at a birthday party, and only I didn't. As they say: "A mother is born, and so is guilt."

My daughter was born four years later and having a son and a daughter has brought me even more clarity about how my role as a mother would also be crucial in the education of individuals with a more diverse mindset. And how I would like the world of work to change to treat my daughter differently than I had been treated along the way—with no moral harassment, missed opportunities, and situations of disrespect. I knew I could do a lot more for the diversity in organizations and for women than I already did, but I needed more space than I had as a multinational company employee.

The maxim was: "to be successful in a consulting firm, one needs to be a good salesperson; being a hunter opens a lot of doors". So, for a long time, I questioned myself what my future would be like, since I wasn't naturally like that.

Although the supposed security of being an employee of a large multinational company was great, I felt trapped in a cocoon. I couldn't support companies and people the way I wanted to. I needed more freedom and the only way to do it seemed to be creating something of my own.

The daunting word "entrepreneurship" was becoming increasingly present in my life. Entrepreneurship was one of the subjects at the Business Administration college, but I only studied it because it was mandatory. That was not for me, I thought. In fact, now I think it was "my fear of taking risks" that was hidden behind the fear of entrepreneurship. I would have to believe in myself.

"Magic happens out of the comfort zone" – this is the message I got from a client when I communicated my decision to start a business. And it has been utterly amazing! I founded VSX Pessoas three years ago and, when I look back, I recognize that it was the best professional decision I made. There surely is a lot of challenge on the way, but I feel highly fulfilled professionally. Today I am able to deliver even greater value to my clients, who recommend me to others and so on – and I don't need to be that hunter they told me about in the past. I contribute to the growth of companies by supporting the building and development of better teams and helping people reach their full potential. This freedom also allows me to work pro bono to support women-led startups, in addition to being able to dedicate quality time to my family.

They say that Vanessa means butterfly... I think I was able to break out of the cocoon that imprisoned me and be truly myself. To the eyes of many people, it may have taken time to find myself, but I am proud of having chosen this path at the age of 45. I hope to continue inspiring and helping many other women to break out their cocoons and fly. In the cocoon, we grow, protect ourselves, strengthen our wings so that one day, confident that the flight is worth it, we can freely fly, displaying the infinite palettes of colors and our uniqueness in this colorful and diverse world.

VIRNA DIAS PIOVEZAN

Motivational speaker, volleyball commentator, Podcast Pod Vir com Glenda
E-mail: virna10@uol.com.br
Instagram: @virnadd
Linkedin: www.linkedin.com/in/virna-dias-04492825/

DISCIPLINE SURPASSES TALENT

Former volleyball player representing Brazilian National Team. Two-time Olympic medalist. She was the MVP of the 1999 Grand Prix and the world's best receiver in 1994. She worked as a volleyball commentator during the Beijing (2008), London (2012), and Rio (2016) Olympics. Currently, she is a speaker and ambassador for volleyball projects in the interior of São Paulo.

Sports teach a lot. They require discipline, resilience, and teach you how to win and lose. I was never the most talented, the tallest, the most skillful, the strongest, or the most popular. I knew I had to train and work hard if I wanted to achieve my goals in volleyball. It wasn't talent that kept me in the national team for 18 years. It was the discipline to get better one day at a time.

I was a tall and skinny 13-year-old teenager attending the Maria Auxiliadora Institute in Natal/RN, the city where I was born. I wasn't exactly a beauty. Very tall, skinny, braces on my teeth, wore glasses, and was quite clumsy. But during recess, when I played dodgeball with my friends, everyone wanted to be on my team. The strength of my throws - because I was physically larger than most girls and boys my age - made me highly sought after by teams. With a variety of sports to choose from in physical education classes, I became mildly interested in volleyball. It was a beautiful sport and didn't have the somewhat violent contact that I thought handball had. That's how volleyball entered my life. Kind of unintentionally, kind of with the thought of "I think it could be fun." My good academic performance led to an invitation to train with the Rio Grande do Norte State Team, and that's where everything officially began. At the age of 14, I already had a routine of training, competitions, and trips. And I was happy. I had found my "crowd." All the girls were tall and clumsy like me. And finally, I found a place where my height wasn't a reason for mockery. On the contrary, it was an advantage.

The toughest battle of my life up to that point began: convincing my father, who dreamed of seeing his daughter pursue a career in Civil Engineering, that at 14 years old, I was capable of living alone in Rio de Janeiro. During the 1986 vacation, he allowed me to do an internship with the team. In my parents' minds, this "volleyball fever" would pass, and homesickness would prevail. I did feel homesick, yes, for home, for Mrs. Carminha, for Mr. Tarcisio, and for my sisters. But it was a one-way path. The love for volleyball only grew, and I never returned. Just before turning 15, I was called up to the Brazilian Youth National Team. In 1987, the Collor Plan was a blow to the main volleyball sponsors in Brazil, and big teams like Bradesco and Lufking ceased to exist. It was a blow to me as well. I felt afraid: so, is it over? Brazilian volleyball was going through a difficult time. Anxious, I gained eight kilograms. Without a club, without a salary, and without prospects, I missed the comfort of my mother's embrace.

I was already old enough to play for adult teams, and I had just been accepted into the Economics program at PUC-RJ. In the meantime, between the comings and goings of my boyfriend Luiz Antônio visiting me in Rio, at the age of 18, I discovered that I was pregnant. The news hit my father like a bomb. Seu Tarcisio, a proud and conservative Northeasterner, was disappointed with his daughter. But his heart softened when he found out he would be a grandfather - with three daughters at home, his dream had always been to have a son.

Vítor was born on April 6, 1991, in Natal, surrounded by love. I was 19 years old and preparing to be a mother. Then came the invitation to play in the Junior World Championship, under the leadership of none other than José Roberto Guimarães - now a three-time Olympic champion. But Vítor was still very young, and I declined the invitation. Three months later, the option to play in Europe came up. I went to Italy with Vítor, my husband, and a nanny, but the experience wasn't good. It was very cold, and I was exhausted from training and taking care of a small baby, not to mention the delayed salaries. I returned to Brazil and, thanks to a recommendation from my friend Fernanda Venturini, I joined Recreativa, under the coaching of Antônio Rizola. But I had to fight for a spot as a starter.

I would call my father in tears, seeking advice, and he would say, "Just give your best." And that's what I did. I gained 12 kilograms during pregnancy and lost 15; if I had to do 100 sit-ups, I would do more, if I had to run for 30 minutes, I would run for 40. I was called up to the Brazilian National Team again after being left out of the selection for Barcelona (1992). In 1993, I competed in the Grand Prix in Asia. It was 40 days between South Korea and Hong Kong. When I returned, Vítor didn't recognize me. He didn't know that I was his mother.

For the first time, I thought about quitting volleyball. How many more times would I have to endure the pain of my son rejecting me and live with the guilt of being an absent mother? It's the dilemma every working mother faces.

Little did I know that it was the first of many challenges to come, both in my personal and professional life. At the end of 1993, Bernardinho took over the Brazilian National Team and he was straightforward with me: "If you want to play on the team, you have to learn to receive." I was very insecure in that skill. I said it was impossible for an adult to learn how to receive. And he said one of the phrases that I carry with me to this day: "Virna, there is no word 'impossible'. There is the word 'work'. Do you want to receive well? You will have to work hard. I'll help you."

In Atlanta, I wasn't a starter. I inherited the position during the competition after the unfortunate injury of the outside hitter Hilma. It was a difficult situation. I felt the doubt from my teammates. "Will she be able to handle it?" Once again, I called my father. Seu Tarcisio always had the right words for uncertain moments. And he would always say, "Give your best, pray, control your thoughts. Be positive, and help the team." Little did he know that he was building, in my mind, the essential pillars for working as a team. Do your best in whatever way you can, but always think about the collective. How can I help the team?

When I finally understood that I could only become a better player by being a better player for the team, my mindset changed.

Being a high-performance athlete teaches us to live with pain - both physical and emotional - all the time. How many times have I stepped onto the court feeling pain in my foot, knee, muscle, or joints? Countless times. How many times do we step onto the court even when we have to deal with off-court problems? Several times!

Just before Sydney (2000), for example, I fractured my foot. Stress fracture. ItAfter a battery of tests, the diagnosis I didn't want to hear came: I would need surgery, and it would be practically impossible to go to Sydney. Unable to train with the team, I made a promise. I had always been a chocolate lover. But for over a month, I didn't eat chocolate!

After winning bronze in Sydney, when the chocolate abstinence promise was over, Bernardinho and I went to the McDonald's at the Olympic Village and both ordered a chocolate sundae with lots of sauce. We celebrated with ice cream and ended the chocolate fast.

Upon returning from the Olympics in Sydney, Leila, a longtime friend and confidante, and I were invited by the president of Flamengo, through Isabel, to join the team and embrace the project. For me, personally, the invitation was more than special. I wore the number 10 jersey in volleyball because of Zico, my great idol. And Flamengo was my beloved football team. Zico had always been a role model for me, both on and off the field .Leila and I arrived to help build the rest of the team. At the team presentation ceremony for the season, as the captain, I received the number 10 jersey from none other than Zico himself. It was pure emotion. At that moment, the magnitude of the challenge I was accepting became very clear. Leila and I had already played many years together in the national team, but it was there, at Gávea, that our partnership gained strength. It was a duo that marked my career and my life. Today, we are friends and sisters. Many times, on the court, we would say whatever came to mind and argue with each other, but always seeking the best for the team. Flamengo was not the best team in that Superliga. We lost several games in the qualifying phase. But through ups and downs, we made it to the final against the favorite Vasco, with Fernanda Venturini and company, and we won in a thrilling match, in front of a packed Maracanãzinho, with the presence of two of the biggest fan bases in Brazil. I became a champion, lifted the trophy, and was chosen as the best player of the Superliga that year. Sports teach us that it's not always the best who wins, but rather the most prepared in that moment.

The following year, Flamengo couldn't maintain the volleyball sponsorship, and I went to São Paulo to play for BCN, with another exceptional coach: Zé Roberto. Meticulous, detail-oriented, and strategic, Zé was another leader who left a mark on my career and my development. At the same time, my personal life was going through a crisis. I separated from my husband, and one of the most difficult decisions was to separate from Vítor, who went to live with his father for a more stable life. I wouldn't be able to be the present mother he needed at the age of 10 with the amount of games, training, concentration, and travel that volleyball demanded at that time. He lived in Bauru/SP, and I continued playing in Osasco/SP to stay close. I was far, but never absent. However, the guilt of being a distant mother saddened me once again. There is no cure for this feeling. It never goes away.

With Zé Roberto in the Brazilian National Team, I was called up for my third Olympics in Athens (2004). Cuba was no longer the same powerhouse as before, and it was our chance to win gold. In the semifinals, we took a 2-1 lead over the Russians and won the fourth set 24-19. We were one point away from the unprecedented Olympic final. One point. And it didn't come. We lost the set and lost the tie-break. It was one of the biggest disappointments of my life, for sure. Until today, I have never been able to watch that match again.

It was hard to digest. Even today, it is difficult to talk about that score. The following year, I said goodbye to indoor volleyball and started playing on the sand. Make no mistake, it's a different sport. Playing in a pair is different from playing in a team. The pressure is greater. Your mistakes are more evident, and your responsibility is even greater.

Understanding the moment to stop is like facing a mourning process. After all,

I needed to say goodbye to the athlete Virna in order to reinvent myself and continue simply as Virna. I remarried, became a mother twice, and attended three more Olympics as a volleyball commentator. Today, as a motivational speaker and ambassador for some volleyball projects, I find myself facing new challenges: passing on everything that sports taught me.

And sports teach a lot: it requires discipline, resilience, and teaches how to win and lose. Yes, it's important to know how to win and not become complacent, and to know how to lose and use the feeling of failure to learn and improve. It's like life. It's like any other profession. I was never the most talented, the tallest, the most skilled, the strongest, or the most popular. I had good physical condition and focused on my strengths, but I always trained my weaknesses as well. I knew that I had to train and work hard if I wanted to achieve my goals. It wasn't talent that kept me in the national team for 18 years. It was discipline.

VIVIANE DE MARCO

Journalist working for Brazil's TV Globo
LinkedIn: www.linkedin.com/in/viviane-de-marco-956aa824

INTRODUCTION

With so many years writing stories, informing, documenting, when I look at this blank page and the mission is to talk about myself, it becomes difficult!

Perhaps it is modesty. It is easier to inform because that is my profession. I am a journalist. I will not even say how many years. It will be easy to see that this is a long road.

I started at TV Bandeirantes as a political editor and one of my first tasks was to cover the Presidente Tacredo Neves's death. I cried while editing the imagens of the coffin down the Palacio do Planalto's ramp carrying the body of the president-elect .

I also edited all the rallies for "Diretas Já" (Direct Elections Now). I was on duty in Brasília on the day Ulisses Guimarães celebrated the 1988's Constitution.

In each of these moments, it was hard to believe that I was working where I had always dreamed: on television!

After spending a goog amount of time working at the newsroom, today, I am the General Director of "Mais Você", an entertainment news show, hosted by Ana Maria Braga!

I am not an executive like most of the members of this incredible group where "one rises and pulls the other up". However, I can say that I had the privilege of being a professional who transitioned from newsrooms to informative entertainment. I made this transition 24 years ago (2023).

In the artistic field, I had the opportunity to "sniff out" talents. I "pulled" several of them into television and everything went well until today. Luckily, I was "pulled" by Ana Maria because we got along well from our first contacts before Mais Você premiered in 1999.

I even left the program for a year to launch the live version of Vídeo Show. But I was "pulled" back.

Going back in time, when I switched sides - and this expression is literal because Globo's production building is on the opposite side of the journalism building, I believed that would be easier, funny and I would get rid of weekend shift.

The schedule was from Monday to Friday and, above all, I would be free from having to choose between working Christmas or New Year's shift.

However, that impression did not last long. The rigor of working with information is the same, and in a daily program, you cannot relax or disconnect on the weekends because events keep happening and, when one program ends, there is another one the next day. The challenge is to make it better than the previous one in an endless chain. In addition, there is one more detail: the fight for ratings is fiercer.

In spite of everything, I must confess that worth it because I'm lucky to work with the best communicator in Brazil, which is Ana Maria, a partner in ideas and someone who doesn't want to stay in the comfort zone. If she escapes that dangerous comfort zone, her time does too, and that is how we have arrived almost at the 25th anniversary of the program, always reinventing ourselves.

I only got here because I followed a path of hard work, zero laziness, a lot of curiosity, and enthusiasm. That is how I am, a Sagittarius with Sagittarius rising. Those who know a little about astrology will understand. For those who don't or don't believe in "those things," I would simply say that I was "born charged up," enchanted by the world, by people, by stories. Essential attributes to be where I am.

HOW I GOT TO "PLIM PLIM" (nickname for Globo)

Going back a little further in time, I remember the dream of being on TV. It took a while to have a TV set in my house. On weekends, I would watch at my paternal grandparents' house. It was a radio with an image, and that was intriguing. How was that possible?

I looked at the cable plugged into socket and wondered: was that the cable that people use to access the Tv screen? At that time, no one could explain the process to me.

Even without understanding, I remember my fascination and imagining myself being inside that tube one day. I didn't know how, but I was certain that one day it would happen. Without the slightest notion, I think I threw this dream with such force into the Universe that the "Law of Attraction" worked. Look where I am today.

Until the beginning of 1991, I was the Executive Editor of Jornal Bandeirantes. I worked with Joelmir Beting, Marilia Gabriela, Ferreira Martins, Fernando Mitre, Silvia Jafet, Celso Ming, José Augusto Ribeiro, Newton Carlos. The main news program at the station had a considerable length, and closing each edition was an exercise in tenacity. Sometimes the news started and the end wasn't ready yet. That was somewhat scary live. I handled the situation calmly. I never had to activate the "panic button."

This "quality" ended up being my passport to Globo. Knowing my profile, a friend who had moved from Band to Globo (José Emilio Ambrósio) recommended me to be the

Executive Editor of SPTV second edition. I took the position that belonged to Amauri Soares, the current CEO of Globo, and unknowingly, he created space that allowed me to rise to te top in my carrer.

I still remember the butterflies in my stomach on the day I started working. The date couldn't have been more symbolic. After sorting out the hiring paperwork, my first working day at Globo was May 1, 1991, Labor Day!

The Editor-in-Chief of SP2 was Carlos Nascimento, a great journalist. The news program, which precedes JN (Jornal Nacional), is shorter than the lunchtime edition. It was easy for me to adapt.

The following year I joined Bom Dia São Paulo with anchor Carlos Tramontina. The news program was more relaxed, and gradually, I realized that Tramontina was also very open to innovation and curiosities beyond the news.

I came up with the idea of including a recipe in the show because I realized that it would help homemakers save time and even save money.

BLESSED "PANETTONE"

Since the recipe had to be tied to the news, one Christmas, in the "last century" still, I thought it would be cool to uncover how homemakers could make a panettone that wouldn't dry out. It had to be like the ones from supermarkets, fluffy and moist, and cost less. I did some research and found out that there was a mixture of yeast that would give it that texture. We tested it. It turned out very good. The recipe aired in early December so that homemakers would have time to prepare it for their families or to make and sell. In the promo, I wrote that it was a tip for homemade panettone to be just like the store-bought one, but half the price.

It was such a big success that the recipe had to be replayed. This was something unusual, especially on a news program.

Moreover, since there was no internet yet, we made copies and left them at the TV'S entrance. In that day, the lines wrapped around the block !

This "case" gave me even more notoriety and caught the press's attention. After that, my name became associated with the lunchtime news programs for knowing how to speak to families.

In 1999, when Globo closed a deal with Ana Maria Braga to do Mais Você, Amauri Soares (who had returned to the network as Regional Editor in São Paulo) recommended me to be part of the team that was coming with Ana from Record.

I didn't know Ana Maria personally, but in our first meeting, I could feel that we would have a good connection. That's what happened until today because we are two who are driven by the new, by the surprises, the different and, above all, by the truth

A TEACHER CALLED "MINUTE BY MINUTE"

The great learning that gave me confidence in the entertainment industry was observing the audience numbers.

Good rates, besides being a fundamental indicator for the commercial health of the media, is the measure of people's taste. It is obvious that the audience comes when we seek topics of greater interest. That is where the "minute by minute" comes in. You can instantly track what is pleasing or driving away the audience. Having this tool as a guide makes it easier to decide.

Some facts are more attractive, such as sensational news, catastrophes, and major factual coverage. In information and entertainment programs, it is necessary to give something more to the viewer, besides entertainment, provide a service airing content where the viewer gains something.

Airing a live daily program for the whole country is a huge responsibility. Free TV is accessible to everyone, and you have to learn to speak to millions. That is what Ana does every day: she talks to millions about topics that interest millions (this expression is often used by our Director Mariano Boni, who is also driven by challenges).

So imagine the challenge of leading a team that produces this content. Learning happens every day. By observing, I learned that unusual facts or images on TV yield results. I also learned that intuition is as important as being well informed. Intuition accompanied by sensitivity. That is an infallible duo.

In the program's routine, we have a long editorial meeting every week. After 24 years on the air, there is no subject that has not been shown on our screen.

If every time someone suggested something and the response was "oh, we've already done that," it would be a cold shower. I strongly believe that old ideas can be updated and renewed.

That is why all ideas are welcome. We just need to ask ourselves in front of each one: "what will the people watching us gain from this"?

They can gain an important tip for a business, an inspiring idea, and advice to guide them, a situation that entertains or a recipe that makes them salivate with desire.

Here is a curiosity: airing a salad recipe doesn't get the proportional audience to the desire people have to be healthy. Otherwise, if you put a polenta with a juicy rib "ragu", or a beautiful chocolate cake, it yields results. If that happens, it is because we awaken an emotion in those who watch us. TV is a medium that overflows with emotion.

The radar must always be on, capturing what people like to see or are curious to know.

The program must adapt to that, but without losing sight of current events.

Because free TV will always survive when it's live. Otherwise, it is difficult to compete with streaming.

BEFORE CLOSING!

By the time I entered in college, my first choice was Public Relations.

I got closer to the journalism group. By then, I had already realized that my profile would fit much better in a "routine without routine" that only journalism would allow.

It was a classmate who gave me my first opportunity in the profession. His name is Caetano Bedaque. He was the one who recommended me for my first job as a journalist at Bandeirantes. From that opportunity on, I always guided my days believing that the easiest solution is not always the best. This was advice I gave to my journalist daughter, Mariana De Marco, to whom I dedicate this chapter. And also to my lawyer daughter, Danielle De Marco, who is the "voice of reason" in the family.

I grew in the profession. I was pulled into numerous challenges and always tried to meet them. That's why I'm here today, pulled by my friend Natasha Caiado, to whom I say "thank you very much". I enjoyed the experience!

WE INVITE YOU TO TELL YOUR STORY HERE.